Levinas and Literature

Perspectives on Jewish Texts and Contexts

Edited by
Vivian Liska

Editorial Board
Robert Alter, Steven E. Aschheim, Richard I. Cohen, Mark H. Gelber,
Moshe Halbertal, Christine Hayes, Moshe Idel, Samuel Moyn,
Ada Rapoport-Albert, Alvin Rosenfeld, David Ruderman, Bernd Witte

Volume 15

Levinas and Literature

New Directions

Edited by
Michael Fagenblat and Arthur Cools

DE GRUYTER

The free availability of the e-book edition of this publication was made possible by the Special Information Service (SIS) Jewish Studies at the University Library J. C. Senckenberg in Frankfurt/Main and 18 academic libraries that support the open access transformation in the Jewish Studies.

ISBN 978-3-11-108842-6
e-ISBN (PDF) 978-3-11-066892-6
e-ISBN (EPUB) 978-3-11-066899-5
ISSN 2199-6962
DOI https://doi.org/10.1515/9783110668926

This work is licensed under a Creative Commons Attribution 4.0 International License. For details go to: https://creativecommons.org/licenses/by/4.0/.

Library of Congress Control Number: 2020943673

Bibliographic information published by the Deutsche Nationalbibliothek
The Deutsche Nationalbibliothek lists this publication in the Deutsche Nationalbibliografie; detailed bibliographic data are available on the Internet at http://dnb.dnb.de.

© 2022 Michael Fagenblat and Arthur Cools, published by Walter de Gruyter GmbH, Berlin/Boston.
This volume is text- and page-identical with the hardback published in 2021.
The book is published open access at www.degruyter.com.

Cover image: Excerpt from manuscript, used with kind permission of Michael Levinas.
Typesetting: Integra Software Services Pvt. Ltd.
Printing and binding: CPI books GmbH, Leck

www.degruyter.com

Open Access Transformation in Jewish Studies

Open Access for excellent academic publications in the field of Jewish Studies: This is the objective of the joint initiative of the Special Information Service Jewish Studies at the University Library J. C. Senckenberg in Frankfurt/Main and De Gruyter. Thanks to the support of 18 consortia partners, 8 frontlist publications from 2020 can be published as gold open access, among them this publication.

The following institutions have contributed to the funding and thus promote the open access transformation in Jewish Studies to ensure free availability for everyone:

Fachinformationsdienst Jüdische Studien, Universitätsbibliothek J. C. Senckenberg Frankfurt am Main
Staatsbibliothek zu Berlin - Preußischer Kulturbesitz
Universitätsbibliothek der Freien Universität Berlin
Universitätsbibliothek der Technischen Universität Berlin
Universitäts- und Landesbibliothek Düsseldorf
Universitätsbibliothek der Europa-Universität Viadrina Frankfurt (Oder)
Bibliothek der Vereinigten Theologischen Seminare der Georg-August-Universität Göttingen
Niedersächsische Staats- und Universitätsbibliothek Göttingen
Universitäts- und Landesbibliothek Sachsen-Anhalt
Staats- und Universitätsbibliothek Hamburg – Carl von Ossietzky
Gottfried Wilhelm Leibniz Bibliothek – Niedersächsische Landesbibliothek
Hochschule für Jüdische Studien Heidelberg
Universitäts- und Stadtbibliothek Köln
Universitätsbibliothek Mainz
Universitätsbibliothek der Ludwig-Maximilians-Universität München
Universitäts- und Landesbibliothek Münster
Herzog August Bibliothek Wolfenbüttel
Universitätsbibliothek Wuppertal

Open Access. © 2021 Michael Fagenblat, published by De Gruyter. This work is licensed under the Creative Commons Attribution 4.0 International License.
https://doi.org/10.1515/9783110668926-202

Contents

Michael Fagenblat
Introduction: Levinas and Literature, a Marvellous Hypocrisy —— IX

Arthur Cools
The Anarchy of Literature —— 1

Part I: *Eros*

Jean-Luc Nancy
***Eros*, Emmanuel Levinas's Novel? —— 21**

Danielle Cohen-Levinas and Jean-Luc Nancy
Eros, Once Again: Danielle Cohen-Levinas in Conversation with Jean-Luc Nancy —— 37

François-David Sebbah
The Debacle or The Real Under Reduction: The "Scene of Alençon" —— 47

Michaël de Saint-Cheron
From Eros to the Question of the Death of God —— 63

Part II: Biblical Texts

Eli Schonfeld
Languages of the Universal. Levinas' (*scandalous*) Doctrine of Literature —— 77

Michael Fagenblat
The Genesis of *Totality and Infinity*: The Secret Drama —— 93

Marcel Poorthuis
Literature as a Burning Bush —— 117

Part III: Poetry

Annelies Schulte-Nordholt
Levinas and the Poetic Word: Writing with Baudelaire? —— 133

Kevin Hart
"Lès-Poésie?": Levinas Reads La folie du jour —— 147

Eric Hoppenot
Poetic Language and Prophetic Language in Levinas's Works —— 165

Vivian Liska
The Poem, the Place, the Jew: Emmanuel Levinas on Paul Celan —— 175

Part IV: Novel Writers

Danielle Cohen-Levinas
The Literary Instant and the Condition of Being Hostage: Levinas, Proust, and the Corporeal Meaning of Time —— 195

Jan Bierhanzl
Ideology, Literature, and Philosophy: Levinas as a Reader of Léon Bloy —— 209

Luc Anckaert
Goodness without Witnesses: Vasily Grossman and Emmanuel Levinas —— 223

Tammy Amiel-Houser
Reading Fiction with Levinas: Ian McEwan's novel Atonement —— 239

Part V: Literary Theory

Shira Wolosky
Emmanuel Levinas: Metaphor without Metaphysics —— 259

Ashraf Noor
***Apparition*: Aesthetics of Disproportion in Levinas and Adorno** —— 281

Michael Fagenblat
Introduction

Levinas and Literature: A Marvellous Hypocrisy

> Wait for me: I'm going to pull you out of this hell into which I descended.
> Clarice Lispector, *The Passion According to G.H.*

For Ariel

Long before the publication of Levinas's *Inédits* we knew that literature was the philosopher's great temptation. The three volumes of *Inédits*, however, reveal the far-reaching intricacy of this fascination from unsuspected angles, shedding new light on Levinas's singular philosophical style, themes, and argument.[1] In them we find youthful poems written in Russian between 1921–28 (2013, §IV); tender ruminations by the Jewish prisoner of war on the actuality of biblical literalisms (2009, 205–15); surprisingly admiring citations of the ultra-Catholic writer Léon Bloy penned in captivity (2009, 151–162);[2] evidence of the breakthrough provided by Proust, "poet of the social" (2009, 145), in thinking of love without communion, intimacy without knowing (2009, 71–74, 144f., 179–81);[3] extensive, suggestive notes on metaphor that were later modified into publications (2009, 227–42, 296f., 329–31, 350f.; 2011, 323–47);[4] transcriptions of poems by Baudelaire with lines Levinas later incorporated, uncited, into his philosophical essays (2009, 177f.);[5] and revealing references to the writers he so admired from Shakespeare through Dostoevsky to Blanchot. Most intriguing are the lengthy fragments of two novels Levinas began to draft in captivity (2009, esp. *Carnet 5*) and continued to work on through to the early 1960's (2013, §§ I-III),[6] in other words, at the very same time that he was composing major philosophical essays, including *Totality and Infinity* (1961), and those on Judaism published in *Difficult Freedom* (1963).

Research for this volume was generously supported by Israel Science Foundation grant 698/16.

---

1 Levinas, 2009, 2011, 2013. For valuable introductions see Calin and Chalier 2009; Nancy 2013; Davis 2015; Hammerschlag 2019a; Hand 2013, 2019.
2 See *infra* Bierhanzl, this vol.; as well as Hand 2013.
3 See *infra* Cohen-Levinas, this vol.
4 See *infra* Wolosky, this vol. A translation of some of these notes appears in Levinas 2012. For illuminating commentaries see Calin 2012, 201; Faessler 2012.
5 See *infra* Schulte-Nordholt, this vol.
6 See *infra* Nancy, Cohen-Levinas/Nancy, Sebbah, this vol.; as well as Calin and Chalier 2009, pp.14–19; Davis; Nancy.

Configured between philosophy, on one side, and religion, in particular Judaism, on the other, it is now clear that literature provided Levinas with a third way of *enacting* the unique *sens* of the Other. More precisely, as both Levinas's aborted novels and his literary exemplars suggest, the advantage of literature consists not so much in *showing* the moral sense of the other—since its truth is strictly "invisible", falling outside the limits of consciousness, beyond empathy and intuition—but in attesting to the formidable difficulty of discerning this sense. It is as if literature affords a way of tracing the sense of goodness under the conditions of its absence. Levinas's novelistic fragments point to a reality lulled into self-content, mistaking the order of the world for its ground, even in the midst of war, until war proves that there is no stable ground to civilized life and that order—even the "immense stability" that is France (2013 3, 38)—is only a veil for the catastrophic chaos that perennially lurks about. War tears away the drapes of civilization (2009, 112, 160), as Levinas describes it in the "scene of Alençon" he envisaged as the moral center of his novelistic ambitions, a scene that speaks "not simply of the end of illusions but of the end of meaning" (2009, 132). The torn drapes reveal the horror of being without any order whatsoever, existence without a world.[7] Far from presenting the Other, then, as does the psychological novel, the literature that interests Levinas explores the implications of a world deprived of the sense of the Other, a world verging toward the abyss of indeterminate, meaningless existence.

To be sure, the exposure of the real behind the stage of civilization and the drapes of intelligibility points to the constitutive role of the Other in grounding the conditions of possibility for meaning. But the sense of the Other is not realized through empathy or intuition; it is indicated or intimated by a phenomenological reduction of intelligibility to humility, epistemic as much as moral, a reduction of the very possibility of meaning to an acknowledgment, without knowledge, of the Other. Interpretation presumes not only 'distanciation' but also separation; the latter has ontological priority over intuition and thereby renders interpretation endless. Baudelaire's immortal ennui exposes the weariness of existence itself; Shakespeare's tragedies are marked by the diabolical inescapability of being, which is why death is not just feared but also desired (2009, 174); and Marcel's self-regard converts into love only when faced with the mystery of Albertine's evanescence which her absence finally manifests. Blanchot, ever-present when Levinas thinks of literature, epitomizes the risk that literature poses to the very possibility of ethics; the risk of substituting the Other for an image, reducing the sense of the Other to one's own sensations.[8]

---

7 See *infra* Sebbah, this vol.
8 See *infra* Hart, this vol.

"In Blanchot's art reality becomes truly ghostly, while in romantism ghosts appear in a world with real contours. Influence of Hamsun's "Mysteries", of Gogol's "Portrait", "Nevski prospect"? Reality unfolds like a dream. The fluidity of things and space. Words and actions strike, but not by what is striking in them." (2009, 406f.) Around 1953,[9] still echoing the critique of art *and* literature articulated in "Reality and Its Shadow" (1948), Levinas differentiates his account of language from his friends', whose approach occludes the essential role of ethics in the ontology of meaning. "The event of language– . . . <u>Blanchot</u>: Language is situated before the relationship with others – in a strangeness of self to self. <u>Me</u>: Language is . . . invocation. Recognition of the Other as such – Teaching that is not maieutic." (2009, 415)

In *Existence and Existents*, the most important of the works published in the wake of the War (1947), Levinas deploys his critique of literature with greatest effect and in consonance with the contemporaneous "Reality and its Shadow". Literature here serves as an approach to the "limit situation" of a world verging toward elemental *il y a* existence, an eidetic reduction of the historical experience of war, of "a world in pieces," "a world turned upside down," that also recalls "the ancient obsession with an end of the world." (Levinas 1978, 21) For Levinas it was war, radically conceived, that raised the specter of a world reduced to elemental worldlessness. "Hitlerism," he wrote in July 1946, was "the presentiment of the denouement of history . . . the drunkenness of the end of the world" (Levinas, 1946, 1), and it is no doubt for this reason that the fragments of both novels are set amid the debacle of wartorn France. Behind the opening lines of *Totality and Infinity*—"war suspends morality; it divests the eternal institutions and obligations of their eternity and rescinds ad interim the unconditional imperatives" (Levinas 1969, 21)—there is the *mise en abyme* of the tearing away of the drapes of civilization. Today one might think of COVID-19, the virus evoking a phenomenological resemblance to Levinas's descriptions of the *there is*, an indistinct menace from which determinate existents "hypostasize" – binding to themselves in fear, physical pain, egoism, possession (think of the hoarding the virus provoked), being *chez soi*, and so on– thereby individuating a self, an existent, within the indeterminate, elemental existence lurking about.[10] It is as if behind the stage of the world and

---

9 The comment appears on the back of an invitation card dated 1953. For further comments on the dating of the philosophical notes in Levinas 2009 see the editor's note, pp. 224–26.

10 Levinas 1987. The lectures published as *Time and the Other* (1987) were delivered in 1946/47 and are consistent with the conceptual schema published in *Existence and Existents* in 1947 and "Reality and its Shadow" (1948). These works, like *Time and the Other*, constitute "the birth and first formulation" of the descriptions and analyses in *Totality and Infinity* (Levinas 1987, 30).

the drapes of civilization lurks a virus, neither living nor dead, an irreal existence threatening the reality of individuated existents which has made visible the fragile interdependence of sense and solidarity, grounding the individuation of entities—the very condition for intelligibility—on the sense that each other's wellbeing is one's own. The ontologically deficient assumptions of liberalism are thereby also made plain. Or one might think, with no less elemental horror, of nuclear or climate change dystopias, as in Cormac McCarthy's postapocalyptic novel *The Road*, in which a nameless father bears the burden of *"impersonal vigilance"* that Levinas describes (1978, 60/98), watching over a world deprived of beings, a world reverted to elemental being.

> "He walked out in the gray night and stood and he saw for a brief moment the absolute truth of the world. The cold relentless circling of the intestate earth. Darkness implacable . . .The crushing black vacuum of the universe. . .Borrowed time and borrowed world and borrowed eyes with which to sorrow it."

> "One vast sepulcher of salt. Senseless. Senseless."

> "Perhaps in the world's destruction it would be possible at last to see how it was made. Oceans. Mountains. The ponderous counterspectacle of things ceasing to be. The sweeping waste, hydroptic and coldly secular. The silence." (McCarthy, *The Road*, 138, 237, 293)

The nameless father in *The Road*, like the paternal subjectivity defended in *Totality and Infinity*, attains no other redemption from the horror of existence than the desire for his son's life above his own.

> "He carried him up to the camp and covered him with blankets. He tried to get him to drink some water. . . . You'll be alright he said. He was terrified. . . I will do what I promised, he whispered. No matter what. I will not send you into the darkness alone.

> They went on. Treading the dead world under like rats on a wheel. The nights dead still and deader black. So cold. . .He'd stop and lean on the cart and the boy would go on and then stop and look back and he would raise his weeping eyes and see him standing there in the road looking back at him from an unimaginable future, glowing in that waste like a tabernacle. (McCarthy, 264f., 292f.)

Levinas's abandoned attempts to write his own literature of disaster show that the last thing he can be accused of is moral naiveté or being a moral "perfectionist," as has too frequently been thought. "My literary methods: 1) Describe everything at the level of "sensation", in the elementary, in this elementary where the whole complex is already present. 2) The real situation is soberly described . . . over a precipice" (Levinas 2009, 194). Literature attests to humanity's verging from sense to senselessness, even as the transformations it brings to language are the very signs of our always provisional transcendence of the disaster of being. Literature thus has the potency of a *pharmakon*, at once poison and medicine, descent into egoism and senselessness, but also orientation toward the Other.

On the one hand, then, Levinas adopts a cautious, even critical approach to literature which he conceives, like all art, in terms of the work's "formal structure of completion" (1989, 131), the sensations of which draw the subject from reality to its shadow, from objects to their images, from concepts that refer to objects in the world to pure sensations that refer the subject back to the formally complete work of art. Levinas's critique of art and literature is essentially Platonic, reiterating the old suspicion of pleasures roused by mimetic idols. It is articulated most severely in "Reality and its Shadow" and the contemporary work, *Existence and Existents*, where the phenomenological sense of a work of art is again situated in the shadows of being. "Instead of arriving at the object, the intention gets lost in the sensation itself, and it is this wandering about in sensation, in *aisthesis*, that produces the aesthetic effect. Sensation is not the way that leads to an object but the obstacle that keeps one from it . . . In art, sensation figures as a new element. Or better, it returns to the impersonality of *elements*." (1978, 53/85f.) Borrowing a term from Jean Wahl, Levinas proposes that works of art induce a "transdescendence" into an elemental realm in which objects become images accessed through sensations disengaged from their worldly referents (Levinas 1989, 137; cf. 1969 35/24). The idea implies that the experience of art deviates from the moral and epistemic seriousness of the world.

Levinas's critique of art and literature was so opposed to Sartre's account of the writer as paragon of "engagement" that *Les Temps Modernes*, where "Reality and its Shadow" was published in 1948, prefaced Levinas's article with a defense of its esteemed editor, signed under the auspices of the journal *T.M.* but written by Merleau-Ponty.[11] This is not the place to explicate Levinas's critique of aesthetic experience in detail.[12] Two brief observations will suffice. First, *T.M.*'s Sartrean defense of the writer as a creator of means of communicating that foster human liberty somewhat misses the point of Levinas's analysis, whose critique of aesthetic experience does not target the ontologically derivative, psychological uses of art, which may indeed serve worldly values, as much as *the original sense* of something-*as*-art within the economy of being. At stake in Levinas's analysis of aesthetic experience is his lifelong preoccupation with deformalizing the temporal grounds of intelligibility. Approached *as a*

---

11 *Les Temps Modernes* 38 (1948), 769–770, reprinted in in Merleau-Ponty (1997), 121–24. For brief and instructive comments see Séan Hand's introductory remarks to "Reality and Its Shadow" in *The Levinas Reader*, 129. My thanks to Arthur Cools for discussion about this intriguing preface.
12 The best commentaries include Armengaud; Bruns; Charles; Colléony; Hammerschlag 2019b; Hart; Taminiaux.

work of art, an object never accedes to the temporal grounds of meaning but languishes in a "meanwhile" that falls short of reality, as if the essential experience of art suspends or delays time, abiding in "instants" disengaged from the temporality that opens and maintains the intelligibility of objects in the world. "In this situation the present can assume nothing, can take on nothing, and thus is an impersonal and anonymous instant (Levinas 1989, 138). The critique of *littérature engagée* was, then, merely collateral damage to Levinas's purposes, whose real ambition consisted in an oblique reductio ad absurdum of recent, remarkable work by Bataille and Blanchot, both of whom prize literature's unworlliness by embracing the elemental ontology Levinas shuns (Bataille, Blanchot). Or perhaps Levinas had in mind Heidegger's account of the work of art as that which "holds open the Open of the world" (Heidegger 2002, 23)[13]. Far from opening the world, Levinas argues that the work of art induces fascination with the exotic, transforming objects in-the-world into elements of an indeterminate "existence without a world" (Levinas 1978). Art provokes an essentially de-worlding effect, exchanging concepts for de-worlded affects. The second point, of particular relevance to this volume, is that Levinas's critique of aesthetic experience does not differentiate between literature and the other arts. In 1948, poems fair no better than statues, paintings or pieces of music; indeed they exemplify "closed wholes whose elements call for one another like the syllables of a verse . . . disengaging themselves from reality." (Levinas 1989, 132) So too in the contemporary *Existence and Existents* literary examples are extensively deployed and quoted, sometimes without citation, to effect a reversion of phenomena from sense to mere sensation. In poetry, "a word detaches itself from its objective meaning and reverts to the element of the sensible . . . Behind the signification of a poem which thought penetrates, thought also loses itself in the musicality of a poem which has nothing to do with objects and perhaps varies solely in function of what thought sets aside, what it liberates itself from." (Levinas 1978, 54/87) Literature plunges the subject into a sea of words that resembles nothing as much as the ghostly demarcations of the *there is*.

On the other hand, however, Levinas sometimes adopts a conspicuously different approach to the "poetic word," which he singles out among the other arts for its unique ethical sense. Not incidentally, the ethical exigency given to literature, alone among the arts, coincides with Levinas's deepening appreciation of

---

[13] Heidegger's essay "On the Origin of Art" was not published until 1949/50 but was delivered in typed lectures in 1935–36. Whether it circulated before publication or whether Levinas anticipated Heidegger's thought from other publications I have not been able to determine.

the ontological import of religious categories like prophecy, revelation, the Book, exegesis, and commentary. The transcendental advantage of literature consists not in uniting subjects through knowledge or communication between separated states of mind but, uniquely among the arts, in the way it inscribes the Other *in the very instant* of aesthetic disengagement from the world, establishing a relation to the Other *at the very moment* of participation in the anonymous irreality of elemental existence. Alone among the arts, literature is proximity to the Other in the instant of apocalypse, when the relational structure of the world gives way. The transcendental advantage of literature consists in its way of awakening the self to the elusive presence of the Other within the elemental conatus of existence, at the very moment when the sense of the world verges toward senselessness—

> zuweilen, wenn
> nur das Nichts zwischen uns stand, fanden
> wir ganz zueinander

> at times when
> only the void stood between us we got
> all the way to each other

—just like "ethics," the poetic word testifies to the *maintenance* of sense in the midst of the debacle of senselessness. *Il maintient le maintenant*—like a handshake in which the possessive conatus of the body is opened to the other, "ethics" *maintains* the fleeting instant of sensation across the duration of concrete temporality.[14] Citing Celan—"I cannot see any basic difference between a handshake and a poem"—Levinas embraces the possibilities of such a literature; "To make oneself completely into a sign, perhaps that is it." (Levinas 1996, 43)

Levinas's theory of literature thus undergoes a decisive bifurcation. On the one hand, literature is placed on the side of impersonal, elemental existence and primitive religion, along with all the arts. On the other hand, due not least to his ongoing reflections on metaphor and their theological implications, literature is redeemed, as it were, from the shadows of art, just as a certain conception of "religion" is distinguished from the primitive and mystical religions that jettison subjectivity and morality. Literature is now able to enact a Saying that leaps out of the dense shadows in which it transpires. If the characters, narrators, and poetic

---

14 The analyses of "the instant" in "Reality and its Shadow," *Time and the Other*, and *Existence and Existents* provide the background of elemental sensations verging toward senseless images that is finally resolved in Conclusion 9 of *Totality and Infinity*, "The Maintenance of Subjectivity". The maintenance of subjectivity across the discontinuities of the instant is accomplished through fecundity, being oneself for the sake of the Other. One can say, then, that the instant is the now-time of egoism, *le maintenant* the now-time of subjectivity.

figures in literature remain "fixed images" that draw us away from real people and real responsibilities in the world—as the critique of the aesthetics of literature proposes—nevertheless *a certain literature* is regarded as "a door, in this loosened self, leading beyond being" to a place without a world, but where, as Levinas cites Blanchot's saying, we "are together, but not yet" (1989b, 156). Levinas's appraisal of Blanchot's work testifies to this bifurcation.[15] Blanchot's writing no longer attests to the self talking with itself as it drifts endlessly into the irreal oblivion of the space of literature; Levinas now finds in Blanchot's work a door leading beyond being toward the Other, the very temporality of being-toward-the-Other, being together, but not yet. While this second conception of literature is reflected throughout Levinas's later thought, the case of Blanchot is particularly instructive on account of the reversal it clearly marks. We have noted how Levinas at first views Blanchot's writings as exemplifying the literature of existence without a world (see also Levinas 1978, 58n.1). In "The Servant and Her Master," however, published in 1966 in response to Blanchot's *L'attente l'oubli* (1997 [1966]), Levinas adopts an entirely different approach to Blanchot's work and, by implication, to a certain literature, which he personifies as a domestic servant in the house of her master, the Logos, "the speaker of truth," "coherent language," "logic". As servant, she indulges her master's pretentions, his "extravagant behavior," his "reputation for loving wisdom"; and yet she knows "the failures, the absences, the escapades of him whom she serves". She must accordingly attend to the ambiguity of her position; on the one hand she must obey the logic that ensures the master's house is kept in good order—through the use of appropriate rhetoric and grammar, for example—, on the other hand she cannot but admit the disorder which her master refuses to acknowledge. This disorder of the poetic word is a "madness" (*folie*) that the master will not tolerate.[16] Inspired by a poem of Lermontov he could doubtless declaim, Levinas translates "(in bad prose)" and avows the "utterances . . . of the madness of desire (*la folie du désir*) . . . In them the tears of separation, In them the trembling of reunion"

---

15 It is tempting to schematize this bifurcation chronologically, as though Levinas changes his view of literature from the critical appraisal in 1948 through to the ethical appraisal that emerges most clearly from the mid-1960's. It is probably more prudent, however, to speak of shifting emphases. A decisive exception to a chronological periodization of Levinas's two conceptions of literature could be illustrated by "The Other in Proust," also published in 1947, thus in the very midst of Levinas's cautionary, critical appraisal of literature, for it clearly indicates the uniquely ethical potential of "poetry". Even so, the more Levinas reflects on the importance of metaphor, which invariably correlates with an increasing appreciation of the ethical significance of "religion,"—roughly, from the mid-1950's—the more literature is singled out among the arts for its unique contribution to the ethics of being.

16 See *infra* Hart, this vol.

(Levinas 1989b, 158). The essay concludes with a question suggesting that the servant, literature, is less the subordinate than the lover of the Logos she serves.

> Housekeeper or Mistress? A marvellous hypocrite! For she loves the madness she keeps watch over.

There is little doubt that Levinas sides with the servant who loves the madness, the folly, of literature, even if he also respects the need for an order of truth and logic, its status and validity "in the world". *Otherwise than Being* (1991 [1974]) amply confirms this, not only with its quite mad, disruptive, anarchic style, its writing against the logos of the Said, but also with its explicit descriptions of subjectivity, the soul itself, as a madness in the heart of reason occasioned by the inextricable intimacy of the other. "The soul is the other in me. The psyche, the-one-for-the-other, can be a possession and a psychosis; the soul is already a seed of folly" (1991, 191n3; cf. 50, 84). A similar invocation of the folly or madness of subjectivity, "already a psychosis," refers the metaphor to the female lover in the *Song of Songs*, "possessed by the other, sick" (1991, 142), the footnote citing *Song of Songs* 6:8, "I am sick with love" (1991, 198n.5).

We thus find ourselves in a paradoxical proximity to the very disaster Levinas sought to avert. On the first conception, literature opens reality to an existence without order, tearing the drapes of civilization, isolating experience in pure sensations of images detached from objects, approaching and conjuring the *il y a*. By the late 1950's, however, the obverse problem has surfaced, namely, the problem of the excess of order besieging the modern world, the reign of the Said, the inevitable homogenization entailed by concepts and the discursive tyranny of everyday life, modern bureaucracy, and information technologies. It now becomes precisely a matter of the disorderly and disruptive function of literature that is prized, its irony with respect to truth, coherence and logic, its metaphorical extension of thought beyond the correlates of the empirically given, all of which offer a much valued interruption to the merciless orders of the Said in which the singular sense of the Other is suppressed. Levinas thus begins with a critical appraisal of literature's complicity in the dissolution of order and ends with an affirmation of its capacity to disrupt a world that has become immoderately ordered. He begins with an account of literature's collaboration with the conceptlessness of sheer existence without a world and ends with an avowal of literature's way of loosening the concepts that grasp the world so tightly as to stifle the unique sense of the Other. If literature participates in the anonymous, impersonal irreality of aesthetic disengagement, as Levinas still thinks, one nevertheless finds oneself oriented through literature toward the Other—not to others in the world, dear reader, but to the Other, the one without whom no sensibility would make sense—,

> . . . like a man lured on by a syllable without any meaning,
> A syllable of which he felt, with an appointed sureness,
> That it contained the meaning into which he wanted to enter.[17]

Literature is both elemental and personal, poison to a peopled world but medicine to the impersonal, anonymous existence in which we are immersed. Alone among the arts, literature affords the promise of a Saying within the impersonalism of elemental existence, just as monotheism introduces prophetic Saying into primitive and mystical religion. Literature is singled out among the arts for its way of measuring up to the folly of proximity. The "poetic word," like "ethics," like "prophesy," is necessary if one is to evade all that would reduce sense to platitudes—the natural topography of concepts—, dilute it within the insincerity of eloquence, or abandon it to the fallen language that dominates everyday life and so-called social media (Levinas 1993). A late essay, "Everyday Language and Rhetoric without Eloquence," picks up this theme in order to defend the alliance between the simplicity of everyday speech in which the other is approached directly and types of literary rhetoric that rage against the orders of discourse, "taking eloquence and wringing its neck," as Verlaine famously put it, the "anti-literature" that rebels against the repressive stability of the discursive orders that be. One might note, as Blanchot did in the very year this essay was published, that the language of "ethics" is not immune from the very problem it was designed to solve, since what Levinas calls "responsibility" is a "term which the language of ordinary morality uses in the most facile way possible by putting it into the service of order (Blanchot 1995, 26)." Hence the need, *for the sake of the Other*, for a literature that sows seeds of madness into the master morality, which is as much a part of the order of the Said as the discourses of politics, science, social media etc, and sometimes even more so.[18] Indeed, Levinas's essay alludes to the Terror of anti-literature (Levinas 1993, 140), famously analyzed by Jean Pauhan (2006 [1941]), long time accomplice of Blanchot, in his defense of a rhetoric of terror that stands up to false eloquence. *Otherwise than Being* exemplifies this rhetoric of terror without eloquence, "as if in order to regain one's lost sincerity, ordinary language were not enough" (Levinas 1993, 140). Levinas's suspicion of the eloquence of literature, then, left him with no alternative but to be a writer, thus fulfilling Paulhan's dictum that "No writer is more preoccupied with words than the one who at every point sets out to get rid of them, to get away from them, or to reinvent them" (Paulhan, 76). In this lies the marvellous hypocrisy of Levinas's approach to literature, which points not only toward impersonal

---

17 Wallace Stevens, "Prologues to What is Possible" (Stevens, 438).
18 Hence the anarchical function of the literature Levinas prizes; see *infra* Cools, this vol.

existence without a world but also toward the mystery of existence made intelligible only by being personal; not only to the *il y a* but also to *Autrui*; not only to 'primitive religion' but also to prophetic monotheism.

The impetus for a second conception of literature coincides with a growing awareness of how metaphor already steers language away from the fascination that reduces words to worldless images. It is clear that metaphor, for Levinas, is not just one literary trope among others but the essential feature that gives language ontological status equal to thought and perception. Metaphor marks the way language approaches *this-as-that*, a structural relation which, following Heidegger's analysis of the as-structure of intelligibility (Heidegger 1962, §32), integrates metaphor into the hermeneutic circle through which the sense of being is accessed. Metaphor is thus not added to understanding but expresses the as-structure of understanding in linguistic form, unsettling any stable hierarchy between language, thought, and perception. For Levinas, moreover, metaphor not only attests to a linguistic way of articulating an understanding of *this-as-that* but orients the horizontal movement of understanding along its implicit, vertical axis. Metaphor exposes the dimension of "height" within the horizontal movement of meaning (see Faessler). If all art, including literature, transdescends toward the *il y a*, literature, alone among the arts, also transascends toward the Other. Levinas provides a metaphor to express this vertical function. Metaphor is language "standing on tiptoes, in a kind of levitation" (Levinas 2009, 350). Metaphor elevates the as-structure of being, bends the curvature of intersubjective space upward in such a way that "the transitivity of being"—the movement of being through which a being maintains its identity—is oriented toward "height". Stevens gives voice to this elevation of the perceived into the sensed:

> How easily the blown banners change to wings . . .
> Things dark on the horizons of perception,
> Become accompaniments of fortune, but
> Of the fortune of the spirit, beyond the eye,
> Not of its sphere, yet not far beyond,
>
> The human end in the spirit's greatest reach,
> The extreme of the known in the presence of the extreme
> Of the unknown.[19]

Metaphor works as the vertical axis of language, providing an essentially theological orientation, even if God is never invoked, as when the nameless father in *The Road* envisions his anonymous son "glowing in that waste like a tabernacle". The *Inédits* make it clear how Levinas's interest in literature, nurtured from his

---

[19] Wallace Stevens, "To an Old Philosopher in Rome" (Stevens, 432).

youth but intensified in captivity as a Jewish prisoner of war, converged with his emerging conviction that theology, without dogma, was indispensable for coming to terms with the moral orientation of meaning—"without God there would be no metaphor. God is the very metaphor of language – the fact of thought that rises above itself. (This does not mean that God is only a metaphor. For there is no other metaphor than the movement bearing towards Him)." (Levinas 2009 1, 233) Although this strong formulation was excluded from his published writings on metaphor (Calin 2012), the thought persists: the *this-as-that* structure of experience is opened by the inscription of metaphorical height, concealing the trace of God in the as-structure of things, a sense of the Other, the still small voice, in the cleft of the identity of a thing with itself, as in Exodus 33. Levinas's second conception of literature affirms the folly or anarchy of love as a way of interrupting the oppressive, platitudinous or universal orders of the Said; this folly is developed because of his faith in the theological orientation of metaphor as such.[20] Another locution, written on the back of an invitation card from 1953 but omitted from his published essays, dares to wonder if the trace of the Infinite, the endless movement of metaphor that elevates the as-structure of meaning, reaches its finality in the solidarity of a people: "the idea of the culmination of all things in Israel: Love in relation to poetry. The end of metaphors" (Levinas 2009, 343). Cryptic, but clear enough to show how the *Inédits* constantly bring the question of literature to reckon with the biblical and prophetic tradition,[21] even if one might retort that 'Israel' is not the end but on the contrary the carnal origin of metaphor, "split first of all between the two dimensions of the letter" (Derrida, 92). The essays in this volume reflect and extend on themes the *Inédits* provoke, while further interrogating Levinas's relation to literary works and theoreticians.[22]

Bibliography

Armengaud, Françoise. 2000. "Faire ou ne pas faire d'images. Emmanuel Levinas et l'art d'oblitération." *Noesis*, no. 3. http://journals.openedition.org/noesis/11.
Blanchot, Maurice. 1995 [1981]. *The Writing of the Disaster*. Lincoln: University of Nebraska Press.

---

[20] For a different account see Hammerschlag (2016, 2019b), who argues for an antithetical relation between Levinas's conception of literature and religion. The alternative proposed here is that Levinas has two distinct conceptions of literature at work, one aligned with primitive religion and the elemental ontology that ethics opposes, the other allied to prophetic monotheism and the ways of Saying that transcend the Said.
[21] See *infra* Schonfeld, Fagenblat, Hoppenot, Liska, this vol.
[22] See *infra* Amiel-Houser, Anckaert, Noor, this vol.

Blanchot, Maurice. 1997 [1962]. *Awaiting Oblivion*. Translated by John Gregg. Lincoln: University of Nebraska Press.
Bruns, Gerald L. 2002. "The Concept of Art and Poetry in Emmanuel Levinas's Writings." *The Cambridge Companion to Levinas*. Eds. Simon Critchley and Robert Bernasconi. Cambridge: Cambridge University Press. 206–233.
Calin, Rodolphe. 2012. "La Métaphore Absolue. Un Faux Départ Vers l'autrement Qu'être." In *Levinas: Au-Delà Du Visible. Etudes Sur Les Inédits de Levinas Des Carnets de Captivité à Totalité et Infini*. Cahiers de Philosophie de l'Université de Caen 49. Caen: Presses universitaires de Caen.
Calin, Rodophe, and Catherine Chalier. 2009. "Préface." In *Levinas, Emmanuel. 2009. Oeuvres Complètes Tome 1: Carnets de Captivité et Autres Inédits*. Paris: Grasset., 13–40.
Charles, Daniel. 2000. "Éthique et esthétique dans la pensée d'Emmanuel Levinas." *Noesis*, no. 3 (March). http://journals.openedition.org/noesis/12.
Colléony, Jacques. 1991. "Levinas et l'art: La Réalité et Son Ombre." *La Part de l'œil* 7: 81–90.
Davis, Colin. 2015. "Levinas the Novelist." *French Studies* 69 (3): 333–44. https://doi.org/10.1093/fs/knv071.
Faessler, Marc. 2012. "Métaphore et Hauteur." In *Levinas: Au-Delà Du Visible. Etudes Sur Les Inédits de Levinas Des Carnets de Captivité à Totalité et Infini*. Cahiers de Philosophie de l'Université de Caen. Caen: Presses universitaires de Caen.
Hammerschlag, Sarah. 2016. *Broken Tablets: Levinas, Derrida, and the Literary Afterlife of Religion*. New York: Columbia University Press.
Hammerschlag, Sarah. 2019a. "Levinas's Prison Notebooks." *The Oxford Handbook of Levinas*. June 27, 2019. https://doi.org/10.1093/oxfordhb/9780190455934.013.1.
Hammerschlag, Sarah. 2019b. "A World Without Contours: Levinas's Critique of Literary Freedom." *Levinas Studies* 13: 121–39.
Hand, Seán. 2013. "Salvation through Literature: Levinas's Carnets de Captivité." *Levinas Studies*. July 1, 2013. https://doi.org/10.5840/levinas201385.
Hand, Seán. 2019. "Levinas, Literature, and Philosophy." The Oxford Handbook of Levinas. June 27, 2019. https://doi.org/10.1093/oxfordhb/9780190455934.013.51.
Hart, Kevin. 2019. "Levinas, Blanchot, and Art." The Oxford Handbook of Levinas. June 27, 2019. https://doi.org/10.1093/oxfordhb/9780190455934.013.3.
Heidegger, Martin, and Kenneth Haynes. 2002. "The Origin of the Work of Art." In *Off the Beaten Track*. Translated by Julian Young. Cambridge: Cambridge University Press.
Levinas, Emmanuel. 1946. "'Tout Est-Il Vanité?'" *Bulletin Interieur de l'Alliiance Israélite Universelle* 2 (9): 1–2.
Levinas, Emmanuel. 1969. *Totality and Infinity: An Essay on Exteriority*. Translated by Alphonso Lingis. Pittsburgh: Duquesne University Press. Translation of *Totalité et Infini : Essai Sur l'extériorité*. Dordrecht: Kluwer Academic, 1971 [1961].
Levinas, Emmanuel. 1978. *Existence and Existents*. Translated by Alphonso Lingis. Hague: Martinus Nijhoff. Translation of *De l'existence à l'existant*. Vrin. Paris. 1993 [1947].
Levinas, Emmanuel. 1987 [1947]. *Time and the Other*. Translated by Richard A. Cohen. Pittsburgh: Duquesne University Press.
Levinas, Emmanuel. 1989 [1948]. "Reality and Its Shadow." In *The Levinas Reader*, edited by Seán Hand, translated by Alphonso Lingis. Oxford: Blackwell. 129–143.
Levinas, Emmanuel. 1989b [1966]. "The Servant and Her Master." In *The Levinas Reader*, edited by Seán Hand, translated by Michael Holland, 150–59. Oxford: Blackwell.

Levinas, Emmanuel. 1991 [1974]. *Otherwise Than Being or Beyond Essence*. Translated by Alphonso Lingis. Dordrecht: Springer.
Levinas, Emmanuel. 1993 [1981]. "Everyday Language and Rhetoric Without Eloquence." In *Outside the Subject*, translated by Michael B. Smith, 135–43. Stanford: Stanford University Press.
Levinas, Emmanuel. 1996 [1947]. "Paul Celan: From Being to the Other." In *Proper Names*, translated by Michael B. Smith, 40–46. Stanford: Stanford University Press.
Levinas, Emmanuel. 2009. *Oeuvres Complètes Tome 1: Carnets de Captivité et Autres Inédits*. Paris: Grasset.
Levinas, Emmanuel. 2011. *Oeuvres complètes, tome 2: Parole et silence*. Paris: Grasset.
Levinas, Emmanuel. 2012. "Notes on Metaphor." Translated by Andrew Haas. *International Journal of Philosophical Studies* 20 (3): 319–30. https://philpapers.org/rec/LEVNOM-2.
Levinas, Emmanuel. 2013. *Oeuvres complètes, Tome 3: Eros, littérature et philosophie*. Paris: Grasset.
Nancy, Jean-Luc. 2013. "Préface: L'intrigue Littéraire de Levinas." In *Levinas, Emmanuel. 2013. Oeuvres Complètes, Tome 3: Eros, Littérature et Philosophie. Paris: Grasset*, 9–30.
McCarthy, Cormac. 2010. *The Road*. New York: Picador.
Merleau-Ponty, Maurice. Parcours 1935–1951. Lagrasse: Editions Verdier, 1997.
Paulhan, Jean. 2006 [1941]. *The Flowers of Tarbes: Or, Terror in Literature*. Translated by Michael Syrotinski. Champaign IL: University of Illinois Press.
Stevens, Wallace. 1997. *Collected Poetry and Prose*. Edited by Frank Kermode and Joan Richardson. New York: The Library of America.
Taminiaux, Jacques. 2009. "Art et Destin. Le Débat de Levinas Avec La Phénoménologie Dans « La Réalité et Son Ombre »." In *Maillons Herméneutiques: Études de Poétique, de Politique et de Phénoménologie*. 243–62. Paris: Presses Universitaires de France.

Arthur Cools
The Anarchy of Literature

1 Introduction

Let us start with this question: Does it make sense to search for a concept of literature in Levinas's philosophy? As Jean-Luc Nancy has observed, compared with some contemporary philosophers such as Jean-Paul Sartre, Jacques Derrida, and Paul Ricoeur, and despite some essays of literary criticism on Blanchot, Celan, Jabès, Proust, and a few others, the explicit relation of Levinas's philosophy to the literary is quite limited (Nancy 2013, 9). Indeed, Levinas does not – and has no intention to – contribute to a philosophy of literature; he does not examine the nature of the literary work and is not interested in defining it, and he does not raise the question of what literature is or employ any concept of literature in his philosophical argumentations and clarifications.

Yet references to literature are hardly absent in Levinas's writings. He acknowledges the existence of *les belles lettres* and recognizes the importance of national literatures (Levinas 1994, xi). Moreover, in some of his analyses, especially in his descriptions of the presence of being, he refers explicitly to the tragedies of Shakespeare and Racine, to the modernist poetry of Baudelaire and Rimbaud, and to the fictional writings of Dostoyevsky and Blanchot, amongst others. Critically, he integrates notions originating from the field of literary theory into the expression of his central argument, claiming an ethics as first philosophy. Examples include his use of the notion "intrigue" in the expression of "an intrigue of responsibility" (Levinas 1991, 6) and "the plot [*intrigue*] of Ethics" (Levinas 1991, 150), which must be articulated as "the breakup of a fate that reigns in essence" (Levinas 1991, 8), and the use of the notion of "denouement" to qualify "subjectivity" (Levinas 1991, 10). Finally, since the publication of the first three volumes of the *Œuvres*, and especially of the third volume, *Eros, littérature et philosophie inédits* (2013), there has been a growing consciousness amongst Levinas scholars about the importance of Levinas's view on metaphor for his own philosophy and of the literary dimension of Levinas's writing experiments, which include poems, narratives, and drafts of novels.

These various manifestations of literary expression in Levinas's writings have generated a more focused attention to the different stylistic, poetic, and semantic dimensions of his texts, as becomes manifest in the contributions to

Arthur Cools, University of Antwerp

this volume. They may even provoke a radical change in the approach to his work in general, in that the so-called philosophical work appears to be part of a writing process still – and each time again and in a different way – in search of "the intrigue" of an otherwise than being. However, they do not offer the answer to the opening question, for they do not deliver as such a concept of literature. Why is it, then, important to ask this question?

Between Levinas's ethics as first philosophy and the work of literature there is a structural and indissoluble coherence: the appearance of the emergence of meaning into being. The central issue of Levinas's investigations concerns the question of how meaning comes into being, and the answer to this question is provided by his account of ethics, by the significance of the face-to-face relationship to the neighbor. That same question is at stake in the work of literature, which can only come into being by expressing, manifesting, reflecting, scrutinizing, and generating meanings of human relationships. The *raison d'être* of the literary work is nothing more and nothing less than the manifestation of cultural, ethical, social, political, and metaphysical meanings at a certain moment and at a certain place in human history.

If one takes this structural coherence as a starting point, it may not come as a surprise that Levinas did not raise the question "What is literature?". For this is a secondary question as regards the primary question concerning the emergence of meaning in being. Moreover, if one takes this structural coherence as a starting point, the attempt to delineate the literary in Levinas's reflections or to articulate Levinas's reflections on literature may seem to be unfounded. For the literary is already at work in Levinas's ethical inquiry. From the perspective of the question concerning the emergence of meaning into being, the manifestation of the ethical significance appears to be already literary and the manifestation of the meaning of the literary work appears to be already ethical.

It follows from this perspective that it makes sense to search for a concept of literature in Levinas's philosophy, albeit not in terms of an already established, pre-given concept but rather insofar as it originates from Levinas's approach to the appearance of meaning. It may be the case that this approach upsets our pre-understanding of literature, whose Latin origin, as Derrida pointed out (Derrida 1996, 17–20), coincides with the moment of its institutionalization, inviting to a radical transformation.

In my contribution I will thematize some aspects of this transformation and I will do so by means of what I call the deformalization of narrative. I derive this expression from Stefano Micali's article "The Deformalization of Time" (2016). In the first part, I will explain how the deformalization of time changes the conditions of narration and I will show how this is present in

Levinas's writings. In the second part, I will present Levinas's concept of illeity as the most radical outcome of the deformalization of narrative and I will discuss its implications for the art of narration, before returning, in the final part, to the opening question concerning the concept of literature in Levinas's philosophy, which is based, as I will argue, upon an anarchical and insoluble ambivalence.

2 Narrative without Synthesis?

In Levinas's philosophy, narrative and narration lose their evidence. The notion of deformalization is meant to approach this loss. As the notion suggests, it implies as a minimal condition to put into question the primacy of the narrative form over content. The primacy of form in the context of a theory of narrative has been formulated time and again in the history of philosophy. In his *Poetics*, Aristotle distinguishes the formal features of the poetic arts and defines their main general feature as a representation of men in action. More recently, but still in the wake of Aristotle's legacy, Ricoeur, in his theory of narrative, uses the notion of "emplotment" (*mise en intrigue*), which names the formal unity and the synthetic coherence, characteristic of the act of narration (Ricoeur 1983, 66).

It is well known that Levinas criticizes, in light of Husserl's phenomenology, the dominance of the category of representation in the account of the constitution of meaning. Likewise, it is commonly recognized that action is not a basic assumption in Levinas's ethics, which refers to a radical passivity in the human condition. I mention this in order to show how far it would be to go from Aristotle to Levinas if one does not first examine the conditions that provoke the deformalization of time and narrative in Levinas's writings. In what follows I will therefore take Ricoeur's account of narrative as a reference not only because he is contemporary to Levinas and refers to his publications, but also because he explicitly thematizes and analyses the role of time in the construction of narrative.

In *Time and Narrative*, it is Ricoeur's explicit intention to connect what he calls the configuration of narrative to the temporality of lived experience and to re-examine in this regard Aristotle's concept of *mythos*, which he translates as "*mise en intrigue*," in order to draw attention to the specific, verbal, synthesizing productivity of the act of narrating which creates coherence and "concordance" in the floating, dispersing experience of time (cf. Ricoeur 1983, 66–67). In this regard, Ricoeur has in fact already opened the possibility of a deformalization of narrative, since he does not take the formal features of narrative as given once and for all; instead, he thematizes the historical condition of narrative forms, including the possibility of an examination of the history of narrative forms in relation to a changing experience of time and world. Moreover, Ricoeur's theory of narrative is supported by a critical in-depth examination of the different categories in which the western philosophical tradition has thought the experience of time and he carefully clarifies the insufficiency of these categories with regard to what he calls the aporia of time consciousness (cf. in particular the first part of the third volume of *Time and Narrative*: "L'aporétique de la temporalité" (Ricoeur 1985, 17–178)). In this way, his examination reveals a radical rupture and even more an unbridgeable gap between time and narrative. This gap has two main consequences for a theory of narrative: on one hand, narration is needed in the experience of daily life and is a necessary condition in order to create coherence in the disparate, to impose a structure on the chaotic and to comprehend the ungraspable; on the other hand, narratives are challenged and undermined by the very singularity of the experience of daily life.

Because of the intrinsic connection it establishes between narrative and time, Ricoeur's theory of narrative enables us to introduce the theme of deformalization. However, Ricoeur never mentions this notion as such, nor does he elaborate the questions and implications that it entails for his own theory of narrative. This is perhaps because, as he confirms on several occasions, he continues to regard, in the wake of Aristotle's *Poetics*, the "*mise en intrigue*" – the productive power of synthesis – to be the main feature of narrative and defines from the start "the world of action" (Ricoeur 1983, 108) to be the basic, ontological reference in which narrative composition is rooted and from which it emerges.

It is thus critical to examine why and how Levinas introduces and develops the issue of deformalization in his philosophy. He mentions the notion explicitly in order to describe his own approach to time. Micali (2015, 69) notes that Levinas gives a clear definition of what he understands by the deformalization of time in the context of his relation to the philosophy of Rosenzweig:

> In Rosenzweig's work, the abstract aspects of time – past, present, future – are deformalized; it is no longer a question of time, an empty form in which there are three formal dimensions. The past is Creation. It is as if Rosenzweig was saying: to think the past concretely, you have to think Creation. Or, the future is Redemption, the present is Revelation. What I retain is definitely not that second or third identification, but that very precious idea that certain formal notions are not fully intelligible except in a concrete event, which seems even more irrational than they are, but in which they are truly thought. (This quotation is from an interview with Levinas, "Philosophy, Justice, and Love" (1982), published in *Entre Nous* (1991), and quoted here from the English translation.)
> (Levinas 1998, 118)

Levinas returns to the notion of deformalization at the end of his article "Diachrony and Representation" (1985), first presented as a lecture at a conference in honor of Ricoeur, where he situates the notion into a broader context and clarifies his own approach in these terms: "But I have sought time as deformalization of the most formal form there is – the unity of the *I think*. Deformalization is that with which Bergson, Rosenzweig, and Heidegger, each in his own way, have opened the problematic of modern thought, by setting out from a concreteness 'older' than the pure form of time" (Levinas 1998, 176).

Deformalization is, for Levinas, in his approach to time a way of going beyond the abstract evidence of the three dimensions of past, present, and future, and of putting into question the formal categories in which the western tradition of philosophy has thought time as a unity, a flux, or a synthetic apperception. But he adds something important: the emancipation of time with regard to the formal categories of time requires a particular attention to the concreteness of the event "older" than the form of time. This means that there are no universal forms of time applicable to all events. Some events may not fit within the temporality of being-towards-death or may arrive in such a way that they interrupt the formal relation between present, past, and future. And it means, moreover, that formal notions cannot become fully intelligible except in light of the concrete event. This implies not only that the way in which one experiences, for instance, the future in the experience of waiting is radically different from the future lived in the experience of hope, but also that the category of future cannot be abstracted from the lived experiences in which the concrete temporal and embodied senses of the future emerge.

In relating deformalization of time to the concreteness of the event, Levinas contests the primacy and evidence of notions such as presence, representation, and synthesis in the understanding of experience. It implies a particular attention for the sensible qualities of experience, the irreducible indeterminable character of sensations, prior to any conceptual grip. In this regard, Levinas's use of the notion of deformalization leads us directly to the other notion of diachrony and its significance in his philosophy, which may have at least two meanings. It may be used in order to reveal the mismatch between conceptual discourse and experience and to disconnect discursive forms from the disruptive experience of the singular event. As Levinas states in "Phenomenon and Enigma" (1957): "The impossibility of manifesting itself in an experience can be due not to the finite or sensible essence of this experience, but to the structure of all thought, which is correlation." (Levinas 1987, 62) Discourse, because of the coherence it establishes, loses here its primacy and evidence with regards to the event that is perceivable in the sensible.

Yet Levinas also uses diachrony in a more stringent way in the analysis of a concrete event, in order to draw attention to a temporal dimension in the experience of the singular event that blocks, disrupts, or interrupts the ordinary, synchronic, or synthetic time experience. The analysis of the immemorial past, a past that has never been present and cannot be in correlation with a present – the so-called "trace of illeity" (Levinas 1987, 106) – has become dominant in Levinas's philosophy and is for many scholars the privileged way to discuss the significance of the concept of diachrony in his work. But Levinas gives other examples of experiences where the synthetic time experience is in default and where a detailed analysis of a different time structure is required, for instance in his analysis of insomnia in *Time and the Other*. As Micali comments about this analysis, "The phenomenon of differentiation, which, according to Husserl, permits the emergence of the elementary unities in the dimension of passive synthesis, does not function in insomnia in the usual way. The supposed unity of apperception dissolves; an indeterminate 'magma' appears to and dominates the person who is lost in this wakefulness without any aim or project." (Micali 2015, 73) Other examples, apart from insomnia, include Levinas's analyses of the caress, the phenomenon of desire, the encounter of the other, the possibility of pardon, the erotic experience, and fecundity in *Totality and Infinity*, and of the temporalities of substitution and traumatism in *Otherwise than Being*.

Levinas's elaborations of the deformalization of time entail important consequences for the art of narration. It may be clear by now why the traditional concepts of narrative forms are losing evidence: concepts such as representation, plot (*intrigue*) – even in the way Ricoeur understands it, as emplotment (*mise en intrigue*) – destiny, denouement, world, action, character, narrator, drama, tragedy, epos, etc. privilege the idea of a unity of the manifold, a synthesis of the disparate, a chronology of formal time dimensions, or a coherence of being and acting in narrative that are not given as such in light of the concrete experience of the event. Because of the representations and correlations they establish through discourse, narrative forms produce meanings that are insufficient or even misguiding as concerns the significance of the singular event – such as murder, violence, trauma, sexuality, maternity, guilt, mourning, depression, love, repentance, loyalty, responsibility, happiness, and the like – that is experienced in the human condition. In this regard, the deformalization of narrative results from the attention given to the concreteness of the event prior to the act of narration. It requires precisely to put into question the primacy of narrative forms, to break open the coherence that they intend, and to reconsider the art of narration in light of the concrete experience that does not fit in the narrated time.

In fact, this transformation of narrative occurred, as Merleau-Ponty describes it in his essay "Metaphysics and the Novel," in a broader historical context in the wake of a phenomenological and existential philosophy: "Everything changes when a phenomenological or existential philosophy assigns itself the task, not of explaining the world or of discovering its 'conditions of possibility,' but rather of formulating an experience of the world which precedes all thought *about* the world. [. . .] From now on the tasks of literature and philosophy can no longer be separated." (Merleau-Ponty 1964, 27–28) It is Merleau-Ponty who points here at the importance of expressing an experience of the world *that precedes* all thought about the world in order to qualify the transformation of narrative inspired by the phenomenological philosophy. Levinas certainly acknowledged and welcomed these developments in the field of literary narratives in his time, as becomes manifest for instance in the narrative technics of Sartre's *La Nausée*. However, it seems that for Levinas the deformalization of narrative has a more radical outcome. The story as narrative cannot avoid creating a unity and a coherence that is not given in the experience prior to any thought about the world. In his article "Language and Proximity," Levinas mentions this coherence of meaning created by narrative, in order to distinguish it from a language that originates from proximity: "Events which are staggered out according to time and reach consciousness in a series of acts and states also ordered according to time acquire, across this multiplicity, a unity of meaning in narration." (Levinas 1987, 109) Even in the existentialist novel, which Merleau-Ponty terms the metaphysical novel, the story enfolds a world and meaning appears as part of the world already given and manifested within the experience of a singular event. The attention given to the concreteness of the event, as implied in the way Levinas understands deformalization, breaks through these narrative coherences between world, experience, and meaning, and leads to the suspension or even breakdown of all meanings, already given, as related to the world, in order to allow the experience of the event manifest itself prior to the world.

In his book *Postmodernity, Ethics, and the Novel: From Leavis to Levinas*, Andrew Gibson underscores the radical dimension of problematizing and undermining the classic conceptions of narrative such as unity, representation, and wholeness in Levinas's philosophy. In-line with this argument he considers Levinas to provoke "the dissolution of the novel": "It seems to me, then, that, for Levinas, 'dissolution' is not to be conceived of as a static condition or a final end. It is an active principle and a form of intellectual work, to which there is no conclusion. Thus, [. . .], 'dissolution' appears as a median term between a given form and its annihilation." (Gibson 1999, 88)

Although, as I will show in the next two parts, this presentation is one-sided and unable to account for the complex ambivalence of narrative in Levinas's philosophy, it remains the case that the deformalization of time and narrative includes the possibility of the dissolution of the narrative in a dynamic way. Yet, this dynamic way is itself singular in Levinas's writings (not applicable to a category such as the "postmodern" novel). The dissolution is not a disappearance or an annihilation; rather, it is a reduction and destabilization or an interruption of the evidence of given forms. For that reason, it would be interesting to reconsider the literary references and experiments in Levinas's writings in light of his approach to the deformalization of time and narrative.

In his article "The Debacle or the Real under Reduction: The Scene of Alençon" (published in translation in this volume), François-David Sebbah thematizes and examines, in terms that recall the operations implied in deformalization, the reduction at work in what Levinas calls, in his *Carnets de captivité*, "my scene of Alençon." (Levinas 2009, 136) This scene figures in what is considered to be Levinas's unfinished and unpublished "novel," *Sad Opulence* or *Eros* (accessible since 2013 in the third volume of the *inédits*), a work that may not actually have been intended as a novel. The notion of "scene" is more adequate here because it already includes the transformation of narrative as it results from the reduction to a single event which reveals the breakdown of all given meanings of a common world. The scene describes the moment of the defeat, the very event of the suspension of a world having lost its familiarity, where human beings suddenly appear to be no longer following their own trajectory in any meaningful context and practice of daily life, but instead find themselves on the move, as a crowd of refugees, indistinct and encumbered by their baggage, without trajectory, in a derisory and senseless turbulence of movements. The scene is precisely in this sense a scene in that it does not relate the event to the world of yesterday or to a *lendemain* of the defeat, another world that already announces itself as a promise or a combat; likewise, it does not take the event as a starting point from which to narrate the action of a character that restores him as an individual and transforms him into a hero. On the contrary, it is a scene in that it searches for the singular meaning of the event by means of a reduction of narrative meanings that is expressed through one single, recurrent image: the drapes (representative of the power of institutions that guarantee the meaningful world) that are ablaze and that fall (their representative function and the power of institutions have collapsed).

Through reduction, the scene transforms the narrative into something spectacular – a visibility without context; however, it does not stop the reduction there but rather pushes it further in order to express the singular, uncertain, non-evident meaning behind this appearance.¹ Something similar is at stake in the way Levinas introduces literary references into his philosophical argumentation. In fact, as many scholars have observed, Levinas's use of literary references is idiosyncratic. His quotations, whether from the Talmud, a drama of Shakespeare, a novel of Dostoyevsky, or a poem of Baudelaire, are time and again included in philosophical examination without any transition, sometimes without even being identified as quotations. For example: "'The true life is absent.' But we are in the world. Metaphysics arises and is maintained in this alibi." (Levinas 1979, 33) These are the opening sentences of his analysis of desire in the first part of *Totality and Infinity*: the first is a quote from Rimbaud (who is not identified); the second inverts the meaning of the quote of Rimbaud, who originally continued by saying that we are *not* in the world; the third confirms Levinas's commitment to metaphysics. Moreover, Levinas often uses a literary quote via reducing it to a single appearance of meaning – a "scene," as I prefer to say – without any consideration for the narrative context and complexity of the original text. A well-known example is a quote from Dostoyevsky's *The Brothers Karamazov*: "Each of us is guilty before everyone and for everyone, and I more than the others." This reference recurs in various texts of Levinas (cf. Levinas 1991, 146; cf. Levinas 1998, 105), but without consideration of either the character who expresses this sentence or the narrative context in which it is expressed. Other examples are his quotation from *The Song of Songs* at the core of his argumentation on subjectivity as exposition of the self to the other, a quotation reduced to one word: "sick [from love]" (Levinas 1991, 142), and the reference to Isaiah 6:8 in the same context, also reduced to a single expression, "Here I am (*me voici*)" (Levinas 1991, 146). Derrida wondered why Levinas does not specify the contexts of these quotations (for instance the female voice in the *Song of Songs* (Derrida 1987, 167–169)).

Levinas, indeed, is not interested in characters or in the plot-structure of narratives. When he refers to *MacBeth* in Existence and Existents, it is not the main character and his dispositions to act that attract Levinas's attention, but rather the experience of the spectacular presence of existence at the margins of world: "In MacBeth, the apparition of Banquo's ghost is also a decisive

---

1 So, when Levinas defines "the face" as that which breaks at any times through the form that presents it, he is, in a certain way, simply formulating the principle of the method of deformalization and applying it to the encounter of the other person: the event of the encounter is first reduced to the scene of the face, that appears in a spectacular way ("a plastic form," "without context"), and second the reduction is pushed further so as to articulate the singular, non-evident meaning behind this appearance.

experience of the 'no exit' from existence, its phantom return through the fissures through which one has driven it. 'The times have been, that when the Brains were out, the man would dye, and there an end; But now they rise again . . . and push us from our stools. This is more strange than such a murder is.' 'And it is over with' is impossible." (Levinas 1989, 33–34) Similarly, when he comments on Blanchot's *La Folie du jour*, he does not enter into analysis of the complex structure of the narrator's time experience; rather, he highlights one "little scene in which, in front of the courtyard door, a man steps back to let a baby carriage through, is the event of an advent – that is, the moment when something abnormal ensues: one person withdraws before the other, one is for the other. Whence the narrator's lightheartedness, which seems to lift him above being." (Levinas 1996, 165–166)

3 Illeity without Narration?

From this examination of the deformalization of time and narrative, it follows that for Levinas narration is secondary with regard to experience. There is no ontological continuity between the latter and the former. Experience itself is not originally or necessarily correlated to the world or to the beings in the world. What manifests itself in experience lacks the formal and synthetic coherence characteristic of the narrative, hence Levinas's emphasis, in the introduction of *Otherwise than Being*, on the "unsayable" (*l'indicible*) and the "enigmatic" that exceeds propositional language: "When stated in propositions, the unsayable (or the an-archical) espouses the forms of formal logic; [. . .]." (Levinas 1991, 7) The articulation of what manifests itself in experience does not necessarily involve narrative or discursive categories. This is precisely what Levinas's analysis of sensibility intends to demonstrate: "The immediacy of the sensible which is not reducible to the gnoseological role assumed by sensation is the exposure to wounding and to enjoyment, an exposure to wounding in enjoyment, which enables the wound to reach the subjectivity of the subject complacent in itself and positing itself for itself. This immediacy is first of all the ease of enjoyment, more immediate than drinking, the sinking into the depth of the element, into its incomparable freshness, [. . .]." (Levinas 1991, 104). The immediacy of the sensible is what at any time escapes the thematization of experience and does not stop manifesting itself without regard for its thematization. The immediacy of the sensible is in this regard the permanent source of contestation undermining the evidence of already given categories that are used to describe experience.

However, despite the ontological break between experience and narration, Levinas seems to take for granted that narration is dependent on experience, not only in the sense of "arising from" or "having its origin in" but also in the sense of "being the expression of." The act of narration responds to the concreteness of a prior event that is not in itself already narrative, or that is not in itself already part of a meaningful world, but that is witnessed by the act of narration. It seems thus inevitable that the act of narration is first confronted with a "not knowing what to say," with "a not being able to express." However, this way of presenting the narrative's dependency on experience risks suggesting that an adequate articulation of what is original in experience remains ever possible and merely awaiting for the corresponding narrative form. This interpretation is mistaken for two reasons. It assumes the continuity between experience and narration, thereby reducing the (ungraspable strangeness of the) former to the meaning expressed by the latter. Levinas's approach clearly has another direction: considering an ontological gap between experience and narrative, he argues that the meaning of narrative forms is dependent on a significance that exceeds that meaning. Moreover, this way of presenting the relation between experience and narrative risks understanding the prior event of the experience as the origin of narrative forms, thus confusing two distinct questions, namely, that concerning the possibility of narration and that concerning the narration's dependency on experience. In fact, Levinas articulates the relation between experience and narration in two steps. The act of narration is possible only within the context of a commonality: in other words, the reference to the third – the presence of a community – is already required in order to address, to compose, and to interpret a narrative. However, as expression of experience, narration responds to a concreteness that is prior to this commonality. This concreteness is not an origin from which to deduce discursive and narrative forms. It is, as noted earlier, not in itself already part of a meaningful world; rather, it disturbs and undermines the evidence of the already given meanings in the common world. In this sense, it is not originary but "anarchical," as Levinas would say. Yet the act of narration responds to it, responds to this non-origin.[2]

The narrative's relation to experience is thus complex. It requires a two-staged analysis: an examination of the narrative's relation to the cultural context as a whole – an examination which may be able to shed light on the origin of narrative forms; and an examination of the narrative's response to the

---

[2] For an in-depth articulation of the problem of origin in Levinas in relation to the anarchical see Bierhanzl, "Chapter III. L'origine du langage" (2014, 59–80).

anarchical concreteness of experience – an examination of the singularity of the narrative's expression which destabilizes the apparent meanings of its formal qualities. In what follows, I will further focus on the narrative's dependency of the anarchical concreteness of experience, as Levinas articulates it. For Levinas has his own way of thematizing this dependency, namely, by introducing the idiosyncratic concept of "illeity": "Illeity is the origin of the alterity of being," he states in "Meaning and Sense" (Levinas 1987, 106). Illeity is the name of the alterity that is not a worldly being, that does not belong to being, and that does not appear: it transcends the order of being and appearing. Illeity is thus not an experience; there is no experience of the illeity. For that reason, Levinas uses the notion of "trace" in a direct connection with the concept of illeity: "Only a being that transcends the world, an ab-solute being, can leave a trace." (Levinas 1987, 105) The trace signifies the transcendence beyond being: "the signifyingness of a trace consists in signifying without making appear, [. . .] it establishes a relation with illeity" (Levinas 1987, 104) in that it disturbs the order of the world. It is not to be confused with a sign that presents another world behind the actual world. The trace does not refer to the presence of a past event that still is accessible from the present (as in memory and history). It refers to a past that has never been present, an immemorial past, and that in passing has disturbed the order of presence in an irreversible way. "A trace is a presence of that which properly speaking has never been there, of what is always past." (Levinas 1987, 105)

It is clear that Levinas, introducing the notion of illeity, still wishes to say something about the anarchical concreteness of/before experience to which narration responds. And the notion of trace is certainly helpful to approach that which escapes synchronization in experience and disturbs the evident order of meanings, as have various authors, from Nietzsche and Freud to Deleuze and Derrida. However, the concept of illeity adds something new, in that it seems to delineate the ungraspable, destabilizing otherness of the anarchical in experience. Illeity is the substantive form of the French pronoun "il," which can be used for the singular masculine "he" or the neutral "it." It appears that Levinas explicitly limits its meaning to the former, as when he writes "[t]he illeity of the third person" (Levinas 1987, 104), although it is unclear how it is possible to define the alterity beyond being as "personal" and as "male." The "il" of the illeity is not the "it" of a thing (cf. Levinas 1987, 106), nor is it the "you" (the second-person singular) whom the I addresses in the encounter of the other person; nor is it the "there" of the "there is" (the *il y a*), the vague, undefinable, and unescapable presence of existence. It would have been possible to approach and to express the anarchic, non-original, inescapable, and unsayable alterity in each of these relations, as does, for (brief) example, Blanchot in *Thomas l'Obscur*, for the "there is" (cf. Levinas 1989, 36); Ionesco, for the "you" in the encounter with the other person; and Artaud, for the "it." The "il" of the illeity seems to relate to the anarchical – to the concreteness of the event "older" than the world – in yet another way.

It is interesting to note that the reduction given with the deformalization of narrative, as mentioned at the end of the first section, reaches here, in the concept of illeity, its most extreme possibility. The formal indicator "il" is the minimal condition without which it would no longer be possible to state any meaning, not even the meaning of the difference between alterity and selfhood. From the abstraction of this formal indicator, almost all narrative means are erased. In other words, with regard to the concept of illeity, a narrative can only fail, be mistaken, fall short of presenting its relevance or betray it, for it belongs to the essence of narratives to represent an experience, an estrangement, an event, a character, a world . . .

Yet, it is also notable that Levinas refers again to a little scene reduced to its minimal form – the form of a name which is the beginning of all names – in order to express the orientation of meaning that the concept of illeity introduces into being. In *Otherwise than Being*, in the midst of a philosophical argumentation about the glory of the Infinite, the concreteness of the event of which the "il" of the illeity is the trace, Levinas states the following: "like the thickets of Paradise in which Adam hid himself upon hearing the voice of the eternal God traversing the garden from the side from which the day comes, offered a hiding-place from the assignation, in which the position of the ego at the beginning, and the very possibility of origin, is shaken." (Levinas 1991, 144)[3] To be sure, the scene is introduced by "like" (*comme*), indicating the scene's metaphoric use, its secondary relevance as regards the meaning of the illeity. The scene is already a betrayal, but one that reveals something crucial about the origin of the anarchical. Again, all narrative context and presuppositions – including the creation of world, the naming of the creatures, the life of paradise, the love of Eve, the prohibition of transgressing, the face of the snake, the seduction – are eliminated from this scene, including even the consciousness of one's own and the other's nakedness. Reduced in this way, the

---

[3] Levinas refers here to Genesis 3:8 but appears to offer his own translation when he adds "from the side from which the day comes." The Hebrew Bible reads: "the ru'ah of the day" – the wind of spirit of the day. In the French translation of the edition of Rachi, the verse is: "Ils entendirent la voix de l'Eternel-Dieu, parcourant le jardin du côté du jour." And in the French translation of the Bible of Jerusalem: "Ils entendirent le pas de Yahvé-Dieu qui se promenait dans le jardin à la brise du jour." I am grateful to Michael Fagenblat for noting this to me and suggesting that Levinas's translation may be based upon a rabbinic midrash.

scene delivers a single image of Adam's hiding, the meaning of which emerges from the passing of illeity – the traversing of the eternal God – that disturbs the order of the created world. The trace of this passing provokes the sign given to the other in the modality of a hiding that is incapable of undoing in the hiding the response to the passing. It seems thus that Levinas is suggesting that the anarchical – whatever may be the experience it disturbs – relates to this scene, which can be called "primal" both in this sense and in that it expresses "the origin of the alterity of being".

In this way, Levinas is able to delineate in at least three ways the alterity of the anarchical of/before experience as intended by the concept of illeity. First, "the trace of the illeity," the illeity as trace, signifies that the anarchical is beyond representation. In other words, it is not sufficient to describe the anarchical in terms of the unconsciousness, the oblivion, the repression or the displacement of the representational (as is the case in a psychoanalytic and/or deconstructionist context). The anarchical does not belong to the order of representation; it cannot be represented and it escapes any attempt to represent it. Second, the illeity as "origin of the alterity" signifies that the anarchical has its origin outside human experience. The anarchical inverts the movement that starts from and has its origin in selfhood. "*Beyond being is a third person* which is not definable by the oneself, by ipseity." (Levinas 1987, 103) Consequently, the anarchical breaks into the self-relatedness of selfhood before and without the self having any possibility of receiving it or relating to it. Third, the "illeity of the third person," the illeity as third person beyond being, signifies that the anarchical assigns selfhood: "a relationship which is personal and ethical, is an obligation and does not disclose" (Levinas 1987, 104). Here Levinas relates the third person of the illeity to the face. "The *beyond* from which a face comes in the third person." (Levinas 1987, 104) The absence that manifests itself in the face, breaking out of its plastic form, is not a senseless emptiness – "a pure hole in the world" (Levinas 1987, 103), as Sartre would say – but signifies the anarchic in the third person beyond being that summons the self to respond to the other.

The concept of illeity thus concerns and transforms in a singular way the possibility of narration. In fact, with this notion, Levinas brings narration into a relation of contiguity with a radical transcendence that exceeds all narrative forms (beyond representation), that precedes the act of narration (having its origin outside selfhood), and that calls for narration as a sign given in response. I will try to articulate a bit more what this implies for Levinas's understanding of narrative. To the extent that it responds to what Levinas calls illeity, narrative has no primary intention to create synthesis – to invent a plot capable of expressing the coherence of different time-layers; it is, rather, a means of invoking and addressing what exceeds it, as does prayer or poetry, especially love songs and lamentations. Hence, perhaps, the relevance of Levinas's references to the *Song of Songs* and *Lamentations*. Moreover, as address and invocation, narrative already exposes its insufficiency with regard to the addressee. It presents itself as response to a prior call and as a response that recognizes the beyond of the addressee. Levinas articulates this relation of insufficiency in terms of "witnessing." He introduces this notion in relation to the Infinite: "There is witness, a unique structure, an exception of the rule of being, irreducible to representation, only of the Infinite." (Levinas 1991, 146) But while he avers that "[t]he Infinite does not appear to him that bears witness to it" and that "[t]he detachment of the Infinite from the thought that seeks to thematize it and the language that tries to hold it in the said is what we have called *illeity*" (Levinas 1991, 147), witnessing can be understood as the narrative's modality of relating to illeity. In Levinas's view, witnessing has a singular structure which already has its origin in the alterity of the illeity. Witnessing cannot be understood here as the confirmation of a present or past event. It does not presuppose the identification of the one who bears witness. Witnessing implies, on the contrary, a "reversal" (Levinas 1991, 147) of the subject, an "alteration in which identity is brought out" (Levinas 1991, 146). Narrative as witnessing exposes this reversal: it reflects and expresses that it has neither its beginning nor its enclosure in the I of the narrator.

4 The Anarchy of Literature

It should be clear by now that the modern novel does not constitute for Levinas the primary narrative model. The expression and exploration of selfhood and otherness, characteristic of the novelistic form, risks by the very act of narration to reduce transcendence and to assess the self – whatever may be the experience of otherness that the novel addresses. However, this does not imply that Levinas rejects literature as such, as some scholars appear to suggest (cf. Robins 1999, 39). In fact, Levinas brings narration back to an origin that precedes the epic genre as a whole: to the testimonies of biblical texts such as *Genesis*, *Lamentations*, the *Song of Songs*, and the *Prophets*. Let us now return to the opening remarks of this contribution and address the question concerning the concept of literature. What happens when Levinas re-uses the literary notions of "intrigue" with regard to the Infinite and "denouement" with regard to subjectivity?

First, he situates his entire philosophy, including its search for the concreteness of the event older than the world, in the dependency of the literary. The literary is required in order to be able to approach and to articulate the emergence of meaning in being, even when this articulation implies the deformalization of all literary means. In other words, even the significance of the trace of the illeity beyond being is already literary; it cannot be expressed without the literary, as the appearance of the story of Adam's hiding in Paradise has revealed. It follows that in Levinas's philosophy the concept of literature does not coincide with the moment of its institutionalization. It follows even more radically that the literary irreducibly exceeds the concept of literature, preceding the moment of its conceptualization and thematization. As concerns the literary, literature and philosophy are both secondary.

Second, Levinas overwrites the notions of "intrigue" and "denouement," adding a new meaning that undermines and destabilizes their given epic meaning. The power of synthesis, characteristic of this epic meaning, is undermined by a diachronic temporality that becomes manifest by breaking open the representational coherence and enclosure of the narrative. The destabilization is not only a result of the temporal reversal of synchrony in diachrony. It also provokes a semantic inconsistency: the intrigue of fate that appears in being is broken up by another intrigue of the Infinite that precedes it and therefore is not an intrigue in being; the denouement of destiny that appears in being is undone by the denouement of responsibility that precedes it and therefore is not a denouement in being. The apparent meaning of the notions of "intrigue" and "denouement" is shaken by another "prior" meaning that puts into question the manifest sense and use of these notions in being.

The anarchy of literature is thus inescapable and insoluble: this is the paradox that follows from Levinas's approach to the appearance of meaning. It is inescapable, for the literary exceeds the concept of literature, including Levinas's articulation of an otherwise than being that intends to address the sense of transcendence beyond all literary means. It is insoluble, because the meaning that appears has already been preceded by another meaning – a sense of passing of the illeity, the signifyingness of a trace – that disturbs, interrupts, and undermines the order of appearing. In this way, Levinas's account of the appearance of meaning is caught by a double bind: while the articulation of this appearance still depends on the use of literary means, this use cannot be but a betrayal of the sense of transcendence beyond being. Indeed, this paradox is the outcome of the deformalization of time and narrative in Levinas's writings and also motivates it as a radical methodology. The double bind is not a failure of Levinas's thought; it is intended. It has the positive meaning of revealing, in the anarchical moment of disturbance, the possibility of an ethics that precedes ontology and resists any attempt of naturalization. As Levinas writes: "Everything depends on the possibility of vibrating with a meaning that is not synchronized with the speech that captures it and cannot be fitted into its order; everything depends on the possibility of a signification that would signify in an irreducible disturbance. If a formal description of such a disturbance could be attempted, it would have us speak of time, a plot and norms that are not reducible to the understanding of being, which is allegedly the alpha and the omega of philosophy." (Levinas 1987, 63)

Bibliography

Bierhanzl, Jan. *La rupture du sens. Corps, langage et non-sens dans la pensée de la signifiance éthique d'Emmanuel Levinas*. Paris: Editions Mimesis, 2014.
Derrida, Jacques. "En ce moment même dans cet ouvrage me voici." *Psyché. Inventions de l'autre*. Paris: Galilée, 1987. 159–202.
Derrida, Jacques. "Demeure. Fiction et témoignage." *Passions de la littérature*. Ed. Michel, Lisse. Paris: Galilée, 1996. 13–73.
Gibson, Andrew. *Postmodernity, Ethics and the Novel: From Leavis to Levinas*. London: Routledge, 1999.
Levinas, Emmanuel. *Totality and Infinity: An Essay on Exteriority*. Trans. Alphonso Lingis. The Hague: Martinus Nijhoff, 1979.
Levinas, Emmanuel. *Collected Philosophical Papers*. Trans. Alphonso Lingis. Dordrecht: Martinus Nijhoff, 1987.
Levinas, Emmanuel. *The Levinas Reader*. Ed. Seán Hand. Oxford: Basil Blackwell, 1989.
Levinas, Emmanuel. *Otherwise than Being or Beyond Essence*. Trans. Alphonso Lingis. Dordrecht: Kluwer, 1991.
Levinas, Emmanuel. *Beyond the Verse: Talmudic Readings and Lectures*. Trans. Gary D. Mole. Bloomington: Indiana University Press, 1994.
Levinas, Emmanuel. "Exercises on 'The Madness of the Day.'" *On Maurice Blanchot*, bound with *Proper Names*. Trans. Michael B. Smith. Stanford: Stanford University Press, 1996. 156–170.
Levinas, Emmanuel. *Entre Nous: Thinking-of-the-other*. Trans. Michael B. Smith and Barbara Harshav. New York: Columbia University Press, 1998.
Levinas, Emmanuel. *Oeuvres 1: Carnets de captivité et autre inédits*. Eds. Rodolphe Calin and Catherine Chalier. Paris: Grasset/IMEC, 2009.
Levinas, Emmanuel. *Œuvres 3. Eros, littérature et philosophie. Essais romanesques et poétiques, notes philosophiques sur le thème d'éros*. Eds. Jean-Luc Nancy and Danielle Cohen-Levinas. Paris: Grasset/IMEC, 2013.
Merleau-Ponty, Maurice. "Metaphysics and the Novel." *Sense and Non-sense*. Trans. Hubert L. Dreyfus and Patricia Allen Dreyfus. Evanston: Northwestern University Press, 1964. 26–40.
Micali, Stefano. "The Deformalization of Time." *Debating Levinas' Legacy*. Eds. Andris Breitling, Chris Bremmers, and Arthur Cools. Leiden: Brill, 2015. 69–80.

Nancy Jean-Luc. (2013). "Préface. L'intrigue littéraire de Levinas," in Emmanuel Levinas, *Œuvres 3. Eros, littérature et philosophie. Essais romanesques et poétiques, notes philosophiques sur le thème d'éros*. Eds. Jean-Luc Nancy and Danielle Cohen-Levinas. Paris: Grasset/IMEC, 2013. 9–30.

Ricoeur Paul. *Temps et récit. 1. L'intrigue et le récit historique*. Paris: Seuil, 1983.

Ricoeur Paul. *Temps et récit. 3. Le temps raconté*. Paris: Seuil, 1985.

Robins, Jill. *Altered Reading: Levinas and Literature*. Chicago: University of Chicago Press, 1999.

Part I: *Eros*

Jean-Luc Nancy
Eros, Emmanuel Levinas's Novel?

1

Among Levinas's unpublished manuscripts from the period of his captivity, there is a partially developed draft project for a novel. It is contained in a notebook of approximately one hundred pages, the cover of which bears the name *Eros*. This notebook consists essentially of the sketch of a narrative, echoed in other notebooks of the same period that are theoretical notes placed under the sign of *Eros*. There are thus two parts, to read and work on separately. I shall refer solely to the first, the sketch of this novel.

One day when we were in the Levinas archive with Michael and Danielle,[1] we discovered this thoroughly fascinating project for a novel. I propose to carry out an initial exploration of this project, cognisant that the pages of this notebook contain many deletions and are not always legible.

I shall take my point of departure from a single theoretical principal: one should attribute to this sketch the full status of literature and should leave theory aside. Levinas wanted to write a narrative. In a note to the *Carnets de captivité*, he sees the future of his work as a triptych: literature, philosophy, and critical writing. Literature is there. Levinas is undoubtedly a philosopher, but he wants to write a narrative. In the *Carnets*, one can refer to the notes (Levinas 2009, 126, 147) that provide the key: the novel is the locus of mystery. At this moment, Levinas felt that to write a narrative, a fiction, was to allow

---

[1] This visit to IMEC in the Abbey of Ardennes near Caen took place in September 2006. Gérard Bensussan was also present when we consulted the computerised files of the *Carnets de captivité*. It was following this visit, after reading the *Carnets* carefully, that the idea of a publication emerged. The project was submitted for the approval of the academic committee of Levinas's *Complete Works*, presided over by Jean-Luc Marion.

Note: This presentation took place on the basis of notes. The painstaking transcription makes more apparent the occasionally abrupt or summary character of a discourse that has not yet mobilised all the means of analysis. This was my choice: not to claim to penetrate either Levinas's text or its singular situation more than an initial, still rough reading allowed. The lecture by Jean-Luc Nancy was transcribed by Laetitia Meyzen. The final text was prepared and annotated by Danielle Cohen-Levinas. We thank Michael Levinas for authorising the publication of extracts from the unpublished novel by Emmanuel Levinas and we thank IMEC for having provided Jean-Luc Nancy with a photocopy of the manuscript of this novel.
Translation: Translated, from the French, by Ashraf Noor.

ට Open Access. © 2021 Jean-Luc Nancy, published by De Gruyter. This work is licensed under the Creative Commons Attribution 4.0 International License.
https://doi.org/10.1515/9783110668926-002

"mystery," a key word in this draft of the novel, to be welcomed, to grant it a complete place of its own, which is not without consequences.

Why did Levinas not continue? Why did he not continue to write literature? One can perhaps say of this draft that it is clumsy. Indeed, Levinas does not really manage to sustain a narrative; he does not manage to fix upon a particular figure, nor even find a fixed name for it. This could, of course, be understood as the path chosen by the author. In this narrative he is undoubtedly too much of a prisoner, if one can say such a thing, of his own experience, which, moreover, he relates. For this novel is, indeed, autobiographical: as another passage in the *Carnets* indicates, autobiography, when it is not autobiographical, consists precisely in not saying Me but He, as in fiction. In saying He, one has already modified the personal position of subjectivity. This assemblage of thought under the sign of *eros* is definitely nothing other than exit from oneself and access to the other.

Afterwards, post captivity, Levinas will write no further literary experiments, because his thought undergoes a turn following the war. This is a complex and delicate aspect of his work. In the series of unpublished *Lectures*[2] that are included in the second volume of the *Complete Works*, one already sees certain very fine inflections consisting of a movement in which desire and pleasure are pushed towards the side of that which does not transcend enough. Pleasure will bear the tone that it takes on later in *Totalité et infini* (1961), the tone of pleasure as possession.

In the period of this manuscript, if one considers the theoretical notes, Levinas writes that voluptuousness is nothing other than seeking even more voluptuousness. He writes that the supreme moment is the extinction of this infinite desire of voluptuousness. In this period, then, with the novelistic attempt to involve the register of reflection on *eros*, Levinas still thinks of desire as infinite. Then, at a given moment, it seems to him that he can no longer grant to desire the "benefit" of infinity – this is indeed very apparent in *De l'évasion*.[3] In the condition of the prisoner, there is something that opens up, something which is in part imaginary, phantasmal. After the war, there will be a return to reality and above all there will be the discovery of what happened during the war, the discovery of something Levinas had not known about. At the end of the novel, there is, however, an evocation of the camps. There is thus a sort of turn in his work and in his reflection. A displacement takes place, a displacement that also

---

2 See Levinas, *Oeuvres*, 2: *Parole et Silence et autres conférences inédites au Collège Philosophique*, *Oeuvres* II (2011).
3 This text was written in 1935 and published in 1982 by the publishing house Fata Morgana, with an introduction and notes by Jacques Rolland.

goes from the others to the Other. This considerable deepening occurs precisely through the displacement.

What is the novel about? It is above all about others. In his theoretical notes, Levinas envisages something that he does not really do in his subsequent work, or at least he envisages it in another way. It is above all a question of all the possible figures and modalities that the relation to others assumes: conviviality, companionship, friendship, and finally love. Much could be learned from a serious study, both theoretical and historical, of what really happens for Levinas in this period.

In a lecture of 1950, "Les enseignements" (The Teachings), which takes up again the theme of voluptuousness that always tends infinitely to more voluptuousness, Levinas says that one may not reduce the other to the experience of pleasure. A few lines earlier, he speaks of Freud in order to reject him, to say that Freud reduces sex to seeking pleasure, without any inkling of the ontological dimension of sex. Levinas feels obliged to modify his view perhaps not only because of Freud, but perhaps more because of the whole atmosphere of the period, in which he feels the danger of falling into seduction and reduction, into seeking pleasure.

There is therefore this displacement of which I just spoke, this deviation, and at the same time, in the same lecture, Levinas writes: "And the caress takes place, however, as a double-headed sensation felt without confusion by two beings." This sentence is clearly not Freudian yet neither is it really that of the later Levinas. In the balancing of this "however," there is a sort of suspension, an extremely interesting hesitation, which I would associate with other slightly later or contemporary hesitations concerning the complexity of the relation to art, which Levinas always maintained in an ambiguous manner. It is particularly noticeable in the text "Reality and Its Shadow,"[4] written in 1948, which Danielle Cohen-Levinas introduced to me.

Let us return to this sketch for a novel.

The whole work is apparently entitled *Eros*. Let us maintain this hypothesis for the moment. The word "novel" is not written there, but everything has the appearance of a narrative. The first page of this narrative bears the title "Rondeau," which is the first name attributed to the principal character or to one of the characters, because other names appear afterwards. One does not know clearly whether they are other characters or whether it is always the same one. It is a fictitious character whom we will follow at the beginning of the war.

---

4 This text was first published as "La réalité et son ombre," *Les Temps Modernes* 38 (1948): 771–789. It was republished in Levinas's *Les Imprévus de l'histoire*, (1994, 123–148).

The work begins with several pages on the significance of the beginning of the war and its relation to France in particular. One has to hear the tone of these first pages. It is completely nationalist, that of a Frenchman who loves France viscerally, with all his strength, and who is unhappy about the war. More than a Frenchman, he is an *ultra-Frenchman*. As Michael Levinas said to me in a private conversation this summer, it is the little Lithuanian who has arrived and for whom France is everything.

> The ancient earth of France had become moving sands. The foot could not find a purchase anywhere. The enemy was infiltrating through invisible fissures in the soil. He did not come from one direction in order to go in another while crossing the spaces in between. (Levinas 2009, 37)

And France, the France that is thus affected, wounded by the war, what is it? He says what it is. Listen carefully.

> What is France? Immense stability. All the forms of life reaching their fullness, like eternally ripe fruit in a miraculous orchard. The perfection of a sedentary people, purified of all its memories of nomadic existence. (Levinas, 2009, 38)

One believes one is dreaming! One asks oneself what nomadic existence he is speaking about. And following this, there is an elegy to France that is almost like Hugo!

> Where one laughs like Rabelais, where one smiles like Montaigne, or one is noble as in the Cid, torn apart as in Phèdre, fooled like Georges Dandin, all the events of the plot foreseen. The great, the terrible book of destiny circulates in a school edition. Children comment upon it by learning their classics.

I do not know what great book, what terrible book of destiny, he is speaking of here. It is not a question of the Bible, that is certain.

The war is taken as the free point of departure for an incredible rupture within an order or harmony. And this order and harmony were also – this is the beginning of both the narrative and the theoretical motifs – the order of feelings.

> Feelings and the course of passions that have flowed despite the iridescence of their nuances, despite their refinement or their subtlety or their unexpectedness in a form that has waited for them for centuries, a form that is forever. O country where no catastrophe will prevent its civil servants from drawing their pension, where civilised life comes to be self-possessed in such a way that it seems as eternal, as immutable as nature. (Levinas 2009, 38)

This passage is very important. It seems to me that one can say that all the force of the narrative he undertakes is there. A magnificent nature, which is culture itself completely stabilised, has been struck point-blank and destabilised by war. In this nature, passions had flowed and had been in some way stabilised. It is perhaps not far from this to say that they had been deprived of passion. Levinas does not want to say that to himself, but perhaps he nonetheless desires to go in that direction when he writes this, for the rest of the narrative will be the possibility of wakefulness or of awaking once war has been engaged then lost and once the hero has been taken prisoner. The narrative probes the dimensions of feeling, erratic ones, which can no longer be related to this great French culture. It seems as if war proposed or offered the possibility of a sort of return to the lived experience of passion, of desire, beneath all the forms of relation to others. Thus, what is initially disastrous proves itself at the same time to be a possibility that the narrative will enact. War, then, is inadmissible, yet at the same time, at least initially – and here Levinas translates the sentiment shared by many in this period – it liberates unexpected emotions.

> And when it was there, it continued to appear to us as an immense exercise, like manoeuvres where despite the severity of what is enacted one only fires blank cartridges.
> (Levinas 2009, 39)

This is what was called "the phoney war."[5] And here, in Levinas's narrative, this "phoney war" will progressively reveal itself as being other than something staged. At a precise moment in the narrative, it will denude beings and place them in this experience of wakefulness or of awaking of which I spoke. It is here (after several pages) that we meet Rondeau again, whom Levinas now depicts more closely:

> After the 10th of May, Rondeau sensed chaos. He was not one of those, however, who admitted this easily. He belonged to that magnificent lineage, to that masterpiece of creation that one calls the common Frenchman. It was not a matter of intelligence but of reason. Rondeau was the son of a minor civil servant, now retired, who had enriched his spare time with research into Descartes' birthplace, and had not climbed a further step on the social ladder. He was a travelling salesman in silk and, having like everyone once received a travel grant, he had in his youth lived for some time in South America. (Levinas 2009, 39–40)

Rondeau is thus a common Frenchman who has returned to France because he loves France above everything. He is also, by the way, an interpreter. We arrive at the decisive moment that precedes the capitulation. I shall read one of the rare passages with dialogue, where Levinas ventures still further into literary writing. Rondeau goes to the train station, the train station in Paris:

> – The train for Crève Coeur le Grand?
> The railway employee makes a vague gesture.
> – Here is the train to Creil.

---

[5] The period between the declaration of war on September 3, 1939, and the invasion of France on May 10, 1940 – tr.

- And after that?
- You'll see. (Levinas 2009, 40–41)

Rondeau understands. After Creil there is indeterminate land or perhaps even a country to explore, thirty kilometres from Paris.

The enemy is so close that Rondeau understands everything is finished. He thus takes the train, knowing that it is the end and that he is not actually leaving for a front that is capable of holding fast. He leaves amidst the general disarray. Indeed, one is no longer able to say where one is going at thirty kilometres from Paris. Rondeau sees a stationmaster, and Levinas writes:

> In a short time, near a charming train station, he will return to a small house with a garden with white curtains at the windows, one of those houses that one sees through the window and that gives the traveller who may bear troubles or sorrow the impression that all France is on holiday and all France is happy. Perhaps through the open windows one will see a young girl at the piano? (Levinas 2009, 41)

A young girl at the piano: the first, fugitive appearance – there are very few – of an erotic figure. No doubt that is much to say of a young girl at the piano; let us say that it is the first appearance of a figure that evokes charm, amorous charm. Afterwards there will be at least one other young girl.

This is the beginning of a very short series of comments concerned with the gaze. There is Rondeau's gaze in the train; the gaze at the young girl at the piano; the gaze at a quiet house of a still happy France; but, further on, there is also the gaze at complete catastrophe. This is critically important because many, many things are traversed by the gaze. Indeed, the gaze is desire. Perhaps one could continue a little in this direction: vision is desire. It is perhaps in this way that the face becomes invisible. It is at the same time a desiring gaze that also sees what is invisible. One will see this further on.

In Levinas's narrative, we are now at the continuation of this journey leading he knows not where:

> […] in this train one boarded without a ticket and where an inspector did not come, which perhaps ran without a driver, like something absurd, by the abstract chance of the rails. Rondeau murmured:
>
> – I am alone.
> And he added, without knowing why:
> – Alone with God. (Levinas 2009, 42)

Levinas has drawn a line under this last phrase. It should be understood, I think, as the end of the chapter.

Thus: the ruptures of war, the somewhat perplexed gaze at the world that is in the midst of changing completely, and the experience of solitude. On the following page, suddenly, Levinas begins anew:

> Alone with God? Will one be able to find some character who will support this solitude without letting himself be tempted? (Levinas 2009, 42)

At this juncture, strangely, Levinas uses the word "character" (personnage). It is as though he asked himself, as the author: will I be able to find a character? And, at the same time, a character means a person here; it means "someone."

> There was an instant of total void between the disappearance of France and the reappearance of France, an instant of defeat in which nothing recreated itself – a vertiginous void, an interregnum, a hiatus, the absolute interval. (Levinas 2009, 42)

Basically, I think that everything Levinas wanted to narrate in what follows takes place here, in this absolute interval. An order is dismantled, another order has not been reconstituted. It is at the same time a kind of loss, an immense privation, and an opening up of possibilities.

One page further on:

> The sky is empty. It was absolutely evident and one had to think and decide for oneself [...]. (Levinas 2009, 43)

There is a void of culture, of France, of the supports. And there is the void of the sky. Just now, "Alone with God," and now, "The sky is empty."

> No France any longer. She left in a night, like an immense circus tent, leaving a clearing with some scattered debris. (Levinas 2009, 43)

And again, some lines further on:

> Everything is permitted. (Levinas 2009, 44)

An isolated sentence, which we, of course, find difficult not to relate to Dostoyevsky. It is known that Levinas read Dostoyevsky often. Certainly, he read Proust, but he also read Dostoyevsky. Thus, suddenly, everything is permitted.

A new alert. The hero has changed. It is now Jules who makes his entrance and no longer Rondeau. We have returned to town.

> Jules descended into the shelter when some aeroplanes appeared that were purportedly hostile – (to what?). He was next to a schoolgirl, from a Lycée, in a lost corner of the trench [the shelter becomes a trench], and with joy he felt desire without ambiguity, without pathos being born again within himself, as simple as purity. (Levinas 2009, 44)

The second young girl, this time a pupil of a Lycée. Levinas will say nothing more about what takes place between Jules and the schoolgirl, but everything has been said. Everything is said in this tension of the meeting, by chance, in a proximity that is not promiscuity, everything is said of the shelter, of a desire that is like purity. Many reflections file past, and actions in the real sense are always very brief. Levinas does not really follow up on any of them at all. Jules is close to the Lycée pupil and in a sense one does not really know if it is an ellipse. Afterwards, in the following narrative, there are some reflections on the state in which one finds oneself:

> And from now on we shall find in personal happiness the consolation for the unhappiness of our fatherland. (Levinas 2009, 44)

There is ruin, collapse, not only in what was the order but also in what was happiness, affective positivity, in the order of the fatherland. Levinas reverses this state into personal happiness, which thus echoes the desire that has just been mentioned.

> For the first time following a thousand years of the French state, the French all belonged to themselves. (Levinas 2009, 44)

The ruin of order also sends each one back to himself.

> Nothing separated them any more from themselves – none of these obligations that for a thousand years had come regularly to disturb the lives of the inner man – taxes, military service, all these lies that had done so much harm to them, all this universality imposed from without. (Levinas 2009, 44–45)

Naturally, the disappearance of all the beautiful French order – this time not as a cultural order but as one of the state, as universality imposed from without – turns these people back upon themselves. Turned back upon themselves, they are also turned towards the possibility, indeed towards the necessity, of going outside themselves, of opening themselves to their own desires.

A little further on this time (we are not present when they are captured by the Germans), Rondeau or Jules, we do not know which, has been captured, taken prisoner, and is being transported to the camp where he will be imprisoned. He passes through a village.

> At the end of the village the most probable [but without doubt the most improbable] spectacle of History was taking.
>
> A sentimental and patriotic barber cries out to everyone that nothing was of value any longer, that money was of no significance beside the love that one had to feel for France and for its little defeated soldiers. With his two apprentices – interrupting their infernal work with rounds of beer in the bistro – the barber was giving free shaves.

It is the first scene in which Levinas devotes himself to such a description. It is a scene that was seen and heard. It is certainly also a memory, but this terminates strangely with a quip, a sort of French private joke: "Oh, you know, they're giving free shaves tomorrow!"[6] Here, however, the barber is shaving for free on that very day and because of his love for France.

The prisoners march together. They are directed towards a camp that is being built at the end of a village or small town.

> The person marching next to him, completely intoxicated by the end of all the individual passions in the Great Passion that he was preparing himself to live – suggested to Asselin that he carry his heavy, folded great-coat. "Take upon yourself suffering of others" – this captivity will be magnificent, constituted by these noble sentiments. (Levinas 2009, 46)

It is the beginning of captivity as the experience of the other, as the experience of a new relation to the other, which begins simply by offering to carry the other's coat.

One should remind oneself of what a military overcoat of the time was. It could indeed be extremely heavy. There follow a certain number of reflections on the possibility of attaining a new consciousness, a new sense of passion that is at once individual, relation to others, and at the same time becomes in some way mediated by what France had been, the fatherland, and beyond this, destiny itself.

And here is the second desiring vision and without a doubt one of the most important in the narrative:

> In the meantime, one entered into Ostenholz. In the streets, the women were passing by.
> (Levinas 2009, 49)

The context allows one to know that the captive soldiers are in a lorry. Yet this does not seem to be of much importance.

> It was evident that this was an extraordinary spectacle. Each of their gestures was like the rendering evident of their lascivious substance. The women walking were there solely to show how their bodies could walk. (Levinas 2009, 49–50)

There is something in this distinction of the function of the body, as lasciviousness, as an immediately perceived presence, that will also provide the rhythm of the following scene. From a general point of view, throughout this essay, one can see without a doubt that a crucially important role accrues to de-functionalisation. Everything that is seen and that is interesting, everything that awakens desire, begins by being marked as having been subtracted from what is

---

6 A reference to the guillotine – tr.

functional, practical, useful. There are thus all the functionalities of society, of the State, etc., and also the functionalities of ordinary life, reaching as far as the market itself. These women no longer walk for the prisoners. That is why the gaze is important. They walk only to show how a female body walks, how it sets "their lascivious substance" into motion.

And then, a little further on, the convoy of prisoners advances. One sees the little boys and little girls who are playing. At this moment (one does not really know whether it is the narrator, the hero, or whether it is still Rondeau who is speaking), one reads this reflection:

> And then one day this little girl will withdraw from this community of children, which amounts to the meaningful world – the masculine world – in order to enter into her mystery. She will draw herself around herself and will glide there while continuing to fulfil the function that falls on her in the meaningful world – carrying the net bag, typing, combing the children's hair.
>
> Body on leave of absence, on holiday. Each of their gestures, the succession of poses that they struck in order to carry their net bag or their umbrella, was pornographic.
> (Levinas 2009, 49–50)

Levinas thus insists: when a woman detaches, disconnects herself from this role of the social function, she is no longer merely lascivious, but truly pornographic, and at the same time she has entered into her own mystery. In this sketch, in very few words, because there are not many texts to bear witness to this, Levinas establishes a great proximity between the mystery – that is to say, also the alterity, therefore the feminine – and lasciviousness, obscenity (the word will appear later), and desire. It is extremely interesting. Throughout this narrative, we learn nothing other than this: there is a sort of trembling of eroticism, understood in the most carnal, the least transcendent manner, to rejoin what Daniel Cohen-Levinas says elsewhere in this volume. With respect to this point precisely, there is a modification, a difference of accent, in Levinas's following works. The little girls of whom Levinas speaks will later find themselves in this situation of being in possession of their mystery yet completely immersed in their interiority, only showing the functional aspect, while at the same time revealing to the eyes of desire, the essence, the substance, the truly pornographic reality of this substance.

A little later, another important scene takes place, and now it is the flesh that is at issue.

> [...] when passing the brothel, the prisoners jostled among themselves on the lorry in order to admire a pullover that was drying in the wind and sometimes a pair of stockings.
> (Levinas 2009, 50)

The stockings are to some extent the high point of the narrative.

> But the day when through an open window one saw a young girl combing her long hair, one had the impression of something indecent or of a dream, acerbic, wrenching poetry of destructive beauty. Stronger than the Lorelei but not higher. The mixture of great beauty and of great baseness. These useful things, the comb to disentangle the tousled hair, as necessary as a hammer is to insert a nail or a knife to cut a knob of bread, these stockings that keep the wearer warm or that prevent shoes from irritating and injuring the skin and that one wields in everyday life with the precision and the sobriety of a doctor, no longer had anything of their chaste essence as utensils. Another essence pervaded them, repossessed them, that which placed them in the cannibalistic world of eroticism.
> (Levinas 2009, 50–51)

At the time, during the war, when there was a shortage of silk stockings, before the Americans introduced nylon ones, women simulated wearing stockings by tracing in ink a seam behind their legs. For one had to have stockings. There is something extremely powerful in this. The stocking, carefully described in its function of providing warmth or of protecting the foot, finds itself offered as a spectacle to the passing prisoners, once it is hung out. The "stocking" becomes in some way the essence of eroticism, which Levinas defines on the following page in this way:

> [. . .] for the whole human anatomy, which is so admirably adjusted to its biological purpose, returns in eroticism to its massiveness as flesh, almost like the animal for the butcher – the hand, the foot, the abdomen – everything that has another substance outside the so pure and chaste system of the organism and of sport, where the leg serves to run, the muscle to make an effort. Here [in eroticism] everything is as if it should be eaten in the indistinctness of its massive agglomeration of elemental skin. (Levinas 2009, 51)

There is a strong and heavy insistence on the massiveness of the flesh, the block, the lascivious, pornographic weight. This insistence is found continually in the text. The heaviness is the place where it declares itself, announces itself, indicates itself as what has been called the mystery and, even more specifically, the mystery of woman. Later in the text, the moment arrives when the scene in the prison camp unfolds, and here Levinas shows himself more attentive to the relations of the prisoners amongst themselves. He describes them as relations in which one finds oneself with people whom one does not know, with whom one has not chosen to be, and who at the same time represent the privileged essence of alterity.

> [...] the mobilisation often puts you by chance in contact with people whom you have not had the opportunity to come to know in the world and to whom, with a bit of nonchalance, one can say *tu* under the flag. All that is required is a little discernment in order not to suffer from the promiscuity and to come to know men of value [...]

There is evidently this accent on discernment, on choice between people of value and those without value. At the same time, however, there is now this real experience of a relation between the other men. In these theoretical notebooks, a bit like a respondent to the narrative, one finds long analyses on comradeship, on companionship. On the basis of this experience one already envisages what the return to society will be.

> He was to become a member of society again. There were already thousands of invisible threads tying themselves around him. He became united, responsible. (Levinas 2009, 55)

It seems to me that this is the first time that the word "responsible" appears in this context. And at the same time, immediately, quite strikingly, one perceives a beginning of the critique of the society to which one will return, which already bears the stigma of consumerism. Essentially, at issue are advertising pages:

> [. . .] a few leagues away from the concentration camps and the crematory ovens [of which nothing has been said hitherto, so it is really a liberated prisoner speaking, who knows what has happened], the advertising pages of *Illustration*, arriving imperturbably from Paris, teaching the virtues of a new brand of oven. Madam went out . . . baby there . . . dinner cooked by itself . . . when Monsieur returns, the roast will be just right . . . I shall only regret one thing in my life, which is to not have come to know the Universal School earlier. "To commit suicide with our revolver is a pleasure." (Levinas 2009, 56)

We are approaching the end of the narrative, which is also, at the same time, the end of the war. The society of France, so harmonious at the beginning, will be followed by a terrible one: that of the creation of false needs. Between the two there was a sort of fleeting flash of the liberation of desire, as in in the scene of the shelter, or rather of the liberation of the possibility of thinking desire, of representing desire as something other than a need, as something other than what is ranged in, channelled into the order. Two episodes are presented as the end of the narrative; they are not very clear but their significance is quite explicit. On the one hand, there is an episode, to which mention is made elsewhere in the *Carnets de captivité*, which takes place in a château, no doubt occupied by French or American liberation troops. These troops tear down the draperies. The heavy fall of the draperies is like the laying bare of what is behind them: worn stones, a number of destroyed, broken things, remnants of the war. On the other hand, there is an even more mysterious scene, in which Jules returns and causes a scandal during a public lecture by slapping the lecturer. One does not know why exactly he does this, but one can guess and therefore also understand it. If one examines the text closely, one becomes aware that the lecturer is someone who only relates things that are too simple, too comforting, and not very credible after the war. Jules, however, represents someone who knows that, whatever happens, an unquiet will remain from now on. The lady in whose house the lecture is held dies of a heart attack after the violent incident Jules brings about.

We arrive at the end of these pages, at the end of this painting – of which we cannot manage to decide whether it is merely ironic or simply ambiguous – a future world, which will be one where all the houses will be built of glass because we shall have nothing to hide:

> Would we have, by chance, anything to hide? Glass would become the only material permitted in the city, the only substance that is at the same time resistant, exhibiting all the qualities of a thing, and which, however, [is transparent]. (Levinas 2009, 58)

This rather strange interlude on glass is itself followed by a somewhat long "Interlude" (given this title by Levinas), in which all sorts of developments with respect to Faust and Margarete occur. One knows neither where this comes from nor what it is connected to, except that, as we know, Faust and Margarete comprise a love relation.

After this, the following pages do not really still belong to the narrative. I cannot tell, for example, whether this sentence, written on another page, belongs to the narrative or not:

> Obscene – the way others make love. (Levinas 2009, 59)

I think this lapidary formulation, which comes from we know not exactly where, says an enormous amount. It says that obscenity, all that which is more or less seen as pornography, lasciviousness, etc., is what unfolds under the gaze of another who is a stranger to what happens for others. However, that which is the case for a spectacle one should not have actually seen, a spectacle not meant for exteriority, is evidently not the case when it is not a private spectacle, when it is we who are making love.

This note is followed by another. I shall not even try to say whether it is related to what precedes, though it is indeed on the same page:

> He is dead – that means – he will never be my enemy. (Levinas 2009, 59)

2 Conclusion

I have found, perhaps drawing on chance pages, the end of this whole narrative, the end – in the sense of "in the end" but also of "beyond" or "after" – like an intrusion of theoretical notes, a series of pages where, indeed, if I have properly understood the order of the copies, Levinas writes theoretical notes on the left while continuing his narrative on the right, which itself is interlaced with many reflections. They are more reflections than descriptions, narration, or dialogues.

In the final analysis, this sentence "Obscene – the way others make love" says fundamentally something very simple: the love we make is not obscene.

Now, love, *eros*, let us say, has been, in a very veiled manner in the novel, and, in a very clear manner in the theoretical fragments, the only path possible for the self to venture outside the self. Thus, I shall state, in conformity with what is said about *eros* in the, let us say, theoretical, philosophical *Carnets*, this formula:

> The embrace – transubstantiation of myself. (Levinas 2009, 196)

There is, I believe, in the moment of this attempt at writing on Levinas's part, the attempt to touch, in some way, the mystery through literature, rather than to make a sort of literary shutter onto what one would otherwise view through a philosophical shutter, even if this attempt fails because Levinas is not really a writer of fiction. What attracted him, however, and this is certain, is the possibility of touching the mystery through narration and not of illustrating a theory. Precisely because of this, perhaps, narration, this impoverished little narration, which does not narrate much, still touches the mystery. It does so by approaching it with the obscene, with the pornographic, with desire, with this motif of desire as vision – which is not exactly Levinas's theme – something towards which his work in this period and later will be inclined in order to understand what has happened. When I speak of vision, in the sketch of the novel, I am also referring to the passages where there is marked insistence on what he "opposes" to vision, to the "sound" that penetrates and does not keep things at a distance.

There is therefore a very great hesitation, a great uncertainty in Levinas himself. In these pages, this uncertainty falls both on the side of eroticism and on the side of literary writing. The two are intimately linked. After 1947, there will be no further attempts at literature. There will also not be the temptation of literature. I shall not say that there will be no further erotic temptations, but this temptation will no longer have the same accent. The tone will have been modified, changed a little. This is why I consider that these pages in Levinas – and this is what, for me, constitutes their great interest, one's fascination in reading them – are not merely a prefiguration of what he does afterwards, though in many respects they indeed are. Yet there is something else. Because clearly he never again continued along this path. Far be it from me to say that he regressed. This is clearly not the point.

Afterwards, rather, Levinas marked, without knowing it, an extremely discreet moment, for he never published anything about it and we never knew anything of it (and now we find ourselves confronted with these pages). It is a moment prolonged by others and still not exhausted today. He marked the difficult relation of philosophy to literature with respect to the sensible mystery:

that which is connected to *eros*. Or rather, he marked the sensible mystery in general, or the mystery as sensible, or the sensible as mystery.

Bibliography

Levinas, Emmanuel. *Totalité et infini: Essai sur l'extériorité*. Nijhoff: The Hague, 1961.
Levinas, Emmanuel. *De l'évasion*. Montpellier: Fata Morgana, 1982.
Levinas, Emmanuel. *Les Imprévus de l'histoire*. Montpellier: Fata Morgana, 1994.
Levinas, Emmanuel. *Oeuvres*, 1: *Carnets de captivité et autre inédits*. Eds. Rodolphe Calin and Catherine Chalier. Paris: Grasset/IMEC, 2009.
Levinas, Emmanuel. *Oeuvres*, 2: *Parole et Silence et autres conférences inédites au Collège Philosophique*. Eds. Rodolphe Calin and Catherine Chalier. Paris: Grasset/IMEC, 2011.

Danielle Cohen-Levinas and Jean-Luc Nancy
Eros, Once Again: Danielle Cohen-Levinas in Conversation with Jean-Luc Nancy

Danielle Cohen-Levinas: Where should we begin, I am tempted to ask? For nothing is more singular than this literary experience in the heart of captivity, and at the same time nothing is more illuminating than the manner in which Levinas from the outset divided his work into three registers: philosophical, literary, and critical – and this already in 1942. I will begin by evoking our visit at *IMEC* in September 2006. It was the first time that you had discovered the Emmanuel Levinas "deposit." On the computer screen, we went through the digitalised files of the *Carnets de captivité*, and I remember your reaction when faced with the pages of the novel, the one supposedly called *Eros*. We read its pages aloud, not without joy and astonishment, and the more we read the more it became patently clear to you that this proximity of literature and philosophy, far from cancelling or contradicting the specificity of one or the other, already bore the very movement of a thought and of writing that recognises itself in the sharing of singularities. One could even ask if, very early on, the young Emmanuel Levinas, after breaking off from his reading of poetry and Russian literature, from his studies of biblical verse and its narrative wisdom, from his admiration with regard to French literature, which his friend Maurice Blanchot had introduced to him during the Strasbourg years, did not live and undergo the experience of literature as a completely separate experience of thought, as a locus where exigencies and questions are concentrated that can no longer really pass through the philosophical mode or, at any rate, which carry out a displacement that philosophy alone perhaps would not have been able to initiate. Did literature, in the midst of the war, in the midst of captivity, come to work in Levinas against inoperativeness?

Jean-Luc Nancy: I don't know whether I can use these terms. There is a risk of confusing "inoperativeness" with the meaning it has in Blanchot. I don't think this preoccupation was present between 1940 and 1945 or even a little later, either for the one or for the other. If you mean by "inoperativeness" the state of relative inoperativeness of Levinas as a prisoner, then what he did to "occupy" himself – in the midst of a thousand tasks and preoccupations – was related to his "work" to the extent that he was already a man with the task of work. Like

---
Note: Paris-Strasbourg, October 2010.
Translation: Translated, from the French, by Ashraf Noor.

∂ Open Access. © 2021 Danielle Cohen-Levinas and Jean-Luc Nancy, published by De Gruyter. (cc) BY
This work is licensed under the Creative Commons Attribution 4.0 International License.
https://doi.org/10.1515/9783110668926-003

other prisoners (Sartre, Ricœur, and many others), he certainly had the great desire to remain in contact with his projects, with his world of thought. The absence of a habitual context of his work – books, conversations, and encounters – made the desire more acute, that is, he had a fear of feeling himself dulled or blurred. Once again, he shares this with others. However, not every – let's say professional – philosopher felt the desire to write a novel during his time of captivity. This desire is evidently prior to captivity. It must have been nourished by his association with Blanchot, as you say, and with others. But also by the example of Sartre: *La nausée* dates from 1938. It was not only a philosopher's novel but, by the work and by what was said about it, one knew that this fiction issued from a desire to make something of the phenomenological experience sensible. I cannot enter into the theoretical and historical analysis that would be necessary. I do not know whether this question has been studied: how and why philosophy was carried out then and in this literary manner. Sartre had felt the impact of Celine and Kafka, which was to say that literature had made itself philosophical, in a more evident way, I should say, than at the time of Flaubert or Mallarmé. Perhaps already Proust. And Gide. And Thomas Mann and Musil. And Malraux. Without a doubt, the question of literature had haunted philosophy since the beginning of Romanticism (without going back still further). Schelling, Nietzsche, Kierkegaard bear witness to this. But it was never a question of the novel, always rather poetry. In the years we are speaking of here, Heidegger does not think for a moment of the novel, only of Hölderlin, Trakl, George.

In the encounter between a philosophical tendency in literature (which also remained mostly narrative, stories, dramas, and passions) and a literary tendency in philosophy (which also remained mostly the exercise of a concept) there is certainly a phenomenon that reveals something about the time. One could observe that *Sein und Zeit* lent itself well to a denunciation of the novel and of prose under the title of "inauthenticity" (to retain the questionable translation of *Eigentlichkeit*) while this kind of judgement could not be found in Husserl or in his other disciples. There are no doubt lessons to be learned from this contrast between an emphasis placed on the poem and an appeal to the novel, which would offer, rather, a naked truth, bared, even rude.

In any case, it is certain that Levinas, on the eve of the war, is a spirit very largely nourished by literature – all the names that you bring up, all those that one finds in the *Carnets* – which is to say that he is also a philosophical spirit for whom philosophy from the outset overflows the theoretical and academic discipline. He is not alone; it is a movement of the period. Camus, too, makes his debut, between essay and narrative, in the years immediately following the war. I think there was the quest for thought that was concrete, vital, active. One has to consider that this was also the time of great disappointment with regard to philosophical representations. It is really the time, when, in a reprisal (then unconscious) of Nietzsche, one distanced everything one called "metaphysics," a term that had already received so much disapproval in Valéry.

DC-L: One of the questions that poses itself from the outset when reading Levinas's novel is: why did he call it *Eros*, if that indeed is the title? There is still a hesitation. The novel is called *Eros* or it's called *Triste opulence*. The pages of the manuscript of this novel were found in a folder Levinas had marked *Eros*, but there is nothing to say that this folder had not also contained other preparatory work on the question, above all with regard to *Totalité et infini*. The invocation of the erotic motif is, here again, at the heart of Levinas's philosophy. In addition, before you had a photocopy of the manuscript of the novel, you were able to consult some preparatory drafts for his reflection on love, eros, the caress, fecundity, and filiation, which is present in *Le Temps et l'Autre* and in *Totalité et Infini*. You even said to me: "But these pages can't be for a novel!" Don't you find it surprising that Levinas attaches himself to this motif as to an idiom, to the point of displacing it in a narrative frame as the central figure of a world in complete inoperativeness and disorientation? All the more since the erotic question is an old preoccupation, which the history of philosophy has not failed to contest, discuss, avoid or, on the contrary, exalt. If one adds the biblical referent to the philosophical referent, we have a very particular constellation, because in the Jewish tradition there is indeed the trace of a primordial divine *eros* of which one can say that it is incarnated in the biblical text. It is this idea that there is a primordial – divine or human or both, it does not matter – *eros* in the work of Levinas that I would like to discuss with you. *Eros* would refer to an objective order of language from which philosophy and literature would not be able to escape. It is a question of a certain exposition to the "mystery," a question that is essential for Levinas but equally for you. If the word "mystery" imposes itself here, it is because it marks the relation of Levinas to literature, whether it be his relation to Proust, to Léon Bloy, of whom one is a bit surprised to learn that Levinas read him assiduously in the time of his captivity, or to Shakespeare or to the Russian authors. It is also the case for the relation to the other, which remains, however it occurs, an incommensurable and unattainable mystery. It is the case, to take up a motif again that is dear to you, with the "literary absolute."

J-L N: In the philosophical-literary impulse I have just spoken about, I don't know whether anything remains or not of the "literary absolute" in the sense that it could constitute for early German Romanticism an ideal for the realisation of thought that would be adequate to an infinite ground, a real actualising of the infinite. It seems to me that what derives from Romanticism is rather what turns to poetry. This is thought as the true act of the word, the offering of the word itself . . . I do not deny that a trace of this temptation can remain in narrative, prosaic desire. In any case, we then broach discreetly another immense debate, which will afterwards become overt, concerning poetry (hatred of it in Bataille, vituperation of it in Artauld; in general a distrust of its "gooey temptation" – another of Bataille's expressions – will be set to work later).

I imagine that for Levinas the prose of narration would be a sort of poetry in the sense in which it could aim towards the possibility of presenting "the thing" or "the truth": this humble truth of a rough, harsh existence, one that is indeed disenchanted yet enchants itself precisely in its very narration. I imagine, but I do not know. It is impossible for me to conclude this on the basis of the notes we have. Yes, he wants, he would like, to enter into mobile, supple, agile speech that would render experience, its banality, its weight, and its fears and desires. His drafts of dialogues, his images of glimpsed scenes (these young girls, these women).

At the same time, he is guided by a project or by a theoretical plan. This is testified by the notes on the motif of *eros*, which are like the double of the novel (and which, for Levinas, could very well bear this title – we cannot divide them) or of which the novel is rather a double – a double, though, that is slighter and in turn traversed by theoretical remarks. In the lecture in which I presented this text, I expressly rejected reading these notes except for some that really "adhere" to the tissue of the narrative. I wanted to show the movement of the text alone, as unfinished as it is. But one cannot deny the effort, the magnetising, the desire to go towards the development of a thought of what he calls *Eros*.

It is certainly not fortuitous if the form of the novel seeks to impose itself upon him in order to speak of this motif. *Eros* is sensible, it has to be sensible, to let itself be felt. When the figure called Jules finds himself in a shelter next to a schoolgirl, one feels (yes, one feels precisely) that the writer wants us to feel tested by the desire that the situation and the shadow elicit. The text says it: "everything is permitted." One finds oneself thinking that Levinas is using an ellipse in the erotic scene. A major question is perhaps connected to this: is it an ellipse? Or does Levinas not dare? Or does it not happen?

The stakes are very high – all the more so if one recalls this note on the obscene that almost completes this notebook. Because at stake is the question of what one can say, show, of the erotic act, or, put differently, to know if it can speak or show itself. In two senses: whether someone can "say it" (and what does that mean?) or whether the act itself can speak. It is at the same time a reality and a symbol or a metonymy of what is at stake in literature (in literary desire and anxiety): saying "it." It is a question of pornography, a word that appears in the text. It is a question of the obscene: if, as Levinas says, the obscene is others making love, that means it is only "pure," dignified, noble (purity haunts the text of the narrative, just as that of the notes) when I make love, when we make love, when we make love to each other. And perhaps this cannot be said. Not because it is "our" making love but because as soon as it is said, posed, presented, it becomes that of others. Literature would be condemned to being an obscenity – or an ellipse.

Some time later these questions will be agitated, they will agitate the literary scene. Bataille (who had published *Story of the Eye* and *Madame Edwarda* under a pseudonym before the war – what did Blanchot and Levinas know of this at the time? That's a question . . .) or Klossowski, or later Guyotat, and the lifting of censorship on Sade or on Miller (the latter had published *Tropic of Cancer* in 1934; Cendrars, among others, had applauded it . . .). There is here a hive of difficult questions concerning the emergence of *eros* in what I would call public consciousness and thought. And there was also Freud. As I note in my chapter, Freud was not to Levinas's liking when he read him shortly after the war.

What is remarkable, though, with the word or with the title – *Eros* – is that Levinas in effect prepares what will, on the one hand, become a central element of his description of the relation to the other and, on the other hand – amplified, enlarged, and transformed, the very motif of the "other" and of his precedence. From the beginning, it is only a matter of this: the concern is to go out of oneself in order to become oneself, and "self" only comes in relation to the other, to the other *tout court*. This other is, above all, woman, it is the feminine. More precisely, it is the feminine inasmuch as this opens all the virtualities present throughout the other forms of relation – comradeship, fraternity, companionship, friendship (not to forget the animal warmth of a dog). All these notions are analysed in the notes, and the narrative renders sensible how much the war, the mobilisation, and captivity at least contributed to etching them in Levinas's mind.

In fact, something very simple can be said: war and captivity were at the same time the collapse of a social and cultural order (the whole beginning of the text speaks of this) and the experience of other relations: friends cultivated, women desired (glimpsed, brushed against; other women, the women of others). All the proximities one knew became distant, others came to the fore, promiscuity too. But in the end it was, on one hand, the revelation of the camps, and, on the other hand, the return to a life in which it was as difficult to prolong what had just ended as it was to retrieve what was prior to the war. The relation to literature could not but be affected by this also. It is difficult to say more about this, even if it seems that for Levinas the temptation or the literary endeavours continued for some time.

DC-L: How should one speak of mystery in literature? Or, rather, is literature the mystery? Is it literature that no knowledge can claim to master? Do you think that in the highest and purest manifestation of the mystery there could reside a kind of narrative law from which narrative and the novel would flow?

J-LN: What is certain is that for Levinas the novel bears or shelters the mystery. I think he charges this word with that which is subtracted from the concept. I am not sure that I am able to decide whether the mystery itself is narrative, as you suggest. It is highly possible. This is clear enough in the Greek mysteries. I am trying to think of the great Christian mysteries. One can say each of them implies a story; including that of the Trinity, which would be less evident. Narrative would be inherent in the truth of what shows itself (for me, it is the definition of mystery) as distinguished from the truth that demonstrates itself, establishes itself, verifies itself. But one would need to take the time to go more into that . . .

DC-L: Is this question of mystery also constitutive of philosophy as the love of wisdom? Levinas turned the idiom around, turning it into a movement of recurrence, and said of philosophy that it was also the "wisdom of love."

J-LN: Philosophy thinks that it dissipates mystery in the sense of mystical obscurity. But it always ends up finding a narrative again . . . the ascent outside the cavern or the life of the spirit.

DC-L: I would like to return for a moment to this double conjunction very particular to Levinas. Narrative eros and theoretical eros. According to you, is this configuration present in the narrative, several passages of which you have commented on? Is there a trace of the theoretical Eros in the narrative Eros? I am asking you this question because the erotic dimension in Levinas's narrative is bordered by the presence of the pornographic, by visions with an erotic tonality, like that of the young girl at the piano, and these visions give birth to a relation to desire and a search for corporeal pleasure, where the body of a woman is precisely seen as a desired and desirable body, and which will later disappear in Levinas's work or which Levinas displaces onto another problematic by carrying out a sort of detachment in the very interior of the word Eros.

J-LN: This will disappear, you say? Is this completely certain? It would be interesting to go further into it? But there was transformation, that is certain. Transformation and/but continuity. I sense there is extremely delicate work to be done on this transformation. Perhaps it is infinite because it is not at all certain that there's a conclusion to be drawn. The end of captivity and of the war certainly displaced the given circumstances that were Levinas's point of departure between mobilisation and liberation. And there is also the reading of Freud I evoked. This is perhaps the reason for the fear of desire, and *eros* in general being reduced *a priori* to need and impulse (itself understood as a mechanical force . . .). In general, one can follow in Levinas an evolution or an oscillation with respect to the subject of desire: does it open itself to infinity or does it close itself around a sensual pleasure understood as possession? This hesitation is not unique to him. He receives it, rather, from a whole *doxa*. And with respect to this he is somewhat audacious: he attributes or attributed more to desire, up to a certain moment. Here again one broaches a domain that has still to be explored, not only for the history of this thought but for our own thought. I think that we have not yet recognised desire enough. If, indeed, it is "recognisable," identifiable.

DC-L: I would like us to return to the genesis of your reading of Levinas's novel, if I can say this, once you held it in your hands. What were your initial impressions? Could you say that in Levinas the writer you find the trace or the mark or the signature of Levinas the philosopher? And if that is the case, how is the passage from one register to the other carried out? I'm asking you this question because Levinas often explained that literature represented for him what he called pre-philosophical experiences, as if an antechamber of philosophy properly speaking existed that would not be philosophy itself, philosophy complete and whole – systematic, if you prefer – but would be the condition of possibility for this, an exteriority of language and of expression that would come to inspire the exercise of philosophy with another breath, another respiration.

J-LN: Yes, the "pre-philosophical" is also "another breath," it is not very easy to understand this. I believe the determination "pre-philosophical" also derives from a *doxa* to which Levinas submitted in spite of himself. To this – afterwards – another dimension was added, that of a distrust of art and of the sensible. (As you know, there is also much one could say about this). On the other hand, one could think another breath is what Levinas wanted to find for his own thought. This is a character that is not "literary" properly speaking but altered with respect to discourse and the concept. At the same time, he conceptualises and tells a story, an intrigue, as he says. It would be necessary to return to the relation of a whole period to philosophical writing (speech). Heidegger, Sartre, Merleau-Ponty, Deleuze, Derrida: each seeks in his own way to inflect discourse, that is, to displace it or transform it, to tamper with the assurance of the concept, if I can say this in a tone already slightly dated. It is now more semantic (Deleuze), now more syntactic (Derrida), now more poetic, now more narrative, and Levinas participates a little in all of this: he needs his own words and his words are also the operators of sequences that are almost narrative.

But I think at the same time of something very simple: of all those no one is a writer. All are "writing," all are alerted by an unease with respect to discourse (argument, demonstration, consequence, etc.), but no one takes his point of departure in literature such as a Proust, a Joyce, a Beckett, a Brecht, a Melville, a Genet, a Jabès, a Celan – to take some figures who roam in his surroundings. A philosopher constructs (even if he deconstructs), a writer walks, moves, roams (even if he also manufactures). These are neither heterogeneous fields nor overlapping regimes. They are irreducible allures, allures in thought, in feeling, in taste. Certainly, there are points of proximity, that is, of promiscuity, and sometimes crossing, hybridisation. But, profoundly, there is scission. Philosophy announces, opens paths, marks trails, indicates perspectives tentatively. Literature does not announce but gives, offers, lets something be touched, presents, and withdraws . . .

DC-L: In your chapter in this volume you indicate a turn that takes place in Levinas after the war, after captivity, and which would be marked by abandoning, or at least by not pursuing further, his vital interest in literary writing. And at the same time you say clearly that Levinas marked a neuralgic point in the relation between philosophy and literature. It is true, I think, one can underline it, that this is also a characteristic of the period. Sartre's case is completely evident but he is not the only one; one could also cite Merleau-Ponty, who has not received the literary recognition that Sartre has. How do you yourself experience this relation today and do you feel that you belong to a constellation of philosophers – such as Deleuze, Foucault, Derrida, Lacoue-Labarthe, with whom you have worked and shared so much – for whom literature, but also poetry, remain this experience irreducible to the intimacy of thought?

J-LN: I think I have already answered this, more or less. I did not mention Lacoue-Labarthe, but I thought of him. It was important to him to maintain the rigour of philosophy but in all his being – in all his heart – he desired the poem (with respect to which he could be ferocious). He desired a prose that makes waste of poetic prettiness and which would be "thoughtful." For he knew that thought does not live solely of rigour. But he also knew that the writer exposes himself to that which, in him or outside him, still cannot be exposed. Without dramatising excessively (he sometimes did, it's true), he knew something of a life played in writing: that is, as a relation to the impossible. Perhaps one could say that philosophy is always in the possible, even creates possible things.

Literature opens up directly and immediately to the impossible: that is, to what one will never be able to deduce from the given, to take up again this thought of Bergson's that the possible is never other than the real turned back before itself. But that which is not given, that which is not really in front of us but which is coming, which approaches otherwise than "in front of" (behind, within, very far away . . .) is the impossible in the sense that one will not derive it from its own conditions.

DC-L: If I allow myself to open here a door to your intimacy of thought, to your own experience, do you accept my advancing in saying that behind or in front of you – there is no attributable direction – there is a Jean-Luc Nancy who is a writer, right next to, very close to, completely opposed to, or engaged with, the Jean-Luc Nancy who is a philosopher?

J-LN: I don't know who you are speaking about, nor what he is. Seriously!

François-David Sebbah
The Debacle or The Real Under Reduction: The "Scene of Alençon"

> The drapes that fall in my scene of Alençon also concern things. Things decompose, lose their meaning: forests become trees – all that which forest meant in French literature – perishes. The ultimate decomposition of elements – the butts of wood that remain after the circus has left or on the stage [. . .]. But I do not want to speak simply of the end of illusions but rather of the end of meaning. {Meaning itself as illusion.} The concrete form of this situation: the empty houses and staying in these empty houses. Cheese and champagne at 5 in the morning.
> [. . .]
> The looting of shop windows – the people who carry away senseless things: a packet of letter-writing paper [. . .].
> [. . .]
> It is not the situation of the reversal of values that I want to describe – of the change in authority – but of the human nudity of the absence of authority.   (Levinas 2009, 136)

"In a sense, all of X's philosophy is there": a sweeping statement of this kind will always be too inexact – except when one hears in this the risky attempt to grasp a gesture of thought at its living center and as a seminal decision. The hypothesis we should like to defend here is precisely the following: in what Levinas calls in his *Carnets de captivité* the – or "my" – "scene of Alençon" one can say that in "a sense all his philosophy is there."

There are "thought-situations," writes Levinas with respect to Proust, and he gives a precise definition of this with respect to the thought of death: "Proust has a notion of this thought by illness or by ageing, which are a positive {and appropriate} access to a notion and without which we can have only a negative concept" (Levinas 2009, 73). In this way, we can gain access to meaning only through the concreteness, the facticity of the existence of a situation. It is known that, as much in his Talmudic commentaries as in his practice of phenomenology, Levinas does not cease to promote a "drama of phenomena"

Note: This text is a translation of "La débâcle ou le réel sous réduction. La scène d'Alençon," published in *Cahiers de philosophie de l'université de Caen* 49 (2012), 181–96, and reprinted in the book *L'éthique du survivant. Levinas, une philosophie de la débâcle* (Presses Universitaires de Paris Nanterre, 2018). This book has been translated by Mérédith Laferté-Coutu into English and was published in *Levinas Studies* 12 (2018), 3–60.
Translation: Translated, from the French, by Ashraf Noor.

François-David Sebbah, Université Paris-Nanterre

according to which the concept should never be cut off from the singularity of situations and according to which, by the same movement, significations have to be deformalized (cf. Franck 2001, 152ff.). Of course, it is in no way a question of identifying the "situation" in an objective sense and of thus restricting it to an occurrence in the world that can be located in objective time. The "thought-situation" is at work as much, and doubtlessly more so, in the novel or even in the text claimed as philosophical, as it is in the objective exactness of the facts. Moreover, as one knows, the *Carnets* relate very few facts or 'objective' events . . .

The "scene of Alençon," which appears in Levinas's unfinished and unpublished novel *Tristes Opulences*, then in *Eros*,[1] is first of all a *situation* of this kind. One finds traces of it in the *Carnets*: either in the drafts and the fragments of this scene, or in explications of its meaning (formulated in the mode: "in my scene of Alençon" this means that; cf. Levinas 2009, 132, 135, 146). It bears witness to the strangeness of the "event" of the debacle. In truth, there is not much to relate. Initially, the buzz of the habitual occurrences and gestures of the world continues, albeit as if they were suspended (as if suspended on the edge of the abyss). It is rather the calm before the storm: the crowds have not yet been thrown onto the streets – we are in the imminence or in the premises of the upheaval that has not yet taken place. Nothing exceptional happens in the daily life of the town – even if soon the panic of flight and the looting that accompanies it will occur (these events, moreover, which Levinas constantly renders derisory, are barely present).[2] Something happens, however, when almost nothing has yet happened objectively; such is the disruptive "transcendental" or "metaphysical" nature of the event [*événementialité*] of the mundane non-event. Ordinary life is, *all of a sudden,* caught in the raw light of defeat. What happens? *Everything happens as if the operation of the suspension of the world-thesis were produced in the world (this is the situation).*

In the narration of the events of his life, Levinas offers us few "objective" clues with regard to what he really experienced as the "scene of Alençon" (and, fundamentally, it is of little importance . . .). It is on another level that the

---

[1] For factual clarifications regarding this novel and with respect to its status both in philosophy and in the course of Levinas's works, one should refer to the preface, written by Catherine Chalier and Rodolphe Calin, to *Oeuvres* I (Levinas 2009, 14 and following) as well of course as the editing work of D. Cohen-Levinas and the preface by Jean-Luc Nancy in *Oeuvres* III.

[2] On singular empirical event merits note here. It is a question of an event that is objectively not very momentous, involving a barber, of which Levinas will reveal the transcendental bearing and to which we will devote ourselves further below.

scene of Alençon is played out.³ When he evokes his writing of the novel taken in its global character and in its generality, one sees clearly that *all* fiction has the function of an *epochè*: an "irrealization" of the world in the sense of the neutralization of the thesis of existence. The claimed and many times declared attraction for fantasy in literature derives from this *index or this operation of neutralization*.⁴ And, from a certain point of view, the scene of Alençon gathers, carries to its highest point, and, so to say, "instantiates" this work of the *epochè*.

Therefore, the "thought-situation" of the debacle, embodied in the scene of Alençon, very clearly has the function of the phenomenological *reduction*. This reduction itself will not, in turn, emerge unscathed from such a recapitulation. Let us describe in detail this operation, this "Levinassian reduction" and what it gives access to.

Phenomenological reduction can be understood in various senses. The debacle as reduction leads to no foundation nor certainty (and certainly not towards that of the *ego* or of consciousness). On the contrary, it is expressed through a recurrent image: the "drapes that are ablaze and that fall."⁵ The defeat – the defection of all power – has its ultimate power in removing the veil, in unveiling. Under Levinas's pen, the play of the "fall" or the "blaze" of the "drapes" can be formulated, very classically, by the dichotomy of being and appearance – appearance being rendered the equivalent of "illusion." However, this formulation is immediately corrected. Certainly, it is being that is revealed,⁶ but not in such a way that it could be opposed to the lack of being

---

3 In the *Carnets*, it is evoked rather than developed; in other published texts it is carried further, though, and particularly in one of these, to which we will return later. It is nonetheless the case that, in a general sense, this seminal scene is difficult to recognize and to assign. Without a doubt, it is a matter of the persistence or the resurgence of a moment actually lived by Levinas himself, but everything takes place as if this moment could not allow itself to be assigned to a simple origin nor to a precise and univocal mundane determination. This is, doubtlessly, not without relation to its status as a "transcendental" or "metaphysical" event: one is therefore more inclined to follow the occurrences of this "scene" in the works than its chronological resurgence since a datable moment in the life of Emmanuel Levinas and the history of France (that can really be objectified as the debacle of 1940).
4 Cf. for example, *Oeuvres* I (Levinas 2009, 150). In the latter, Levinas evokes what he calls his "literary procedures": "The real event is described in a sober fashion. [. . .] But a small final image, on which one should never insist [. . .] makes something fantastic circulate in it like a rapid current of air. The whole 'real' situation appears above a precipice." (Ibid., 190)
5 Calin and Chalier comment on this expression in their preface (Levinas 2009, 16).
6 From this point of view, one senses a true proximity to Heidegger's problematic of the a-letheia, of being, and of the forgetting of being – which one would no doubt have to explore further on.

that is illusion. On the contrary, what the revelation shows is shown insofar as it does not present itself in full presence: its nudity or its truth is a matter of an essential characteristic of the foundation of being: *to not be enough or not really* (we shall return to this). And a crucial precision is made: if being in the debacle, being at issue because of the debacle or the defeat, as one could say, is deprived of something, it is not of a deceptive appearance that would have both hidden and clothed it, but of its meaning. *Being in its foundation, revealed as what it "is," struggles to be and in the same movement, "is" senseless.*[7]

Under reduction, in the situation of the debacle, beings are presented as having two characteristics which are in appearance, and in appearance only, contradictory. From a certain point of view, the cold light of defeat outlines their contours in a too raw way, freezes their shapes into caricatures, and, by exaggerating their traits, reveals what is derisory about them. The cold light of the debacle makes the different beings get stuck in their being, prohibits them from freeing themselves or escaping. This is the reason why the crowds who take the road, encumbered by their baggage, are pathetic and derisory, as when circuses leave town, Levinas writes (cf. Levinas 2009, 104). Every word counts here. Each individual human is encumbered by their baggage and leaves traces in being – traces of being in being – that express the impossibility of escape (and therefore opposing themselves radically to the "trace of what has never taken place").[8] The debacle is the impossibility and incapacity of a departure from the world and from being; demobilization that is only the reverse side of mobilization, or movement of beings in being; being is revealed in the same movement for what it is: derisory circus, meaningless or absurd, stuck within itself, tangled up on itself. And this weight or burden, as being stuck, is the impossibility of foundation or of the hypostasis, or of substantiality. This is the reason for the second characteristic of these beings: their being tangled up in being – and this is contradictory only in appearance – in fact de-realizes them. They hardly exist, they struggle to exist: they are phantoms, caricatures of themselves, always on the edge of fading into an indeterminate existence.[9]

---

[7] This is why the very term "scene" in Levinas's expression "scene of Alençon" should be understood at least as much in the sense of theatre (even as far as its apparatus) as in the sense of the novel. Suddenly, the world appears as being nothing more than a stage on which a derisory game is played. As soon as one no longer adheres to the spectacle, or again, as soon as the circus is gone (the term "circus" used in this occasion by Levinas is certainly significant), there remains only a derisory stage voided of all substantial reality (the elements decompose themselves) and of all meaning.

[8] On the heavy trace of "existence bearing baggage" cf. Levinas 2009, 133.

[9] Cf. the motif of the "phantom," evoked here with regard to the whole year in captivity (Levinas 2009, 126).

The over-determination of the role, the trait applied too heavily, are always on the edge of collapsing into what is neither truly being nor the frank negation of being, and certainly not "otherwise than being": being that hardly exists, *il y a* – in its double characteristic of a deficiency of both being and meaning.

The *il y a*,[10] of which Levinas shows precisely that it always "holds" itself "there" (as phantoms do – hardly, but inevitably and indefinitely) under the thin skin, the fine surface where the circus puts on its play: the play of being (of substance) and the play of meaning (of thematized signification).

Can one not read there, in the thought-situation of the debacle, the description of this "broken world" that provides the beginning of *Existence and Existants*, as Chalier and Calin note in their preface (cf. Levinas 2009) ? Can one not even maintain that, "shining" into the whole work, the "scene of Alençon," so to say, "offers something to see," "renders an image," for the phenomenological descriptions of being that are mentioned at the beginning of *Totality and Infinity* (cf. Levinas 1979, 21), then in *Otherwise than Being or Beyond Essence* (cf. Levinas 1991, chapter one, section II)?

Let us return to the description of the scene of Alençon. What strikes one is the underlying idea that the "drapes" are pomposity and decorum. They are the expression of the authority of the official order (of which it is suggested that it basically maintains itself in what should be only its sign or its appearance) or even of the officiality of order. One imagines the "golden insignia of the Republic" – this French Republic which, as we know, meant so much to the young Lithuanian Jew who had just taken up French citizenship.

In a sense, for Levinas, the real perfects itself and is accomplished in institutions: the French Republic, the State of Law, the homeland of Human Rights, where the signs are those of the legitimate authority that fundamentally guarantees the consistency of all that is real. Professors, judges, and lawyers inhabit and incarnate a world of education and justice guaranteed by a police force under the orders of a measured, enlightened, and legitimate power. They are authorities who watch over the social order, the cultural order, and the order of civility (where one goes to the theatre), the order of those who are active and industrious (where the "bakers bake" but also "where the viscounts tell the stories of viscounts"). Such is the very "consistency" of the real (an inauthentic consistency) in ordinary times. We know how much Levinas as a young man believed in this order, the one guaranteed by the French Republic, the guardian

---

10 For Levinas, as is well known, the notion of the *il y a* is like the dark side of the notion of the element or of the elemental. It is thus highly significant that he evokes the decomposition of things into elements and even the decomposition of the elements themselves, which occurs "after the circus has left or on the stage."

of Human Rights, and how much Levinas as a mature man never stopped being loyal to this order that guarantees the real and ordinary life. But one measures how much in the same movement he emphasized its *insufficiency* – or again how much he emphasized that what truly counted in it never originated from it.

This is precisely what the Levinassian reduction reveals: being is not sufficient, is not sufficient for meaning – for signifying-ness – and not even, from a certain point of view, for being.

In the preface of *Totality and Infinity*, the pivotal image of the scene of Alençon returns, the scene of the "drapes ablaze." And what does the fire reveal? I return to this well-known passage: "Harsh reality (this sounds like a pleonasm!), harsh object-lesson, at the very moment of its fulguration when the drapings of illusion burn war is produced as the pure experience of pure being" (Levinas 1979, 21).

One only needs to read the beginning of *Otherwise than Being* in order to find this description, that I will not reproduce in detail and of which I only indicate the main aspects: being is the confrontation of beings, each being persevering in its being, ineluctably colliding with others. This substantial confrontation derives from the indeterminate anonymity of the *il y a* as much as it threatens to return to it. In the order of being, the anonymous *il y a* is precisely neutralized and domesticated in an intrinsically fragile way. Being is order, distinguishing substances and juxtaposing them in space, retaining each of them in its limits. Being is *legein*, gathering, which produces thematized meaning (cultural significations) and civility, but also justice understood as a measure and a sharing guaranteed by a State. Being is peace, insofar as peace is only the reverse side of war and this war, which is the allergy and the collision of individual substances, can at every instant return them to the terrifying anonymity that ceaselessly threatens to lock them up in the phantom existence of the *il y a*.

The debacle thus reveals the foundation of being for what it is and, by contrast and as a consequence, it reveals the surface of being for what it is: the comedy of a harmonious order or the harmonious order as comedy, as theatre and in this sense a stage. It is on the "stage of being" that there is order, peace, and quite simply a world and a space where substances can arrange themselves next to one another. Being in the debacle, however, sees the official order collapsing, revealed to be nothing but a fragile, lacerated, and interrupted film: the stage of being is actually only a very thin surface where, doubling itself as *logos*, being strives to persevere. It is a surface that, once it tears, allows the worst and at the same time reveals itself as a fragile and derisory play. From this point of view, Levinas's claim is radical. Along with this human order, which seemed guaranteed by reason from all eternity, along with this "reasonable world," it is the world as such – beginning with perception – that collapses. The roads taken by those who flee not only do not lead beyond being but, already, do not even lead from place to place; they belong to a bad *no man's land* (not to an u-topia but to the indeterminacy of all place).[11] Without a doubt, one could go as far as saying that in a sense it is the peace of the *logos*, of the philosophers, the judges, and lawyers that "maintains" the world of perception.

If the thought-situation of the scene of Alençon, of the debacle, has this key role, if it truly embodies the "Levinassian reduction," then it is not surprising that it is disseminated in a more or less explicit manner throughout Levinas's texts: in the literary texts of course, but also in the philosophical texts and, in addition, in the texts that I would characterize as "Jewish." I designate by this latter in a very precise sense all the texts that Levinas has written from the position of his being Jewish (and which are often addressed to the Jewish community).

Let us examine two occurrences of the scene of Alençon and let us attempt to clarify what they teach us and what the displacement and the transplantation to which they are submitted teach us about the Levinassian reduction as debacle. It is a matter of considering them "variations" of this scene and of the operation that it embodies.

1 Occurrence 1

"Sans nom," a text published in *Les Nouveaux Cahiers* in 1966,[12] is, at least from a certain point of view, a Jewish text, in the sense that its author, and

---

[11] For a tracing and above all a very fine reading of Levinas's texts on the place and the non-place, particularly on the *no man's land* and its ambiguities, cf. Jean-Louis Chrétien, "Lieu et non-lieu dans la pensée de Levinas" (2007). Cf. also Sebbah, "Emmanuel Levinas. L'utopie du chez-soi" (2009).

[12] This text is republished in *Noms Propres* (Montpellier: Fata Morgana, 1976). It is translated by Michael B. Smith as "Nameless" in *Proper Names* (1996, 119–123). The explicit and primary addressee is indeed – as it is called – the "Jewish community," to which the text's first publication in a journal that identifies itself with French Judaism, bears witness. Levinas, who addresses himself to a "we" to which he belongs, identifies himself as the sender of the text from the position of his being Jewish. It is no less the case, however, that by definition – as *published*, and capable of being read by everyone – this text is called to address the universality of the community of possible readers (something that, moreover, is testified by the fact that it is included in a collection with no privileged addressee other than its reader). It seems illuminating to distinguish the different kinds of texts written by Levinas according to his situation as sender and according to the privileged addressee. It is self-explanatory, however, that tracing the borders between types of texts produces necessarily a schematic identification and that such borders are, of course, not impermeable.

addressor, identifies himself from the position of his being Jewish and asks himself what should be communicated to the Jewish community concerning the experience of concentration camps and the clandestine Jewish experience after having survived the horrors of the Nazis.

I shall not take up the description in these pages of the abandonment that took place between 1940 and 1945. Let us simply indicate that, in this abandonment, everything appears as if the event of the debacle, the traumatic interruption that it constitutes, had been "continued" in a strange suspension.[13] Everything is there, unchanged from a certain point of view, but deserted of all meaning, rendered derisory. "Interregnum or end of the Institutions, or as if being itself had been suspended. Nothing was official anymore. Nothing was objective. Not the least manifesto on Human Rights." (Levinas 1996, 119–120) And for Levinas, as one knows, after this suspension, there was the feeling of the "unjustifiable privilege of having survived six million deaths" (Levinas 1996, 120). Life from then on was lived as a "stay of execution," in which the "reality of normal life" reconstituted itself (newspapers, chats, values, and the force of public order to protect them), but in such a way that "nothing has been able to fill, or even cover over the gaping pit" (Levinas 1996, 120). In this way, the reduction of being, or to being (as *il y a*), that we have represented above as it is grasped by Levinas in the situation of the debacle which is in some way punctual and paroxysmal (there is something like an instant of the debacle, a before *and* an after: all things are in their place *and* the crowds are on the roads), is also the situation of *desolation* of the Jew, of the person who assumes being Jewish. The desolation temporalizes itself, first in the punctum of the debacle, then as duration of five years. More radically, in a sense, once revealed it always lasts: the debacle continues, the desolation is there. Nothing of the life that begins again (as legitimate inauthenticity) can really cover the abyss. Once the drapes have caught fire, the texture of a new coat of decorum, of authority, and of civility cannot but bear the indelible mark of rupture and let discern what it strives to cover up.

It is a question of radical desolation: not only that I am separated from the other or enclosed in my world, not only that I am alone in the world, but I am alone without even the world any longer. I am alone. The situation is not one where I am struck by injustice in such a way that the violence of its blow is

---

[13] Here one finds a temporal characteristic of the phenomenological reduction distributed in its different stages, a characteristic expressed, moreover, by the emphases borne respectively by two translations of the term *epochè*: interruption and suspension. The reduction is a matter of a radical discontinuity and/then of a suspension of the time of the world (through which this interruption is paradoxically "continued").

attenuated by the certitude that somewhere there is justice and there are just persons, other human beings who cannot hear me for the moment but whom I can hope to rejoin. The situation of radical desolation is such that the very idea of justice has collapsed.

In this way, one of the "variations" of the Levinassian reduction relates it to being Jewish, puts it to work under the particular guise of this facticity, of this specific situation. And what, then, do we learn from this? Something appears in this text that did not directly appear in other evocations of the "scene of Alençon": as a residue of a reduction that has not been perceived hitherto.

Let us clarify what is at issue. The desolation is *also* designated as the internalization of the values that collapsed Outside and with this very Outside – an internalization in "the hidden recesses of subjective consciousness" (Levinas 1996, 119). The broken world, the real under reduction or in the debacle, where everything seems similar and is neutralized in its thesis of existence, is also a world, so to say, without its ethical orientation. This world no longer constitutes a world: "[w]e returned to the desert, a space without countryside" (Levinas 1996, 121).[14] This annulling of the whole world, however, leaves a residue untouched: the irreducible "remainder" of the subjectivity that endures the trauma of such a reduction. Being Jewish allows the subjectivity in question to be understood in two ways. First, as being riveted. Being riveted means, first, "negatively" as a being that cannot escape, first of all from itself, or as a being for which its own being is a prison and a malediction (*il y a* as the hyperbole of the "being laden with baggage"). Such a being is assigned to a space, but it is by no means a question of being extended or deployed. On the contrary, it is a matter of space as receptacle, "a space made to measure – like a tomb – to contain us" (Levinas 1996, 121): suffocation in being and by its being – like being buried alive. Subjectivity about to succumb to the burden of its own being. But already – this is the second characteristic of this subjectivity – one can read, as if on dotted lines, the reversal of this assignation to oneself, of this being "riveted to oneself." It is thus a question of what the reduction of being to being (of being and its order to the *il y a*) has no hold on, of what precisely does not belong to being: to *believe* in the return of values, a "feeling oneself responsible"

---

14 Let us indicate that the description proposed by the "Jewish" text is completely homologous to the one proposed in the "philosophical" texts (*Totality and Infinity*, *Otherwise than Being*) recalled in the first part: the human order that guarantees peace collapses and, with it, space itself, letting the desert emerge without place and orientation. One lesson is thus gained from this: the human being does not need civilization in order to live – the civilization that exhausts itself as a simple sign or appearance of itself, and not even of comfort . . . (cf. Levinas 1996, 121).

for values even when they have collapsed outside, along with anything else outside, with the whole World. The "inner life," Levinas says, in ancient and conventional words in order to say that the true interiority is not of the World, and certainly not something as an "interior" that could again be "situated" in the World. Hope and responsibility resist when nothing in the world remains upright – or which does so only in the raw light of the derisory – because they are not from the World nor from being. Hope and responsibility through which, in a sense, interiority is evasion itself.[15]

2 Occurrence 2

I would like to consider another "transplant," another variation of the scene of Alençon, of the debacle, this time in a text the reading of which clearly identifies as philosophical. As far as the texts published by Levinas are concerned I believe that it is the most explicit version of the evocation of the debacle. In particular, this version takes up the markers of this scene extremely clearly (the places, the details mentioned), and exhibits them. The same situations are evoked, exactly in the same terms, but in a more thorough manner than in the renderings of the scene more directly connected to what was experienced biographically.

When does Levinas live, as if for a second time, the "thought-situation of the debacle"? When does he live a second debacle – or rather relive the debacle? When reading Derrida. The effect of deconstruction on the world of significations is not only compared to the debacle of 1940 but it is in a sense identified with it. The text on Derrida of 1972, "Wholly otherwise"[16] (which one can say is contemporary to *Otherwise than Being or Beyond Essence*), is highly

---

[15] Here, I leave out an issue that is, however, decisive: the relation between being Jewish in its particularity and the "human soul" in its generality, the relation between the situation of the Jew in the facticity of his/her existence and that of all human being. Cf. in particular "Être juif" (a text that appeared in the community revue *Confluences* in 1947) and was taken up again in "Judaïsme et altruism" (Levinas 2003).

[16] "Jacques Derrida / Tout autrement," first published in *L'Arc* 2 (1973), and then in *Noms Propres*. The English translation, "Jacques Derrida: Wholly Otherwise," is included in *Proper Names* (Levinas 1996, 55–62). This text devoted to Derrida thus first appeared in the special number on Derrida of one of the leading journals concerned with what was "very contemporary" in the arts, literature, and philosophy in the 1970s. It is not without significance, certainly, that these two texts ("Nameless" and "Jaques Derrida: Wholly Otherwise"), whose heterogeneity we have emphasized, met each other in their "recovery" within the same issue, which is precisely to a large extent a "gathering" of "friends."

eloquent on this matter. One finds all the characteristics of the debacle (this time "circumscribed" by the domain of thought): the abolition of place and the desolation of all landscapes – there are landscapes of thought – rendered uninhabitable. The image of the *no-man's land* used in the *Carnets* returns: "In the meantime, we tread a *no-man's land*, an in-between that is uncertain even of the uncertainties that flicker everywhere. [. . .] At the outset, everything is in place; after a few pages or paragraphs of formidable calling into question, nothing is left inhabitable for thought [. . .]. In reading him [Derrida], I always see the 1940 exodus again." (Levinas 1996, 55–56) It is not in the notes of the *Carnets* nor in the other pages that here and there narrate and comment on historical events, but on page 56 of a text on Derridian deconstruction that one finds the most complete restitution of the scene of Alençon in the published work of Levinas. In this way, the "thought-situation" brings together the episode lived in the world by the man Levinas – *hardly* locatable empirically, "[s]omewhere between Paris and Alençon" in 1940 – and the situation of deconstruction. And if, according to the hypothesis guiding our reading, the debacle is indeed a guise of reduction (the "Levinassian reduction"), then one can measure how much deconstruction is related to reduction, remains a reduction, even if it is a reduction that "happens to" the subject rather than being operated by it – a Derridaean reduction in intimate affinity with the Levinassian reduction: the debacle or the real under reduction; deconstruction or the text under reduction (the one continues the other and vice versa).

What is at stake in this contact between debacle and deconstruction – what is the case of, using Levinas's expression, "[p]hilosophy as defeat" (Levinas 1996, 57)? One can no longer believe in, nor adhere to, the regime of deconstruction, as is the case in the debacle: the thematized meanings collapse, leaving the order of the signifier voided of sense. Here, something is in play that is not a dialectic of being and appearance but – the terms are almost identical with those used in the description of what the debacle in the "scene of Alençon" reveals – a lack of "originary" presence that undermines being (the Derridaean text explicitly cited at the time by Levinas is *Voice and Phenomenon*).

One point deserves our attention: an episode sometimes mentioned in other versions of the debacle acquires an absolutely decisive status at the heart of the revisiting of Derridaean deconstruction. It is part of the event, literally as strange as anecdotal, that I was alluding to in the beginning (cf. footnote 5). It seems to me that one can accredit this event a bearing that is "transcendental" or "metaphysical" in the sense of Levinas. It is a strange episode: "[A] half-drunk barber invited the soldiers who were passing by on the road (the 'boys' [les '*petits gars*'] as he called them, in a patriotic language gliding above the waters, or keeping afloat in the chaos) to come into his little shop for a free shave." (Levinas 1996, 56) The hypertext is neither very "learned" nor very "old." It concerns, very prosaically, "tomorrow one shaves for free." It is with respect to this that the very title of the section, "Today is tomorrow," gains its meaning. "Tomorrow one shaves for free or: 'messianism!'" Levinas comments in these terms: "The essential procrastination – the future *difference* – was reabsorbed into the present. Time was reaching its end with the end, or the interim, of France." (Levinas 1996, 56)

Let us extract the meaning of "tomorrow one shaves for free." It is work done freely for the other, like a gift of oneself: this is what is impossible for the "calculating rationality" of the ordinary economy and social relations. That is what the expression in its ordinary usage denounces kindly but ironically: the illusory character of such a hope. The person who hopes for the advent of the impossible cradles himself in illusion. Now, in the event of the debacle – more or less continuous in its suspended duration – in the here and now of a place itself put into parenthesis ("[s]omewhere between Paris and Alençon"), the impossible as such takes place. It "takes place" in a manner that is necessarily strange and paradoxical: it dismantles time. It derives from the in-between-time (suspension of the normal course of time) and from counter-time: interruption but also upheaval and "crash" in the forced scansion of time. Today and tomorrow collide, melt into each other without, however, being absorbed into each other: a today that acquires the strength of a future after tomorrow as such, a "tomorrow" that takes shape as the present, as today, without cancelling itself as a pure to-come. An impossible advent that arrives as the advent of the impossible. Can one not identify here the very structure of the messianic moment, that to which the prophetic intervention opens?[17]

And what arrives is then certainly not a surplus of presence or a super-presence. The preceding descriptions of the debacle have taught us this – rejoining clearly from this point of view an idea that is at the heart of "deconstruction": that what arrives is the defeat or the debacle of presence. Presence is missing the call: it defects. And this is why what comes in the debacle comes as if it were not coming. It is that of which the non-arrival constitutes the event and thus the *quasi-*presence. The collapse of presence is an event.

I shall not insist further here on the quasi-identity of the debacle and/or the defeat, on the one hand, and the messianic event, on the other. This is a proximity tied, if the description is correct, at the heart of the thought-situation

---

[17] On the temporality of the prophetic and of the messianic cf. Gérard Benussan, *Le temps messianique* (2001), particularly page 57 and following.

of a certain phenomenological thought that reveals itself in this very movement as *closest* to Derridaean "deconstruction."

The feeling attached to this debacle is characterized by its intrinsic ambivalence: it is a trial that afflicts you and that is not chosen (in contrast to the operation of the "phenomenological reduction" understood in the Husserlian sense – thus synonymous with mastery). It is a terrifying trial of desolation and collapse. And yet this trial is necessary because it does indeed carry out a reduction (despite everything that opposes it to the Husserlian *operatio princeps*). It is a reduction even in the sense that it opens and gives access – be it through desolation or the defection of presence.

The complexity of the relation of Levinas to Derrida has something to do with this ambivalence – with this "contact at the heart of a chiasmus" (Levinas 1996, 62).[18] Up to a point, Levinas suggests that Derrida, in a sense better than anyone, "inscribes" the thought-situation of the debacle at the heart of philosophy. In Levinas's description of deconstruction, there is, moreover, a quasi-confusion between these two gestures, as though intermingled with his own philosophical gesture. It is absolutely clear: certain sequences of the description of deconstruction, in the terms that are used as much as in the meanings that are suggested, are indiscernible from the descriptions to which Levinas proceeds in his "own" philosophical gesture. Deconstruction as the back-and-forth between Saying (the event of the otherwise than being) and the Said (*legein* gathering being), the "flickering" through which the Saying compromises itself with the Said – and already the "pullback" of the "Unsaid" that delivers, reduced to the Saying . . . In these lines that speak about the philosophical gesture, there is almost the avowal, the confession or perhaps – also indirectly addressed to Derrida – something like the implicit declamation of a "he is me and I am him."

And yet nothing of the harshness that can be identified in the deconstruction of 1940, in the debacle, is effaced. The intermingling of the friendship between the gestures of thought, which cannot be unraveled, however, leads – without cancelling anything of itself – to the point of disagreement, or at least of extreme reticence. Without a doubt, Levinas shares with Derrida the idea that in a sense one does not rise up from defeat, that the debacle is without "*Aufhebung*" and does not promise new troops in combat formation – neither restoration nor revenge of substantial presence. Whoever has once been exposed to the devastating afflatus irreducibly remains locked in the feeling of the debacle (whether he be "covered up" again by the reconstituted veneer of

---

[18] These are the final words of "Jacques Derrida / Tout autrement."

the world and culture). However, as we have seen, this feeling is also hope and even the condition of possibility of hope: hope maintained at the heart of the impossible and even hope that cannot emerge as such except when it is at the heart of the impossible, against all odds. It is here that the point of the disagreement is located: Levinas, in his text of 1972, suspects that the defection of presence carried out in Derrida's deconstruction does not open onto a one-for-the-other, to "ethics," "goodness," or "love" (the terms and emphases have varied), which, for him, so to say, already break through the evidence of war and the trial of defeat – without, however, cancelling them.[19]

The two debacles, that of Levinas and that of Derrida, in fact do not coincide. The paths diverge. Levinas suspects that deconstruction, after having liquefied the world, demobilized beings, thrown on the roads the phantoms encumbered by their baggage, stops there and does not open onto the positivity of what has no subsisting presence but gives itself in this way precisely in its very positivity: in faces and ethics. Deconstruction would remain with the specters (and, indeed, in Levinas the motif of the specter always has a negative connotation – one has to avoid the world of specters – while Derrida attached himself to this motif, giving it the positive connotation of saying the absenting of all presence as the event).[20]

Between the two debacles, that of Levinas and that of Derrida, there is indeed a point of contact at the heart of a chiasmus. One cannot fail to notice how, in the course of time, tangentially, a convergence tends to be produced within

---

[19] One thus understands that Levinas ambivalently appreciated the deconstruction of his own text by Derrida, qualifying "Violence et métaphysique" (Derrida's commentary on *Totality and Infinity*) as an "assassination under anesthetic" rather than an unsaying leading back to the Saying.

[20] It would be necessary, far more than we are doing here, to reflect on the *superposition* of the two exoduses – the biblical one and that of 1940. One knows that the event of the biblical Exodus is "inaugural and that of a matrix", that it "makes a metonym out of all the events that are homologous to it" (according to Bensussan's words in *Le temps messianique*). Yet, what the "original form" of the "prophetic event" promises is the interruption of the disaster through liberation and then redemption. Without a doubt, the trial of the suspension between 1940 and 1945, of that desert, would have disrupted Levinas's understanding of the messianic moment. The latter perhaps reveals itself to be terribly "without the promise of redemption," but, as we have insisted, not without hope – on the contrary! This is a fragile messianism, but it is maintained in this sense. The problem is not to be saved by a God whose death Levinas confirms with the horror of Nazism, but hope is preserved. Even more, hope only emerges from the depths of the abyss, in and through its very fragility: as the ethics of the face of the Other. Such would be the dispute with what Levinas suspects in Derrida: "deconstruction" would denominate the risk of an exodus that breaks any link with the Exodus . . . the exodus of phantoms without a face.

the very irreducibility of the gap. Levinas explicitly assumes proximity between deconstruction and his own practice of the unsaying (with which Levinas responds to Derrida's critique with respect to the "ontological naivety" of *Totality and Infinity*). Inversely, one cannot fail to notice how Derrida understands "deconstruction" progressively as an "ethics" in the sense of Levinas: "deconstruction" that, in exposing itself to what does not arrive, exposes itself, however, to what arrives in this way (as not arriving) and says "yes" to it, "unconditionally."

In conclusion, I hope that, despite the necessarily approximate and abusive manner of formulating this, there will have been some sense in saying that "all the philosophy of Levinas is there, in the scene of Alençon", if this scene is indeed something like a – the? – seminal "thought-situation," that of the debacle as reduction (and thus of the reduction as debacle). It is this seminal "thought-situation" that disseminates itself throughout the diversity of Levinas's texts and that we have tried, for example, to designate at work in two moments of extreme importance, two decisive palpitations or flickers: in the description of being Jewish *and* in the contact with Derrida's thought – a contact in which Levinas's philosophical gesture is at play and displays its living center.[21]

Bibliography

Benussan, Gérard. *Le temps messianique*. Paris: Vrin, 2001.
Chrétien, Jean-Louis. "Lieu et non-lieu dans la pensée de Levinas." *Emmanuel Levinas et les territoires de la pensée*. Eds. Danielle Cohen-Levinas and Bruno Clément. Paris: PUF, 2007. 121–138.

---

21 A name that mattered for Levinas as much as it did for Derrida, does not appear in this text. In a sense, it is missing to such an extent that one would have to justify its absence by the necessity of constructing another set of remarks: Blanchot. Indeed, in many respects, literary writing according to Blanchot and above all on the part of Blanchot – the "writing of the disaster" – is the debacle itself: beyond affirmation and negation, the arrival of that which only arrives by disappointing, by lacking its very presence (cf., for example, *L'attente, l'oubli*). While reading in Blanchot something of the ethical gesture, Levinas does not accompany his friend all the way because, precisely, Blanchot's reduction as a debacle succeeds in a way only too well, since it no longer preserves the remainder of subjectivity as responsibility. Blanchot leads back to radical anonymity through literary writing at that point at which Levinas requires for philosophical writing a remainder of irreducible subjectivity – as responsibility and testimony to the trial of the otherwise than being. This bifurcation, which relies to a large extent on the possibility of distinguishing philosophical from literary writing, will doubtlessly have to be taken into account in understanding Levinas's novel – and the difficult relation that he maintained, it seems, to his own literary writing.

Franck, Didier. *Dramatique des phénomènes*. Paris: PUF, 2001.
Levinas, Emmanuel. "Etre juif." *Confluences* 15–17 (1947): 253–264.
Levinas, Emmanuel. *Totality and Infinity*. Trans. Alphonso Lingis. The Hague / Boston: Nijhoff, 1979.
Levinas, Emmanuel. *Otherwise Than Being or Beyond Essence*. Trans. Alphonso Lingis. Dordrecht/Boston/London: Kluwer, 1991.
Levinas, Emmanuel. *Proper Names*. Trans. Michael B. Smith. London: The Athlone Press, 1996.
Levinas, Emmanuel. "Judaïsme et altruism." *Cahiers d'Etudes Lévinassiennes* 2 (2003): 197–206.
Levinas, Emmanuel. *Œuvres complètes*, Volume I: *Carnets de captivité et autres inédits*. Eds. Rodolphe Calin and Catherine Chalier. Paris: Grasset/IMEC, 2009.
Levinas, Emmanuel. *Œuvres complètes*, Volume III : *Eros, littérature et philosophie. Essais romanesques et poétiques, notes philosophiques sur le thème d'éros*. Eds. Jean-Luc Nancy and Danielle Cohen-Levinas. Paris : Grasset/IMEC, 2013.
Sebbah, François-David. "Emmanuel Levinas. L'utopie du chez-soi." *Le territoire des philosophes*. Eds. Thierry Paquot and Chris Yours. Paris: La Découverte, 2009. 255–274.

Michaël de Saint-Cheron
From Eros to the Question of the Death of God

I would like to explore two essential themes in Levinas's philosophy. First, I will examine how Levinas, in the outline of his attempt at fiction, *Eros*, or *Sad Opulence*, manages to join the erotic and the ethical. Secondly, I will argue that the rhetoric of the prophetic in Levinas's discourse takes aim at the end of the rhetoric of the promise and should be read in light of the unfathomable question concerning the death of God in the Nazi extermination camps. My aim here is to demonstrate how Levinas, the philosopher, found in literary texts, as exemplified by Vassily Grossman's monumental work *Life and Fate*, the possibility of an anti-rhetoric of the prophetic that led him to conceive God as still audible after the Shoah.

1 The Erotic and the Ethical in Dialogue

In the fragment *Eros*, which is actually entitled *Sad Opulence* (Levinas 2013), our novelist-philosopher sets the action during the spring of 1940. The major character in the beginning of the work, the recently mobilized Paul Rondeau, enters into a dialogue with France and also with history. The plot, from which eroticism is not absent, is psychological. We encounter Joan of Arc and General Weygand. The narrative gathers momentum when Rondeau's battalion is captured and he becomes a *Kommando* in charge of a group of prisoners, several of whom are Jewish. In the course of these pages, Levinas introduces a passage devoted to women and a "soft" eroticism – an eroticism bathed in poetry: "Mais le jour où à travers une fenêtre ouverte on a aperçu une jeune fille qui peignait de longs cheveux on avait l'impression d'une indécence ou d'un rêve, d'une poésie aiguë et déchirante de la beauté qui fait mal. Plus fort que la Lorelei, mais pas plus haut. Le mélange d'une grande beauté et d'une grande bassesse. [But the day when across an open window one caught a glimpse of a young girl who was combing her hair, one had the impression of an indecency or a dream, of a sharp and

---
Translation: Translated from the French, by Dr. Karen D. Levy, Professor Emerita of French Studies, University of Tennessee and by Pr. Alan Astro, Trinity University, San Antonio.

Michaël de Saint-Cheron, Histara/École Pratique des Hautes Études

Open Access. © 2021 Michaël de Saint-Cheron, published by De Gruyter. This work is licensed under the Creative Commons Attribution 4.0 International License.
https://doi.org/10.1515/9783110668926-005

rending poetry, of beauty which causes pain. Stronger than the Lorelei, but not higher. The blending of a great beauty and a great baseness.]" (Levinas 2013, 50).

Let us now examine how the phenomenologist analyzes the utility of the pair of stockings that is drying in the wind: "ces bas qui réchauffent ou qui empêchent que la chaussure n'irrite la peau et ne la blesse et que dans l'usage quotidien on manie avec la précision et la sobriété de médecin n'avaient plus rien de leur chaste essence d'ustensiles. [these stockings that keep one warm or prevent the shoe from irritating the skin and wounding it and that daily use treats with the precision and sobriety of a physician ... no longer had anything left of their chaste essence as tools.]" (Levinas 2013, 50–51) It is not the "[m]onde cannibale de l'érotisme [cannibalistic world of eroticism" (Levinas 2013, 51) of which Levinas speaks, but, beginning with an erotic allegory, a return to things themselves. A pair of stockings is there foremost not to excite the erotic imagination of the man, but rather as protection for a woman's legs.

In this fragment of his novel, Levinas returns to Boby, the little dog who, in the stalag, had glommed onto the *Kommando* of the Jewish prisoners: "ce fut le seul être qui ne faisait pas de différence entre les prisonniers et les aryens qui les gardaient. [. . .] Il reconnaissait seul le droit de l'homme et la dignité de la personne de ces juifs. [the only being who did not discern a difference between the prisoners and the Aryanss who were guarding them [. . .] He only recognized human rights and the dignity of the Jewish person.]" (Levinas 2013, 51) We can compare this page to the particular text in *Difficult Freedom*, which draws as much from the genre of the story, as from the novella, the press, and philosophy and which is titled "The Name of a Dog, or Natural Rights". "But we called him Bobby, an exotic name, as one does with a cherished dog. [. . .] For him, there was no doubt that we were men." (Levinas 1990, 153)

There is in these strictly speaking non-philosophical texts a rift between moral conduct and the forbidden, between narration and reflection, between prose in its pure state and a speculative discourse such as that between the psychology of the characters and the action that drives them. Love of literature again assumes here in a brief instant its place in the imagination of a man nourished from his earliest years by the great Russian novelists. Beyond these novelistic fragments, there is, as there was in his Russian youth, a Levinas who was a poet – as can now be read for the first time in the third volume of the *inédits* (Levinas 2013) that I wish to acknowledge for including an impressive number of unedited poems and especially some one would not inevitably expect to find. It is an impressive collection that gives a more complete and almost definitive vision of Levinas the philosopher, more in keeping with the man, the thinker, that he was, for they grant him the secret share of literary ambition and of efforts to produce non-philosophical writings. Jean-Luc Nancy examines the transgression linked in part to the erotic "à la fois emblème et lieu effectif [at the same time emblem and actual site]," but, on the other hand, connected as well to a form of writing employed here because "[l]a littérature permet la transgression: c'est-à-dire qu'elle la transporte hors de tout cadre moral ou légal et en permet l'expression. [Literature permits transgression, that is to say, it transports transgression outside any moral or legal framework and allows for its expression.]"(Nancy 2013, 28). It is as if literature, for the philosopher, incarnates eros in its dimension of mystery, of desire, of the quest for going beyond being for being.

However, contrary to Sartre, Levinas did not seek to make these literary premises parallel to his philosophical work, which is already doubled by a strong Talmudic and Jewish content – and by a book so close to being literature: *Proper Names*. In his "Philosophical Notes on Eros", Levinas strongly separates himself from Heidegger, who in *Being and Time* outlines a phenomenology in which, so to say, there is no relationship between beings. On the contrary, Levinas defines the relationship with the shopkeeper, or the artisan, as an act of sociality (Levinas 2013, 165). He distinguishes, for example, "cette relation interpersonnelle de commerce économique ou intellectual [this interpersonal relation of economic or intellectual commerce]" from social, non-commercial relations (Levinas 2013, 167). There exists in these pages a play on the polysemic meaning of the word commerce, as when Levinas writes, "le commerce intellectuel est essentiellement une communion [intellectual commerce is essentially a communion]" (Levinas 2013, 166–167), before using the word several lines later to speak of commercial relations, which, if they are sometimes similar, are opposed to one another more than they can be considered mutual substitutes, communion being only rarely a commercial relationship.

On the level of eros itself, we find marvelous expressions, such as these: "Autrui – c'est négativement le caché. Et l'éros c'est la communion avec le caché. Le caché n'est pas seulement ce qui est caché pour la connaissance; ce qui est ignoré: c'est la caresse qui est en quelque manière l'accès à autrui. [The Other is negatively the hidden. And eros is communion with the hidden. The hidden is not only what is concealed from knowledge; it is what is not known: it is the caress, which, in a certain way, gives access to the other.]" (Levinas 2013, 179) Quite paradoxical as well as strange is the development of sexuality that Levinas sees as "une relation sans 'avoir' et par conséquent une relation sans responsabilité. Dans l'événement sexuel – la volupté et la caresse – le moi sort du règne de la possession – il sort de lui-même, de la tautologie moi-soi. [a relationship without possession and consequently a relationship without responsibility. In the sexual experience, in the sensual pleasure of the caress, the self leaves the domain of possession and goes out from the tautology of the I-Self.]" (Levinas 2013, 181) Despite these paradoxes, Levinas insists on the fact that nudity is not only "le fait d'être sans vêtements. Elle est l'apparition et l'appel du mystère, le fait pour le Mystère de se révéler. [the fact of being without clothes. It is the apparition and the summons of mystery, the way for mystery to reveal itself.]" (Levinas 2013, 181) From which follows the total rejection of pornography, which denies all mystery, where flesh, reduced to being only a receptacle for pleasure as well as sexual pain, has nothing to reveal in its nudity. In these non-dated "Notes", close in time to the writing of *Totality and Infinity,* there arises the rustling of the "there is" in its association with night, as we found in Blanchot, but which goes back further to *From Existence to Existents*, written right after the war. Levinas clearly distinguishes between the anonymity of the "there is" and the "assumption du present à travers la distance de l'instant [taking on of the present via the distance of the instant]" (Levinas 2013, 162).

2 The Prophetic Function and the Question of the Death of God

How can we now approach Levinas from the precise point of view of the prophetic function with, as a surplus, the testimonial function? An entire part of his work can be read under the aegis of prophetic philosophy or of testimonial rhetoric, even when the testimonial function breaks in some way with the entire prophetic function in our time, which we can qualify as postmodern, if it is true that it is situated beyond modernity, the contemporary, and the current. Can we speak of a prophetic rhetoric in Levinas, and if so, what do we make of his ethical rhetoric? As I will attempt to demonstrate, there is a fundamental break from the prophetic to the ethical, namely, the break in history constituted by the years 1939 to 1945. I will begin with the rhetorical function, from the acknowledgment of the death of God in the extermination camps, in order to reach what we see as the end of any rhetorical, prophetic function: Levinas's encounter with the masterpiece by the Russian novelist Vassily Grossman: *Life and Fate.* Philippe Nouzille, a Catholic theologian and philosopher, in his last work titled *Beyond the Self* and subtitled *Revelation and Phenomenology* (2014), brought in from the very first page these words of Levinas, speaking about 1941, as from a "a hole in History, a year in which all the visible gods had abandoned us, in which god was really dead or gone back into his non-revealedness." (Levinas 1987a, 93) But is there not between these two concepts in Nouzille's subtitle an antinomy, a radical opposition, that of Revelation and Phenomenology? Through phenomenology, he aims to approach the fact of revelation. What is in the realm of revelation, however, cannot belong to phenomenology, and the same goes for our question – what is in the realm of revelation was canceled by the Shoah.

Let us take serious Levinas's formulation on the veritable death of God, as if Nietzsche had moved forward in a tempestuous or visionary or prophetic manner – or what he calls "his non-revealedness." God returned to the state of the underside of revelation. If biblical Revelation carries in its heart a promise made to men, made to his [God's] people in the broadest sense, or to his peoples, because no single people has the privilege or the presumption; to say that this God, the God of Revelation, returned to his non-revealedness, signifies something much more serious that Levinas took a long time to formulate: there are no longer any promises possible. The end of the promise requires then, for the philosopher of *Totality and Infinity* who still uses the language of ontology, the construction of an ethics that is capable of responding to the absence of any promise. This end undoubtedly does not signal the end of metaphysics or the end of the prophetic function, except as regards the belief that nothing means anything. Be that as it may, neither of these two functions can endure any longer in the same way after recognizing this acknowledgement. Levinas is not proposing a hypothesis here; he is setting forth a theological affirmation. Thus it is necessary to take him at his word. Yes, after Auschwitz, there is no longer any covenant possible, only the illusion of a covenant.

There is a great distance between Nietzsche's discourse on the death of God and that of Levinas. If by "the death of God," Nietsche intended to hasten the presupposed end of religion as we had understood it until then, what Levinas means implicitly by the end of the promise is even much more hallucinatory and terrifying. Certainly, Franz Rosenzweig, in "Das neue Denken: Einige nachträgliche Bemerkungen zum *Stern der Erlösung*," affirmed, immediately after the First World War, that "God hat eben nicht die Religion geschaffen, sondern die Welt." (Rosenzweig 1925, 442) But what can a religion be when it is emptied of its power to announce a *happy ending*? What does it serve, what is its ultimate goal?

If we can still speak of prophecy, of the prophetic function after Auschwitz, it must take into account the no longer simple question of *tsimtsum*, of the hidden God of the cabalists, but but rather the notion of a God who is no longer the God of promise, but the one who abandoned His children, His people, in the most appalling abyss.

Let us reread the words of the madman in *The Gay Science*: "Where is Gott? I'll tell you. We have killed him – you and I! We are all his murderers." (Nietzsche 2001, 119–120) In his fifth book, subtitled *We fearless ones*, Nietzsche added a second declaration: "The greatest recent event –that 'God is dead'; that the belief in the Christian God has become unbelievable – is already starting to cast its first shadow over Europe." (Nietzsche 2001, 199) Nietzsche attached great importance to his a-theological discovery. Heidegger, however, so profoundly antisemitic, anti-Judaic, glosses the quotation thus: "It is clear from this sentence that Nietzsche, in speaking about the death of God, means the Christian God. But it is no less certain and no less to be kept in mind beforehand that Nietzsche uses the names 'God' and 'Christian God' to indicate the supersensory world in general. God is the name for the realm of ideas and the ideal. Since Plato, or more accurately, since the late Greek and the Christian interpretations of the Platonic philosophy, this realm of the supersensory has been considered the true and actually real world. [. . .] 'God is dead' means: the supersensory world has no effective power. It odes not bestow life. Metaphysics, which for Nietzsche is Western philosophy understood as Platonism, is at an end." (Heidegger 2002, 162)

Let us now return to *The Humanism of the Other Man*. The last chapter, "No Identity," opens with words quite Nietzschean but perhaps also anti-Nietzschean: "The end of humanism, of metaphysics – the death of man, the death of God (or death to God) – these are apocalyptic ideas or slogans of intellectual high society." (Levinas 1987b, 141) Levinas takes up in his own way a rhetoric that has biblical accents, which resonates with unbelievable force in our time, torn precisely between ethics and no more ethics. We are facing an opposition that it is difficult not to consider essential. This marks the end of theodicy, the "end of all theodicy," (Levinas 1986) as Levinas specifies in a rare untitled text, to which he never returned, on the scandal of evil.

> Voici l'être vidé de Dieu et qui n'en finit pas de finir – selon Maurice Blanchot. Voilà un Dieu qui s'est "laissé vider" plus lamentablement que le Dieu qui s'est laissé mourir chez Nietzsche. Cette petite fille sur l'écran de la télévision qui se noie lors de la récente catastrophe de Colombie est sans doute seule à appeler encore sa maman, vainement, au secours : "Mon Dieu, mon Dieu, pourquoi m'as-tu abandonné ? ". Il n'y eut plus de Dieu là où les faibles périssaient. Mais, dans les camps d'extermination, Emile Fackenheim a vu le Diable. [Here is being emptied of God, who never finishes finishing – according to Maurice Blanchot. There is a God who "let himself be emptied" more lamentably than the God who let himself die in Nietzsche's writings. This little girl on the television screen who is drowning in the recent catastrophe in Colombia is undoubtedly alone in vainly calling again to her mother for help: "My God, my God why have you abandoned me?" There is no longer any God there where the weak perish. Rather, in the extermination camps, Emil Fackenheim encountered the Devil.] (Levinas 1986)

The question posed to us is this: who is the God who returned to his non-revealedness or the dead God of whom the philosopher speaks here? Because in any epoch we could not speak of God "there where the weak were dying" even if we were to do so, out of weakness perhaps. What absolute change has occurred in order for discourse, for biblical but also philosophical rhetoric, to thus lose its power of persuasion?

A German journalist interviewed Levinas for *Spuren* seven years before his death. Let us reread the strong words he spoke in answering the interviewer:

> Questioner – Le Dieu qui révèle ici son sens, c'est encore et toujours le Dieu positif de la toute puissance, le Dieu d'une existence suprême. Vu à partir de Nietzsche, c'est donc le Dieu dont la pensée passait les voies du nihilisme, en le poussant vers une crise désespérée. [The God who here reveals his meaning is always the positive, all powerful God, the God of supreme existence. Beginning with Nietzsche, he is seen thus as the God whose thought passed through the paths of nihilism, pushing it towards a desperate crisis.]

> Emmanuel Levinas – Ce Dieu a encore une voix. Il parle avec une voix muette, et cette parole est écoutée. Mais ce Dieu est le Dieu mort de Nietzsche. Il s'est suicidé à Auschwitz. Cependant l'autre Dieu qui ne peut pas être prouvé statistiquement et celui qui seul figure en tant que fait de l'humanité, c'est une protestation contre ce qui seul figure en tant que fait de l'humanité, c'est une protestation contre Auschwitz. Et ce Dieu apparaît dans le visage de l'autre. Dans ce sens précis, Dieu fait irruption dans la pensée, mais dans la pensée conçue phénoménologiquement, d'une manière rigoureuse. Et cela, c'est l'éthique. [This God still has a voice. He speaks in a mute voice, and his word is listened to. But this God is Nietzsche's dead God. He committed suicide at Auschwitz. However, the other God, who cannot be proven statistically and who alone figures as a fact of humanity, is a protestation against which humanity signifies as protestation against Auschwitz. And this God appears in the face of the other. In this precise way, God bursts into thought, conceived of phenomenologically in a rigorous way. And that is ethics. (Levinas 1995, 134–135)

Through this reply, Levinas refutes any prophetic function. But he touches here upon the basis of the aporia/impass of the end of meaning, the limit of discourse that he took up only once, in 1986, with an accent of endless hopelessness. It is a forbidden question, which becomes, in this way, the sole question that dominates everything and which presupposes the ultimate question: "Can one remain a Jew before God who breaks the covenant, who stops answering, who refuses help, and who lets you die as if he abandoned you? Do we not, by remaining Jewish, take lightly the despair – and perhaps the doubts – of those who were going to die?"

It matters little here the reply Levinas offers to Fackhenheim. The ultimate question remains and signals the ultimate reply. But did he not go to the end of aporia, of the logical incompatibility of the question he posed, of the infinitude of the question? After that, how can one redeem a God who allowed Himself to die lamentably along with His children, His chosen people from time immemorial? This people had been for all time the people of the promise. Does not letting this people die thus amount to killing the promise that they carried in themselves for three thousand years?

The depth of the abyss presented here is to reply no longer to a God who has broken the covenant, but rather to a God who let himself die at Auschwitz-Birkenau or, worse yet, to a phantom of a one and only God whom men have been addressing since Abraham and Moses, but who is a utopia. Let us take up the rest of the text:

> Emil Fackenheim pense pourtant que ne pas assurer la continuation d'Israël reviendrait à parachever l'entreprise criminelle du national-socialisme, à combler les vœux de Hitler: anéantir Israël pour annuler son message. Oublier la Bible, oublier la Thora, oublier la miséricorde qui, à travers la Loi, est ordonnée aux hommes. D'où devoir impérieux : rester juif, maintenir Israël, accomplir les conditions morales et politiques de cette existence. Bâtir la nation et l'Etat – formes modernes de cette survie du people. [Emil Fackenheim, however, thinks that not to assure the continuation of Israel would be equivalent to putting the finishing touches on the criminal enterprise of National Socialism, to fulfilling Hitler's vow: to annihilate Israel in order to destroy nullify its message. To forget the Bible, to forget the Torah, to forget mercy, which through the Law is commanded to men. From that point comes the imperious duty: to remain Jewish, to support Israel, to live up to the moral and political conditions of its existence. To build the nation and the State – modern forms of the survival of the people.] (Levinas 1986)

Today we ask ourselves – how can we not raise this question? – the way in which Israel replies to these questions. But in doing so, we would be going beyond our problematic. Thus, let us come back to Levinas.

We can take note of the fact that the written form of the word God is different in *Humanism of the Other Man*, where "god is truly dead or has returned to His non-reveleadness" (Levinas 1987, 93) is written in small letters, in relation to all his other texts, including this last one, where God who breaks the covenant is once again written in capital letters.

The presupposition that leads Levinas to speak of a God who breaks the covenant is quite paradoxical and raises numerous questions, as do Paul Celan's poetry and Elie Wiesel's *Night*. However, in the interview cited above, the philosopher definitely concedes that "[u]n certain Dieu et une certaine façon de penser Dieu, telle qu'elle est propre aux instances religieuses positives, a certainement pris fin [a certain god, a certain way of thinking about God (...) appropriate to positive religious moments has certainly ended]" (Levinas 1995, 135); but on the other hand, he notes that the entity "speaks in a mute voice," even if "this word is listened to. But this God is the dead God of Nietzsche. He committed suicide at Auschwitz." (Levinas 1995, 135) "La négation de Dieu par Nietzsche a été confirmée par le XXe siècle; le Dieu de la promesse, le Dieu donnant, le Dieu comme substance – tout cela ne peut être maintenu, bien entendu. [Nietzsche's negation of God was confirmed by the twentieth century, the God of promise, the giving God of substance – all that cannot be maintained of course.]" (Levinas 1995, 133)

In these two texts Levinas ends with a philosophical way-out, an intentional aiming. In fact, this dead god, preached about by churches and religious authorities, is definitely dead, but he is not the true god. It is as if Levinas, confirming the death of this God, who is the God of theologians, had an obsessive wish to found a new relationship with the divine, with a God who comes to mind and does not preach.

What then is the high point of all of the rhetoric on presence (parousie)? That it is as if the Apocalypse – or revelation – were no longer at the end of history but at the beginning or in the middle.

If theologians of different religions proved their inability to speak of a God who died at Auschwitz, arriving at the aporia (impass?) of their discourse, then we can say either that they are incapable of taking into account what destabilizes and essentially contradicts them, and thus they destroy themselves, or that they take this into account but do not draw any lesson that has true meaning, that can be heard by those who call their rhetoric into doubt. Of course, there exist exceptional theologians who worked with great courage to define possible Christian theologies after the death of God during the Shoah. But we find only a few rabbis after the Shoah who have made theological advances, taking these questions into account, such as Emil Fackenheim, Abraham Yeshoua Heschel, and Leo Baeck, who was deported in 1943 to Theresienstadt. These questions were above all taken up by certain poets, musicians, philosophers, and writers, among whom Levinas is one of the most important, but also by other writers, Yiddish or not, such as Yitskhok Katzenelson, killed at Birkenau in 1944 and author of the terrifying *Song of the Murdered Jewish People*; Benjamin Fondane, who died several months later in the same gas chambers; and Paul Celan, who took his own life in Paris in 1970. Can we say that Levinas was wrong the day he replied that religion could offer more consolation than philosophy (cf. Levinas 1998a, 86) ?

At this time I would like to open another path in our exploration. Nothing would be more absurd than to oppose philosophy to literature, because, for more than a century now, so many philosophers and writers have built bridges between these two disciplines, two fields of action and thought. If it is true that fundamental questioning of being, of the self but also of the other as the source of all morality of all ethics, is the formidable contribution of philosophy, which elaborates with phenomenology all questioning, it does the same with regard to things in themselves and first causes, as well all things in an ultimate sense, which pertain to metaphysics. Philosophy has a powerful relationship with the prescriptive, the juridical, and with rhetoric. On the other hand, contrarily perhaps to literature, to poetry, it does not assume any power/right regarding prayer. But let us go a bit further. So many contemporary and likewise more classical philosophers knew how to reach transcendence in non-conceptual discourses, such as literature, poetry, mysticism, sacred writings, not to mention art and music.

Among the many philosophers who found in writers and poets a sustenance for their exploration of the conceptual, epistemological, analytical, phenomenological and metaphysical realms, Heidegger encountered in Hölderlin and in Trakl two poets who marked, by means of another rhetoric, a unique story and related it to Greek mythology. Levinas found in the Torah and the Talmud – more so than in the greatest literature, from the Greek tragedies to Celan and Jabès – elements that nourished his philosophical discourse, and his ethics, in particular. Dostoevsky, not Kant, in this realm brought him the idea of a universal responsibility of men for one another. He regularly quoted the eternal words of the staretz, Father Zossima, in *The Brothers Karamazov*: "Each of us is guilty before everyone and for everyone, and I more than the others." (cf. Levinas 1991, 146; cf. Levinas 1998, 105) Responsibility is already present in the Torah, naturally, but here it takes on an altogether universal form. Then, in 1982, at the dawn of his last and so fruitful decade, reflecting on "God who comes to mind," we see the concept of saintliness assume an all-important place, which is nothing less than totally anti-rhetorical, because we either scorn it or scorn ourselves in the depths of our human conscience, or we aspire to it from afar, or we embody it, without knowing so, of course. In 1980, Levinas discovered a final Russian masterpiece, by Vassily Grossman, titled *Life and Fate*, which brought to fruition the last part of his own work on the beyond of ethics, a meta-ethics altogether contemporary with the moment when the term "saintliness" appeared in his writings, and which we could qualify as the sublime epiphany.

All of his discourse on the epiphany of the face, of God who comes to mind, if it brings no new proof of the existence of God, does speak of the irreducible place of an invisible presence, of a "new breath," which lets itself be heard and perceived. There remained for Levinas an evidence, that of a summoning to human gratuitousness, which assumed a new name for him: the small goodness.

What is conceived of as a concept can still be induced from a homiletic rhetoric. On the contrary, what escape a concept, a dogma by nature can in no way enter into a rhetoric if it is not by breaking it open. Levinas knows that there are rituals in life, in particular in Judaism, which escape all rhetoric; he likewise knew that there were human actions that similarly escaped it. With Vassily Grossman, it is necessary to leave the realm of rhetoric, that is the great instituted Good, whether it be ecclesiastical, ideological, political, or philosophical.

Let us note that at least in contemporary philosophy since Bergson, there is a moment when "diachrony [. . .] will turn out to be love of one's fellowman." (Levinas 1998b, 208) But how can philosophy, which is not a religion and offers so little wisdom in our time, put in place love for one's neighbor? To answer this question, let us come back to Levinasian presuppositions, to that which is above all essential for him. Levinas always wished to read the word philosophy as the wisdom of love, which, for all that, did not exclude the wisdom of knowledge or science, as epistemologists understand it. Let us read as signature and prolepsis his lines:

> He [the author of *Totality and Infinity*] then asked himself whether all that was dear to the love of "the love of wisdom," or the love that is the philosophy of the Greeks, was the certainty of fields of knowledge directed toward the object, or the even greater certainty of reflection on these fields of knowledge; or whether knowledge beloved of and expected from philosophers was not, beyond the wisdom of such knowledge, the wisdom of love or wisdom in the guise of love. Philosophy as love of love. A wisdom taught by the face of the other man ! (Levinas 1998b, 200)

We can be surprised by the at once questioning and affirmative phrasing chosen by the philosopher, who concludes with a period, not a question mark. Levinas echoes Plato: "It is in view of the Good that each soul does what it does" (cf. *The Republic*, 505 d-e). Once again, we are in the midst/context of the rhetorical function. But soon the end of all rhetoric shows up, when he invokes Grossman in *Life and Fate*. Here are several of the anti-conceptual words that the author of *Otherwise than Being* uses: mercy, goodness, kenosis (humbling oneself?), epiphany, and finally, saintliness. Where does he find them? They do not come from the philosophical lexicon. He found them, he read them in works of theology, in Russian and French literature, and above all in the Torah, except for the words kenosis and epiphany, which come from Greek. We understand here the metaphor of *Ruah hakodesh*, the spirit of saintliness, so striking in the book of Ezekiel, when God says: "Spirit, come from the four winds, breathe on these dead, so that they might live again!"

Then, let us say that the *Ruah hakodesh*, the spirit of saintliness did breathe and still breathes highly and sublimely through the pen of Vassily Grossman, at a level rarely reached in the twentieth century. Levinas reads Grossman for us, with us:

> He thinks that "the small goodness" from one person to his fellowman is lost and deformed as soon as it seeks organization and universality and system, as soon as it opts for doctrine, a treatise of politics and theology, a party, a state, and even a Ccurch. Yet it remains the sole refuge of the good in being. Unbeaten, it undergoes the violence of the evil, which, as small goodness, it can neither vanquish nor drive out. A little kindness going only from man to man, not crossing distances to get to the places where events and forces unfold! A remarkable utopia of the good or the secret of its beyond. (Levinas 1998b, 230)

Levinas, philosopher, phenomenologist, as Grossman the writer, sought untiringly the trace of the "*for-the-other* [. . .], in which, in the adventure of a possible holiness, the human interrupts the pure obstinacy of being and its wars."

(Levinas 1998b, 231) In this way, it is possible to show how Levinas's philosophy of saintliness (the for-the-other) stems from the rhetorical function and, in a certain way, also from the prophetic function. Confronted with the question of Auschwitz and the death of God (by suicide), this development of his thought leads up to the theme of the epiphany of the face, of saintliness in the sense that I specified, but never in an ecclesiastical, religious sense and finally in the small goodness found in Grossman.

Bibliography

Heidegger, Martin. "Nietzsche's Word: 'God is dead (1943)", in *Off the Beaten Track*. Trans. Julian Young and Kenneth Haynes. Cambridge: Cambridge University Press, 2002. 157–199.
Levinas, Emmanuel. *Totality and Infinity: An Essay on Exteriority*. Trans. Alphonso Lingis. The Hague: Martinus Nijhoff, 1979.
Levinas, Emmanuel. "Le scandale du mal". In *Les nouveaux cahiers*. Paris, 85 (1986). 15–17.
Levinas, Emmanuel. "Meaning and sense", in *Collected Philosophical Papers*. Trans. Alphonso Lingis. Dordrecht: Martinus Nijhoff, coll. « Phaenomenologica » vol. 100, 1987a. 75–108.
Levinas, Emmanuel. "No Identity", in *Collected Philosophical Papers*. Trans. Alphonso Lingis. Dordrecht: Martinus Nijhoff, 1987b. 141–151.
Levinas, Emmanuel. *Difficult Freedom*. Essays on Judaism. Trans. Séan Hand. Batimore: The Johns Hopkins University, 1990.
Levinas, Emmanuel. *Otherwise than Being or Beyond Essence*. Trans. Alphonso Lingis. Dordrecht: Kluwer, 1991.
Levinas Emmanuel. "Visage et violence première (phénoménologie de l'éthique), entretien avec Hans Joachim Lenger," in Arno Münster (réd.), *La différence comme non-indifférence. Ethique et altérité chez Emmanuel Levinas*, Kimé, Paris, 1995, 129–143.
Levinas, Emmanuel. *Of God Who Comes to Mind*. Trans. Bettina Bergo. Stanford: Stanford University Press, 1998a.
Levinas, Emmanuel. *Entre Nous: Thinking-of-the-other*. Trans. Michael B. Smith and Barbara Harshav. New York: Columbia University Press, 1998b.
Levinas, Emmanuel. *Oeuvres 1: Carnets de captivité et autre inédits*. Eds. Rodolphe Calin and Catherine Chalier. Paris: Grasset/IMEC, 2009.
Levinas, Emmanuel. *Œuvres 3. Eros, littérature et philosophie. Essais romanesques et poétiques*, notes philosophiques sur le thème d'éros. Eds. Jean-Luc Nancy and Danielle Cohen-Levinas. Paris: Grasset/IMEC, 2013.
Nancy Jean-Luc. (2013). "Préface. L'intrigue littéraire de Levinas," in Emmanuel Levinas, *Œuvres 3. Eros, littérature et philosophie. Essais romanesques et poétiques, notes philosophiques sur le thème d'éros*. Eds. Jean-Luc Nancy and Danielle Cohen-Levinas. Paris: Grasset/IMEC, 2013. 9–30.
Nietzsche, Friedrich. *The Gay Science. With a Prelude in German Rhymes and an Appendix of Songs*, ed. by Bernard Williams, Cambridge, Cambridge University Press, 2001.
Nouzille, Philippe. *Au-delà de soi. Révélation et phénoménologie*. Paris: Hermann, 2014.
Rosenzweig, Franz. "Das neue Denken: Einige nachträgliche Bemerkungen zum *Stern der Erlösung*", in *Der Morgen: Monatsschrift der Juden in Deutschland*, 1 (1925), 426–451.

Part II: **Biblical Texts**

Eli Schonfeld
Languages of the Universal: Levinas' (*scandalous*) doctrine of Literature

> Ma condition – ou mon in-condition – est mon rapport aux livres. C'est l'a-Dieu même.[1]
> Levinas, *L'au-delà du verset* (9)

Literature occupies a privileged role in Levinas' life and work. Classic authors such as Racine, Shakespeare, Dostoyevsky, Cervantes, but also modern writers such as Blanchot and Celan appear time and time again throughout his oeuvre. Alongside, of course, with references to the Bible. In the opening pages of *Ethics and Infinity* Levinas tells us how much literature counted for him, and how it shaped his relation to the world: ". . . the Russian classics – Pushkin, Lermontov, Gogol, Turgenev, Dostoyevsky and Tolstoy, and also the great writers of Western Europe, notably Shakespeare, much admired in *Hamlet*, *Macbeth* and *King Lear* [. . .] is it a good preparation to Plato and Kant registered in the degree program in philosophy? It takes time to see the transitions" (Levinas 1985, 22). The transition from Shakespeare to Plato is not immediately perceptible. Nevertheless, for Levinas, literature paved the way to philosophy. "Let no one ignorant of Literature enter," would be the inscription engraved on the door of Levinas' academy, had he one.

The centrality of literature in Levinas' oeuvre is an undeniable fact.[2] Some commentators have understood it merely in terms of illustration: his recourse to literature would be a means to illustrate philosophical ideas.[3] This study will challenge this view. It will try to demonstrate how literature is not only a means for Levinas, but that one can find, in his corpus, a theory of literature, or at least

---
[1] "My condition – or my un-condition – is my relation to books. It is the very movement-towards-God [*l'a-Dieu*]" (Levinas 2007b, xv).
[2] Despite Jill Robbins's claim that "Levinas speaks very rarely about the literary, and when he does it is almost always in dismissive terms" (see Robbins 1999, 39 (see also xxi)). In order to sustain her claim, Robbins draws heavily on Levinas's article "Reality and Its Shadow." Nevertheless, if indeed Levinas's 1948 article is critical about art in general, the object of his critique is not literature, but, precisely, art. And literature in Levinas cannot simply be understood, as Robbins claims, as a "genre of art" (Robbins 1999, xxi). In confusing between art in general (which is, indeed, strongly criticized by Levinas) and literature, she misses the fundamental place of literature in Levinas's philosophy. In this paper, I will try to elucidate this place. For a nuanced analysis of art in Levinas, see Gerald L. Bruns, "The Concept of Art and Poetry in Emmanuel Levinas' Writings" (2002).
[3] See for instance, Robbins, *Altered Reading* (2009, xx).

an implicit doctrine of literature. This doctrine – that is to be found mainly in his Jewish texts – is sustained by an explicit phenomenology of the book.[4] Revealing this phenomenology of the book, therefore, amounts to stressing the *philosophical* centrality of literature in Levinas's thinking.

Before broaching the subject I wish to highlight again the textual fact just mentioned, a fact that will orient this study: Levinas's phenomenology of the book – as well as its related doctrine of literature – is to be found mainly and almost exclusively in his Jewish texts. Attentive to this textual symptom, the following lines will be guided by the following hypothesis: In order to be understood fully, Levinas's doctrine of literature should be interpreted in light of one of the central theme of his Jewish philosophy, namely, the theme of chosenness and universality. Levinas's theory of literature is part of his philosophical struggle with the question of the relation between universality and singularity. Moreover, in his theory of literature Levinas is perhaps formulating, under cover, his most extreme version of the relation between singularity (Israel) and universality (the nations). Its *scandalous* version. This is what I will try to demonstrate in this chapter.

1 Levinas' Phenomenology of Writing: Literature and Inspiration

In the introduction to *Beyond the Verse*, in a very original – and unique – passage, Levinas formulates a phenomenology of *the act of writing*.

> A contraction of the Infinite in Scripture [. . .] Scripture would begin with the line which is outlined in some way, and thickens or emerges as a verse in the flowing of language – no doubt of every language – in order to become text, as proverb, or fable, or poem, or legend, before the stylet or quill imprints it as letters on tablets, parchment or paper. A literature before the letter! (Levinas 2007b, xiv)

A line that emerges as a verse, as a contraction of the infinite into a text. This is what every act of writing does: "A contraction of the Infinite in Scripture." The term "contraction," and even more so "contraction of the Infinite," sends us

---

[4] The question of the relation to literature could be addressed to most contemporary French thinkers – Sartre, Barthes, Foucault, Deleuze, or Derrida, to name just a few, each of whom, in his own way, reserves a particular place for literature in his *oeuvre*. It would be enlightening to understand when and why this reference to literature started to play such a central role in Philosophy.

immediately to the Kabbalistic horizon – the deepest of Jewish wisdoms, its interior wisdom (*hohmat ha'pnim*) – and more specifically to the Lurianic concept of צמצום [*tsimtsum*]. God, or the Infinite, contracted Himself, in order for the world to be created, in order to *make space* for the world. The Same contracts in order for otherness to be.[5] The infinite does not incarnate itself here, but retreats, contracts. Like a maternal body, contracting itself in order to make place for alterity: an other-in-the-same, to speak the language of *Otherwise than Being*.[6]

But in the text from *Beyond the Verse* the stakes are different: The *topos* of divine contraction is Scripture: "A contraction of the infinite in Scripture" (Levinas 2007b, xiv). God contracting himself means: God in-scribes His self on a piece of parchment.

Hence, the act of writing – the act of drawing a line, of tracing a line (*kav*) – implies the whole drama of creation. Or in Levinas's words: the act of writing, when it is truly an act of writing (which is very rare, and can by no means be identified with the prosaic gesture of inscribing words on a piece of paper or typing them on a computer) is, *by definition*, inspired: "[. . .] the marvel of inspiration where man listens, amazed, to what he utters" (Levinas 2007b, xiv). Again we find here the structure of otherness within the same. To write means to be animated by alterity. As if in writing I make the experience of not being the author of my own speech, of my own words. It is my mouth that utters those words, it is my pen that traces those lines that becomes letters, words and phrases. Nevertheless, I experience language as coming to me *from the other*. I speak, and while speaking, or writing, I surprise myself, I hear myself speaking, I read what I write as if it was dictated by another, written by another. It is not completely me who speaks, not completely me who writes. This is the original act of writing. Inspired writing

---

5 This idea is alluded to once in Levinas's whole corpus, in one of the most enigmatic passages of *Totality and Infinity*. In order to articulate the metaphysical relation between the same and the other, Levinas speaks of "creative contraction": "Infinity produces itself by withstanding the invasion of a totality, in a contraction that leaves a place for the separated being" (Levinas 1979, 104 (translation slightly modified)). In order for a separated being to exist (the Same), the Infinite (or the Other) has to contract. What is described here is nothing short of the genesis of the metaphysical relation itself: at the beginning, there is a "creative contraction." But Levinas will never repeat this idea, and the notion of creative contraction never reappears in his philosophical texts. As if he here crossed a line. On the concept of creative contraction in Levinas, see Michael Fagenblat, "Transcendental *Tṣimṣum*: Levinas's Mythology of Meaning" (2020).
6 In this very text (*Otherwise than Being, or Beyond Essence*), the *psyche* is described as structured as a maternal body: "Here the psyche is the maternal body" (Levinas 1998, 67). The maternal body: a body that contracts itself in order to make space for another being. A creative contraction, *in existence*.

occurs whenever the words written are experienced as not being my own. Paradoxically, one becomes an author only when one experiences oneself as not being the author of one's own words.

Inspiration describes the actual *Erlebnis* of writing as an event where the subject is retiring, where the subject, by contracting himself, makes space for transcendence. And thus – inspiration being the condition of possibility of literature – makes space for literature itself.

In his address following the reception of the Jerusalem Prize in 1985 at the Hebrew University, Milan Kundera proposed:

> Now, not only is the novelist nobody's spokesman, but I would go so far as to say he is not even the spokesman for his own ideas. When Tolstoy sketched the first draft of *Anna Karenina*, Anna was a most unsympathetic woman, and her tragic end was entirely deserved and justified. The final version of the novel is very different, but I do not believe that Tolstoy had revised his moral ideas in the meantime; I would say, rather, that in the course of writing, he was listening to another voice than that of his personal moral conviction. He was listening to what I would like to call the wisdom of the novel. Every true novelist listens for that suprapersonal wisdom, which explains why great novels are always a little more intelligent than their authors. Novelists who are more intelligent than their books should go into another line of work. (Kundera 2000, 158)

What Kundera calls "the wisdom of the novel," *la sagesse du roman*, is exactly what Levinas calls inspiration: to be traversed by alterity, to be transpierced by otherness. I am writing, but already I am listening, and reading what I myself am writing. Literature, the true event of the literary, in this sense, always occurs "before the letter" (Levinas 2007b, xiv).

We are affected by language before we express ourselves. The self is transcended by literature: language precedes us. This is the truth of Heidegger's radical formulation: "Die Sprache spricht" (Heidegger 1985, 11 *et al.*). And between Heidegger and Levinas, the crucial question is not whether inspiration is at the heart of writing and literature (or poetry), but rather: what/who inspires? Being or the Other? Who is the subject of the fundamental experience of language, the poet or the prophet? Or rather: in its core, is subjectivity poetic or prophetic? Levinas's answer is clear: subjectivity, in its essence, is prophetic, i.e., inspired by the Other. The Other is the source of inspiration, of language. From this we can draw our first conclusion, our first thesis: language, *every language* (and not only the Greek of the pre-Socratics, or the German of Trakl and Hölderlin) is prophetic. Levinas formulates it explicitly: "That is the resonance of every language 'in the name of God,' the inspiration or prophecy of all language" (Levinas 1998, 152).

Inspiration is universal. This truth is taught not by pre-Socratic fragments, or by German poets, but by the Hebrew prophet: "'God has spoken, who can but prophecy?' (Amos 3:8) Prophetic receptivity already lies in the human soul" (Levinas 2007b, 141).[7]

Inspiration and prophecy are universal categories. Therefore, as such, they function as fundamental categories in Levinas's *philosophy*: in *Otherwise than Being or Beyond Essence*, for instance, he develops, in a purely philosophical language, the thesis of subjectivity as inspiration, of the soul (âme, *anima*) as *animated*, affected by otherness. In a paragraph called "inspiration," Levinas writes:

> There is a claim laid on the same by the other in the core of myself, the extreme tension of the command exercised by the other in me over me [. . .] Through this alteration the soul animates the object; it is the very *pneuma* of the psyche. The psyche signifies the claiming of the same by the other, or inspiration, beyond the logic of the same and the other, of their insurmountable adversity. It is an undoing of the substantial nucleus of the ego that is formed in the same. (Levinas 1998, 141)[8]

This is my starting point: inspiration and prophecy are universal categories that appear both in Levinas's philosophy of subjectivity and, as part of his doctrine of literature, in his phenomenology of the act of writing.

2 From The Book to Books: Levinas' Doctrine of Literature

After having stressed the universality of inspiration and prophecy, after having pointed out the sameness of these categories, let us look deeper into the text and try to detect the difference, the otherness.

The line, writes Levinas, "emerges as a verse in the flowing of language – no doubt of every language – in order to become text, as proverb, or fable, or poem, or legend, before the stylet or quill imprints it as letters on tablets, parchment or paper" (Levinas 2007b, xiv). From the verse to the poem and the legend; from the tablets to paper. This is not a random inventory. It is a meticulously calculated sequence which establishes a gradation: from the more to the less, from the inspired text *par excellence*, to what echoes it, to what stands in its light or in its shadow. The verse written on tablets: this is the event of inspiration in its full intensity. Scriptures, Holy Scriptures (*Ecritures saintes*), are the exemplary model of an inspired text. Unique in its kind, this text is inspired by the infinite and has

---

[7] Levinas refers to this verse time and time again in his later texts.
[8] Further, Levinas develops the notion of prophecy, in the paragraph called "Witness and Prophecy" ((Levinas 1998, 149–152).

an infinite potential to inspire.⁹ In this typology of inspired texts, *literature comes second*, even if immediately after Scriptures. As if in its trace:

> A religious essence of language, a place where prophecy will conjure up the Holy Scriptures, but which all literature awaits or commemorates, whether celebrating or profaning it.
> (Levinas 2007b, xiv)

There is a continuity between Scriptures and literature. Both inspired, each in its own way, each in its own degree, inspire. In other words: those texts invite interpretation, those texts are an invitation to propose readings (or midrash). This is what singularizes an inspired text: its ability to inspire, its propensity to generate speech, to oblige the subject to answer. Where there is a possibility of exegesis, something of the inspired quality of Scriptures is present. And literature, exactly like scriptures, has this quality.

> Hence, in the very anthropology of the human [. . .] the eminent role played by so-called national literatures, Shakespeare, Molière, Cervantes, Goethe and Pushkin. Signifying beyond their plain meaning, they invite the exegesis that is spiritual life.
> (Levinas 2007b, xiv)

From the Book of books to (simply) books, from the Hebrew Bible to literature, the continuity of inspiration is attested by exegesis. Exegesis is a modality of meaningfulness: it is through reading and interpreting that meaning is made manifest. Pushing this logic to its last consequences, Levinas eventually writes: "The fact that sense comes through the book testifies to its biblical essence" (Levinas 2007b, 110). A book – βιβλίον – is essentially biblical. This is Levinas's radical thesis. Hence the status he accords to books as such in his thinking:

> One may wonder whether the book, as a book, before becoming a document, is not the modality by which what is said lays itself open to exegesis, calls for it; and where meaning, immobilized in the characters, already tears the texture in which it is held.
> (Levinas 2007b, 110)

The book is an extraordinary entity. In the world of objects, it transcends objectivity from within. A book can of course be apprehended as an object among objects (it has dimensions, color, content, weight, even smell; like the human body, it is a *res extensa*). One can use a book as a mere object (for decoration, or for any other possible usage). Nevertheless, taken for what it is, in its original givenness, the book defies the rules of objectivity. It is not seen, or apprehended, as a tool among tools, and this sense it defies Heidegger's

---

9 Levinas develops this theme of the infinite potential of Scriptures to inspire in "On the Jewish Reading of Scriptures" (Levinas 2007b, 101–114).

categories of *Vorhandenheit* and *Zuhandenheit*. It is not, says Levinas, "one thing amongst others, demonstrating in handbooks – like a hammer – its affinity with the hand" (Levinas 2007b, xiv). And in *Ethics and Infinity* this idea is pushed even further: "I think that in the great fear of bookishness, one underestimates the 'ontological' reference of the human to the book that one takes for a source of information, or for a 'tool' of learning, a *textbook*, even though it is a *modality* of our being" (Levinas 1985, 21–22). The book is a modality of our being, says Levinas: our relation to books is not identical to our relation to things in the world. We respect books, we handle them with care, but not in order to not damage them (as one would handle furniture with care, or any fragile object), but as an act of respect for what they are. As if the fragility of books is fully interior. As if books are fragile because they can so easily be profaned (like the face, like transcendence itself). The book, therefore, curves ontology, it requires us to think anew human existence: "Aristotle's 'animal endowed with language' has never been thought, in its ontology, in terms of the book" (Levinas 2007b, xiv). What would this ontology thought of in terms of the book look alike? Levinas answers: it is "a modality [of Being] by which what is said lays itself open to exegesis" (Levinas 2007b, 110). And he carries on, describing exactly this modality: the book, he writes, "tears the texture in which it is held" (Levinas 2007b, xiv).

The careful reader will easily recognize the following point: Levinas's descriptions of the book (as an ontological event) are *exactly the same* as his most classical descriptions of the apparition of the face. The face, writes Levinas in "Meaning and Sense," "detaches itself from its own form in the midst of the production of its form" (Levinas 1996, 53); it "breaks through its own plastic essence" (Levinas 1996, 53); its presence consists in "divesting itself of the form which does already manifest it" (Levinas 1996, 53). The similarity is striking. Whereas the face tears itself as it where from the texture of visibility, the text – writing, Literature – tears itself from the very texture which allows it to be inscribed: "In propositions which are not yet – or which are already no longer – verses, and which are often verse or simply literature, another voice rings out among us, a second sonorous voice that drowns out or tears the first one" (Levinas 2007b, 110). A voice within a voice, a saying beyond the said. Exactly as in the phenomenological description of the face: "This is what the formula 'the face speaks' expresses. The manifestation of the face is the first discourse. To speak is before all this way of coming from behind one's appearance, behind one's form an opening in the openness" (Levinas 1986, 352).

This analogy between writing and the face – as *events of transcendence* – is explicitly formulated in *Ethics and Infinity*:

> The sentiment that the Bible is the Book of books wherein the first things are said, those that *became* said so that human life has a meaning, and are said in a form which opens to commentators the same dimension of profundity, was not some simple substitution of a literary judgement onto the consciousness of the 'sacred.' It is that extraordinary presence of its characters, that ethical plenitude and its mysterious possibilities of exegesis which originally signified transcendence for me. And no less. (Levinas 1985, 23)

But let us return to the question of the difference between the Book of books and the book. As we have seen, in his text, Levinas suggests a hierarchy: the books are in the trace of the Book of books, literature is in the trace of the verse. Or, as we have just seen, books are in their essence biblical (the Bible functions here as the prototype of writing, as the father of all literature, transcending as it where literature as such). We should try to understand this difference further.

First, I wish to stress a textual fact: the term Levinas uses whenever he characterizes literature is not "general literature," or "world literature," or "classic literature," but "national literature," *literature nationale*. In *Beyond the Verse*, for instance, we read:

> The infinite life of texts living through the life of the men who hear them; a primordial exegesis of the texts which are then called national literature and on to which the hermeneutics of universities and schools is grafted. Above and beyond the immediate meaning of what is said in these texts, the act of saying is inspired. The fact that meaning comes through the book testifies to its biblical essence. The comparison between the inspiration conferred on the Bible and the inspiration towards which the interpretation of literary texts tends is not intended to compromise the dignity of the Scriptures. On the contrary, it asserts the dignity of "national literatures." (Levinas 2007b, 110)

National literatures: this locution is carefully chosen. The plural form is used here: national literatures. There is a plurality of literatures, many literatures. Why is this important for Levinas? Because the plurality of literatures articulates the plurality of languages. The plurality of literatures reflects the (factual) plurality of languages. In the inventory of authors Levinas quotes, this plurality is clearly manifested: Shakespeare, Molière, Cervantes, Goethe and Pushkin. English, French, Spanish, German, Russian. And one could go on. But – and this is the second point – the plurality of languages echoes, although indirectly, esoterically one may say, *the plurality of nations*. In biblical Hebrew, *Am* (nation) and *Lashon* (language) are synonymous (as for instance in Isaiah 66:18). For each language, a nation. Nations are first and foremost languages (and not states, political entities). The plurality of languages corresponds therefore to the plurality of nations. And if language, in its essence, is an implicit reading of the world, then we can propose the following *definition* of a nation: in its metaphysical essence, a nation is a particular, possible, reading of the world.

This metaphysics of nations is an explicit teaching of the masters of the Talmud. In the beginning of his introduction to *In the Time of the Nations*, Levinas refers to it:

> Seventy nations, or seventy languages. This is a metaphor that in the Talmudic manner of speaking, in the oral Torah, designates all mankind surrounding Israel; mankind taken as a whole, in its entirety, although split up by differences that group men into nations.
> (Levinas 1994, 1)

In order to articulate the meaning of mankind, one needs to refer to the plurality of languages. A plurality that is not – if one follows the Talmudic teaching – indefinite. In other words: there is a limit to the possible readings of the world. Not everything is possible, not every reading is a reading, not every language is a language. Against the nihilistic vision of the world (for which plurality rhymes with relativity, with the renouncement of truth – "everything is interpretation," "everything is subjective," etc.), the Talmudic vision of the world proposes the idea of a *limited plurality*, reflected concretely in the fact there are limited possible readings of the world: seventy languages. No more, no less. Accordingly, there are seventy nations, no more, no less.

We understand better Levinas' usage of the term "national literatures." Indeed, if we add up what we have established until now – national literature, i.e., language in its inspired modality, expressing a particular reading of the world which is not subjective, even though it passes through particular subjects (Racine, Shakespeare, Goethe, etc.) – and once the Talmudic subtext of Levinas's text is revealed, it is not difficult to recognize the metonymic relation between what Levinas refers to as "national literatures" and the Jewish definition of the nation (*goy*) as such. But one should add to this account a last point, probably the most difficult one, not theoretically, but existentially: the fundamental difference between the Book of books and national literatures. If nations are in their essence languages, and if languages express themselves first and foremost in what is called national literature, then, for Levinas, the nation whose essence is expressed in the Hebrew Bible, is Israel. In other words: the separation of the separated language (*lashon ha-kodesh*, which is the language of Scripture, the very language revealed *as* Scripture) corresponds to the separation of the biblical people, i.e., the people of Israel. In the language of the talmudic sages, this is expressed by the idea that there are not seventy languages, but seventy-one languages. And accordingly, seventy-one peoples, the one being separated from the seventy.

This is what can be called Levinas' scandalous thesis. Scandalous, at least to the western ear, to the universalistic-philosophical ear, which immediately interprets separation or hierarchy in a political way; which is incapable of hearing the asymmetry of election as an asymmetry of responsibility and obligations and not as an asymmetry of rights. This scandalous thesis – central to the wisdom of Judaism – appears therefore only in Levinas's Jewish corpus. Moreover it appears there in a hidden form (i.e., in terms of a doctrine of literature). In terms of literature, this asymmetry can be expressed in the following manner: whereas the sacred text (the verse) is *saturated with meaningfulness* – and this is where its sacredness resides – national literatures, each in their *particular* way, only echo this event of meaningfulness, this event of transcendence. The plurality of languages, as Levinas puts it, is in the aftermath of the one language: they "await or commemorate" Scriptures, "whether celebrating or profaning it" (Levinas 2007b, xiv).

Without excluding other languages (or other nations) from the economy of inspiration (all literatures, by definition, are inspired), the sacred language, given though the Book of Books, and the separated nation, are designated as a principle of unity that allows the plurality of nations to exist *as a plurality* open to the infinity of meaning [*sens*]: "mankind taken as a whole, in its entirety, although split up by differences that group men into nations." (Levinas 1994, 1).[10] Seventy-one: this is the cipher of the universal.

Through his reflection on literature, Levinas is able to formulate a *concrete* thinking of the universal. The plurality of languages, which cannot be reduced to unity, which testifies to the singularity of every nation, suffices to cast doubt on the *abstract* idea of universality (universal reason, universal truth, universal man, etc.). Universality – this is the underlying theoretical assumption of all of Levinas's reflection here – can be thought only if the essential difference of humanity, the plurality of humankind, is taken into account (and not in terms of divisions *per genus proximum et diferentiam specificam*). Against the myth of sameness, of a universal nature of man in general, Levinas – inspired by the Talmudic sages – theorizes the reality of difference within sameness. But in order to do this, he has to suggest – even if through hiding it – the scandalous thesis of election. Seventy-*one*.

---

10 Of course – and this is a fundamental teaching of Levinas – if one interprets this dissymmetry, this separation, as a privilege, or as an advantage, everything is lost. This separation, this chosenness, is always understood by Levinas as a surplus of duties, as a surplus of responsibilities. In this respect, the one nation should be envisaged – if to speak in topological terms – not as above the seventy nations, but as responsible for the seventy nations, and therefore, strictly speaking, as below the seventy (the ethical relation being, by essence, asymmetrical: the other, who commands me, is always higher than me).

3 Literature as Profanation: Otherwise Inspired

Literature, writes Levinas, "awaits or commemorates" Scriptures, "whether celebrating or profaning it." In order to complete this study of Levinas's doctrine of literature, I wish to look closer into that passage. The question to be asked is: what does it mean that literature, a certain modality of literature, commemorates Scriptures *through its profanation*?

In order to answer this question, let us look, through a concrete example, at how literature functions in Levinas's text. The Talmudic reading "And God created woman" permits us to examine closely the relation between scriptures and literature, because Levinas opposes there a passage from Racine's *Phèdre* to some verses from *Psalms*.

Racine's *Phèdre* is quoted several times in Levinas's corpus. The first occurrence is in *Existence and Existents*:

> The pure nothingness revealed by anxiety in Heidegger's analysis does not constitute the *there is*. There is horror of being and not anxiety over nothingness, fear of being and not fear for being; there is being prey to, delivered over to something that is not a "something." When night is dissipated with the first rays of the sun, the horror of the night is no longer definable. The "something" appears to be "nothing." Horror carries out the condemnation to perpetual reality, to existence with "no exists."
>
>> The sky, the whole world's full of my forefathers.
>> Where may I hide?
>> Flee to infernal night.
>> How? There my father holds the urn of doom . . .
>
> Phaedra discovers the impossibility of death, the eternal responsibility of her being, in a full universe in which her existence is bound by an unbreakable commitment, an existence no longer in any way private. (Levinas 1995, 62)

In this passage, Levinas distinguishes himself from Heidegger, and more precisely, he distinguishes his notion of *there is* (*il y a*), from Heidegger's nothingness as revealed through anxiety. The central feature of *il y a* is the impossibility to escape, the experience of being irremissibly trapped in Being. Phèdre's phrases catch this experience in all its intensity: Phèdre does not find a place to hide from the gaze of the oppressive father, of the angry father. She has no place in-the-world. But she cannot flee this world. This is her tragedy. And this is – according to Levinas – the essence of tragedy itself: the impossibility of escape. Tragedy – in Racine, or in Shakespeare – expresses the in-humanity of the experience of Being as *il y a*: an otherness that crushes the subject, that does not let one be. The tragic experience of being is inhumane.[11]

Let us now turn to Psalm 139:

> You hedge me before and behind; You lay Your hand upon me.
> It is beyond my knowledge; it is a mystery; I cannot fathom it.
> Where can I escape from Your spirit? Where can I flee from Your presence?
> If I ascend to heaven, You are there; if I descend to Sheol, You are there too.
> If I take wing with the dawn to come to rest on the western horizon,
> even there Your hand will be guiding me.

The contrast is striking: Like the tragic experience of the world, like Phèdre, the biblical experience is an experience of the impossibility to hide, an impossibility to escape. Nevertheless, there is, a fundamental difference. Levinas, in his Talmudic reading, writes:

> Always the hand of God grabs me and guides me. It is impossible to escape from God, not to be present before his sleepless gaze. A gaze which is not experienced as a calamity, in contrast to the terror felt by Racine's *Phaedra*! (Levinas 1990, 167)

Racine and the Psalmist are equally exposed to otherness, to transcendence. But – this is what the text reveal, this is what literature reveals, this is what scriptures reveals, when one is attentive to its voice – the tonality of the experience is radically different: oppressive, as "terror[12]," for the one; for the other: a stretched hand, a guiding hand, a providential presence. Transcendence is experience in *Psalms* as a gesture of tenderness, as the caring proximity of the Other. Or as a call, as an address. And Levinas goes on, quoting the next verses of *Psalms*:

> If I say, "Surely darkness will conceal me, night will provide me with cover," darkness is not dark for You; night is as light as the day; darkness and light are the same. It was You

---

[11] In *Time and the Other* – a text that is strictly contemporaneous to *Existence and Existents* – Levinas refers to Shakespeare in order to manifest the oppressive ambiance of the *il y a*. Hamlet, in his famous monologue, expresses the "tragedy of tragedy": the impossibility of escape, even in death. The horror of the perspective to live forever. The impossibility of death itself: "Hamlet is precisely a lengthily testimony to this impossibility of assuming death. Nothingness is impossible. It is nothingness that would have left humankind the possibility of assuming death and snatching a supreme mastery from out of the servitude of existence. 'To be or not to be' is a sudden awareness of this impossibility of annihilating oneself" (Levinas 1987, 73). Tragedy in general, for Levinas, is this literary genre that repeatedly expresses the impossibility of escape (fate), the entrapment in Being.

[12] From the Proto-Indo-European *tre* (to shake), or *tres* (to tremble), which might not be far from this experience of "fear and trembling" that Rudolf Otto describes in his famous analysis of the sacred.

who created my conscience; You fashioned me in my mother's womb. I praise You, for I am awesomely, wondrously made.

Levinas comments: "In the biblical passage, certainly God's presence means: to be besieged by God or obsessed by God. An obsession which is experienced as chosenness [. . .]" (Levinas 1990, 167). This is the fundamental point: the experience of exposure, in *Psalms*, is a *positive* experience. Or in Levinas' lexicon: an experience of chosenness. Exactly the same way in his phenomenology of the face, the encounter with the other is experienced as a *positive* impossibility of escape (the impossibility of avoiding the commandment emanating from the face of the other, the impossibility of indifference), which constitutes – for Levinas – the very *Erlebnis* of chosenness. The verse – contrarily to the tragic drama – conveys this experience. Pushing the analysis to its last consequence, we can now reformulate Levinas' (scandalous) thesis: there is *a particular Hebrew experience of the absolute*, which is radically opposed to the Greek (tragic) experience of the absolute.

> He [God] does not let you go or He catches up with you again. You are always exposed! But in this spirited psalm you are discovered with joy; it is the exaltation of divine proximity that this psalm sings: a being exposed without the least hint of shadow.
> (Levinas 1990, 167)

The absolute exposedness to the Absolute – the obsession of the Absolute – is experienced as joy. Rather than provoking terror, "fear and trembling," transcendence, *as an experience of the impossibility of escape*, provokes exaltation. This "unexpected reversal from curse to exultation" is what characterizes the Hebrew *experience* of the Absolute.[13] This is what differentiates the psalmist from the author of tragedies: not the Event itself (the radical exposure to transcendence, to otherness), but the way the Event is experienced. For the one, terror; for the other, exaltation.

We can now return to the enigmatic passage of *Beyond the Verse*: literature, writes Levinas, can be a profanation of transcendence. Indeed: profanation is *a possible modality of the relation to transcendence*. A modality that is expressed, for instance, in tragedy. In this sense, literature, national literature, on occasions, expresses *the other side* of transcendence, or what Levinas calls: *il y a*. From Shakespeare and Racine to Blanchot, literature is inspired (by transcendence) – but instead of experiencing transcendence, the (oppressive) presence of the Other, as chosenness, it is experienced as tragedy, or as absurdity. The total

---

[13] See Levinas, "Being Jewish" (2007a, 208 (translation slightly modified)). For an in-depth reading of this problematic in Levinas see Benny Lévy, *Etre Juif: Etude Levinassienne* (2003).

exposure of subjectivity to otherness, in this horizon, is experienced as an exposure that crushes subjectivity (like the alterity of death).[14] Nevertheless, for Levinas, all those experiences (tragedy, absurdity, anxiety of death, *il y a*, anonymous Being, etc.) are *effects of a primordial exposure to transcendence*.[15] In *Otherwise than Being*, Levinas formulates this relation between positive transcendence (the face, transcendence as experienced by the psalmist) and negative transcendence (the *il y a*, transcendence as experienced by the tragedian) in its most striking way:

> But the absurdity of the *there is*, as a modality of the-one-for-the-other, signifies. The insignificance of its objective insistence, recommencing behind every negation, overwhelms me like the fate of a subjection to all the other to which I am subject, is the surplus of nonsense over sense, through which for the self-expiation is possible, an expiation which the oneself indeed signifies. The *there is* is all the weight that alterity weighs supported by a subjectivity that does not found it. (Levinas 1998, 164)

Subjectivity is originally affected by transcendence. Even when the subject does not acknowledge it. Even when transcendence is veiled, and appears as *il y a*, or Being. Even when profaning transcendence, subjectivity is *in its trace*. Even when profaning transcendence, (national) literature is in the trace of the (Hebrew) verse.

4 Languages of the Universal

At least one thing is clear: national literature, in Levinas, does not mean simplistically ethical literature, literature with an ethical message. Literature is not literature because it illustrates anything having to do with morality. Levinas's doctrine of literature is far more complex and fundamental: Literature, is the site of a

---

14 See Levinas, *Time and the Other* (1987, part III).
15 The passage from *Totality and Infinity* to *Otherwise than Being* can be understood as a deepening of this fundamental intuition. Separation in *Totality and Infinity* (synonym in this text to the concept of atheism) conditions the metaphysical relation: it is only as a separated being that a genuine relation to otherness is possible (against the idea of fusion, or participation). Thus, atheism, even though being a mode of being that exists away from transcendence, conditions at the same time the possibility to enter into a relation with transcendence. In *Otherwise than Being*, this intuition is radicalized: subjectivity, in this text, is described as anarchically affected by otherness (there is no moment of separation anymore). From the beginning, even before it begun, subjectivity is for the other. Or, in the language of *Otherwise than Being*, the other is in the same. This otherness can be experienced either as the otherness of being (*il y a*), or as the otherness of transcendence.

plurality of fundamental expressions (literatures), of the original (and universal) exposure to otherness. This exposure can manifest itself through a radical ethical language, as for instance in the famous passage from Dostoyevsky's *The Brothers Karamazov* that Levinas quotes time and again: "Each of us is guilty before everyone for everyone, and I more than the others" (Levinas 1998, 146). But literature can also exist as profanation (of transcendence, of Scripture), as for instance in tragedy, both ancient and modern. In either case, what characterizes literature—or language as such—is the effect of a primordial exposure to otherness. And this is the reason why, ultimately, literature testifies to *the ethical structuring of subjectivity* (its essential "being-for-the-other"). Either positively (as attention to transcendence), or negatively (as profanation of transcendence).

Levinas's doctrine of literature is intimately linked to the question of the relation between universality and particularity. More precisely – if read without ignoring the Talmudic horizon that inspires Levinas throughout all of his writing – this doctrine is intimately related to the question of the relation between Israel and the nations. By changing registers (from the existential phenomenology of subjectivity as being-towards-transcendence to the question of language and literature), Levinas is able to express the relation between the one and the multiple, between chosenness and universality, *without ambiguity*.[16] This thinking detaches itself from the (philosophical) universality of the idea of "man in general," in order to think through *concrete humanity*, i.e., the unity of separated, distinct and concrete nations, who express their uniqueness through actual languages and specific literatures. In articulating the relation between Israel and the nations through the question of language and literature, Levinas is able to think universality in all its concreteness. He is able to think radically – even at the risk of proposing a scandalous thesis: the uniqueness of the Hebrew (language), the seventy-*one*, Israel's *concrete* election – the *Languages of the Universal*.

Bibliography

Bruns, Gerald L. "The Concept of Art and Poetry in Emmanuel Levinas's Writings." *The Cambridge Companion to Levinas*. Eds. Simon Critchley and Robert Bernasconi. Cambridge: Cambridge University Press, 2002. 206–233.

---

[16] For the question of the ambiguities in Levinas's relation to the universal, a subject that touches on the core of Levinas's Jewish philosophy, see Benny Lévy, "Judaïsme et philosophie: La septante n'est pas une tâche" (2004).

Fagenblat, Michael. "Transcendental *Tṣimṣum:* Levinas's Mythology of Meaning." *Tsimtsum and Modernity: Lurianic Heritage in Modern Philosophy and Theology*. Eds. Agata Bielik-Robson and Daniel Weiss. Berlin: De Gruyter, 2020.

Heidegger, Martin. *Unterwegs zur Sprache* (Gesamtausgabe Band 12). Frankfurt am Main: Vittorio Klostermann, 1985.

Kundera, Milan. "Jerusalem Address: The Novel and Europe." *The Art of the Novel*. Trans. Linda Asher. New York: Perennial Classics, 2000. 157–165.

Levinas, Emmanuel. *Totality and Infinity: An Essay on Exteriority*. Trans. Alphonso Lingis. Pittsburgh: Duquesne University Press, 1979.

Levinas, Emmanuel. *L'au-delà du verset*. Paris: Editions de Minuit, 1982.

Levinas, Emmanuel. *Ethics and Infinity*. Trans. Richard A Cohen. Pittsburgh: Duquesne University Press, 1985.

Levinas, Emmanuel. "The Trace of the Other." Trans. Alphonso Lingis. *Deconstruction in Context*. Ed. Mark Taylor. Chicago: University of Chicago Press, 1986. 345–359.

Levinas, Emmanuel. *Time and the Other*. Trans. Richard Cohen. Pittsburgh: Duquesne University Press, 1987.

Levinas, Emmanuel. *Nine Talmudic Readings*. Trans. Annette Aronowicz, Bloomington: Indiana University Press, 1990.

Levinas, Emmanuel. *In the Time of the Nations*. Trans. Michael B. Smith. Bloomington: Indiana University Press, 1994.

Levinas, Emmanuel. *Existence and Existents*. Trans. Alphonso Lingis. Dordrecht: Kluwer Academic Publishers, 1995.

Levinas, Emmanuel. "Meaning and Sense." Trans. Alphonso Lingis. *Emmanuel Levinas: Basic Philosophical Writings*. Eds. Adriaan T. Peperzak, Simon Critchley, and Robert Bernasconi. Bloomington: Indiana University Press, 1996. 33–64.

Levinas, Emmanuel. *Otherwise than Being, or Beyond Essence*. Trans. Alphonso Lingis. Pittsburgh: Duquesne University Press, 1998.

Levinas, Emmanuel. "Being Jewish." Trans. Mary Beth Mader. *Continental Philosophical Review* 40.3 (2007a): 205–210.

Levinas, Emmanuel. *Beyond the Verse: Talmudic Readings and Lectures*. Trans. Gary D. Mole. London: Continuum, 2007b.

Lévy, Benny. *Etre Juif: Etude Levinassienne*. Paris: Verdier, 2003.

Lévy, Benny. "Judaïsme et philosophie: La septante n'est pas une tâche." *La confusion des temps*; Paris: Verdier, 2004. 73–98.

Robbins, Jill. *Altered Reading: Levinas and Literature*. Chicago: University of Chicago Press, 1999.

Michael Fagenblat
The Genesis of *Totality and Infinity*: The Secret Drama

> "It is forbidden to interpret the Act of Creation in front of two people."
> *Mishnah Hagiga* 2.1

> "No stories will be told here."
> Husserl, *Ideas I*, fn. 1

> "One must unroll the *Archē* like a genesis."
> Jacques Derrida, *Heidegger: The Question of Being and History*, 35

1 Behind the Scenes

In the first substantive footnote to *Totality and Infinity* Levinas proposes that his thought might be understood as a type of drama, were drama not usually bound to the notion of action.

> In broaching, at the end of this work, the study of relations which we situate beyond the face, we come upon events that cannot be described as noeses aiming at noemata, nor as active interventions realizing projects, nor, of course, as physical forces being discharged into masses. They are conjunctures in being for which perhaps the term "drama" would be most suitable, in the sense that Nietzsche would have liked to use it when, at the end of *The Case of Wagner*, he regrets that it has always been wrongly translated by action. But it is because of the resulting equivocation that we forego this term.
> (Levinas 1971, 13–14 n. 1; Levinas 1969, 28 n. 2)[1]

The prospect of a drama behind the scenes of action coincides with the overarching goal of *Totality and Infinity*, which consists in discerning a structure of subjectivity – "ethics," as Levinas calls it – *prior to its enactment* as consciousness, Dasein, or incarnate existence. The footnote points to a drama that takes place in the backstage of the intelligible activity of being or consciousness. This chapter attempts to expose the drama behind the stage of meaning. I begin by presenting the philosophical reasoning that motivates Levinas's recourse to "essentially nocturnal events"

---

[1] My interest in this footnote was sparked by Simon Critchley's lively book *The Problem of Levinas* (2015).

Note: Research for this chapter was generously supported by Israel Science Foundation Grant 698/16

Open Access. © 2021 Michael Fagenblat, published by De Gruyter. This work is licensed under the Creative Commons Attribution 4.0 International License.
https://doi.org/10.1515/9783110668926-007

(Levinas 1971, 13; Levinas 1969, 28) behind the scenes of meaning. The way toward such "nocturnal events" consists of two stages, a critique of the correlation between intelligibility and activity (section 2), and a way of approaching the drama behind the activity of meaning (section 3). Levinas's usual way of approaching the subterranean ground of meaning is via "ethics." Our footnote, however, suggests another way: a drama or holy story that is structured without action or plot. What does it mean to think of drama without action or plot? The footnote cited above points to this possibility of a nocturnal drama whose events provide "conjunctures in being" (Levinas 1971, 13 n. 1; Levinas 1969, 28 n. 2) that do not form a story but a structure. My argument is that Levinas not only implicitly alludes to such a drama but indeed *produces* it. The "defense of subjectivity" that *Totality and Infinity* undertakes consists not only in phenomenological descriptions of how meaning is constituted in relation to the Other but also of a dramatic backstory comprised of *fragments* of the holy history of Genesis 1–11 (section 4). While Genesis 1–11 is of course a *narrative* (indeed several) of divine and human *acts*, the fragmented allusion that *Totality and Infinity* makes to this story prevents such fragments from becoming acts in a story behind the scenes. The fragments point to ways of beginning without acts that begin "once upon a time" or "in the beginning . . ." In similar fashion the rabbinic tradition points to interpretations of creation concealed behind the acts of creation:

> "In the beginning God created" – R. Jonah said in R. Levi's name: Why was the world created with a *beth* [the first letter of *br'šyt*, "in the beginning"]? Just as the *beth* [ב] is closed at the sides but open in front, so you are not permitted to investigate what is above and what is below, what is before and what is behind.   (*Midrash Rabbah: Genesis* 1939, 9)

The midrash suggests that behind the Act of Creation lies a secret teaching, which is prohibited, according to Mishnah Hagigah 2:1 cited in the epigraph above, from being expounded before more than two people. The rabbinic texts point to the possibility of a secret teaching behind the Act of Creation, prior to its narrative form. It is in this esoteric sense that one can approach the relation between *Totality and Infinity* and the narrative form of Genesis 1–11.[2] Levinas's text extracts

---

[2] Critchley proposes that in *Totality and Infinity* "Levinas is trying to write a drama, a holy story" (Critchley 2015, 10) and finally locates this drama in the *Song of Songs*, which he thinks Levinas *should* have relayed but did not. Critchley favours a mystical interpretation of the *Song* in which the enjoyment (*jouissance*) of God displaces the tyranny of egoism and thereby gives way to ethical subjectivity (Critchley 2015, 115–132). Instead of *contrasting* enjoyment and ethics, then, as Levinas does, Critchley wants them to commingle. His reading of the *Song* as "a staging of the erotic" (Critchley 2015, 12) seeks to bring to light the eros which, he proposes, remains *backstage* in Levinas's thought, an eros that founds ethics and thereby founds society. But even as Critchley, following Lacan, avows that eros is "not a matter of fucking," he offers no account of how mystical eros might distinguish between *jouissance* and justice.

fragments of the narrative of Genesis which it then orders, without a plot, into the "nocturnal" form of subjectivity. This production does not consist in telling a story that can be acted or embodied but in de-forming the plot of Genesis 1–11 in order to expose the "conjunctures in being" that make meaning possible. This dramaturgical "structure," precisely because it precedes the subject of experience in order to render experience intelligible, does not lend itself to action or imitation by a subject.[3] It is a drama produced, as it were, in the folds – in the binding – of Levinas's text, illegible in itself but able to be glimpsed when the text is looked at from a certain angle. In view of the subterranean aspects of this drama subtending Levinas's text, I conclude by considering the idea, rarely entertained, that *Totality and Infinity* is an *esoteric* work (section 5).[4] Levinas's is an unusual esotericism, which reverses the conventional structure of the secret. Whereas esotericism usually conceals a secret teaching deemed inappropriate for widespread consumption, in the case of *Totality and Infinity* there is an exoteric philosophical meaning that conceals the secret truth of the childlike "story" of Genesis 1–11. This amounts to an inverted form of esotericism that conceals a *critical naiveté*,

---

Without in the least wanting to forgo the *jouissance en plus*, I am not convinced that mysticism makes for morality. It is perhaps preferable, with Heidegger, Bataille, and Lacan, simply to prize ecstasy over ethics. Critchley reads the *Song* in line with the Christian tradition as a *lock* that can be opened, allegorically, to reveal the theological core of human eros, in the hope that this will make us all one. But I imagine Levinas reading the *Song of Songs* not as a lock to be opened but as a *key* that opens a backstage door to the theatre of life as it is lived less in its mystical ecstasies than in the banality of respect for difference. For a nuanced reading of this Jewish/Christian difference see Daniel Boyarin, "The Song of Songs: Lock or Key? Intertextuality, Allegory and Midrash" (1990). In any case, it may be premature to determine Levinas's precise relation to the *Song*. According to Salomon Malka, there is a "handwritten reading and translation of the Song of Songs" among Levinas' unpublished material (Malka 2006, 284), but these have not yet appeared. Critchley's reading is stimulating and suggestive, though too speculative to succeed as an interpretation of Levinas's text. If there is a holy story or a sacred drama concealed in *Totality and Infinity* is that of Genesis 1–11; the *Song of Songs*, I would suggest, is more likely to provide a key to interpreting *Otherwise than Being*.

3 The category of "experience" is ambiguous in *Totality and Infinity*. On the one hand, the approach and sense of the Other falls outside the subject's capacity for action and understanding. On the other hand, this exteriority affords access to "absolute experience" (Levinas 1969, 219). For example: "Metaphysics approaches without touching. Its *way* is not an action, but is the social relation. But we maintain that the social relation is experience preeminently" (Levinas 1969, 109).

4 Esoteric in the sense of a coded text which conceals meanings that are only appropriate for a subset of readers. The Jewish tradition is replete with esoteric approaches to Torah and in particular to the Act of Creation. For a conceptual and taxonomic overview, see Moshe Halbertal, *Concealment and Revelation: Esotericism in Jewish Thought and its Philosophical Implications* (2009).

what Levinas elsewhere calls "the secret of angels," behind the transparent philosophical sophistication of the text. The philosophical meaning of the texts masks a truth that exceeds the meaning of philosophical analysis. This truth is conveyed by allusion to the *"holy story"*—the *heilige Geschichte* of Genesis 1–11 reconfigured as a structure without a plot.

Admittedly, the argument of this chapter does not find confirmation in Levinas's explicitly stated intentions. It is nevertheless supported by significant textual evidence from *Totality and Infinity* and the posthumous notebooks and is, it seems to me, consistent with Levinas's view on the relation between phenomenology and Scripture. His confessional account of the "holy history" of the Jews illustrates this consistency, as do his subsequent descriptions of ethics as an "intrigue" or "divine comedy," which likewise intimate the drama-like character of "ethics." Even so, I do not claim that Levinas *intended* to convey the secret of the holy story of Genesis 1–11 in the interstices of his phenomenological argument. It is possible that such a secret was not only kept by him but also from him. Just as the meaning of a great work exceeds the intentions of its author, so a wise man bears more wisdom than he knows.

2 Critique of "thought as act"

The footnote cited above opens the gates to an interpretation of *Totality and Infinity* that takes seriously a certain drama-like quality of Levinas's work, if only we think of drama in Nietzsche's anti-Wagnerian fashion. For Nietzsche, Wagner's infatuation with *Handlung*, the action or plot around which the work is organized, betrays a type of aesthetic idolatry of the visible: "he begins with a scene that will *knock people over* [*umwirft*]," Nietzsche notes sardonically, "*eine wirkliche Actio.*" In contrast to this potent sense of dramatic action, Nietzsche proposes an older, subtler notion:

> It has been a real misfortune for aesthetics that the word *drama* has always been translated "action" [*Handlung*]. It is not Wagner alone who errs at this point. . . Ancient drama aimed at scenes of great *pathos* – it precluded action [*Handlung*] (moving it *before* the beginning or *behind* the scene). The word *drama* is of Doric origin, and according to Doric usage it means "event" [*Ereignis*], "story" [*Geschichte*] – both words in the hieratic sense. The most ancient drama represented the legend of the place, the "holy story" [*heilige Geschichte*] on which the foundation of the cult rested.[5]
>
> (Nietzsche 1997, 174; Nietzsche 1988, 32)

---

[5] Judith Norman's more recent translation for Cambridge University Press renders *Handlung* as "plot." Levinas translates it, as did Kaufman, as "action," which accords better with the philosophical contrast he draws between his position and philosophies of action. Nietzsche's

Alluding to this passage, Levinas implies that *Totality and Infinity* can be understood as a drama that form a holy history – so long as one does not confuse such terms with a sequence of actions that form a plot. *Totality and Infinity* aims at a different, more ancient drama behind the scenes of action, resistant to plot, indeed behind the stage of thought. This ancient alternative contrasts not only with Wagner's brawny conception of drama but also with the Aristotelian construal of drama as *mimesis praxeôs*. Following Nietzsche, Levinas aims at a drama or story that does not lend itself to mimetic action and for that reason can take place *only* off-stage, beyond the presence of the visible, as a type of broken backstory that cannot be plotted into a series of actions. Aristotelian drama gives narrative form to the likeness between idea and act, but the drama Levinas has in mind conveys an inimitable, inactive sense that can neither be displayed on the stage of "consciousness" or "world" nor represented through signs, symbols, or metaphors referring to another dimension of ideality. It is a matter, rather, of accessing the way intelligibility opens in the first place, as the curtain of the real is drawn, at the threshold of consciousness, worldhood, and ideality, as formlessness takes form. The scene of Alençon in Levinas's aborted novel, superbly analysed by François-David Sebbah,[6] is in the final analysis another example, in literary form, of the idea that drives Levinas's entire project: Events on the stage of meaning are *in truth oriented* from behind the curtain of intelligibility. "Ethics" affords *orientation – sens* – toward the backstage of meaning, where there is a *structure* that cannot be converted into action or plot: "the irreducible structure on which all other structures rest" (Levinas 1971, 77; Levinas 1969, 79), "the ultimate structure of being" (Levinas 1971, 104, Levinas 1969, 102). The structure here invoked has nothing to do with structuralism, whose formal holism lacks reference to subjectivity. For Levinas, rather, the structure of subjectivity consists in the way of individuating oneself as for-the-Other, being-answerable to- and for-the-Other. The structure of subjectivity consists of the way one opens (to meaning) by being oriented (to the Other). Subjectivity is structured as being-answerable to the claims of meaning in virtue of being exposed to the Other. Like the content of the note itself, the footnote points from behind the stage of Levinas's philosophical argument to a drama of an entirely different order. It is here that the "real action," the *inimitable inaction*, of "ethics" takes place.

The way toward the "nocturnal events" behind the stage of meaning consists of two stages. The first involves a philosophical critique of the correlation

---

"Doric" alternative to *Handlung* refers to a different type of plot/action, a plot without action, akin to what Levinas will later call an "intrigue."
6 See his chapter to this volume.

between intelligibility and activity. The critique holds that intelligibility – the experience of meaning, of something *as* something – cannot be explained on the basis of the possibility of activity but requires recourse to another ground, beyond the horizon of all possible action. To this critique, however, there must be added a second, positive stage that not only legitimates or even necessitates resort to such nocturnal events but also approaches them. Let us take each stage in turn.

Levinas's novel sense of ethics distinguishes itself from similar projects that attempt to ground meaning in action, whether through *acts* of consciousness (Husserl), the *activity* of being (Heidegger), or the *enactive* body (Merleau-Ponty). As Levinas construes it, "ethics" consists of a way of grounding the possibility of meaning or intentionality – the experience of something *as* something, such that it is available as an object of perception, thought, talk, imagination, and so on – *prior* to the intelligibility that shows up in acts of consciousness, the activity of being, or the embodied enactment of existence. Against his nearest philosophical rivals, Nietzsche's critique of Wagner is invoked in order to put distance between his and the dominant approaches to transcendental phenomenology, each of which seeks to ground the conditions for the possibility of meaning in modes of pre-reflective activity. In the final analysis, Levinas proposes that despite its compelling explanatory and descriptive power, transcendental phenomenology begs the question concerning the possibility of intentionality. It helps itself to the fact of intelligibility merely in virtue of being, in the lifeworld, incarnate; but it never answers the question of how intelligibility is possible. Like a speculative realist *avant la lettre*, Levinas takes his stand against the correlation of thought and the pre-reflective activity that wraps itself around the real. Indeed, he goes further, for he does not merely speculate but proposes a metaphysics that is *concretely produced* through the relation with the Other. The metaphysical claim is that meaning, mind, intentionality, and subjectivity are founded in a relation to the Other that comes from beyond the horizon of the synchronic totality of one's own existence, beyond implicit acts of consciousness, beyond the horizons of phenomenological evidence – "beyond the face," as he indicates in our footnote, alluding to the title of Section IV of *Totality and Infinity*.

3 Deduction to Drama

Following the critique of transcendental phenomenology comes the positive alternative, usually called "ethics" but here called "drama." In Levinas's view, the grounding of meaning in action misconstrues the role of subjectivity as a power able to constitute intelligibility, even if it does so in implicit, passive, or receptive ways. In his alternative view, subjectivity has access to meaning only on the basis of an antecedent "production" of sense, the idea of infinity or the sense of the Other, imposed from outside and beyond the transcendental horizon of possible acts of thought. The intelligibility I access is not only grounded in acts of consciousness, the activity of being, or the enactments of my embodied existence; its origin also requires separation from all such activity, for only such separation makes it possible to experience the difference between how things appear and how they ought to appear. Only the distance between the activity I undergo and its intelligibility makes it possible for such activity to be measurable, be it as valid, erroneous, sufficient, illusory, or whatever. Separation makes intentionality possible. My own access to meaning is illuminated from beyond the horizon of my possible activity. It is produced in and from the dark. "No prior disclosure illuminates the production of these essentially nocturnal events," Levinas says in the paragraph that concludes with the footnote guiding our study, before avowing that this recourse to the nocturnal constitutes his *departure* from phenomenology to another origin of intelligibility: "Phenomenology is a method for philosophy, but phenomenology . . . does not constitute the ultimate event of being itself" (Levinas 1971, 13; Levinas 1969, 28).[7] The phenomenological and ontological reduction to the grounds of meaning are thus supplemented by a "deduction" (Levinas 1971, 14; Levinas 1969, 28) to another, *metaphysical* origin that cannot be accessed through evidence, intuition, consciousness, experience, flesh, or being.[8] This other, metaphysical locus of meaning which lies behind the stage of "thought as act" (Levinas 1971, 12; Levinas 1969, 27 (translation modified)) has a structure appropriate to its nocturnal truth.[9] The "deduction" consists in finding the right fit in the dark.

---

7 Disclosure refers to *Erschlossenheit*, as Heidegger uses the term in *Being and Time* and related texts. Disclosure opens the horizon of possibility within which beings can be discovered.
8 Levinas uses "deduction" in the context of the Preface where he speaks of deducing "ethics" from the structure of the approach he is analysing. Deduction here is compatible with Kant's use of the term in that it seeks to justify the use of the concept, in this case "ethics," as appropriate to the sense of transcendence, which strictly speaking falls outside the horizon of experience and thus strictly speaking falls outside the phenomenological reduction. The distinction between a deduction and a reduction in nevertheless not entirely stable, as the remarkable admission by Jacques Taminiaux implies; see his "La genèse de la publication de *Totalité et Infini*" (2012, 81).
9 Levinas's critique of "thought as act" in this passage alludes to Heidegger, Husserl, and Merleau-Ponty; indirectly to Gabriel Marcel too. The notion of intelligibility as "incarnation" is announced by Merleau-Ponty's in "La philosophie de l'existence (1959, 307–322), where it is explicitly derived from Marcel's work yet modified, in view of the work of Husserl, Scheler, Heidegger, and Sartre, in the direction of his emerging conception of "the flesh of the world,"

Such a deduction, Levinas proposes, is "necessary yet non-analytical . . . it is indicated by expressions such as 'that is,' or 'precisely,' or 'this accomplishes that,' or 'this is produced as that'" (Levinas 1971, 14; Levinas 1969, 28). This crucial admission requires scrutiny. The claim is that the critique of the sufficiency of transcendental phenomenology *amounts to* – is accomplished as, is produced as, implies – "ethics." One may doubt, however, whether "ethics" is the *only* way of concretizing the nocturnal events in virtue of which the structure of subjectivity can be deduced. There seems no prima facie reason why some other way of rendering concrete the backstage of meaning could not be conveyed. Later, in *Otherwise than Being*, Levinas will admit that the structure he seeks is independent of "moral experience" and therefore that the privilege he gives to "ethics" involves a certain contingency, a looseness of fit or a certain distance between the sense of "ethics" and its concretion in "moral experience." Ethics is no longer deemed "necessary" but "adequate" to the structure of subjectivity.

> The ethical language we have resorted to does not arise out of a special moral experience, independent of the description hitherto elaborated. The ethical situation of responsibility is not comprehensible on the basis of ethics. [. . .] The tropes of ethical language are found to be *adequate* for certain structures of the description: for the sense of the approach in its contrast with knowing, the face in its contrast with a phenomenon.
> (Levinas 1991, 120 (emphasis added))

Might there then be other structures that are also "adeqaute" for approaching the backstage of meaning *without* converting this approach into an *act* of thought? Might the "essentially nocturnal events" that supplement acts of thought be concretized by other means? In the eulogy Derrida delivered many years later we glimpse such a possibility in the words relayed in Levinas's name: "what really interests me in the end is not ethics, not ethics alone, but the holy, the holiness of the holy" (Derrida 1999, 4). Here, again, the deduction from a critique of transcendental phenomenology to ethics no longer seems "necessary." This does not make it arbitrary; there must be an adequate fit from the structure of subjectivity, called into being from behind the scenes of its own activity, to its concretion. Such a structure can be "multiply realizable." It can be realized concretely in "ethics," but also in the approach to the holy, or the holiness of the holy. It is not surprising, then, that a certain construal of Revelation would likewise be

---

intelligibility as it is given "charnellement, *leibhaftig*" (Merleau-Ponty 1959, 312). Marcel was a member of the committee that judged and accepted *Totality and Infinity* as Levinas's *doctorat d'état*. Merleau-Ponty was scheduled to be there but died unexpectedly shortly before the committee convened.

"adequate" to the sense of the structure of subjectivity behind the stage of its activity as being-there, consciousness, or enactive body. Admittedly, Levinas argues that ethics, holiness, and Revelation all exhibit the same structure of being answerable one-for-the Other, the primordial *me voici* that his work constantly seeks. But rather than assume that there is only one pure or true name name – "ethics" – for rendering this primordial answerability concrete, one should acknowledge the essential ambiguity that constitutes answerability as such. After all, "ethics" is not restricted to *moral* accountability but concerns the grounds of answerability as such.

Let us gather our findings so far. We have seen (1) that Levinas develops a critique of transcendental phenomenology, and in particular of the correlation it assumes between intelligibility and activity, including acts of consciousness; (2) that this critique motivates him to search for a "structure" that is adequate to the nocturnal access of subjectivity to the claims of meaning; (3) that such a structure is ordinarily but not always or exclusively concretized as ethics; (4) that these nocturnal events *could* be articulated in the form of a drama or holy story, so long as such a drama was dissociated from *Handlung*, action or plot. Such, in brief, is the reconstructed rationale for Levinas's postphenomenological deduction to the possibility of a drama in which the nocturnal advent of meaning is conveyed.

4 The Genesis of *Totality and Infinity*

Levinas's allusion to Nietzsche's alternative conception of drama not only precludes action, it also founds the cult. "The most ancient drama represented the legend of the place, the 'holy story' [*heilige Geschichte*] on which the foundation of the cult rested." We find an analogy to the founding cult in the concept of "religion" deployed throughout *Totality and Infinity*. For Levinas, religion is a way of relating to the Other as inaccessible source of the intelligibility that I am able to access. The drama or holy story of religion founds the cult of humanity, the cult of those who are able to experience meaning (something *as* something). The cult of humanity rests on "ethics." But before "ethics" becomes conflated with "moral experience," before its foundational status converts into the *ritual* of banal moral conventions and courtesies – *Apres vous!* and so many other everyday acts – the cult is founded on the holy story, the drama of Genesis 1–11, the "primeval history" from creation to the election of Abram.[10]

In one sense, such an interpretative proposal will come as no surprise. Some will no doubt be disappointed, suspicious, as happens when the obvious suddenly appears. That Levinas could be suspected of having disseminated the old oracle of "creation" is indeed hardly surprising. As word and theme, "creation" is rife in *Totality and Infinity*, where it is interlaced with an elaborate lexicon of scriptural metaphors and secularized theological concepts that Levinas discerns in multiple, concrete phenomenological form.[11] But it is one thing to invoke the terms and themes of creation; it is quite another to convey (without narrating) *all the main elements* – episodes, stories, and motifs – of the primeval history of Genesis. Much more than the idea of creation, it is the major elements of the entire primeval history of Genesis 1–11 that constitute the nocturnal drama produced in *Totality and Infinity*. These all too familiar yet apparently still generative elements include:

- Genesis 1 – creation *ex hylus* (from *tohu wa'wohu*); "separation" from the primeval, "mythic elements" of water, wind, earth, and sky; the creation of the human, male and female; the separation of sexual difference; the injunction of fecundity;
- Genesis 2–3 – the paradisiac enjoyment and satisfaction of the "egoism" of terrestrial life; the problem of knowledge as it emerges from the point of view of egoistic existence; the ambiguous transcendence of erotic union; the productive value of exile from paradise; the possibility of "sabbatical existence" outside paradise;
- Genesis 4, the story of Cain and Abel – the temptation, prohibition, and banality of murder;
- Genesis 5, the genealogies, "this is the genealogy of *Adam* from the day he was created in the divine image" – a redoubled emphasis on the sense of transcendence accomplished through "fecundity";

---

10 The notion of a primeval history has been a mainstay of higher criticism of the Pentateuch for generations, where it is conspicuously, though by no means only, associated with Priestly authors. Joel Baden offers a recent recap: "The primeval history in P comprises the genealogy of humankind from Adam through Abraham . . . primeval history for P is the basic presentation of the state of nature and humanity. The elements established in this section are unalterable and serve as the background for the rest of P's history" (Baden 2012, 170).

11 I sought to elucidate this in *A Covenant of Creatures: Levinas's Philosophy of Judaism* (2010). At that stage, however, I did not see how the full array of the major episodes of Genesis 1–11 enter into the structure of *Totality and Infinity*. The present essay, along with another on the allusion Levinas makes to the Kabbalistic concept of *tsimtsum* (Levinas 1971, 107; Levinas 1969, 104), constitute additional excavations of the secularized creation theology at work in *Totality and Infinity*.

- Genesis 6–9, the flood – a dramatization of the possibility of reverting to the pre-created chaos of "existence without a world";
- Genesis 8 – a vision of postdiluvian peace as a plurality of creatures;
- Genesis 10 – the human kinship issued from monotheism;
- Genesis 11, the tower of Babel – the dystopia of monolingual humanism and the utopia of cacophonous peace among the plurality of creatures; the election of the father, Abram, called to journey to an unknown land.

What we see, in rough outline that I will presently augment, is the primeval history of Genesis 1–11 arrayed *without plot or action* behind the stage of *Totality and Infinity*. The holy history of Genesis splayed, not displayed; the narrative form of its plot and action (*Handlung*) broken apart like beads of a necklace and reworked into the subterranean *structure* of his philosophical work. The holy story, broken into nonnarrative fragments, constitutes the "essentially nocturnal events" that form the "conjunctures in being" behind the stage of the transcendental activity of signification and so too behind the scenes of the text of *Totality and Infinity*. By breaking the holy story of Genesis 1–11 into episodic fragments, *Totality and Infinity* disseminates it esoterically, in nonnarrative form. This constitutes its nocturnal drama, behind the stage of the phenomenological argument. Let us briefly elaborate on the more salient of these nocturnal events.

Consider first the major arc of the philosophical argument of *Totality and Infinity*, summarized by Levinas in the 1963 version of "Signature." "Light and *meaning* (*sens*) are born with the emergence and positing of existents in this horrible neutrality of the *there is*. They are on the road that leads from existence to the existent and from the existent to others – a route that delineates time itself" (Levinas 1966, 31).[12] Thus summarized, *Totality and Infinity* consists of the "ontogenesis" of meaning, to borrow a phrase Ricoeur used in a related context.[13] *In the beginning . . . il y a l'existence* (Levinas 1947, 99), "before the light comes" (Levinas 1995, 61), as Levinas said in 1947, "before creation," as he later put it (Levinas 1985, 48), as in Genesis 1:2, where creation takes place against the background of the mythic elements of primordial *tohu wa'wohu* – "welter and waste," as Robert Alter translates it (Alter 1996, 3) – the primordial dark and the abyss (*tehom*). In *Totality and Infinity*, the genesis of meaning is not constituted in a linear fashion but consists in deformalizing the experience

---

12 This 1966 translation of Levinas's "Signature" differs somewhat from the version published in *Difficult Freedom: Essays on Judaism* (see Levinas 1990, 292). Levinas's original article appeared in the volume *Les Philosophes Francais d'aujourd'hui par eux-mêmes: Autobiographie de la philosophie française conternporaine* (1963).
13 See Ricoeur, *The Symbolism of Evil* (1967).

of separation from formless, elemental existence "prior to discourse" (Levinas 1969, 190). It consists of a "deliverance from the horror of the *there is*" (Levinas 1969, 191) that amounts to the continuous creation of subjectivity.

By the same token, such a deliverance attests to the spectre of decreation, reversion to the formlessness of "existence without existents." The biblical text dramatizes this possibility in the story of the flood, where creation reverts to the primordial abyss (*tehom*) before creation (Gen. 7:11). The arc of Levinas's account of the *genesis of meaning* recapitulates fragments of the Act of Creation in Genesis, which likewise involves a deliverance from the nocturnal elements and can equally revert to the primordial condition of elemental existence. In *Totality and Infinity*, as in Genesis, creation *is* the fragile deliverance from the "mythical format" of "existence without a world."[14]

Zooming in from the broadest arc of *Totality and Infinity* to Section II, "Interiority and Economy," we find a series of allusions and phenomenological recapitulations of Genesis 2–3, the garden of Eden, where Levinas develops a phenomenology of being "innocently egoist." "At the origin there is a being gratified, a citizen of paradise" (Levinas 1969, 145). The idea that basic needs such as hunger are not merely the function of lack or need but are constitutive of the *jouissance* through which one is affectively individuated *within* the indeterminacy of existing renders the experience of selfhood innocently materialist, carnal and sinless. "It is not that at the beginning there was hunger; the simultaneity of hunger and food constitutes the paradisal initial condition of enjoyment" (Levinas 1969, 136). The references to paradise are not incidental. Unpublished notes from the *Inédits* make the biblical allusion clear. "An egoist movement irreducible to negation: *paradisal subjectification of Adam, innocent egoism*, immanence: dwelling in oneself while borrowing from the world only a place for being in oneself" (Levinas 2009, 245, emphasis added). The phenomenological descriptions of the egoism of enjoyment, of satisfaction without sin, point backstage to the paradisiac life of Genesis 2, the edenic egoism where the subjectification of Adam begins.

Levinas might have found inspiration for this phenomenology of paradisiac life in the writings of the ultra-Catholic thinker Léon Bloy, whose *Lettres à sa fiancée* provided an example of how to generate philosophical anthropology on the basis of religious categories (Levinas 2009, 151). The conservative writer's way of deriving a non-confessional spiritual anthropology on the basis of his understanding of Catholicism impressed Levinas profoundly: "Same work to be undertaken for j[udaism]," he anticipates for himself (Levinas 2009, 151). One wonders,

---

14 As Ricoeur says of Ancient Near East cosmologies, "salvation is identical with creation itself" (Ricoeur 1967, 172).

then, if section II of *Totality and Infinity* has Genesis 2–3 behind the stage on which Levinas unfolds the problem of objective knowledge in terms of "the lust of the eyes," the role of labor, dwelling, and eros on the way to knowledge, and the implied exile from the innocent "frisson égoïste" (Levinas 2009, 245) of paradisiac life that is finally required to account for the experience of meaning that we in fact already possess. Bloy's retrieval of Genesis was clearly the inspiration for the rich account of the ambiguity of the erotic, equivocating between alterity and possession, veneration and profanation,. In the *Carnets* we read: "The second chapter of Genesis where one finds terrestrial paradise described is, in my eyes, a symbolic figure of *Woman*. This is one of the discoveries of which I am most proud" (Levinas 2009, 153, citing Bloy's *Lettres* 3 November 1889). *Time and the Other* acknowledges "the admirably bold pages of Léon Bloy in his *Letters to his Fiancée*" (Levinas 1987, 86), which were subsequently elaborated in *Totality and Infinity* into a phenomenology of eros and, I suggest, of the edenic quality of innocent egoism independent of knowledge.

To Genesis 4, the story of Cain and Abel, *Totality and Infinity* makes explicit reference in the phenomenology of hatred that accounts for the will to annihilate, rather than merely defeat, the Other. Whereas phenomena can be opposed, circumvented, destroyed, and so forth, just as the manifest, empirical other can be contested, ignored, and even killed, the Other, as the transcendent source of my own subjectivity as being-answerable, cannot be annihilated. One can kill and thus reduce the other to nothingness, but the Other, as non-phenomenological source to whom one is finally answerable, "expresses my moral impossibility of annihilating" (Levinas 1971, 258; Levinas 1969, 232). Ontically facile, murder is ontologically impossible since the sense of the Other as origin of my answerability cannot be reduced or eliminated. "The face resists possession, resists my powers" (Levinas 1969, 197), because it consists in a way of being that falls outside possibilities of possession or horizons of understanding. Defying appropriation, the Other introduces "the temptation of murder, not only as a temptation to total 'destruction,' but also as the purely ethical impossibility of this temptation and attempt" (Levinas 1969, 199). While murder is one of the banalities of history, it is ethically impossible to annihilate the Other, for that would amount to *justifying the negation of one's own access to justification*. The transcendence of the Other consists in this irreducible source of normativity which founds subjectivity. The thought, central to *Totality and Infinity*, implies an almost indiscernible but pervasive reference to Genesis 4, for the ethical impossibility of murder "looks at me from the very depths of the eyes I want to extinguish, looks at me as the eye that in the tomb shall look at Cain" (Levinas 1969, 233). In his commentary on *Totality and Infinity* Blanchot puts it well: "man facing man like this has no choice but to speak or to kill . . .

Cain killing Abel is the self that, coming up against the transcendence of *autrui* (what in the other exceeds me absolutely and that is well represented in biblical history by the incomprehensible inequality of divine favor), attempts to confront it by resorting to the transcendence of murder" (Blanchot 1993, 61).[15]

Just as the implied thematics of Genesis 4 stand behind the stage of the phenomenology of hatred and the temptation of murder, so too the notorious genealogies of the Priestly author, recurring throughout primeval history, find their correspondences in the decisive notion of fecundity and its associated concept of election. In Genesis, the genealogies of primeval history are explicitly linked to the divine likeness. "When God created mankind, he made them in the likeness of God . . . .When Adam had lived 130 years, he had *a son in his own likeness, in his own image*; and he named him Seth" (5:1–3). Levinas renders concrete this notion of being in the likeness of God by describing it as a way of being oneself diachronically, across the discontinuity of generations, thus being unlike oneself. Subjectivity is concretely founded on the temporality of fecundity through which one *is* for the sake of the Other. "Paternity is a relation with a stranger who while being Other . . . *is* me, a relation of the I with a self which is yet not me. . . . In existing itself there is a multiplicity and a transcendence. In this transcendence the I is not swept away, since the son is not me; and yet I *am* my son. The fecundity of the I is its very transcendence" (Levinas 1969, 277). To be oneself is to be *fecund and multiple* by being temporally oriented beyond oneself, for the sake of the Other to come. On this view, it is not the case that an individual as such *is* an image of God but that the divine image is rendered concrete through the transcendence of the self in its being fecund and multiple. This way of being oneself by transcending oneself for the sake of the Other distinguishes Levinas's "defense of subjectivity" from rival accounts that ground subjectivity in its transcendental activity. Accordingly, although we discern elements of primeval history throughout *Totality and Infinity*, fecundity constitutes a privileged access to the "conjunctures in being" of the drama behind the activity of intelligibility, as we will see in the next section.

From Genesis 5, primeval history moves into a lengthy account, or accounts, of the deluge, whose narrative premise is that the covenantal structure of creation can collapse into the primordial formlessness of mythic elemental existence.[16] In the Deluge, the worldhood of creation reverts to the primordial abyss (*tehom*) before there was Saying (Gen. 7:11). This is, as it were, the primal

---

[15] Cf. *Totality and Infinity* (Levinas 1969), pages 198–201 and especially 232–236.
[16] For a classic explication see Jon. D. Levenson, *Creation and the Persistence of Evil: The Jewish Drama of Divine Omnipotence* (1994). I have written about this at greater length in "The Ethics of Creation: Biblical and Post-Biblical Views" (2012).

scene of the "epoché of debacle" that obsessed Levinas from his ruminations on the *il y a* in the mid-1940s to the narrative form he gave it in *Sad Opulence* to his location of its historical traces in radical evil, the "total chaos" of a world "fallen apart," as happened in "a world put in question by Hitler's triumphs," "as if being itself had been suspended" (Levinas 1996, 119).[17] The Deluge *is* decreation, existence without existents, a possibility not only for myth but also for historical existence, indeed a spectre accompanying the egoist enjoyment of life (Levinas 1971, 160ff.). Once again, then, a major axis of the arc of *Totality and Infinity* is anticipated by the primeval history of Genesis. Levinas occasionally makes this explicit, as for example when describing the return of the primordial *il y a* as a reversion to a mythic time "before the light" (Levinas 1947, 99; Levinas 1995, 61) or "before creation" (Levinas 1985, 48).

The final episode in primeval history is the Tower of Babel, which is found in Levinas's critique of the monolingual universalism of impersonal reason, whose ideal is the Hegelian state. "In accomplishing its essence as discourse, in becoming a discourse universally coherent, language would at the same time realize the universal State, in which multiplicity is reabsorbed and discourse comes to an end, for lack of interlocutors" (Levinas 1971, 239; Levinas 1969, 217). The first name of the Hegelian state is Babel, whose towering ambition implies a suppression of the multiplicity of singular voices that constitute the original possibility of communication.

What is striking is not only the philosophical rendering of this or that episode in the primeval history of Genesis but their accumulation. All the main elements of the primeval history of Genesis 1–11 can be discerned within the texture of *Totality and Infinity*. Crucially, the presence of these traces of Genesis does not amount to a repetition of its narrative structure, as if it were a matter of repeating the plot of the biblical story. Beginning with a critique of the primacy of action, one could hardly progress by repeating the ancient plot. What we find, rather, is that the "holy story" of Genesis 1–11 has been stripped of

---

17 See also Levinas, "Tout est-il vanité?" (1946). Later, in the historical event of Destruction, the created world again reverts to the primordial state of elemental existence, before the light and without the individuation of creatures, this time on account of war. Jeremiah bears witness to this reversion:

> I look at the earth,
> It is unformed and void [*tohu wa'bohu*];
> At the skies, And their light is gone.
> I look at the mountains, They are quaking;
> And all the hills are rocking. I look: no human [*eyn ha'adam*],
> And all the birds of the sky have fled [*nadadu*]

(Jer. 4:23)

potent acts and disemplotted. Produced in its nocturnal profile, *Totality and Infinity* records a drama that Nietzsche called "hieratic," in accordance with the priestly writings that are so prevalent in Genesis 1–11, recording those "conjunctures of being" behind the stage of meaning and behind the scenes of Levinas's phenomenological descriptions.

5 Holy History

In Nietzsche's comment on Wagner, the drama without action is called *heilige Geschichte*. Holy history is not to be confused with a "sacred drama," if the word sacred connotes participation in, or the possibility of imitating the holy. The *heilige Geschicte* to which Levinas alludes does not consist of the familiar narratives of Genesis 1–11 in their canonical form but in fragments of episodes from primeval history whose re-contextualization supports the backstage structure of Levinas's argument. The fragments of holy history lie broken behind the stage on which subjectivity becomes consciousness and agency, before one becomes an ability to act and thereby enter the theatre of life, before psychological stories and the plot of secular history are played out. Yet Levinas often speaks of *histoire sainte* in a manner that seems to diverge from the pre-philosophical sense we have discerned in *Totality and Infinity*. In the philosophical work, it refers to fragments of the backstage structure of subjectivity, but elsewhere it quite explicitly refers to the history of the Jews, which prima facie seems to transpire empirically where it is registered in terms of action. In fact, however, the two conceptions are not so distinct.

Levinas's *explicit* notion of "holy history" emerges in 1947 in critical dialogue with Sartre's view of Jewish history before it becomes a recurring feature of his essays in Jewish thought.[18] Here, holy history marks the difference between Sartrean "facticity" and Levinas's understanding of Jewish "election." Whereas facticity enables the free reception of one's past, election is yoked to a metaphysical sense that no act of freedom can overcome. Facticity converts into freedom and *amor fati*, but to be elected is to be answerable to someone else, from another time, to the Father, whose call is constitutive of who one is – "personhood as a son and as elected" (Levinas 2007, 2010). To be elected is to be bound to the time of the Other; it is to *be* metaphysical, that is, to maintain

---

[18] See especially Levinas "Being Jewish" (2007) and "Existentialism and Anti-Semitism (1999), both published in 1947. For a fine commentary see Schonfeld 2006.

oneself at a distance from historical existence, to be answerable beyond the horizon of the present and thus to be oneself in virtue of holy history. Through election, "the very mystery of personhood" (Levinas 2007, 210), subjectivity, enters holy history. Accordingly, as Eli Schonfeld observes, it is not only the case that the concept of holy history belongs to Levinas's confessional writings, as if it were simply a matter of describing and vindicating Jewish history. Rather, the concept of holy history undergoes "philosophical translation" into *Totality and Infinity*, where it takes form of the "election" of subjectivity in the mode of "fecundity" – being oneself in virtue of being answerable to the time of the Other, "while occluding the Jewish reference" (Schonfeld 2006, 142).

The "confessional" appeal to the holy history and election of being Jewish thus translates into descriptions of the structure of subjectivity as individuated or elected through fecundity, which means being answerable to a time beyond the horizon of political and historical existence. This explains why the footnote we have been explicating refers the notion of drama, which Nietzsche identifies with the drama of a holy history, to "the end of this work, the study of relations which we situate *beyond the face*." The reference points to Section IV of *Totality and Infinity*, "Beyond the Face," where Levinas describes the individuation of subjectivity as elected in virtue of its fecundity, as being oneself answerable to the time of the Other. Whether as the "election" of the Jews into "holy history" or, philosophically, the individuation of subjectivity through "fecundity," in both cases it is a matter of maintaining subjectivity in its temporal being for the sake of the Other, standing under the judgement of those of a different time, the Father and the Child. This temporal structure of subjectivity, which *Totality and Infinity* calls fecundity, being answerable "beyond the face" and thus beyond the horizon of the present, translates and secularizes the holy history of Jewish election. It refers subjectivity beyond the horizon of historical existence and thus beyond the category of historical *agency*. Ultimately, it refers subjectivity from its constitution as an historical agent to its election under the judgement of holy history, to "the story of *Genesis* . . . of the transmission of the blessing" (Schonfeld 2006, 147). The prospect of a drama "beyond the face" implied by Nietzsche's appeal to *heilige Geschichte* as a drama behind the scenes of action thereby points to a notion of holy history consonant with Levinas's conception of Jewish election as metaphysical rather than empirical and its transposition into an account of subjectivity as founded on the temporality of the Other, the elected structure of fecundity. Here too, then, the primeval history of Genesis is concealed amid the phenomenological descriptions of *Totality and Infinity*.

Moreover, like the opening eleven chapters of Genesis, and so too like the metaphysical "holy history" of the Jews to which Levinas appeals in his confessional writings, *Totality and Infinity* recalls the drama of humanity at large. One can thus view Levinas's writings as a recapitulation of the work of the ancient Priestly authors, recording a "drama . . . in the hieratic sense," as Nietzsche proposed. In both cases, it is a matter of a "universal" drama that founds the cult of humanity: "ethics," as Levinas calls it, or "the Noahide laws," as rabbinic Judaism calls those seven basic laws given to pre-diluvian humanity, among them the prohibition on murder and the injunction to establish institutions of justice. Finally, one should note that the primeval genesis is ritualized by the priestly cult of the Israelite sanctuary described in Exodus 39–40, which provides a "microcosm" of the creation story from Genesis 1.[19] The priestly cult of Israel and its sanctuary thus become an icon of the drama of the creation of the world, just as, for Levinas, the holy history of the Jews is an icon of the drama of subjectivity at large. The priestly enactment of the holy story of Genesis in the Tabernacle of the Book of Exodus well illustrates the "hieratic" drama that Nietzsche discerned in Doric antiquity. It is a drama that founds the cult, performed *behind the curtain* and in *silence*, intimating the Act of Creation without imitating it, without the pretence of *mimesis praxeos*.[20] *Totality and Infinity* effects a transposition of this logic. The cult of humanity–the cult of the experience of meaning–is founded on the primeval history of Genesis and ritualized in moral experience.

6 As if we were children

A drama or holy story founds subjectivity from behind the stage of its transcendental activity. Levinas calls it ethics, but we have seen that it is constituted in no small part from the fragmented primeval history of Genesis 1–11. This does not mean that ethics depends on, much less reduces to, the stories of Genesis. For one, the validity of the descriptions depends only on the eidetic evidence they exhibit to a subject, including the sense of the limits of experience that such evidence provides. Scripture exercises no authority over these descriptions it merely provides allusions to how such "conjunctures in being" beyond the horizon of evidence might be "formally indicated," much like Heidegger's allusions to St Paul or Kierkegaard show how ontological structures might be indicated. Moreover, in the backstage of *Totality and Infinity*, the allusions to holy history never amount to telling a story behind the visible. The episodes from

---

[19] The microcosmic reiteration of the drama of creation in the priestly cult is a common feature of ancient near eastern ritual. For a lucid account of the biblical case, see Levenson (1994, 78–99).
[20] On the Priestly drama see Knohl 2007.

Genesis have been disemplotted from the biblical narrative and placed in a new structure behind the curtain of the activity of signification. Recourse to fragments from the primeval history of Genesis behind the stage of the activity of being does not amount to recourse to a primordial story of the genesis of being.

Accordingly, *Totality and Infinity* does not violate the founding gesture of phenomenology, which consists in distinguishing between the validity of meaning and the genetic stories that explain our access to meaning, whether through evolutionary biology and cognitive science or through historical accounts of the development of concepts, values, institutions, and so forth. Husserl opens *Ideas 1* by declaring: "No stories will be told here. Neither psychological-causal nor historical-developmental genesis need be, or should be, thought of when we speak here of originality (*Ursprünglichkeit*)" (Husserl 1983, 5 n. 2).[21] The originality of meaning or intelligibility – that consciousness is always intentional, that there is always already meaning – is not explained by appeal to a causal story, for such stories always presuppose other antecedently valid meanings. For the same reason Heidegger brings the question of being to light by emphasizing the difference between the transcendental-ontological account of being and alternative, ontic ways of understanding entities. Alluding to *Sophist* 242c, he proposes that "our first philosophical step consists in not *mython tina diēgeisthai*, in not 'telling a story' [*keine Geschichte erzählen*] – that is to say, in not defining entities as entities by tracing them back in their origin to some other entities, as if Being had the character of some possible entity" (Heidegger 1962, 5). Since being – the ways of being in virtue of which a being is intelligible as what it is or might be – is not itself a being, it cannot be explained by appeal to entities that cause and materially constitute it. No developmental story, whether naturalistic or historical, can account for the fact that there is sense to being. The hermeneutic circle of intelligibility is "primordial" (*ursprünglich*) (Heidegger 1962, 195).

Even so, what is gained by this elaborate allusion to fragments of primeval history behind the scenes of transcendental phenomenology? Two points in particular, and with them we can conclude. First, by appealing to a drama or holy history behind the philosophical scene while refusing the narrative form of a story, *Totality and Infinity* invites the reader to recover a pre-philosophical sense of wonder without resorting to pre-philosophical naiveté. It is not just Husserl and Heidegger who refuse to tell stories. Philosophy begins by breaking with mythos and refusing to tell stories. Plato makes the point against his precursors who try to explain being by telling a story of its origin in another being.

---

[21] This discussion is indebted to Jacques Derrida, *Heidegger: The Question of Being and History* (2016).

"Every one of them seems to tell us a story (*muthon*) as if we were children" (*Sophist* 242c), he objects.

Elsewhere, however, Plato concedes that the philosopher is not always true to his or her ambitions, for the philosopher needs a good story as much as the common run of people: in *Timaeus*, he states that "we should bear in mind the fact that I and all of you, the speaker and his judges, are no more than human, which means that on these matters we ought to accept the likely account [*muthos*] and not demand more than that" (Plato 2008, 18). Derrida puts forth two ways of understanding this concession to story or mythos. First, philosophers, being mortal, must resign themselves to a likely story about the origins of meaning:

> Very remarkable in this respect is the *Timaeus*, in which, when it comes to explaining the origin of the *world*, the origin of the beings that appear to us, the origin of the ordered system (*Cosmos*) of phenomena, Timaeus, responding to Socrates who was asking for a true story (*aléthinon logon*) at last, and not a *muthon*, announces (29 c-d) that, when it is a question of the origin of beings, a philosophical discourse adequate to the origin is impossible, a true and exact discourse is impossible, and so one must be content to recite, to unroll like a genesis, like a becoming-real of things, something that is not becoming, but the origin of things. One must unroll the *Archē* like a genesis. One must produce a discourse, a narrative in terms of becoming, in what is already here, already born, even though one would need to speak of the origin and of the birth of the world.
>
> (Derrida 2016, 35)

No less than ordinary people, philosophers cannot live without stories. They too find themselves always already within the domain of meaning. They cannot pull themselves up by the bootstraps, they were not witness to the genesis of meaning, and so they too must surmise a likely story about the origin of meaning. They speak, for example, about the "emergence" of intelligibility from biological life, the "emergence" of biological life from chemical elements and of chemical elements from physical forces – a likely story, but "emergence" only obscures the enigma of intelligibility, as transcendental phenomenologists since Husserl have insisted.

Alternatively, even if the philosopher is able to avoid telling a story of the origin of meaning, there may be reason, Derrida proposes, to tell such a likely story – not to console philosophers but to control the non-philosophical mass of people. The philosopher may have need for an "esotericism," for plausible stories whose "expository necessity" unroll the inaccessible origin like a genesis in order to justify basic exigencies of social and political life, such as answerability, accountability or responsibility, in short, ethics (Derrida 2016, 36).

The elaborate allusion *Totality and Infinity* makes to the holy story of Genesis 1–11 brings these two alternatives to converge in the form of an inverted esotericism. On the one hand, it unrolls the *Archē* like a genesis; more precisely, it unrolls the *archē* of intelligibility like a Genesis. The story it articulates, without plot, action or narrative, adheres to the primordial orientation of the Good, which every child knows. In a radio talk from September 25, 1945, reflecting on his experience as a Jewish prisoner of war Levinas marvelled at this recovery of a childlike reception of Revelation. Old biblical stories, "unlearned" since the age of Bar Mitzvah, suddenly reappeared "true in their elementary truth, their truth for children . . . their popular truth . . . And this truth itself, this truth taught from childhood that the unjust and the strong succumb, that the weak and the poor are saved and triumph appeared marvelous in its simplicity . . . . seeing it confirmed by world events – it takes your breath away, it grabs you by the throat. Good becomes Good; Evil, Evil. The dismal masquerade is over" (Levinas 2009, 214). With immeasurably more sophistication, the defense of subjectivity that *Totality and Infinity* produces behind the stage of meaning provides the philosopher with a likely mythos, the story that he or she needs to be oriented within the activity of being. But at this point one should ask, with Derrida, "Why the value of philosophical discourse is spontaneously measured by the yardstick of adult maturity is a question to which it is not so easy to reply seriously. Why, fundamentally, is an *adult's* discourse better than a *child's* discourse? And why would philosophy make common cause with maturity?" (Derrida 2016, 34). Elsewhere Levinas calls the primordial orientation to the Good "the secret of angels," a "childlike trust," the "reception of Revelation" (Levinas 2019, 46–48). It consists in affirming the structure of subjectivity as being-for-the-Other, prior to knowledge, without guarantee, and before the success or failure of one's actions, a childlike trust in the Other without naïveté. This has nothing to do with blind deference to the authority of other people. The recursion from philosophy to the backstage structure of subjectivity does not revert to naïveté but to integrity, an affirmation of the orientation of subjectivity, prior to the knowledge of good and evil, toward the Other. "The question is not to transform action into a mode of understanding but to praise a mode of knowing which reveals the deep structure of subjectivity . . . *Temimut* [integrity]" (Levinas 2019, 43). "Integrity, taken in its logical meaning and not as a characteristic of a childlike disposition, indicates, if it is thought through to the end, an ethical configuration" (Levinas 2019, 48). Integrity consists in maintaining one's answerability to the Other in the course of one's everyday activities, even when no one is around, or in the face of the dishonesty of others, or under pressure from economic, social, or biological factors. This ethical configuration is the subterranean structure of subjectivity, its adherence to the Other from behind the stage of its active ways of being in the world. *Temimut*, or integrity, maintaining one's answerability to the Other in the face of the temptation to yield to the pressures of life, is structured as fecundity, an orientation to some*one* still to come. At issue, then, is a *critical naiveté*, the integrity of a vision that sees beyond the needs of the instant, an integrity that is therefore "different from that which would consists in a return to childish naiveté . . . It is a perfectly adult effort" (Levinas 2019, 42).

Thus, on the other hand, the numerous evocations and allusions that *Totality and Infinity* makes to the most likely of all stories, the primeval history of Genesis, as orienting subjectivity from behind the stage of its activity, suggests the possibility of an esotericism of the Good hidden from philosophers. For in making common cause with maturity, philosophers not only forgo stories but also risk forgetting the angelic secret of a critical naiveté that is answerable to the Other beyond the horizon of knowledge. To return to the zero-degree of answerability is to awaken philosophers from the great midday slumber of reason. It is to convey a secret way of being answerable in the dark. Traditional esotericism conceals the truth from the mass of people by secreting it within a holy story where it can be disclosed by those 'in the know'. But *Totality and Infinity* conceals fragments of the holy story from the philosophical elite in order to awaken an integrity that is dispelled by the light of knowledge. In an intellectual climate pervaded by the ideal of total disclosure, where nothing is as sacred as harsh truth, *Totality and Infinity* orients the philosopher back to that primordial trust, adherence to the Other, as if philosophers were not only rational mortals but also children.

Bibliography

Alter, Robert. 1996. *Genesis: Translation and Commentary*. New York: Norton.
Baden, Joel S. 2012. *The Composition of the Pentateuch: Renewing the Documentary Hypothesis*. The Anchor Yale Bible Reference Library. New Haven: Yale University Press.
Blanchot, Maurice. 1993 *The Infinite Conversation*. Trans. Susan Hanson. Minneapolis: University of Minnesota Press.
Boyarin, Daniel. 1990. "The Song of Songs: Lock or Key? Intertextuality, Allegory and Midrash." *The Book and the Text: The Bible and Literary Theory*. Ed. Regina M. Schwartz. Oxford: Blackwell. 214–230.
Critchley, Simon. 2015. *The Problem of Levinas*. Ed. A. Dianda. Oxford: Oxford University Press.
Derrida, Jacques. 1999. *Adieu to Emmanuel Levinas*. Trans. Pascale-Anne Brault and Michael Naas. Stanford: Stanford University Press.
Derrida, Jacques. 2016. *Heidegger: The Question of Being and History*. Trans. Geoffrey Bennington. Chicago: The University of Chicago Press.
Fagenblat, Michael. 2010. *A Covenant of Creatures: Levinas's Philosophy of Judaism*. Stanford: Stanford University Press.

Fagenblat, Michael. 2012. "The Ethics of Creation: Biblical and Post-Biblical Views." *Monotheism and Ethics: Historical and Contemporary Intersections among Judaism, Christianity and Islam*. Leiden: Brill. 107–140.
Halbertal, Moshe. 2009. *Concealment and Revelation: Esotericism in Jewish Thought and its Philosophical Implications*. Princeton: Princeton University Press.
Heidegger, Martin. 1962. *Being and Time*. Trans. John Macquarrie and Edward Robinson. New York: Harper.
Husserl, Edmund. 1983. *Ideas Pertaining to a Pure Phenomenology and to a Phenomenological Philosophy: First Book: General Introduction to a Pure Phenomenology*. Trans. F. Kersten. Dordrecht: Springer.
Knohl, Israel. 2007. The Sanctuary of Silence: The Priestly Torah and the Holiness School. 1st Edition. Winona Lake, Ind: Eisenbrauns.
Levenson, Jon. D. 1994. *Creation and the Persistence of Evil: The Jewish Drama of Divine Omnipotence*. Princeton: Princeton University Press.
Levinas, Emmanuel. "Tout est-il vanité?" *Bulletin Intérieur de l'Alliance Israélite Universelle* 2.9 (July 1946): 1–2.
Levinas, Emmanuel. 1947. *De l'existence a l'existant*. Paris: Vrin.
Levinas, Emmanuel. 1963. "Signature." *Les Philosophes Francais d'aujourd'hui par eux-mêmes: Autobiographie de la philosophie française conternporaine*. Eds. G. Deledalle and D. Huisman. Paris: Centre de Documentation Universitaire. 325–328.
Levinas, Emmanuel. 1969. *Totality and Infinity: An Essay on Exteriority*. Trans. Alphonso Lingis. Pittsburgh: Duquesne University Press.
Levinas, Emmanuel. *Totalité et Infini : Essai Sur l'extériorité*. Dordrecht: Kluwer Academic, 1971 [1961].
Levinas, Emmanuel. "Signature." *Philosophy Today* 10.1 (1966): 30–33.
Levinas, Emmanuel. 1985. *Ethics and Infinity: Conversations with Philippe Nemo*. Trans. Richard A. Cohen. Pittsburgh: Duquesne University Press.
Levinas, Emmanuel. 1987. *Time and the Other*. Pittsburgh: Duquesne University Press.
Levinas, Emmanuel. 1990. *Difficult Freedom: Essays on Judaism*. Trans. Séan Hand. London: Athlone. 291–295.
Levinas, Emmanuel. 1991. *Otherwise than Being or Beyond Essence*. Trans. Alphonso Lingis. Dordrecht: Springer.
Levinas, Emmanuel. 1995. *Existence and Existents*. Trans. Alphonso Lingis. Dordrecht: Kluwer Academic.
Levinas, Emmanuel. 1996. "Nameless." Proper Names. Trans. Michael B. Smith. Stanford: Stanford University Press. 119–123.
Levinas, Emmanuel. "Existentialism and Anti-Semitism." Trans. Denis Hollier and Rosalind Krauss. *October* 87 (Winter, 1999): 27–31.
Levinas, Emmanuel. "Being Jewish." Trans. Mary Beth Mader. *Continental Philosophy Review* 40.3 (2007): 205–210.
Levinas, Emmanuel. 2009. *Oeuvres complètes*, Vol. 1: *Carnets de captivité et autre inédits*. Eds. Rodolphe Calin and Catherine Chalier. Paris: Grasset.
Levinas, Emmanuel, 2019. "The Temptation of Temptation." *Nine Talmudic Readings*. Trans. Annette Aronowicz. Bloomington: Indiana University Press. 42–72.
Malka, Salomon. 2006. *Emmanuel Levinas: His Life and Legacy*. Trans. Michael Kigel and Sonja M. Embree. Pittsburgh: Duquesne University Press.
Merleau-Ponty, Maurice. "La philosophie de l'existence." *Dialogue* 5:3 (1959): 307–322.

Midrash Rabbah: Genesis, Vol. I. Trans. H. Freedman. London: Soncino, 1939.
Nietzsche, Friedrich. 1988. *Sämtliche Werke. Kritische Studienausgabe in 15 Einzelbänden*, Vol. 6. Eds. Giorgio Colli and Mazzino Montinari. Munich: Deutscher Taschenbuch Verlag.
Nietzsche, Friedrich. 1997. *The Birth of Tragedy and The Case of Wagner*. Trans. W. Kaufmann. Toronto: Random House.
Plato. *Timaeus and Critias*. 2008. Trans. Robin Waterfield. Oxford: Oxford University Press.
Ricoeur, Paul. 1967. *The Symbolism of Evil*. Trans. Emerson Buchanan. Boston: Beacon Press.
Schonfeld, Eli. "Histoire et facticité juive: À propos d'un dialogue entre Lévinas et Sartre." *Cahiers d'Études Lévinassiennes* 5 (2006): 137–151.
Taminiaux, Jacques. "La genèse de la publication de *Totalité et Infini*." *Levinas: au-delà du visible. Études sur les inédits de Levinas des* Carnets de captivité *à* Totalité et Infini. Eds. Emmanuel Housset and Rodolphe Calin. *Cahiers de philosophie de l'Université de Caen* 49 (August 2012): 69–85.

Marcel Poorthuis
Literature as a Burning Bush

> hierarchitectitiptitoploftical, with a burning bush abob off its baubletop.
> (James Joyce, *Finnegans Wake*)

1 Introduction

Imagine a transcendent moment which astonishes man but does not infringe upon his freedom to decide, as the natural world remains intact. This may be an apt description of how the divine word, using as its medium a natural element (a bush), came to Moses at the burning bush, which burned without being consumed. Moses was free to ignore the message, as he was not forced into his decision by any lasting infringement upon the natural order. Moses could not even point to the ashes of the burning bush, because the very thing remained as it was. The call to responsibility was so personal as to border on a phantasmagorical vision. Moreover, the truth conveyed was radically personal: no one else heard or saw anything that could corroborate Moses' vision. The proximity to its message cannot be figured by historico-critical tools alone: At the burning bush, Moses was reminded of the fate of his brothers and sisters, even as he was spatially far removed from them. The transcendent message of the divine name, which cannot be pronounced, almost coincides with Moses' awareness of this responsibility.

In a way, the spirit hidden within the letter is similar to this radically personal revelation. The reader unveils a truth that is felt to be meant for him or her alone, and which was perhaps not even explicitly intended by the writer. In a way, the writer is the medium of the truth rather than the originator of the truth. The poet who transmits words without completely understanding them can be compared to an oracle in Antiquity who conveys divine messages without being at their origin. This latter description fits Heidegger's idea of poetry being an access to Being and of the poet being neither an active forger nor a passive recipient of poetry but rather a medium through which the language becomes speech: "die Sprache spricht." Undoubtedly, historico-critical methods which attempt to pinpoint the meaning of a text by treating it as a historical residue of bygone times cannot do justice to the "Anspruch" of poetry. For Heidegger, Hölderlin's complaint, "What use are poets in times of need?" (in his elegy *Bread and Wine*), does not evoke a long-forgotten past, but is in fact more present and more a herald of the future than contemporary writers.[1] In a way, Levinas's approach to literature/poetry shows similarities with that of Heidegger. Both discover in poetry essential elements of their own philosophy, as if it were preluding upon their own thought. Heidegger demonstrates the difference between Being ("Sein") and the totality of beings ("Seienden") in Hölderlin's poetry as well as in pre-Socratic maxims. Levinas points to the difference between I and the other as the experience par excellence, forgotten in philosophy but expressed in poetry. Rimbaud's "Je est un autre," a quotation from his letter of May 15, 1871, may be read as the experience of alienation of the subject without specific reference to the other human being; in Levinas's reading it becomes an allusion to the intrigue of the uniqueness of the subject as being-for-the-other. This *re-contextualization* of lines of poetry allows for a creative renewal by which poetry becomes "food for thought," transcending the mere intention of the author. In a way, this re-contextualization is quite similar to how the Talmud reworks biblical quotations. In the famous story of Rabbi Joshua and Rabbi Eliezer, in which even a heavenly voice cannot decide their difference of opinions (Babylonian Talmud *Bava Metsia* 59b), Rabbi Joshua underlines his position with the statement, "the decision follows the majority" (Ex 23:2).[2] On closer scrutiny, however, the biblical quotation in question states "you shall not follow the multitude to do evil." Implicitly, the rabbis take this to mean that one should follow the multitude in good cases, but this of course raises the question of how one can be sure of that. Hence this quotation does not conclude the debate but instead deepens it in such a way that the reflection is continuously enriched and open to new perspectives, without coming to a conclusion. This "infinite reading" of the Talmud, in which quotations are sometimes molded in such a way that they may state the opposite without betraying the original, is similar to how Levinas refers to literature. The world literature of Shakespeare and Molière, Cervantes and Dante, Goethe and Pushkin, form a national treasure, Levinas states, yet contain significance beyond their primary meaning and invite exegesis (Levinas 1982a, 8).[3] Rimbaud's famous line "The true life is elsewhere," the opening lines of the same page of Levinas's *Totalité et infini*,

---

[1] See Martin Heidegger, "Wozu Dichter?" (1980). About Hölderlin as "Vor-gänger" Heidegger states: "Sowenig überholbar der Vorgänger, so wenig vergänglich ist er auch" (Heidegger 1980, 316).

[2] Levinas adduces the story several times. See for one example "La révélation dans la tradition juive" in *L'au-delà du verset* (Levinas 1982a, 175).

[3] All literature is perhaps an anticipation of remembrance of the Bible, Levinas states. See Levinas, "Philosophie, justice et amour" (1983, 64). See also Rudi Visker, *Lof der zichtbaarheid* (2007, 183).

are followed by "But we are in the world" ("La vraie vie est absente. Mais nous sommes au monde"), although Rimbaud had stated: "La vraie vie est absente. Nous ne sommes pas au monde."[4] For both philosophers, philological and historical considerations are anything but decisive. Poetry escapes as if it were the general "Seinsvergessenheit'" (Heidegger) or the ignorance of the Other (Levinas), from which Western thought suffers. This is not to say that there is an "agreement" between Levinas's thought and poetry – as noted, Rimbaud stated more or less the opposite of Levinas; rather, there is a Wahlverwantschaft, an intellectual affinity in the search for a truth that is not ready at hand.

Although Levinas denies to poetry the status of the privileged medium to transmit the ultimate meaning of life, we may safely conclude that in the rejection of historico-critical tools Levinas and Heidegger agree. A historico-critical approach does not know about this proximity of text and reader. It fails to consider the unique position of the reader of the text; instead, it favours an objectifying approach to the truth of a text which can be unearthed without resorting to the position of the subject. This leads to a thoroughly truncated understanding of a literary text. For Levinas, the model and archetype of any literary text is the Bible. Hence, reading a text is more than just one activity among others; it is an ontological event, a modality of being.[5] Hermeneutics have taught us to take into account the position both of the subject and of the text, stressing that it is precisely the historical distance which enables proper understanding. Nonetheless, Levinas's approach to the text of the Talmud should not be regarded as a hermeneutical understanding in the sense by which Gadamer has introduced it, although the latter's hermeneutics may already be understood as a correction of a one-sided historical-critical approach in which the significance of the text would remain enclosed in the past.[6]

---

4 On Levinas's transformative reading of these lines from Rimbaud, see Eric Marty, "Emmanuel Levinas avec Shakespeare, Proust et Rimbaud" (2016, 5–9).
5 See also Levinas, *Éthique et infini* (1982b, 16). Hence there is no real gap between the Bible and other literature, for in a way, the meaning of life constitutes the core of all literature.
6 According to Levinas, philology reduces the text to an object and does not invite the reader to a genuine application of the text to his or her own life. See for example Levinas, *Difficile liberté* (1976, 50, 77, 95, 122, 284, 330, 343–344). See also my *Het gelaat van de Messias. Messiaanse Talmoedlezingen van Emmanuel Levinas. Vertaling, commentaar, achtergronden* [*The face of the Messiah. Levinas's Messianic Talmud Commentaries. Translation, Commentary, Backgrounds*] (1992, 265).

2 Levinas's "Hermeneutics"

The merging of historical "horizons," which is at the basis of a hermeneutical process, does not play a role in Levinas's interpretation of either the Talmud or literature in general. Levinas even claims that the Talmud, in contrast with the Bible, directly addresses the reader without resorting to supernatural manifestations to impose the truth.[7] In contrast with popular – or, rather, Christian-theological opinion – the Talmud is not a chauvinistic document limited to the well-being of the Jewish people; rather, it opens up the universal dimensions of the Hebrew Bible, which would otherwise remain a mere national history.

> Why was the Torah given in the wilderness? Because if it would have been given in the land, each tribe might have said to the other tribes: "I am better than you." It was given in the wilderness because there all are equal. (Numeri Rabba 19:26)

The book in the desert: here is the purity and renouncement of the so-called civilization, which makes a truly ethical existence possible, according to Levinas. The rootedness in this book would uproot all dichotomies between autochthonous and allochthonous existence in favour of the naked face of the other. However, the relationship to the Torah cannot be exhaustively interpreted as being rooted in the book and being uprooted from the soil, as the promise of the land remains a central element in it.[8] Still, even then the obligation of hospitality to the stranger remains in force, "for you yourself were strangers in Egypt" (Lev 19:34).

The historical distance of – let us say – fifteen hundred years is not decisive for Levinas, who claims for the Talmud the same critical attitude as for modern philosophy. The traditional division of history into a pre-critical period, ending either with Descartes or with Kant, and a post-critical one, does not seem to affect the status of the Talmud for Levinas.[9] The fact that the Talmud quotes biblical verses as authorities should not be considered as the end to critical thinking; on

---

[7] For an analysis of the differences and the similarities between Levinas and a fundamentalist approach to a holy text, see my study "The Holy Text and Violence: Levinas and Fundamentalism" (2015b).
[8] Levinas's well-known polemics against Heidegger about the rootedness in the soil, negatively contrasted with being a "stranger on earth," betray characteristics of Jewish thought as developed in the Diaspora and fail to account for the new situation of Judaism in the political arena. See for example Levinas, "Heidegger, Gagarin et nous," *Difficile liberté* (1976, 301). For the same polemics against paganism and rootedness against Simone Weil, see Levinas, "Simone Weil contre la Bible," *Difficile liberté* (1976, 183). See also my *Het gelaat van de Messias* (1992, 182). Visker takes up this issue without completely resolving it (Visker 2007, 184).
[9] Spinoza's criticism of the Bible hardly impresses Levinas, who is convinced that Spinoza has not understood the Talmud at all.

the contrary, each quotation adds a new dimension to the debate by introducing a new context.[10] By exploring the context some arguments may receive a wholly different meaning: the initial harmony of Psalm 104 turns out to be an evocation of human animalism.[11] After such a quotation the Talmudic debate simply continues with another quotation. Hence it is clear that the biblical quotations do not serve as a conclusive proof; rather, they should be considered as providing "tonality" to the debate, more or less comparable to the status of a specific human experience in phenomenology. By exploring the context of each biblical quotation, this tonality becomes ever more apparent and comprehensive. Still, there is a difference between the traditional study of the Talmud and Levinas's approach. Traditional Talmudic study, intricate as it may be, is generally confined to Jewish piety and halakhic rules that are valid only for Judaism, and fails to take into account the universal dimensions of Talmudic reasoning. It is probably Levinas's Lithuanian background, in which strict reasoning about the Talmud gets its due, which explains why he views piety and charismatic claims as not offering adequate access to Talmudic debate. He advocates instead a constant alertness to review venerated opinions in the light of universal problems.[12]

The reason why Levinas distances himself from a mere historico-critical reading becomes clear from his philosophy: neither the object/text nor the subject/reader can be understood solely from their historical contexts, not even by merging the two historical horizons. This holds well for the understanding of the Talmud and for understanding literature tout court. In a way, the Bible offers a model for understanding literature as such, by emphasizing the status of the book (and any book) as a living reality, opening up the reader to that living reality. The Talmud offers an access to the living reality in all its details and paradoxes, without being submerged into pre-critical adherence to miracles

---

10 Searching the biblical context of each quotation in order to assess the tonality of the argument is one of the hermeneutical devices that Levinas learned from his Talmud teacher Chouchani. See also the debate between Rabbi Joshua and Rabbi Eliezer, a battle of quotations from Scripture, each adding an aspect of freedom versus constraint, in *Babylonian Talmud* Sanhedrin 97b–98a, and my *Het gelaat van de Messias* (1992, 76–97 and 162).
11 See Levinas, *Quatre lectures talmudiques*, (1968, 26–33, 120). The reference to Chouchani is on page 26.
12 Here again the influence of Chouchani may be felt, who constantly and bluntly confronted his disciples with different conclusions of the same debate, mocking pious readings. See also Elie Wiesel, "Le juif errant" in *Le chant des morts* (1966), for a romanticized picture of this legendary teacher-clochard. Salomon Malka, in *Monsieur Chouchani: L'énigme du maître du xx siècle* (1994), offers many anecdotes, but apparently the Talmudic method remains for the writer an enigma.

and dogmas. Reading literature is being confronted with "sense," sense of life and sense of the other. The subject confronted with the other is ultimately confronted with a sense that transcends horizons. Levinas's understanding of the Talmud displays considerable distance from a hermeneutical process in which the subject is merely enriched by broadening his horizon. Levinas understands literature as a serious matter, dealing as it does with the meaning of life and uprooting the reading subject from its comfortable instalment in the world. On one hand, philological and historical tools as such are not sufficient to realize this confrontation. On the other hand, a traditional Talmudic approach fails to acknowledge the universal dimension of the Talmud, which in that respect shares with all serious literature the dimension of world literature, not limited by ethnic or linguistic barriers. Levinas's Talmudic lectures should not be regarded as merely another addition to the vast Rabbinic and midrashic sea of commentaries (in which they do not stand out for their intricacies). They receive their specific meaning from a philosophical perspective only, and in that respect should not be viewed as addressed solely to a Jewish audience, despite Levinas's own affirmations.[13] It is only by resorting to Levinas's philosophy that his Talmudic readings display their significance. Viewed as Talmudic readings only, they do not reach the heights of the yeshiva learning.[14] Still, his approach to the Talmud contains certain dynamics that can be of relevance even to traditional Talmudic study. The inner-Jewish debates about agriculture, prayer, repentance, and days of rest do not exhaust the multiple meaning of the Talmud, in which universal topics like human responsibility are debated through daily issues. When my ox wounds someone, am I responsible? And when a fire destroys the land of my neighbour without me knowing it, am I still responsible? Both examples transcend my consciousness of my actions and thus refer to a responsibility even for what I have not committed myself.[15]

---

13 See Levinas's first Talmudic lectures in *Difficile liberté* (1976, 83–129) and my *Het gelaat van de Messias* (1992). These lectures were followed by *Quatre lectures talmudiques* (1968); *Du sacré au saint. Cinq nouvelles lectures talmudiques* (1977); *L'au-delà du verset : Lectures et discours talmudiques* (1982a); *À l'heure des nations* (1988); and *Nouvelles lectures talmudiques* (1996).
14 Levinas limits his use of traditional Talmudic commentaries to Rashi (1040–1105) and to Maharsha (Edels) (1555–1631).
15 See Levinas, "Les dommages causés par le feu," in *Du sacré au saint* (1977, 149–180).

3 Translating Jewish Wisdom into Greek

Levinas's project: translating Jewish wisdom into Greek presupposes a paramount importance of both elements: the Jewish and the Greek. Opting for only one of them is not in order, despite the many attempts to contrast a supposedly superior Jewish thought with a Greek thinking by facile polarities, such as time versus space, concrete versus abstract, and so on.[16] Levinas's aim cannot be to consider one or two cultures as a privileged access to truth, which would then be denied to other cultures. Although Heidegger considered both Greek and German as privileged to communicate truth precisely because of their etymological reservoir which would hide-and-unveil a truth hidden to other cultures, Edmund Husserl cherished another perspective of "Greek," one which seems to be closer to Levinas's own idea. "Greek" stands for philosophy as such, not because Greece is a superior culture, but because Plato and Socrates succeeded in transcending the boundaries of their culture by addressing universal problems. To put it differently, the universal concept of mankind has been discovered by Greek philosophy. The concept of "human being" stresses the fundamental equality of all human beings, irrespective of race, language, and gender. In that perspective, all wisdoms of the world should be translated into "Greek" in order to assess their universal significance, transcending mere intuitions or chauvinist claims to truth meant for a few elect only.[17] The precarious enterprise of translating Jewish wisdom into Greek becomes immediately apparent: what could the Jewish particularism of election and being chosen add to the universal significance of humanity? The radicalism of Greek universalism should either dispense with such particularistic claims altogether or integrate them into a universal perspective, which may amount to the same. Here we encounter a central hermeneutical device of Levinas, the *transposition*. Levinas claims that the expression "Israel" should not be taken primarily as a description of an empirical reality of a given culture. Rather, it should be understood from an asymmetrical responsibility which ultimately refers to the subject: I am more responsible than the other. This responsibility cannot be described on the level of mankind or of the

---

[16] See Thorleif Boman, *Das Hebräische Denken im Vergleich mit dem Griechischen* (1952). Abraham Joshua Heschel, in *The Sabbath: Its meaning for Modern Man* (1951), likewise contrasts Jewish predilection for time with Greek affinity with space. However, this polarity does not clarify Greek culture, but merely serves as a rhetorical tool to highlight Judaism and the Sabbath as a "palace in the time." Reference to the land of Israel, the Temple, and the present Western Wall should be sufficient to discard the idea that Judaism would refrain from holy places.

[17] There is a certain Eurocentrism involved in both Husserl's and Levinas's assumption that Indian or Chinese philosophy would not be sufficiently universal to be called philosophy. However, for Levinas, the same holds for Jewish philosophy, which remains mere wisdom without being confronted with Greek philosophy.

concept "human," as I would attribute to the other the same surplus of responsibility. This would ultimately benefit myself and thereby would annul my surplus. This asymmetrical responsibility is the inequality between me and the other which lies hidden under the concept of man, serving even as the foundation of the equality of all human beings. This forms the cornerstone of Levinas's philosophy and explains why expressing this asymmetry in philosophy, i.e., in universal language, is so difficult: this asymmetrical responsibility is only valid *for me*. We should not, however, assume that this foundation of Levinas's philosophy has merely been read into the Talmud later on. More precisely, all great literature, all "world literature," according to Levinas, delves into the meaning of life, by posing the question of the humanity of mankind, sometimes even by testifying to a transcendence leading to asymmetrical responsibility.[18] Great literature is never merely national, but contains universal dimensions and is in that respect genuinely "world literature." This holds for the Bible as well. Far from being a chauvinistic plea for prerogatives destined for the Jewish people, it emphasizes the surplus of responsibility, at least if read through the lens of Rabbinical commentaries, Levinas maintains.

Indeed, this asymmetrical responsibility lies at the heart of the following Talmudic expression. The Talmud recommends passing over my rights and increasing my duties beyond a legal obligation: "lifnim mishurat ha-din."[19] The moment I would use this exhortation to remind the other of his responsibility, this would result in benefit for me: the other would refrain from his rights towards me and hence my duties would be alleviated. Perhaps this ethical attitude cannot be preached, but only applied to myself? The Sermon of the Mount contains the same asymmetrical responsibility Levinas is referring to: the exhortation to detect the beam in my own eye and not the splinter in the eye of the other can only be applied to myself (Mt 7:5). The moment I turn it into a general rule about mankind or into a sermon to be preached to others I turn my own beam

---

[18] Most frequent is Dostoyevsky's *Brothers Karamazov*, which includes the line "Everybody is responsible for all others, and I more than anyone else." Next to the importance of the great authors like Pushkin, Shakespeare, and Proust, one should note that during the pre-war period Levinas showed a remarkable interest in French Catholic writers who stress the importance of self-sacrifice, such as Léon Bloy. See also Levinas, *Oeuvres*, 1: *Carnets de captivité et autres inédits* (2009, 154, 159). About this "renouveau catholique" in France see my article "Self-Sacrifice between Constraint and Redemption: Gertrud von Le Fort's *The Song at the Scaffold*" (2016) and Richard Griffiths, *The Reactionary Revolution: The Catholic Revival in French Literature, 1870–1914* (1966, especially 149–222).

[19] See my *Het gelaat van de Messias* (1992, 102 and following) and my article "Asymmetrie, Messianismus, Inkarnation. Die Bedeutung von Emmanuel Levinas für die Christologie" (1998, especially 206); and Levinas, *Quatre lectures talmudiques* (1968, 53 and following).

again into a splinter and the splinter of the other into a beam. It is this strategy which prompted the philosopher Nietzsche to denounce Christian charity as a hidden self-interest, a criticism which holds only when this would be preached to others instead of applied to oneself. Likewise, the concept "Israel" does not primarily refer to an ethnic entity which would be bestowed with more privileges than other peoples, but should be transposed towards this asymmetrical responsibility. Hence, Israel is not so much a predicate that can only be appropriated in its ethnical sense, but should be interpreted as an ethical challenge, which can be transposed to a universal meaning by indicating *my* surplus of responsibility.[20] "The lasting significance of Israel rests in the conscience of sanctity and in the possibility to judge history; this eternity of Israel is not a privilege but a human possibility" (Levinas 1982a, 37).[21] According to Levinas, Israel is certainly a specific ethnic group, but at the same time this concept stands for a people having received the Law and as such stands for mankind being conscious of its obligations.[22] The universality of the concept "Israel," its translation into Greek, cannot be realized by a mere equation of Israel and mankind. Such an approach would come down to an assimilation of Jewish values to Western insights, by which Judaism would lose its prophetic potential. The "burning bush" would then be no more than an illusion instead of an attachment to transcendence which goes beyond self-preservation. The universalism of the concept "Israel" happens when I realize that implicitly the ethical challenge to Israel denotes *my* strictly personal – but in that respect without any limitations as to religion, ethnicity, and so on – responsibility towards the other. The patriarch Jacob – later named Israel – was not prompted by mere self-interest when he took the clothes of his brother, Esau, in order to deceive their father; he took over the responsibilities of his brother (Levinas 1968, 181). And when Jacob was afraid to meet his brother at the Jabbok, he had not forgotten the divine blessing that God would

---

[20] There is a striking similarity between this idea of Levinas and the patristic criticism of the concept of Israel as a mere ethnic category, as appropriated by the Jewish people. However, the patristic emphasis upon "Israel" as a divine surplus that cannot be appropriated by the Jewish people has led to an appropriation of the same concept by the Church! In addition, this appropriation is only partial, for when it comes to the biblical judgments and condemnations of Israel, the Church Fathers relegate them to the Jewish people. For a biblical debate about who the "children of Abraham" actually are, but without subsequent appropriation, see John the Baptist in Mt 3:9.
[21] See also Levinas, *Quatre lectures talmudiques* (1968, 181).
[22] See Levinas, "Judaïsme et révolution," in *Du sacré au saint* (1977,18) as well as "Textes messianiques," in *Difficile liberté* (1976, 112), and my *Het gelaat van de Messias* (1992, 122–124). Levinas learned this insight from his Talmud teacher Chouchani. Regrettably, the publications on Chouchani delve into the mythical, without paying attention to his approach to the Talmud.

protect him, but his conscience dictated to him that he had not yet realized his responsibility towards his brother (Levinas 1976, 112; Poorthuis 1992, 122–124). It is clear that Jacob's numinous encounter with the nightly opponent (Gen 32), which offers ample room for connecting the divine with the tremendous and mysterious, receives instead a wholly ethical interpretation in rabbinic tradition, followed herein by Levinas. For Levinas, the numinous coincides with idolatry. This seems to me one of the highly debatable elements in Levinas's philosophy.[23]

The divine revelation at the burning bush and even the revelation of the Torah cannot be viewed as a possession entrusted to a specific people while excluding the rest of mankind. Again we should speak of a translation of Jewish wisdom into Greek by *transposition*: the Torah is not a specific knowledge but a relationship with the Infinite. The Talmud teaches: "the Torah is not an obligation for you" (Babylonian Talmud *Menakhot* 99b). This is explained as: it is not an obligation that can be fulfilled in order to get rid of it. It is a relationship with the other that becomes more demanding in the measure that I deepen it. In earlier texts, even in the previously unpublished documents, Levinas even speaks about the "felix culpa," a happy guilt. The expression stems from the Christian liturgy of the Easter night in which Adam is said to have a "happy guilt," because it made the redemption necessary.[24] This should, however, not be interpreted as an alibi for one's own failures! According to Levinas, "felix culpa" presupposes the fertility of time and the Messiah as the apogee of history, without destroying time, but making forgiveness as a rupture with the past possible.

4 Biblical Humanism

Transposed towards the relation of the other human being, the Torah as an obligation that cannot be fulfilled testifies to a responsibility which increases the more I respond to it. To put it in relational terms: the more I understand the other by approaching him, the more I will realize his needs, which merely

---

[23] Not only Levinas's attitude towards non-biblical religions, but even his attitude towards other Jewish strands such as Hasidism and Kabbala are highly influenced by his Lithuanian Talmudic background. See my article "Gott steigt herab. Levinas über Kenose und Inkarnation" (2006).
[24] See Levinas, *Carnets de captivité et autres inédits*, Oeuvres 1 (2009, 81); *Difficile liberté* (1976, 91,94, 188); and my *Het gelaat van de Messias* (1992, 48–49, 60, 107, 253). See also my article "De betekenis van de recent gepubliceerde vroege notities van Levinas" [The significance of the recently published early annotations of Levinas] (2015a). It seems that Levinas had been quite impressed by Christian notions of forgiveness and rebirth before the war, as is also clear in his "Quelques réflexions sur la philosophie de l'hitlérisme (1934).

enhances my responsibility.²⁵ The Torah evokes the relationship with the transcendence as an infinite obligation towards the other. In that respect, the Talmud is loyal to the biblical message, in which the obligations towards the other human being are accompanied by the solemn assurance: "I am the Lord" (Lev 19). Levinas refers to "biblical humanism," while indicating how the obligation towards the fellow human being is ipso facto religious, even without me realizing it. Levinas recognizes this biblical humanism in the famous scene of the Last Judgement when both the righteous and the wicked stand before the Son of Man (Mt 25: 31–46). The wicked people had not met the Son of Man during their lives, but neither had the righteous recognized him when they visited the sick and the prisoner, fed the hungry, etc.²⁶

We should be aware that Levinas does not use the concept of the Son of Man to clarify the "condition humaine," but to indicate the status of the other, which can only be understood from an I–thou-perspective and which increases *my* responsibility, not that of the other. Undoubtedly this can be of great significance for Christology. Other texts about Christ likewise do not clarify the "human condition" either, nor do they portray Christ exclusively as the other who has done it all for me (and possibly creating an alibi for my responsibility). These texts focus instead upon *my* position, by increasing *my* responsibility without enabling me to demand that of *the other*.²⁷ This transposition of concepts from a descriptive level to the level not of ethics as such but of asymmetry between me and the other, creating as it were a schism in the universe, constitutes the kernel of Levinas's Talmud hermeneutics and of *world literature* dealing with the meaning of life. Simultaneously, this asymmetry constitutes the cornerstone of his philosophy.

No doubt the hermeneutical device of transposition leaves much to be debated: what is the relation between a historical people (Israel) and the subject? In what way does this paradigmatic status of Israel allow other peoples and wisdoms to fulfil a similar role? It seems obvious that Israel as paradigm for a responsible humanity should not claim any exclusivism, at least not insofar as it concerns the philosophy of Levinas. The famous Talmudic story about the peoples of the world being present at Sinai and, although having been offered the Torah, refusing to accept it, whereas Israel willingly accepts the Torah,

---

25 See Levinas, *L'au-delà du verset* (1982a, 46) and my *Het gelaat van de Messias* (1992, 102).
26 See "Discussion d'ensemble" in *La révélation* (1977, 224–225).
27 A striking example is the key text of the kenosis (Phil 2:6–11), which should not be read as an event that exclusively concerns Christ, but is introduced by: "Let the same attitude be in you as was in Jesus Christ ... " See my article "Asymmetrie, Messianismus, Inkarnation" (1998). The concept of the Messiah in Levinas's "Textes messianiques" in *Difficile liberté* (1976) likewise clarifies my position in respect to that of the other, in both cases increasing my responsibility.

reflects a staunch chauvinism, historically perhaps fostered by rival claims of the Church to be the true heir of the revelation. It is striking then that the Talmud adds another story in which the people stands *under* the mountain, being threatened with death if they refuse to accept the Torah (Babylonian Talmud *Avodah Zarah* 2b). Hence it was not because of moral superiority and not from free will that Israel accepted the Torah!

Levinas recognizes here a responsibility based not upon a free decision but upon a relationship preceding it, without, however, identifying it with slavery.[28] This relationship even precedes the consciousness of oneself and hence opens up an immemorial past, a past that has never been in the full light of the present, and hence can be considered as an-archic. Again, what is at stake here is not a description of the special status of Israel receiving the Torah, but a debate about human freedom vis-à-vis my responsibility towards the other. In this one sentence both the Jewish wisdom of my unique responsibility and the Greek realm of reflecting upon the human being as a universal and egalitarian concept come together. Although my unique responsibility may seem to evaporate in front of the universal and collective and political realm of the human society, in reality the latter egalitarian level is tributary to the asymmetrical responsibility that precedes it. The full light of reason and Western philosophy may be oblivious to this notion, but the Jewish religion needs this light to bring to the fore the universal dimensions of its religion.[29] No wonder, then, that Levinas quotes the Talmud in a slightly ironic fashion. A student, Ben Dima, comes to ask his master and uncle, Rabbi Ishmael, whether he is allowed to learn Greek. Overly confident, the student professes to have "finished" his study of Torah. His master then quotes the Bible: "the words of Torah will not leave your lips and you will meditate them day and night" (Jos 1:8), and recommends his disciple to find a time in which it is neither day nor night (Babylonian Talmud *Menakhot* 100a). Although the story intends to state that this is impossible, Levinas detects here his own project of translating Jewish wisdom into Greek, which requires neither the option of remaining completely in the dark nor of entering the clear daylight, but embracing the domain of the twilight.[30] Neither the blind subjection to religious authority

---

28 See Levinas, "'La tentation de la tentation'. Texte du traité 'Chabat'," *Quatre lectures talmudiques* (Levinas, 1968, 80–84).
29 Commentators of Levinas such as Derrida in his "Violence et métaphysique" refer to James Joyce's *Ulysses*, which in a way describes Western culture in search of its Hebraic origin: "Japhet in search of a father." The identities of the two main protagonists, Stephen Daedalus and the Jewish Leopold Bloom, are inextricably intertwined: "Jewgreek is greekjew. Extremes meet."
30 See Levinas, *L'au-delà du verset* (1982a, 42). In a different context, this idea of philosophy in the twilight is strikingly similar to Hegel's famous assertion, in the preface to *Elements of*

nor an autonomous rejection of religion in favour of an enlightened reason form the valid alternatives here. The Greek language spoken at the royal courts, stands for the political realm which tends to suppress the individual in favour of the collective. A protest in the name of the individual seems unable to challenge the political order. Unless a certain notion of the individual is at stake, without which the political order, with its sense of justice and of equality of all human beings, is not even thinkable. Unless it is the justice done to the individual other which constitutes the *raison d'être* of the political order as such. What prompts the individual to accept the collective realm of the state if not as a necessary guarantee of his own responsibility towards the other and towards all others? Even my individual responsibility towards the other in front of me would remain an *egoisme à deux* if it would not be extended to the third and fourth, in short to the realm of society, even risking an anonymous administration instead of a personal solidarity. The objection that Levinas's philosophy would ignore the political realm fails to recognize the prime importance of the Greek language vis-à- vis the Jewish wisdom and the indispensable ambition to translate Jewish wisdom into Greek. To be precise, Levinas distinguishes between the Greek language, into which the Jewish wisdom should be translated, and the Greek wisdom, which is considered incompatible with Jewish wisdom. In other words: for the suppression of alterity in Western philosophy to be denounced by Jewish wisdom, translation into Greek is necessary.[31] It is only in that in-between that the burning bush can be the medium of revelation rather than being what it afterwards seemed to be: a thorny bush without any visible trace of something special.

Bibliography

Boman, Thorleif. *Das Hebräische Denken im Vergleich mit dem Griechischen*. Göttingen: Vandenhoeck & Ruprecht, 1952.
Griffiths, Richard. *The Reactionary Revolution: The Catholic Revival in French Literature, 1870–1914*. London: Constable, 1966.
Hegel, Georg Wilheim Friedrich. *Elements of the Philosophy of Right*. Ed. Allen W. Wood. Trans. H. B. Nisbet. Cambridge: Cambridge University Press, 1991.
Heidegger, Martin. "Wozu Dichter?" *Holzwege*. Frankfurt am Main: Klostermann, 1980. 265–316.

---

the Philosophy of Right, that "the owl of Minerva begins its flight only with the onset of dusk" (Hegel 1991, 23).
31 See Levinas, *À l'heure des nations* (1988, 64–65), a distinction that can be found in Babylonian Talmud *Baba Kamma* 83a as well.

Heschel, Abraham Joshua. *The Sabbath: Its meaning for Modern Man*. New York: Farrar, Straus and Giroux, 1951.
Levinas, Emmanuel. "Quelques réflexions sur la philosophie de l'hitlérisme. *Esprit* 2.26 (1934): 199–208.
Levinas, Emmanuel. *Quatre lectures talmudiques*. Paris: Minuit, 1968.
Levinas, Emmanuel. *Difficile liberté*. Paris: Albin Michel, 1976.
Levinas, Emmanuel. *Du sacré au saint. Cinq nouvelles lectures talmudiques*. Paris. Minuit, 1977.
Levinas, Emmanuel. *L'au-delà du verset: Lectures et discours talmudiques*. Paris: Minuit, 1982a.
Levinas, Emmanuel. *Éthique et infini*. Paris: Fayard, 1982b.
Levinas, Emmanuel. "Philosophie, justice et amour" (interview with R. Fornet-Betancourt and A. Gomez-Müller). *Concordia* 3 (1983): 59–73.
Levinas, Emmanuel. *À l'heure des nations*. Paris: Minuit, 1988.
Levinas, Emmanuel. *Nouvelles lectures talmudiques*. Paris: Minuit, 1996.
Levinas, Emmanuel. *Oeuvres*, 1: *Carnets de captivité et autre inédits*. Eds. Rodolphe Calin and Catherine Chalier. Paris: Grasset, 2009.
Malka, Salomon. *Monsieur Chouchani: L'énigme du maître du xx siècle*. Paris: J.C. Lattes 1994.
Marty, Eric. "Emmanuel Levinas avec Shakespeare, Proust et Rimbaud." *Cairn* 5 (26) (2016): 5–9.
Poorthuis, Marcel. *Het gelaat van de Messias. Messiaanse Talmoedlezingen van Emmanuel Levinas*. Vertaling, commentaar, achtergronden [*The face of the Messiah. Levinas's Messianic Talmud Commentaries. Translation, Commentary, Backgrounds*]. Zoetermeer: Boekencentrum, 1992.
Poorthuis, Marcel. "Asymmetrie, Messianismus, Inkarnation. Die Bedeutung von Emmanuel Levinas für die Christologie." *Emmanuel Levinas – eine Herausforderung für die christliche Theologie*. Ed. Joseph Wohlmuth. Paderborn et al.: Ferdinand Schöningh, 1998. 201–213.
Poorthuis, Marcel. "Gott steigt herab. Levinas über Kenose und Inkarnation." *Apres vous. Denkbuch fur Emmanuel Levinas (1906–1995)*. Eds. F. Mieting and C. von Wolzogen. Frankfurt am Main: Neue Kritik, 2006. 196–212.
Poorthuis, Marcel. "De betekenis van de recent gepubliceerde vroege notities van Levinas." *Mededelingen van de Levinas Studiekring / Journal of the Dutch-Flemish Levinas Society* XX (2015a): 10–18. http://www.duyndam.demon.nl/E-Journal_Mededelingen_van_de_Levinas_Studiekring_Jrg20_2015.pdf (20 November 2019).
Poorthuis, Marcel. "The Holy Text and Violence: Levinas and Fundamentalism." *Debating Levinas' Legacy*. Eds. A. Breitling, C. Bremmers, and A. Cools. Leiden: Brill, 2015b. 144–163.
Poorthuis, Marcel. "Self-Sacrifice between Constraint and Redemption: Gertrud von Le Fort's *The Song at the Scaffold*." *Sacrifice in Modernity: Community*, Ritual, *Identity: From Nationalism and Nonviolence to Health Care and Harry Potter*. Leiden: Brill, 2016. 241–254.
Ricoeur, Paul, et al. (Eds.). *La révélation*. Brussels: Presses de l'Université Saint-Louis, 1977.
Visker, Rudi. *Lof der zichtbaarheid*. Amsterdam: SUN, 2007.
Wiesel, Elie. *Le chant des morts*. Paris: Seuil, 1966.

Part III: **Poetry**

Annelies Schulte Nordholt
Levinas and the Poetic Word: Writing with Baudelaire?

1 Introduction

When Levinas's youth works were first published, it was a surprise to discover that he had also been a poet. The volume *Eros, littérature et philosophie* (Levinas 2013) includes a series of poems in Russian, written in the beginning of the 1920s, when Levinas was sixteen or seventeen. Poetry – and literature in general – was Levinas's first love, and these unpublished works show how, in his youth, he hesitated for a time between literature and philosophy. This biographical fact explains both his sensitivity to poetry and literature and his incisive comments on his favourite authors: Shakespeare, Baudelaire, Proust, Celan, Blanchot and several others. It also explains the great number of literary quotations in his philosophical works.

These literary references have been recorded with great precision, for instance in the *Levinas Concordance* (Ciocan & Hansel 2005), but few commentators have studied them closely. Behind the detailed examination of these references, what is at stake is Levinas's relationship to literature, which is, at the very least, ambiguous, as many readers of Levinas know. In an earlier article, I called it the ambiguity between "aesthetical temptation" and "ethical resistance" to this temptation (Schulte Nordholt 1999). Repeatedly, Levinas insists on how poetry, with its enchanting rhythms, fascinates and carries away the artist (and the reader) to a realm where he is no longer responsible for himself; at the same time, however, he sees art, and especially poetry – or, perhaps we should say, some art, some poetry – as a language which may make an ethical relation of proximity and responsibility possible. This explains how Levinas is alternately full of admiration and full of horror for the literary work.

In *Altered Reading: Levinas and Literature* (1999), Jill Robbins provides a thorough examination of Levinas's relationship to literature. Like Robert Eaglestone (1997), she underlines how Levinas's positions on literature shifted over the years, from his condemnatory views in his early article "La réalité et son ombre" (Levinas 1948) to the much more positive views in his later essays on Celan and Agnon in *Noms propres* (Levinas 1976), where poetry seems able to realize the ethical relation to the other. Robbins pays close attention to Levinas's practice of quoting and what it means for his relationship with literature. This culminates in a perceptive interpretation of Levinas's repeated quotation of Rimbaud's famous formula "Je est un autre." More recently, the question has been taken up by Alain Paul

∂ Open Access. © 2021 Annelies Schulte Nordholt, published by De Gruyter. This work is licensed under the Creative Commons Attribution 4.0 International License.
https://doi.org/10.1515/9783110668926-009

Toumayan (2009), who provides a rather swift but clear survey of Levinas's readings of nineteenth-century French literature, focusing on the Baudelaire case.

In the following, while relying on these former studies, I wish to more closely examine Levinas's reading of Baudelaire, especially in *De l'existence à l'existant* (Levinas 1947).[1] In this early work, the network of literary quotations is markedly dense, especially in the chapter "Existence sans monde." Literary quotations form an intertextual network here and include Shakespeare, Racine, Rimbaud, Hoffmann, Huysmans, Maupassant, Valéry, and Zola. This is also where Baudelaire is most present. This seems therefore the appropriate text by which to investigate the impact of Baudelaire's poetry on Levinas's thought and writing practice. How do Levinas's quotations of Baudelaire function? Are they mere illustrations of his argument and shared cultural references? Or does Baudelaire's poetry have a different, more incisive status, determining Levinas's thought more profoundly? These questions require not just contextual reading but also an examination of how these quotations are inserted into the text. As Robbins observes, Levinas's literary quotes are mostly "covert, non-citational references to a shared literary heritage" (Robbins 1999, 90). Baudelaire is often quoted literally, but without quotation marks and without mentioning the title of the poem or reproducing the disposition of the verses. In this way, Levinas integrates verse into his prose, weaving it into his writing. In some cases, as Robbins shows, he may "overturn" or even betray what he is quoting. The real question, however, is not so much Levinas's fidelity to the literary text but what is at stake in his practice of literary texts, of Baudelaire's poems in particular.[2]

2 Poetry, Totality, and Infinity

Ah! ne jamais sortir des Nombres et des Etres![3] This final verse of "Le Gouffre" is the most frequently quoted Baudelaire line in Levinas's work, from *De l'évasion* to *De l'existence à l'existant*, *Totalité et infini*, and to his essays on Maurice Blanchot. Levinas rightly sees this realm of numbers and beings as an expression of what he calls the atmosphere of Being, of totality, and reads Baudelaire's exclamation as a desperate cry: "how terrible it would be never to get out of numbers and beings!" His whole philosophy, from its very start – as the title *De*

---

[1] In my quotations I will use the English translation by Alphonso Linguis, published in 1978.
[2] Baudelaire, *Les fleurs du mal* (1961). For the English quotations from Baudelaire, I will use the translation by William Aggeler, *The Flowers of Evil* (1954).
[3] "Ah! Never to go out from Numbers and Beings!" ("The Abyss," Baudelaire 1954).

l'évasion shows – is an attempt to escape this atmosphere, to go beyond it. In *De l'évasion*, he speaks of "a profound need to get out of Being" ["un besoin profound de sortir de l'être"] (Levinas 1982, 97) and to break with Heideggerian ontology. Here, Toumayan goes astray when interpreting the Baudelaire line as "the exclamation of ironic nostalgia for empiricism" (Toumayan 2009, 138). There is no irony in Levinas's quoting of this line, but the recognition of a longing for the Infinite that he shares with Baudelaire. But the question remains: may literature, poetry, be one of the ways of quitting the atmosphere of "numbers and beings"? Or are they bound with totality?

We may take this question further by examining the two poetry quotations that open and close *Totalité et Infini*: a Rimbaud and a Baudelaire quotation from, respectively, the *incipit* and *excipit* of the book. The first is: "'La vraie vie est absente.' Mais nous sommes au monde."[4] This famous phrase from Rimbaud's "Une saison en enfer" is a confession put in the mouth of Verlaine, who complains about his ruined life and says farewell to writing. But Rimbaud's original line runs slightly differently: "La vraie vie est absente. Nous ne sommes *pas* au monde." Levinas's quotation is thus a contrapuntal one, as if to say that Rimbaud's "real life" is but an illusion since one cannot escape the world, since we are irremediably bound to the world. But this being bound to the world enables us to feel a metaphysical longing for the infinite, for something beyond the world. This is an example showing how Levinas's quotations are certainly more than a mere illustration.[5] The same goes for the last sentence of the book, where the "heroic existence" of the individual is described in Baudelaire's words as the victory of "l'ennui, fruit de la morne incuriosité qui prend les proportions de l'immortalité" (Levinas 1980, 284) – the two last lines of the second strophe of "Spleen" no. 76:

> Rien n'égale en longueur les boiteuses journées
> Quand sous les lourds flocons des neigeuses années
> *L'ennui, fruit de la morne incuriosité,*
> *Prend les proportions de l'immortalité.*[6]

---

4 "Real life is absent. But we are in the world."
5 See also the detailed analysis by Robbins of this line and of the much quoted "Je est un autre." In her diachronic reading, she comes to a different conclusion: Levinas overturns, betrays the Rimbaud line, making it express the dismissal of any ethical meaning of literature (Robbins 1999, 119–131).
6 In all quotations, the verses quoted by Levinas are in italics.

> Nothing is so long as those limping days,
> When under the heavy flakes of snowy years,
> Ennui, the fruit of dismal apathy,
> Becomes as large as immortality.   (Baudelaire 1954, v. 17–20)

In the conclusion of *Totalité et Infini*, the quote is used as a last recapitulation of the opposition between totality and infinity. In his chapter on Eros, Levinas has just described fecundity: through Desire, we have reached "being for the Other" and goodness. To this being for the Other, he opposes the "isolated and heroic individual" imprisoned in his own subjectivity. For Levinas, the Baudelaire verses about *ennui* are the very expression of that identical I imprisoned in itself.

Baudelairian *ennui* (or Spleen) is not an accidental reference here. It plays a primordial role in Levinas's elaboration of being and of his conception of the self as an identity closed within itself, "condemned to being." This self and its "birth" out of the "there is" is the departure point of Levinas's reflexion. This is most clearly visible in *De l'existence à l'existant*, and it may account for the great density of Baudelaire quotations. Let us now see how, in this text, *The Flowers of Evil* accompanies the successive moments of Levinas's demonstration, from fatigue to work and from work to "the horror of the night."

3 Fatigue and Spleen

The first reference to Baudelaire is in the first part of *De l'existence à l'existant*. Here, Levinas tries to understand the relationship of the existent with his/her existence, with the mere fact of existing. This relationship is experienced in phenomena that precede reflexion, such as fatigue and laziness. To Levinas's view, fatigue is not accidental, and laziness is not a moral choice. More essentially, they are "positions taken with regard to existence" (Levinas 1978, 24). Fatigue is a "weariness [that] concerns existence itself" (Levinas 1978, 24), it is "the reminder of a commitment to existence [. . .]" (Levinas 1978, 24). This explains why Levinas sees fatigue as a refusal of that contract, as a desire to escape existence itself. It is a first sketch of evasion, but it remains aimless at first. At this point, a Baudelaire quote is inserted: "Like for Baudelaire's true travellers, it is a matter of parting for the sake of parting" (Levinas 1978, 25). This is a clear reference to "Le Voyage":

> *Mais les vrais voyageurs sont ceux-là seuls qui partent*
> *Pour partir* ; cœurs légers, semblables aux ballons,
> De leur fatalité jamais ils ne s'écartent,
> Et, sans savoir pourquoi, disent toujours: Allons!   ("Le Voyage," v. 17–20)[7]

---

[7] But the true voyagers are only those who leave
     Just to be leaving; hearts light, like balloons,
     They never turn aside from their fatality
     And without knowing why they always say: "Let's go!"   (Baudelaire 1954, v. 15–18)

The theme of the journey seems quite innocent at first view: an invitation to evasion.[8] But let us remember that "Le Voyage" is the last poem of *The Flowers of Evil*: it closes part VI, the title of which is "La Mort." It is a huge poem of 144 verses, divided into eight parts, and begins with the nostalgic picture of the child with his atlas, dreaming about far countries:

> Pour l'enfant, amoureux de cartes et d'estampes,
> L'univers est égal à son vaste appétit.
> (v. 1–2)[9]

But "Le Voyage" is a journey denouncing all journeys – be they imaginary or real – as an illusion, since under different skies – tropical or polar – "Nous nous sommes souvent ennuyés, comme ici" (v. 60).[10] Wherever we were, we were bored; we suffered ennui, in the strong, Baudelairian sense of the word, of a *taedium vitae*. Travelling around the world is nothing else but travelling around one's prison – to quote the words of Marguerite Yourcenar's Zeno in *The Abyss*[11] – since it is impossible to get rid of oneself:

> Le monde, monotone et petit, aujourd'hui,
> Hier, demain, toujours, nous fait voir notre image :
> Une oasis d'horreur dans un désert d'ennui.
> (v. 110–112)[12]

Travelling is an illusory evasion, since we are riveted to ourselves, imprisoned in our poor identity with ourselves: here we already find the heroic and isolated individual of which Levinas speaks in the last lines of *Totality and Infinity*. For Baudelaire, at the end of "Le Voyage," the only exit (but is it an exit?) is death.[13] We are here at the darkest, most desperate point of *The Flowers of Evil*. Levinas, in his turn, will find a very different solution to the monotonous "plot" ("intrigue") of the subject: the revelation of the face of the Other, of Infinity. But on the side of Totality, he does share Baudelaire's experience of being riveted to being, and thinks the utter consequences of this in *De l'existence à l'existant*.

---

8 Toumayan sees it as "a poetic icon of evasion" (Toumayan 2009, 139).
9 "To a child who is fond of maps and engravings, / The universe is the size of his immense hunger" (Baudelaire 1954, v. 1–2)
10 "[. . .] we were often bored, as we are here." (Baudelaire 1954, v. 60)
11 "Who would be so besotted as to die without having made at least the round of this, his prison?" (Yourcenar 1976).
12 "The world, monotonous and small, today, / Yesterday, tomorrow, always, shows us our image: / An oasis of horror in a desert of ennui!" (Baudelaire 1954, v. 110–112).
13 Toumayan misses this by seeing "Le Voyage" as merely providing Levinas with "a salient poetic figure of evasion" (Toumayan 2009, 138).

The experience of being riveted to being is the very definition of Baudelaire's Spleen or "Ennui." Originally, Spleen was a Romantic malaise, but in *The Flowers of Evil* it becomes the existential feeling of imprisonment in being and in a circular, irremissible temporality. The volume is constructed as a series of grandiose attempts to escape Ennui and to access another dimension, which he calls the Ideal. The Ideal takes on many different forms, from memory to sensation, eroticism, travelling, dreaming, imagination, music, painting, drunkenness (wine and "artificial paradises"), and poetry, to the infinite and finally to death. They are all manifestations of the Ideal, routes of evasion that may only offer a provisional relief. That is why the tension between Spleen and Ideal – the two terms are juxtaposed in the title of the first part of the volume – will never be resolved.

In the Levinas passage on laziness, the reference to Baudelaire's "Voyage" is therefore less banal than it seems at first sight. In the same passage, he states clearly that "in weariness, we want to escape from existence itself [. . .]" (Levinas 1978, 25). That is exactly what Baudelaire does at the end of *The Flowers of Evil*: to abdicate existence.

4 From Fatigue to Work

In the next chapter of *De l'existence à l'existant*, "Fatigue and the Instant," Levinas shows how fatigue is intimately linked to its opposite, work and effort. He tries to get hold of the event of fatigue, the instant of its accomplishment, and compares fatigue to "a hand little by little letting slip what it is trying to hold on to [. . .]" (Levinas 1978, 30). Fatigue thus exists only in its relationship to effort and work. But for Levinas, work is very far from being a self-realization where the slave discovers that he is a master, as in Hegel's *Phenomenology*. On the contrary, work and effort "reveal a subjection which compromises our freedom. [. . .] We are yoked to our task" (Levinas 1978, 31) This slavery is due neither to the nature of the task (which may be heavy or light) nor to the fact that work is imposed upon us. It may be freely chosen, light, and yet it is a servitude because of its relation to the instant: working is acting and acting is "[to take up] an instant as an inevitable present" (Levinas 1978, 34). In that sense, work is a yoke, a "condemnation" (Levinas 1978, 34). This present is unavoidable; therefore Levinas sees it as an "eternity." At this point, he turns to Baudelaire once more:

> This is at the bottom of Baudelaire's profound meditation on skeleton's digging. Existence seems to him to be both irremediably eternal and doomed to pain: unceasingly, alas, we shall perhaps have to upturn the stony soil in some unknown land and to push at the heavy spade with our naked and bleeding foot. (Levinas 1978, 34)

The last three lines are a literal quotation from Baudelaire's "Le Squelette laboureur." This poem was inspired by an engraving of a skeleton ploughing the earth with a spade. One may think of Holbein's engraving "Adam Cultivating the Soil": an image of Adam after the Fall (Fig. 1). He cultivates the earth, with Death at his side.

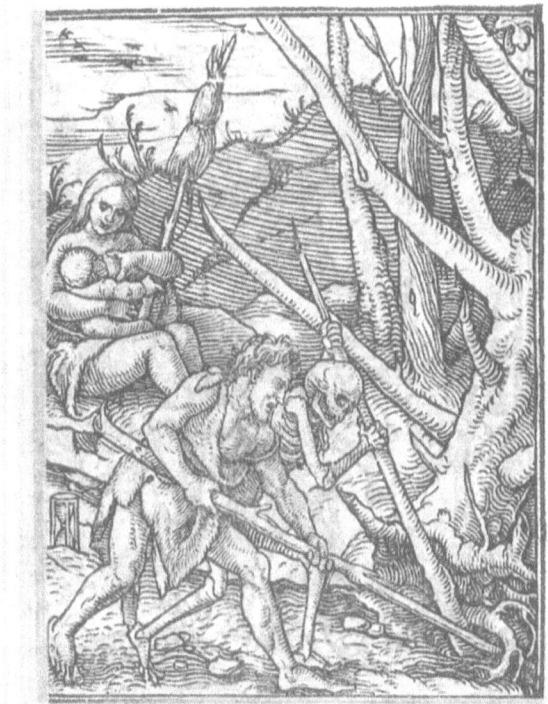

Fig. 1: Hans Holbein, "Adam Tills the Soil," woodcarving from *The Dance of Death* (1538), Collection of the Rijksmuseum, https://publicdomainreview.org/collections/hans-holbeins-dance-of-death-1523-5/, consulted on 12–11–19.

In the poem the lyrical I addresses the skeleton and rhetorically asks him what lesson he wants to teach mankind. Does he want to show that even death is not the end?

> Qu'envers nous le Néant est traître ;
> Que tout, même la Mort, nous ment ;
> Et que *sempiternellement*,
> Hélas ! il nous faudra peut-être

Dans quelque pays inconnu
Ecorcher la terre revêche
Et pousser une lourde bêche
Sous notre pied sanglant et nu ?
　　　　　　　　(v. 25–32)[14]

Though he does mention Baudelaire and the title of this poem, and reproduces its literal phrasing, Levinas integrates these verses into his own text. He does not use quotation marks or italics and makes prose of it. In this way, Baudelaire's lines become an integral part of Levinas's own meditation on work and labour. It is not clear where the quotation starts or ends, unless one knows the poem quite well.

In Baudelaire, the skeleton with a spade is a cruel image of human condition after the Fall. The skeleton pictures the mortal condition of Man: while waiting to die (and to be buried in his turn), men are condemned to cultivate the soil "to the sweat of their brow," as is said in *Genesis*. Like Adam, men are exiled from Paradise ("in some unknown land"); they suffer and there is no end to their labour, which is subjected to time. Also, to Levinas's view, work is "an ancient curse" (Levinas 1978, 34). Man does not work in order to feed himself but the instant of the effort "condemns" him to the present, therefore to endless existence. The word "sempiternellement," counting six of the eight syllables of this line, beautifully expresses this endlessness. However, the idea of the instant also implies that the present of fatigue may be assumed by the subject. This first happens in something very simple: rest. Levinas etymologically reads the word "repos" as "re-pos": literally "the act of positing oneself on the ground" (Levinas 1978, 36). It is the first step of the "hypostasis," leading to the birth of the subject. This is where Levinas clearly leaves behind Baudelaire, for whom there is no rest, not even beyond death.

5 "Silence and the Horror of Darkness"

The following chapter of *De l'existence à l'existant* is about the world: the reign of all that is given, and not only as a tool for action or work. It is the world

---

14 "That Annihilation betrays us, / That all, and even Death, lies to us, / And that, forever and ever, / Alas! we shall be forced perhaps / In some unknown country / To scrape the hard and stony ground / And to push a heavy spade in / With our bare and bleeding feet?" (Baudelaire 1954, v. 25–32).

where we act, walk, enjoy; in brief, it is the world where we live. This is what Levinas will later call totality. While examining this dimension, he once more takes up his favourite Baudelaire quotation from "Le Gouffre": "Western philosophy and civilisation never get out of 'numbers and beings,' remain conditioned by the secular world" (Levinas 1978, 38). Indeed, only the "sanctity" of the face of the Other may enable us to go beyond totality. But here we are already anticipating, since the word "sanctity" does not appear at this stage, where Levinas has a single aim: to get hold of the event, the birth of the subject in the anonymity of being. In order to get there, he first goes back to what lays below being: "existence without a world." He then proceeds to describe two experiences that enable us "to withdraw from the world" (Levinas 1978, 52) and confront us to the "there is" (*il y a*). One of them is art (painting, poetry), the other is the night.

I will not repeat here Levinas's well-known and much commented analyses of art[15]: as an image distancing itself from representation, modern art "makes [things] stand out from the world" (Levinas 1978, 52), it makes them literally "exotic," by bringing them back to their original materiality, their thickness. Painting lapses into forms and colour, poetry gives priority to "the musicality of verse" (Levinas 1978, 54), that is, to prosody, rhythm and rime. Here, Levinas elaborates a theory of art but does not refer to any concrete work of art. Only in the following paragraph, the famous description of night as "the very experience of the 'there is'" (Levinas 1978, 58), do we see a plethora of literary references appear, to Baudelaire and Shakespeare but also to fantastical literature. The central question is: why does night have a vaguely threatening character? Where does the instinctive fear of darkness, which is so beautifully described in fantastical tales like Hoffmann's, Poe's, or Maupassant's come from? Here is Levinas's answer:

> The things of the day world then do not in the night become the source of 'the horror of darkness' because our look cannot catch them in their 'unforeseeable plots'; on the contrary, they get their fantastic character from this horror. Darkness does not only modify their contours for vision; it reduces them to undetermined, anonymous being, which sweats in them. (Levinas 1978, 59)

The end of this passage gives the explanation: night horrifies us because in it, we sense the undetermined, anonymous, and ineluctable "there is." The key

---

15 See for instance Schulte Nordholt, "Tentation esthétique et exigence éthique. Lévinas et l'œuvre littéraire" (1999).

words of this passage – "the horror of darkness" – come directly from Baudelaire, from his poem "Les Chats":

> Les amoureux fervents et les savants austères
> Aiment également, dans leur mûre saison,
> Les chats puissants et doux, orgueil de la maison,
> Qui comme eux sont frileux et comme eux sédentaires.
>
> Amis de la science et de la volupté
> Ils cherchent le silence et *l'horreur des ténèbres* ;
> L'Erèbe les eût pris pour ses coursiers funèbres
> S'ils pouvaient au servage incliner leur fierté.
>
> (v. 1–8)[16]

This admiring portrait of cats posits them as the proud companions of man but also, of course, as nocturnal, mysterious animals. Loving darkness, they are related to night and therewith to death, to the point that the god of the underworld would have liked them to help transport the dead. But this context is less important here than in the former quotations. The formula "the horror of darkness" is between quotation marks but Levinas does not give the source: it is only the formula that he finds important here. He uses it in order to underline the central thesis of this first part of *De l'existence à l'existant*: the disappearing of things and beings in the night (or in art) does not result in nothingness but in an "anonymous and impersonal existence," which Levinas calls "obsessive and horrible."[17] The horror of being questions Heidegger, criticizing his "Angst" in the confrontation with death. The original and strongest experience, to Levinas's view, is not the fear of nothingness but the fear of endless being, of "the impossibility of death" (Levinas 1978, 62):

> We are opposing then, the horror of the night, "*the silence and horror of the shades*," to Heideggerian anxiety, the fear of being to the fear of nothingness. While anxiety, in Heidegger, brings about "being toward death," grasped and somehow understood, the horror of the night "with no exits" which "does not answer" is an irremissible existence. "*Tomorrow, alas! one will still have to live*" – a tomorrow contained in the infinity of today. (Levinas 1978, 63)

---

16 "Both ardent lovers and austere scholars / Love in their mature years / The strong and gentle cats, pride of the house, / Who like them are sedentary and sensitive to cold. / Friends of learning and sensual pleasure, / They seek the silence and the horror of darkness; / Erebus would have used them as his gloomy steeds: / If their pride could let them stoop to bondage." (Baudelaire, "The Cats," 1954, v. 1–8)

17 Preface to the second edition.

Levinas repeats the quotation from "Les Chats" but adds a line from another Baudelaire poem, "Le Masque": "Demain, hélas, il faudra vivre encore!" 'Le Masque', like 'Le Squelette laboureur', is an ekphrasis of a work of art: a sculpture by Ernest Christophe representing a beautiful naked woman; she is the very expression of love but she is a misleading figure. (Fig. 2). When we look at her from a different side, we see that she wears a mask, and behind the mask she is crying. In Baudelaire's poem, the lyrical I wonders why she cries, this woman of a perfect beauty:

> Elle pleure, insensé, parce qu'elle a vécu !
> Et parce qu'elle vit ! Mais ce qu'elle déplore
> Surtout, ce qui la fait frémir jusqu'aux genoux,
> C'est que *demain hélas ! il faudra vivre encore !*
> Demain, après-demain et toujours – comme nous !
> (v. 32–36)[18]

Once more, Baudelaire elaborates on the opposition between Spleen and the Ideal: perfect beauty belongs to the Ideal but it is misleading; it is just a provisional evasion from Spleen. The two-faced sculpture is an allegory of human existence as Baudelaire conceives it: a life riveted to being, "condemned" to pain and sin. In this perspective, death is seen as deliverance, as is said in the final lines of "Le Voyage." In "Le Masque," Levinas finds the perfect expression of existence as the impossibility not to be.

Closely examining these quotations from *The Flowers of evil*, it seems that Baudelaire's presence in *De l'existence à l'existant* and in *Totalité et infini* is far from accidental. These quoted verses are not mere illustration of his argument but inform it, sometimes becoming an invisible intertext. Almost all of them express Baudelaire's central experience of Spleen and Ennui. This intense experience certainly played a role in shaping Levinas's first intuitions about the "there is" and the ineluctable character of being ("existence"). In that sense, Baudelaire was determining for Levinas's first philosophy, as we find it in *De l'existence à l'existant*. However, when Levinas describes the birth of the subject ("the hypostasis") out of existence, as he does in the second half of the essay, he turns from Baudelaire. The same goes for *Totalité et infini*, where the next, decisive step is taken, from the subject to the incursion of the Other. One may

---

18 "She is weeping, fool, because she has lived! / And because she lives! But what she deplores / Most, what makes her shudder down her knees, / Is that tomorrow, alas! she still will have to live! / Tomorrow, after tomorrow, always! – like us!" (Baudelaire, "The Mask," 1954, v. 32–36)

Fig. 2: Ernest Christophe, "La comédie humaine ou le Masque" (1876), Musée d'Orsay, https://en.wikipedia.org/wiki/File:The_Human_Comedy_Mask_by_Ernest_Christophe.jpg#/media/File:Le_Masque-Ernest_Christophe-IMG_8121-black.jpg, consulted on 14–11–19.

regret it, since many poems of *The Flowers of Evil* – especially those about the modern city – are about the encounter of the lyrical I with what one may call the face of the Other, in all its vulnerability: beggars, widows and orphans, blind people, old women . . .

In *Le temps et l'autre*, when apologizing for quoting Shakespeare so often, Levinas says that "all philosophy is a mere meditation of Shakespeare" (Levinas 1979, 60). Might he have said the same about Baudelaire? We may conclude, more prudently, that Levinas's first philosophy – especially his conception of the "there is" as the impossibility of nothingness – is (amongst others) a meditation on Baudelaire's Spleen.

Bibliography

Baudelaire, Charles. *Les fleurs du mal*. Paris: Classiques Garnier, 1961.
Baudelaire, Charles. *The Flowers of Evil*. Trans. William Aggeler. Fresno: Academy Library, 1954.
Ciocan, Christian, and Georges Hansel. *Levinas Concordance*. Dordrecht: Springer, 2005.
Eaglestone, Robert. *Ethical Criticism: Reading After Levinas*. Edinburgh: Edinburgh University Press, 1997.
Levinas, Emmanuel. "La réalité et son ombre." *Les Temps Modernes* 38 (1948): 769–789.
Levinas, Emmanuel. *Noms propres*. Montpellier: Fata Morgana, 1976.
Levinas, Emmanuel. *De l'existence à l'existant*. Trans. Alphonso Lingis. Dordrecht: Kluwer Academic Publishers, 1978.
Levinas, Emmanuel. *Le temps et l'autre*. Paris: Fata Morgana, 1979.
Levinas, Emmanuel. *Totalité et infini*. The Hague: Martinus Nijhoff, 1980 [1961].
Levinas, Emmanuel. *De l'existence à l'existant*. Paris: Vrin, 1981 [1947].
Levinas, Emmanuel. *De l'évasion*. Montpellier: Fata Morgana, 1982 [1935].
Levinas, Emmanuel. *Essais romanesques et poétiques, notes philosophiques sur le thème d'éros*. Eds. Jean-Luc Nancy and Danielle Cohen-Levinas. Paris: Grasset, 2013.
Robbins, Jill. *Altered reading: Levinas and Literature*. Chicago: University of Chicago Press, 1999.
Schulte Nordholt, Annelies, "Tentation esthétique et exigence éthique. Lévinas et l'œuvre littéraire." *Etudes littéraires* 31.3 (1999): 69–85.
Toumayan, Alain Paul, "Levinas and French Literature." *Levinas and Nineteenth-Century Literature: Ethics and Otherness from Romanticism through Realism*. Eds. Donald R. Wehrs and David P. Haney. Newark: University of Delaware Press, 2009. 125–147.
Yourcenar, Marguerite. *The Abyss*. Trans. Grace Frick. New York: Farrar, Straus and Giroux: 1976.

Kevin Hart
"*Lès-Poésie*?": Levinas Reads *La folie du jour*

Maurice Blanchot's short narrative "Un récit" – or "Un récit?": the difference has attracted considerable comment – first appeared in the short-lived Parisian review *Empédocle* in May 1949, and was reissued by Fata Morgana under the definitive title *La folie du jour* in 1973.[1] Only as a little book, published in the wake of May 1968 and at a highpoint of Blanchot's intellectual standing in France, did it begin to attract attention beyond avant-garde literary circles.[2] One significant instance of this new awareness and esteem is Emmanuel Levinas's "Exercices sur 'La folie du jour,'" which was published in the February 1975 number of *Change* and became the final of four texts devoted to his old friend gathered in *Sur Maurice Blanchot* (1975). That Levinas admired Blanchot's narrative works, especially the first edition of *Thomas l'obscur* (1941), is amply testified, not least by the wartime notes written in captivity in which he planned to launch a career as a novelist.[3] And that, after the war, he distanced himself from most art, including a great deal of literature, is also evident from even the most cursory reading of "La réalité et son ombre" (1948). "Art," he writes in that fierce essay, is "essentially disengaged, is a dimension of escape in a world of initiative and responsibility" and, worse, "There is something nasty, selfish, and cowardly in artistic pleasure" (Levinas 2004, 89, 90).

Yet Blanchot largely evades his friend's strictures because his work disrupts any authorial pretension to classical literary mastery and *le beau style*. There is a world, Levinas tells us in 1971, in which "no human suffering keeps from being in order [*n'empêche de s'ordonner*]," and yet in the same breath he recognizes that Blanchot "reminds that world that its totality is not total – that the coherent discourse it vaunts does not catch up with another discourse which it fails to silence." In the five brief sentences that follow he nicely captures much of what Blanchot wishes to tell us.

---

[1] In particular, see Jacques Derrida, "Title to be Specified" (2011, 214–215).
[2] One index of the esteem in which Blanchot was held at this period is the special issue of *Critique* (volume 229, June 1966) that was consecrated to his work.
[3] See Emmanuel Levinas, *Oeuvres*, 1: *Carnets de captivité et autre inédits* (2009, 98).

> That other discourse is troubled by an uninterrupted noise. A difference does not let the world sleep, and troubles the order in which being and non-being are ordered in a dialectic. This Neuter is not a someone, nor even a something. It is but an *excluded middle* that, properly speaking, is not even [*n'est même pas*]. Yet there is more transcendence than any world-behind-the-worlds ever gave a glimpse of. (Levinas 1996, 154–155)

Presumably religious transcendence merely ends in a higher state of immanence, and this is not so with the Neuter.

Earlier, in "Le regard du poète" (1956), a long review of *L'Espace littéraire* (1955), Levinas was more nuanced in his estimation of his friend's achievement. He drew attention, amid much insight and much praise, to a squint in Blanchot's gaze. The stricture is less to do with him as a reader of Mallarmé and Kafka, Hölderlin and Rilke, than as a diagnostician of the figure of the modern writer, in particular the ground – which for Levinas is at best a playground – for his or her authenticity. "If the authenticity Blanchot speaks of is to mean anything other than a consciousness of the lack of seriousness of edification," Levinas pointedly says, "anything other than derision – the authenticity of art must herald an order of justice, the slave morality that is absent from the Heideggerian city" (1996, 137). Presumably, Blanchot's narrative writing up to that time, from *Thomas l'obscur* (1941) to *Celui qui ne m'accompaignait pas* (1953), including "Un récit" (1948), announces, directly or indirectly, positively or negatively, "an order of justice." The same cannot be said for all of his critical writing, it seems.

What upsets Levinas when reading *L'Espace littéraire*? He seizes upon a footnote towards the end of the book, where Blanchot specifies the artist's mission. An artist should "call us obstinately back to error, to turn us toward that space where everything we propose, everything we have acquired, everything we are, all that opens upon the earth and in the sky, returns to insignificance, and where what approaches is the nonserious and the nontrue, as if perhaps thence sprang the source of all authenticity"(1982, 247 note 8). "Error" here is written in full awareness of its root in Latin, *errare*, "to wander, to go astray." The art we need today, art that is nourished by Lautréamont and Sade, as well as by the authors already mentioned, enables us to move away from a world fixed by God or the gods, from traditional norms of literature, even from "being" as rigorously determined by philosophers such as Hegel and, above all, Heidegger. Blanchot's phenomenology of art seems to be couched in terms ("earth," "sky") that Heidegger had made familiar in "Das Ding" (1950).[4] Yet it also contests those very terms, for it consists in indicating something other

---

4 See Martin Heidegger, "The Thing" (1971, 171). Levinas is of course aware of this aspect of Blanchot's thought. See Levinas, "The Poet's Vision" (1996, 137).

than the truth of being, as Heidegger would have it, namely, that mysterious excluded middle he calls the "Neutral" or the "Outside." It would be better to say, then, that Blanchot offers a counterpart to phenomenology, for the Outside only ever approaches and never appears as such.

There are at least two reasons why Levinas might take umbrage with his friend. In the first place, he might well hear, a little too quickly, Heidegger's word *Eigentlichkeit* whispered behind Blanchot's *authenticité*.[5] Blanchot does not use the word to translate Heidegger's German in *Sein und Zeit* (1927), for he does not look to that which is true (or genuine) or to the true state of being but rather to that which escapes both "truth" and "being." Nor does he distance himself sufficiently for Levinas from the Heidegger who thinks that *Dasein* is in each case mine, and for whom *Mitdasein* and *Miteindersein* are derivative of *Dasein*.[6] The truth that the other person's face silently commands "Do not kill me!," along with the moral seriousness of this command, are not acknowledged. In the second place, Levinas, as advocate of ethics as first philosophy, recoils from Nietzsche's view, adapted by Blanchot, that with the abolition of the "real world" the "apparent world" also crumbles.[7] Henceforth, for Blanchot, to live authentically in accord with an uncompromising nihilism one must look to the non-serious and the non-true, which derive from the approach of the Outside. This is the view of thoroughly demystified existence that one finds elsewhere affirmed as "the ultimate insignificance of lightness" [*l'ultime insignifiance de la légèreté*] (Blanchot 1993b, 43), and that troubles the self-ordering of the Heideggerian city.

Reflecting on Levinas's sharp reaction to Blanchot's note, we begin to see that the philosopher does not grasp all the aspects of the notion of the Outside that he acclaims. He affirms its status as an excluded middle, a third that frustrates any dialectical drive to totality, yet fails to appreciate how strongly it conflicts with his own views. For Blanchot, the Outside can be discerned in various ways: in ordinary suffering, when time seems to stall; in the midst of the everyday; and in intransitive – literary – writing; yet also in the ceaseless oscillation of being and non-being, which happens when something becomes an image of itself. For him, this awareness of the relation between being and non-being signals the approach of the non-world of image, a neutral state that can only fascinate us and, in doing so, bind us to itself. Yet it cannot concern us; it does not offer itself to us by way of experience, only as something impossible to bring into that realm, and therefore comes to be dubbed "the impossible."[8] Levinas

---

5 See Heidegger, *Being and Time* (1973, 167).
6 See Heidegger, *Being and Time* (1973, 68).
7 See Friedrich Nietzsche, "How the 'Real World' at last Became a Myth" (1968, 41).
8 See, for example, Blanchot, *The Infinite Conversation* (1993a, 45–48).

had already rejected that specter in no uncertain terms in "La réalité et son ombre" where he recognizes that it precedes the workaday world of initiative and action, and thereby has the ability to mire characters in a temporal "meanwhile" and to hold readers immobile before it.[9] In some respects, it resembles what he calls the *il y a* at about the same period, the inability to cancel being, for even when something is absent, even permanently absent, one nonetheless intuits the presence of that absence.[10] For Levinas, one escapes the *il y a* by responding to another person, and yet it seems that for Blanchot that avenue is not available. Certainly, in "Exercises on 'The Madness of the Day'", Levinas comes to affirm what he calls the "extra-vagant" (1996, 170) dimension of narrative, and his hyphen recalls the Latin patrimony of the French – *extra* ("outside") and *vagari* ("wander") – yet he does so without fully endorsing, perhaps without fully realizing, what motivates Blanchot's affirmation of radical error in literature.

Of course, Levinas in quite right to say in "Le regard du poète" (translated as "The Poet's Vision") that the Blanchot of *L'Espace littéraire* abstains "from ethical preoccupations, at least in explicit form" (1996, 137).[11] When Blanchot turns to consider ethics more directly it will be in terms of an adjustment of the program of *Totalité et infini* (1961) by way of the Outside. He will not accept that the asymmetry of the other person with respect to me is properly basic.[12] One important step on the path to this discussion will be the writing of "Comment découvrir l'obscur?" (1959), in which Blanchot will indicate a peculiar phenomenology of this Outside, of something quite other than light and being, and this will enable him to chart a different course from the one that Levinas undertakes in his insistence that ethics, as first philosophy, revolves around the other person as enigma, rather than as phenomenon.[13] When the other person speaks to me I hear the irreducible strangeness of the Outside, and that strangeness orients me to think of community rather than any individual.

Yet in 1975 Levinas finds an ethical moment, a call for justice, in *La folie du jour*, and makes it the thesis of his reflections on the *récit*. His main idea is, as

---

9 See Levinas, "Reality and Its Shadow" (2004, 84–89).
10 See Levinas, *Existence and Existents* (1988, chapter 4).
11 Blanchot's post-war left-wing political commitments are evident, though, in at least one text that precedes the publication of this book. See Blanchot, "Dionys Mascolo: *Le Communisme*" (1953).
12 See Blanchot, "Tenir parole" (1962) and "L'Interruption" (1964). The first "dialogue" and part of the second were republished in *L'Entretien infini* (1969, 84–93, 106–112).
13 See Blanchot, "Comment découvrir l'obscur" (1959), reprinted in *L'Entretien infini* (1969, 57–69). Also see Levinas, "Phenomenon and Enigma" (1987).

he says, that even though texts are always open to various interpretations, "the irreducible (inspired) exoticism of poetry refers back to [*en appelle à*] a saying *properly so-called*, a saying that thematizes, even if it may be obliged to unsay itself in order to avoid disfiguring the secret it exposes" (Levinas 1996, 157). Actually, he goes further than this claim in his fourth exercise, finding in the *récit* "a way out" of the endless suffering of the human condition, co-ordinate with interiority. This interiority is one with "the *closure of being*" (Levinas 1996, 158), the Western obsession with being which runs from Parmenides to Heidegger and which he had identified as early as *De l'évasion* (1935). This exit is found, he says, by developing a "relation to the other" (Levinas 1996, 165). Is his reading of the *récit* justified?

*

When we see that Levinas entitles his commentary "Exercises" we might, at a pinch, think of Epictetus's two-stage model of philosophical education. First, we master theory and then, through spiritual exercises, seek to apply it to our own lives.[14] And we might entertain the idea that he is led to title his piece in this manner because of a Stoic element in *La folie du jour*. For we are told, almost at the very start, "this life gives me the greatest pleasure. And what about death? When I die (perhaps any minute now), I will feel immense pleasure . . . I experience boundless pleasure in living, and I will take boundless satisfaction in dying" [*cette vie me fait le plaisir le plus grand. Alors, la mort? Quand je mourrai (peut-être tout à l'heure), je connaîtrai un plaisir immense . . . j'éprouve à vivre un plaisir sans limites et j'aurai à mourir une satisfaction sans limites*] (Blanchot 1981, 5). Yet Stoic pedagogy also rings very faintly in the idea of a schoolboy's exercise: Levinas, remember, was Director of the École Normale Israélite Orientale (ENIO) from 1945 to 1961. ("Exercises on 'The Madness of the Day,'" however, would be an unorthodox example of pedagogy, written, as it is, in jagged French and moving in a halting manner, at once overly compressed and sometimes unclear in its passage from sentence to sentence.) Also, while Blanchot's narrator claims to be indifferent to the accidents of life and death, his tranquility does not seem to have been brought about by adherence to virtue for its own sake and one does not look even to Seneca for finding satisfaction in death; at the most one's demise brings release from desire and pain.[15] And yet perhaps an echo of Stoicism is not a mere distraction, at least with regards to Levinas, as we will see.

---

14 See Epectetus, *Dissertationes*, 1. 26. 3. Also see Musonius, *Dissertationum a Lucio Digestarum Reliquiæ*, 6.
15 Blanchot, in *The Space of Literature*, distances himself from Stoicism (1982, 101). Also see Seneca, *Epistulæ Morales ad Lucilium*, 12.4.

Appropriately enough, Levinas begins by commenting on the title of the *récit*: "Madness of today, but madness of the day also in the sense that, in it, day is madly desired, and in the sense that day – clarity and measure – goes made there, and, hence, especially, in the sense that the madness of day is contrasted with the madness or panic of night" (Levinas 1996, 158). Perhaps it needs to be brought out a little more strongly that the expression "*folie du jour*" also names the madness or extravagance of light, especially of daylight. Exactly what "*folie*" means for Levinas, and for Blanchot, for there is no reason to think that they agree at all points, is left unmarked; but let us remain with "*jour*" for the moment. To which day or days does it refer? Not to France after the Occupation, Levinas says, but rather it "seems to bear a greater resemblance to 1968" (1996, 159), a claim to which he returns ("inanity and madness, twenty years later" (1996, 169)) but which is left to dangle, even while we recall the remark about "the lack of seriousness of edification." Levinas continues: "These pages do not even reflect what was going on in 1948 on the level of the history of ideas. . . . *The Madness of the Day* might therefore be said to be free from any temporal limitations" (1996, 159).

If *La folie du jour* does not take on one or another of the primary philosophical colors of post-Liberation Paris – neither that of Camus, Marcel, and Sartre, nor that of Raymond Aron – it certainly is of a piece with Blanchot's own itinerary. "Un récit" was composed in the midst of dense reflection on Lautréamont, Sade, and Hölderlin, texts in which the question of madness is seldom absent, even when not explicitly posed.[16] One might look, for instance, to the very end of "L'Expérience de Lautréamont" (1948), parts of which appeared over the same few months that saw the publication of "Un récit." Blanchot concludes his long essay by comparing Hölderlin and Lautréamont. The German poet, he thinks, was "truly and absolutely united with the light to which he had the strength to sacrifice all his forces and that, in return, brought him this unique glory of a child's reasoning wherein all the splendor of impersonal clarity shines forth" (Blanchot 2004, 163).[17] The French poet, however, "was unable to disappear within madness, being born of madness." He too had the "force of light within him" which was "an unlimited aspiration, which the extreme moment designates the sole, ideal and real point at which, ceasing being himself, he can become, outside of himself, completely himself, in the end coming

---

16 For the importance of Hölderlin to Blanchot's *récit*, especially the essay "La Parole 'Sacrée' de Hölderlin" (1946), see Leslie Hill, *Blanchot: Extreme Contemporary* (1997, 95–102).
17 Also see Blanchot, "La Folie par excellence" (1951).

forever into the world at the ultimate moment that makes him disappear from it" (Blanchot 2004, 163–164).

Connections between light and madness are at the very heart of *La folie du jour*, but we would do well to approach them with caution. We first hear of madness when the narrator recalls having lost people he has loved, presumably in the recent war: "I went mad when that blow struck me, because it is hell" [*Je suis devenu fou quand ce coup m'a frappé, car c'est un enfer*] (Blanchot 1981, 6, 20). Indeed, the war is characterized directly thereafter as "the madness of the world" [*la folie du monde*] (Blanchot 1981, 6, 20). Note, though, that the extreme moment of that violence, when the narrator is almost executed, is precisely the point when he stops "being insane" [*être insensé*] (or foolish, senseless . . .)] (Blanchot 1981, 6, 20).[18] He appears to be on an even keel when later "a lunatic" [*un fou*] (Blanchot 1981, 8, 22) stabs him in the hand and, still later, again for no apparent reason, another person crushes glass in his eyes. After that second event he becomes convinced that [he] is "face to face with the madness of the day" [*je fus convaincu que je voyais face à face la folie du jour*] (Blanchot 1981, 11, 25). This is no sudden vision but rather a making evident of the truth of a situation, regardless of whether the judgment is made correctly or incorrectly. When recovering from his injury in half-light, the narrator longs for daylight, which would be perfectly normal: "and if seeing would infect me with madness, I madly wanted that madness" [*et si voir c'était la contagion de la folie, je désirais follement cette folie*] (Blanchot 1981, 12, 25). It is an extreme desire, to be sure, yet I draw attention to the "*et si*"; he has not lost his power of reason or perhaps the power to feign reason. Finally, after the narrator agrees to be locked up, one of the doctors sees another inmate, an old man with a white beard, jumping on his shoulders and hears the narrator say, impatiently, "Who are you, Tolstoy?" [*Tu es donc Tolstoi?*] (Blanchot 1981, 16, 29), which makes the doctor think (according to the narrator) that he is "truly crazy" [*bien fou*] (Blanchot 1981, 16, 29). But we are not invited to trust the doctor's supposed judgment. (Presumably, he does not know Tolstoy's *On Insanity*, to which the narrator most likely alludes. We read there something that he might well recall: "Recently I happened to visit two large establishments for the mentally deranged, and the impression I received was that I saw establishments built by mentally deranged people suffering from one common epidemic form of lunacy, for patients suffering from different forms of lunacy which do not resemble the common epidemic form" (Tolstoy 1936, 31).) And when, at the very end, "a specialist in mental illness" [*un spécialiste des maladies mentales*] (1981

---

[18] Blanchot recounts the attempted execution in his *The Instant of My Death* (2000).

18, 31) interrogates the narrator, we have no particular ground to think that the specialist is called for.

One should take care before saying that the narrator is clinically mad, and should certainly consider his black humor, which tends to deflate situations: for example, *le sang dégouttait sur mon unique costume* ["the blood was dripping on my only suit"] (Blanchot 1981, 22, 8), he says in response to having his hand cut with a knife, and *C'étaient de joyeux moments* ["Those were happy times"] (Blanchot 1981 29, 16), which he remarks by way of concluding the episode of his being beaten by inmates in the hospital. Also, one should be circumspect in categorically denying that the narrator is a little touched; the mad can sometimes appear quite reasonable if one accepts the confines of their disorder, and this man experiences delirium when seeing a perfectly ordinary occurrence: the conjunction of a woman with a pram and a man entering a building. He interprets this banal event eschatologically. "Here it comes, I said to myself, the end is coming: something is happening, the end is beginning" [*Voici qu'elle arrive, me disais-je, la fin vient, quelque chose arrive, la fin commence*] (Blanchot 1981, 10, 24). Equally eccentric is his reaction to facing the end: "I was seized by joy" [*J'étais saisi par la joie*] (Blanchot 1981, 10, 24). And yet we have been prepared for this sort of response from the opening paragraph: "I will take boundless satisfaction in dying" [*j'aurai à mourir une satisfaction sans limites*] (Blanchot 1981, 5, 19).

Is there other evidence than the direct allusions to *folie* in the *récit* that should be taken into account before coming to a conclusion? There is: the second figure of the law as recounted in the latter part of the story. We hear that the narrator was "attracted to the law" [*la loi m'attirait*] (Blanchot 1981, 9), perhaps as a profession, or perhaps he found her charming. (We know already that he prizes women, "beautiful creatures" [*belles créatures*] (Blanchot 1981, 7, 21), for their equal acceptance of life and death.) In any case, it is abnormal for someone to call to the law, "Come here; let me see you face to face" [*Approche, que je te voie face à face*] (Blanchot 1981, 9, 22). Only Moses, who receives the Law from the Most High and talks with him "face to face" and "mouth to mouth," comes to mind (Exod. 33: 11, Num. 12: 8). The law, in *La folie du jour*, would be what Levinas comes to call *autrui*, higher than the one addressing her, but of course she does not respond, for which the narrator is thankful. (A little later we hear the narrator seeing the madness of the day "face to face" (Blanchot 1981, 11), but it too cannot be *autrui*, despite its height.) The narrator declines engaging with the law by not suing the man who crushed glass in his eyes, and disapproves of a doctor who litigates a patient who fooled him by taking a drug without telling him. In addition, he dislikes thinking of his various talents as judges "ready to condemn" him [*prêts à me condamner*]

(Blanchot 1981, 14, 27), and, from the beginning, observes the power of the medical profession, which imposes its own protocols on him regardless of the pain it causes him. Yet the most disturbing evocation of the law comes when the doctors, who act as kings, are interrogating him. "Behind their backs I saw the silhouette of the law. Not the law everyone knows, which is severe and hardly very agreeable: this law was different" [*Derrière leur dos, j'apercevais la silhouette de la loi. Non pas la loi que l'on connaît, qui est rigoureuse et peu agréable: celle-ci était autre*] (Blanchot 1981, 14, 28). His former attraction to the law, the first law, must have faded.

How is this second law different? Because the narrator seems "to terrify her" (Blanchot 1981, 15); she is "perpetually on her knees" before him (Blanchot 1981, 15), as though he is now *auturi*. At times their relationship has the character of *une folie*, a fling. "Once she had made me touch her knee – a strange feeling. I had said as much to her: 'I am not the kind of man who is satisfied with a knee!' Her answer: 'That would be disgusting!'" [*Elle m'avait une fois fait toucher son genou: une bizarre impression. Je le lui avais déclaré: Je ne suis pas homme à me contenter d'un genou. Sa réponse: Ce serait dégoûtant!*] (Blanchot 1981, 16–17, 30). Certainly, the first sight of the law has a romantic element to it. The narrator sees her in silhouette – a black and featureless shadow – as if in a scene in a *film noir* of the period, and if we take the narrator, being neither learned nor ignorant, as fulfilling Diotima's requirement for being a lover, we should not be surprised at this turn of events.[19] Of course, an unusual light would be needed to produce a silhouette of the law, something that contrasts sharply with its exteriority. Call it the light of consciousness. There is some textual support for the claim, since the law takes the narrator's gaze to be "a bolt of lightning" [*la foudre*] (Blanchot 1981, 15, 28), recognizing, perhaps, what Derrida was to remark years later with respect to Levinas, that phenomenology relies on "the violence of light."[20]

If we closely follow what the law says to the narrator, we find that she sets him above authority, that she praises him outrageously, that she commends justice to him, that the two of them are forever bound together, and that she is intent upon his glory. I take it that the silhouette of the law, which is all the narrator sees, is a figure for writing, which, for Blanchot, contests all rules, plays games – "*ce jeu insensé d'écrire*," as Mallarmé says, and as Blanchot likes to quote – creates an author only to let him fade the moment he stops writing,

---

19 See Plato, *Symposium*, 204a. On this motif, see Sarah Kofman, *Comment s'en sortir?* (1983, 97–98).
20 See Derrida, "Violence and Metaphysics: An Essay on the Thought of Emmanuel Levinas" (1978, 84–92).

remains forever bound to the one who writes, converges with left-wing demands for justice, and that forever is capable of resurrecting his consciousness, whether he is alive or dead, in a ghostly half-life.[21] Writing is the silhouette of the Outside, which our mundane laws seek to contain and which nonetheless irrupts through them and imposes its own law on us in various ways.

*

Madness, for Blanchot, is therefore several things at once: insanity, experience of the measureless light of divine inspiration, whether as a return to childhood or as an extravagant struggle to overcome constraints, and erotic adventure. It is also the "absence of work," not simple laziness but *désœuvrement*, in which a text or a person resonates with the Outside in its approach and becomes disengaged from any dialectic. In that absence of work, we are told by Blanchot in 1960, "discourse ceases, so that, outside speech, outside language, the movement of writing may come, under the attraction of the outside"(1993a, 32).[22] This is madness in the sense of being unhinged from an established order.

Levinas is attentive solely to the last of these senses of "madness," which in "Exercises on 'The Madness of the Day'" he regards as a symptom of the "*closure of being*," a "hellish unfreedom" (Levinas 1996, 159), a suffocation in selfhood that "lurks at the very heart of the joys, the day, and the unshakable happiness described in the opening lines of our text" (Levinas 1996, 160). He approaches this madness under the sign of weariness:

> Weariness [*la fatigue*] keeps recurring in the text; the void fills itself with itself, repose doesn't settle down. Weariness [*Lassitude*] – precisely. There is no progressive dialectic, in which the moments of the story spring up in their newness, before contracting their freshness by all they conserve. The circular return of the Identical does not even follow a long-term cycle. It is a twirling on the spot: happiness is obsessed in its very permanence, the outbreak of madness sinks back into madness, into oppression, into an unbreathable interiority without exterior. Is madness a way out, or is the way out madness?
> (Levinas 1996, 161–162)

Levinas's concern with the "presence of the present" being "immobilized" (1996, 159) is familiar to readers of "La réalité et son ombre" (1948); it is at the hub of his criticism of art. And the inability of someone to break free from the fatigue associated with the *il y a* is of course a dominant them of *De l'existence à l'existant* (1947). If *La folie du jour* does not, for Levinas, "reflect what was

---

21 Stéphane Mallarmé, "Villiers de l'Isle-Adam" (2003, 23). Also see the conclusion of Blanchot's "Dionys Mascolo: *Le Communisme*" (1953).
22 See Blanchot, "La Marche de l'écrivisse," (1960, 93).

going on in 1948" (1996, 159), it seems to resonate with precisely what *he* was thinking and writing at that time. He does not seem to recognize this as a "temporal limitation" of the story, however.

In the late 1940s Levinas recognized that the only way of escaping the stultifying oppression of the *il y a* was to leave the suffocating solitude of the self and move towards the Good, which can occur only when one salutes another person and recognizes and values his or her irreducible otherness. Madness is not the way out of banal existence, as it was for Artaud and van Gogh, and before them the Breton of *Nadja* (1928), let alone for proponents of Dionysian excess such as Bataille. Rather, a rethinking of philosophy – so that ethics, not metaphysics, is first philosophy – will indicate that exit, and this turning upside-down of the intellectual world doubtless seemed to some of Blanchot's contemporaries to be nothing short of madness. In order to assimilate *La folie du jour* to his own thought, Levinas must find a "way out" that is delineated in the story. The fourth exercise does precisely that. "Relation to the other – a last way out. From one end to the other of the story, this relation is present" (Levinas 1996, 165). He points to the narrator's experience of the loss of loved ones, which causes the narrator such pain, but gravitates on one brief scene, which I have already mentioned. "The little scene in which, in front of the courtyard door, a man steps back to let a baby carriage through, is the event of an advent – that is, the moment when something abnormal ensues: one person withdraws before the other, one *is* for the other. Whence the narrator's lightheartedness, which seems to lift him above being" (Levinas 1996, 165–166). Let us look more closely at this scene.

The narrator certainly sees the man think twice and step aside so that a woman can enter a door with a pram. Notice, though, that the narrator does not do anything except observe, and while it has extraordinary significance for him – it "excited me to the point of delirium" [*me souleva jusqu'au délire*] (Blanchot 1981, 10, 24) – exactly what it means is beyond him. The man who steps aside is "for the other," we might agree, and we might think of this by way of *la transascendance*, but we have no reason to say the same of the narrator.[23] He merely enters the courtyard after the woman has disappeared, takes in how very cold it is, and lingers there "in the joy and perfection of this happiness" [*la joie et la perfection de ce bonheur*] (Blanchot 1981, 10, 24). Far from seeing moral action as an exit from his situation, the narrator remains

---

23 The word "transascendance" was coined by Jean Wahl and taken up by Levinas. See Wahl, *Existence humaine et transcendance* (1944, 37) and Levinas, *Totality and Infinity: An Essay on Exteriority* (1979, 35 note 2).

pleasurably within himself. What strikes him is not the goodness of the event he has witnessed but its *reality*, and that the day "having stumbled against a real event, would begin hurrying to its end" [*ayant buté sur un événement vrai, allait se hâter vers sa fin*] (Blanchot 1981, 10, 24). In case we overlook the statement, the narrator underlines it in the very next paragraph, "All that was real; take note" [*Tout cela était réel, notez-le*] (Blanchot 1981, 11, 24). Reality, for the narrator, would seem to be purely sensory. The only thing he dislikes about the prospect of dying is that "Suffering dulls the senses [or 'stupifies']" [*Souffrir est abrutissant*] (Blanchot 1981, 6, 19). He says, "I see the world – what extraordinary happiness! I see this day, and outside it there is nothing" [*je vois le monde, bonheur extraordinaire. Je le vois, ce jour hors duquel il n'est rein*] (Blanchot 1981, 6, 20); in other words, all that there is is sensory: no past, no future, and surely no transcendent realm. What disturbs him most of all about the medical experiment of covering him with mud is that "My sense of touch was floating six feet away from me" [*Mon tact errait à deux mètres*] (Blanchot 1981, 7, 21). Immediately before the scene of the woman with a pram, "the gloomy spirit of reading" [*sombre esprit de la lecture*] (Blanchot 1981, 9, 23) insults him and, being at a low point, he could not even have answered the question "Who was I?" [*Qui étais-je?*] (Blanchot 1981, 10, 23). (Of course, it can be a hard question to answer even if one is at a high point in life.[24]) So when he sees the woman, the pram, and the man, when he feels the cold in the courtyard, he is impressed by the sensuous reality of these things; they have a solidity that the realm of spirit does not have. Time seems to click into gear once more; if it has stalled with the encounters with the lunatic and the spirit of reading, and with a loss of selfhood, it now picks up speed and finds a direction.

I return to Levinas's remarks on weariness as a dominant motif in *La folie du jour*, at least until the narrator sees the woman with a pram. Now the narrator does not speak of fatigue; on the contrary, his testimony is given with noticeable vigor, returning time and again to declarations given in the first-person ("I am not learned; I am not ignorant" [*Je ne suis ni savant ni ignorant*] (Blanchot 1981, 5, 19), "I have wandered" [*J'ai erré*] (Blanchot 1981, 5, 19), "I have loved people" [*J'ai aimé des êtres*] (Blanchot 1981, 6, 20), "I am not timid" [*Je ne suis pas craintif*] (Blanchot 1981, 8, 22), "I must admit I have read many books" [*Je dois l'avouer, j'ai lu beaucoup de livres*] (Blanchot 1981, 9, 22) and so on) or posing questions in order to answer them ("Is my life better than other people's lives?" [*Mon existence est-elle meilleure que celle de tous?*]

---

24 See, for quite different examples, Blaise Pascal, *Pensées* (2005, S567/L688), and André Breton, *Nadja* (1928, 7).

(Blanchot 1981, 6, 20), "Can I describe my trials?" [*Puis-je décrire mes épreuves?*] (Blanchot 1981, 7, 21) "Am I an egoist?" [*Suis-je égoïste?*] (Blanchot 1981, 8, 21)). Almost frenetic, the testimony lurches from one statement or evocation to another, sometimes so briefly as to perplex the reader as to its significance for either the narrator or the story he is telling. The episode of the woman with a pram is exemplary here; and yet the narrative runs on, past this episode, as though seeking a *dénouement*. Throughout, the narrator appears to be distanced from the very events he undergoes. It is less a matter of alienation from the world than something stranger: a sense of not having any agency, of being thrown from one event to another, which results in the staccato narrative. It is this relentless self-interrupting of the narrative by the narrator himself that becomes the true "subject" of *La folie du jour*, a technique that Blanchot probably learned from Kafka.[25] It reaches its apotheosis when, at the end, the narrator begins to retell his story. There is a disjunction between events we presume to have occurred (but which are perhaps taking place only in the story) and the significance of them for those who know who they are and who embody institutional power. For the narrator, some of those events, the ones that most interest the medical world, may have been lived through but not at the center of his consciousness. They fall outside the bounds of his story.

So we only apparently reach a point when the plot becomes unlaced, which is when the narrator has glass crushed into his eyes, for we are never told who injures him or why. The shards of glass seem to intensify the daylight, making it as though immediate and without measure, and when they are removed he must rest with a film under his eyelids for seven days – the biblical number of fullness, and especially of the seven seals in Revelation – which becomes for him "the spark of a single moment" [*la vivacité d'un seul instant*] (Blanchot 1981, 11, 25).[26] Notice that the narrator takes himself to be called "to account" [*comptes*] in that week, yet his judges, the seven days, perhaps a metaphor for the seven angels of Revelation, who act as one, light itself, are mad and without any restraint. On waking in hospital, the very idea of engaging with a lesser law – that of suing for special or general damages – strikes him as risible; and in his convalescence, when he must wear dark glasses, he finds that he would experience the fire of the seven days, the

---

25 See Blanchot, *The Infinite Conversation* (1993a, 384). On the nature of the *récit*, see Blanchot, "The Song of the Sirens" (2003, 6).
26 It is worth noting that for Levinas an immediate contact with the sacred, without the mediation of reason, would be an instance of *la folie*. See Levinas, "To Love the Torah More than God" (1990, 144).

transcendent luster of the seven angels, again if only he could see properly. In seeing that the days or angels are without ground, the narrator is unmoored from the usual anchors, ropes and cables, undergoes *désœuvrement*, and so disorientation becomes his task.

It seems then that the Outside is acknowledged in two distinct ways in *La folie du jour*. One recognizes its approach in the distance between the "I" and the apparently random events that occur to him, which becomes a distance within himself, dividing him from himself. The narrator does not experience this disunion by way of fatigue, however, although such a thing is possible. In a later *récit* attuned to weariness a speaker ironically observes, perhaps to himself, that he is too fatigued to affirm that weariness can prompt a reduction to the non-world of the Outside. He simply overhears, as it were, a voice whispering that it is so, a voice that is close to the Outside:

> Do you really believe you can approach the neutral through weariness, and through the neutral of weariness, better hear what occurs when to speak is not to see? I do not believe it, in fact; I do not affirm it either. I am too weary for that. Only, someone says this close to me, someone I do not know; I let them talk, it is an inconsequential murmur. [Crois-tu vraiment que tu puisses t'approcher du neutre par la fatigue et, par le neutre de la fatigue, mieux entendre ce qu'il arrive, quand parler, ce n'est pas voir? Je ne le crois pas, en effet; je ne l'affirme pas non plus; je suis trop fatigué pour cela; quelqu'un, seulement, le dit près de moi, que je ne connais pas; je le laisse dire, c'est un murmure qui me tire pas à conséquence.] (Blanchot 1993a, xx–xxi)

Yet if the Outside is indicated in a passive non-relation to oneself, it also presents a counterpart to itself in sheer intensity, in being "face to face" with a mad light: the Most High is revealed to be crazy, like the doctors as Tolstoy sees them, and in any case hiding us from the Outside as it truly gives itself (in withdrawal). Even here, in this false encounter with the Outside, the narrator bespeaks a distance from himself: "At times I said to myself, 'This is death. In spite of everything, it's really worth it, it's impressive'" [*Parfois, je me disais: 'C'est la mort; malgré tout, cela en vaut la peine, c'est impressionnant*] (Blanchot 1981, 11, 25).

*

Levinas writes on *La folie du jour* in 1975. Some years before then Blanchot had devoted several dialogues to his friend's mature thought in *Totalité et infini* (1961). One of the voices in "Tenir parole" (1962) ponders the relation between "myself" and *Autrui*. Of this relationship, one voice says, "Emmanuel Levinas would say that it is of an ethical nature, but I find in this word only secondary meanings. That *autrui* should be above me, that his speech should be a speech of height, of eminence – these metaphors appease, by putting it into perspective, a difference so radical that it escapes any determination other than itself" (Blanchot 1993a, 63). The primary meaning of the encounter with another person is given in speech when it is figured as primary, not derived from sight. Another dialogue, "L'Indestrucible" (1962), augmented in *L'Entretien infini* (1969), argues that I and another person subsist in a "third relation," given neither by way of dialectic nor by way of absorption by the other person. This third relation holds the two parties together and apart in the activity of speech; it is, as he says, "the very extent of the Outside" (Blanchot 1993a, 69). He goes on to erode Levinas's claim that the ethical height of another person is a phenomenological given, insisting that the other person and I abide in a relation of double dissymmetry, one that does not flatten the ethical sphere into a plane, and rephrasing the object under scrutiny from *Autrui* to the community (Blanchot 1993a, 70–71).[27] In short, Blanchot is clear that there is no exit from the Outside, and that it is only by way of the Outside that one can properly encounter another person: we may speak of justice but only if we do so in the awareness that it derives from a more fundamental situation than ethics ever countenances. For what is crucial is not meeting the other person as a stranger but regarding him "*as a man in his strangeness – that which escapes all identification*"(Blanchot 1993a, 74).

To be sure, Blanchot's understanding of the Outside develops over the years from 1948 to 1969, in part through the intellectual rapport he has with Levinas's philosophy. Yet it does not change in major ways. The conversations about Levinas's *magnum opus* at the start of *L'Entretien infini* can be read as an oblique response to his reservations about *L'Espace littéraire*. Yet in "Exercices sur 'La folie du jour'" Levinas makes no reference to this response, and writes as though Blanchot were following the philosophical position outlined in *De Existence à la existent*. Levinas wonders if he might be accused on "*lès-poésie*" in his reading of *La folie du jour*, because he plans to consider only a few passages of it and respond to their texture (1996, 157). But the charge would be more surely justified on the ground that Levinas does not acknowledge the story's affirmation of the inescapability of the Outside. In the end, Levinas does not read *La folie du jour*; he applies his own philosophy to it, seeing there a story written by a version of himself, perhaps the novelist he never became, and not the story written by his friend Blanchot.

---

27 The difficulty of thinking community is explored by Blanchot in *The Unavowable Community* (1988, 12).

Bibliography

Blanchot, Maurice. 1951. "La Folie par excellence." *Critique* 45 (February 1951): 99–118.
Blanchot, Maurice. 1953. "Dionys Mascolo: *Le Communisme*." *La Nouvelle Revue française* 12 (December 1953): 1096–1099.
Blanchot, Maurice. 1959. "Comment découvrir l'obscur." *La Nouvelle Revue française* 83 (1959): 867–879.
Blanchot, Maurice. 1960. "La Marche de l'écrivisse." *La Nouvelle Revue française* 91 (July 1960): 90–99.
Blanchot, Maurice. 1962. "Tenir parole." *La Nouvelle Nouvelle française* 110 (February 1962): 290–298.
Blanchot, Maurice. 1964. "L'Interruption." *La Nouvelle Nouvelle française* 137 (May 1964): 869–881.
Blanchot, Maurice. 1969. *L'Entretien infini*. Paris: Gallimard.
Blanchot, Maurice. 1981. *The Madness of the Day*. Trans. Lydia Davis. Barrytown: Station Hill Press.
Blanchot, Maurice. 1982. *The Space of Literature*. Trans. Ann Smock. Lincoln: University of Nebraska Press.
Blanchot, Maurice. 1988. *The Unavowable Community*. Trans. Pierre Joris. Barrytown: Station Hill Press.
Blanchot, Maurice. 1993a. *The Infinite Conversation*. Trans. Susan Hanson. Minneapolis: University of Minnesota Press.
Blanchot, Maurice. 1993b. *The One Who was Standing Apart from Me*. Trans. Lydia Davis. Barrytown: Station Hill Press.
Blanchot, Maurice. 2000. *The Instant of My Death*, bound with Jacques Derrida, *Demeure*. Trans Elizabeth Rottenberg. Stanford: Stanford University Press.
Blanchot, Maurice. 2003. "The Song of the Sirens." *The Book to Come*. Trans. Charlotte Mandell. Stanford: Stanford University Press. 1–24.
Blanchot, Maurice. 2004. *Lautréamont and Sade*. Trans. Stuart Kendall and Michelle Kendall. Stanford: Stanford University Press.
Breton, André. 1928. *Nadja*. Paris: Gallimard [reprint 1945].
Derrida, Jacques. 1978. "Violence and Metaphysics: An Essay on the Thought of Emmanuel Levinas." *Writing and Difference*. Trans. Alan Bass. London: Routledge and Kegan Paul. 79–153.
Derrida, Jacques. 2011. "Title to be Specified." Trans. Tom Conley. *Parages*. Ed. John P. Leavey. Stanford: Stanford University Press. 192–215.
Heidegger, Martin. 1971. "The Thing." *Poetry, Language, Thought*. Trans. Albert Hofstadter. New York: Harper and Row. 165–186.
Heidegger, Martin. 1973. *Being and Time*. Trans. John Macquarrie and Edward Robinson. Oxford: Basil Blackwell.
Hill, Leslie. 1997. *Blanchot: Extreme Contemporary*. London: Routledge.
Kofman, Sarah. 1983. *Comment s'en sortir?* Paris: Galilée.
Levinas, Emmanuel. 1979. *Totality and Infinity: An Essay on Exteriority*. Trans. Alphonso Lingis. The Hague: Martinus Nijhoff.
Levinas, Emmanuel. 1987. "Phenomenon and Enigma." *Collected Philosophical Papers*. Trans. Alphonso Lingis. Dordrecht: Martinus Nijhoff. 61–74.

Levinas, Emmanuel. 1988. *Existence and Existents*. Trans. Alphonso Lingis, corrected edition. Dordrecht: Kluwer.

Levinas, Emmanuel. 1990. "To Love the Torah More than God." *Difficult Freedom: Essays on Judaism*. Trans. Seán Hand. Baltimore: Johns Hopkins University Press. 142–145.

Levinas, Emmanuel. 1996. *On Maurice Blanchot*, bound with *Proper Names*. Trans. Michael B. Smith. Stanford: Stanford University Press.

Levinas, Emmanuel. 2004. "Reality and Its Shadow." *Unforeseen History*. Trans. Nidra Poller. Urbana: University of Illinois Press. 76–91.

Levinas, Emmanuel. 2009. *Oeuvres*, 1: *Carnets de captivité et autre inédits*. Eds. Rodolphe Calin and Catherine Chalier. Paris: Grasset.

Mallarmé, Stéphane. 2003. "Villiers de l'Isle-Adam" *Oeuvres complètes*, 2 volumes. Bibliothèque de la Pléiade. Ed. Bertrand Marchal. Paris: Gallimard.

Nietzsche, Friedrich. 1968. "How the 'Real World' at last Became a Myth." *Twilight of the Idols*, bound with *The Anti-Christ*. Trans. R. J. Hollingdale. Harmondsworth: Penguin.

Pascal, Blaise. 2005. *Pensées*. Ed. and Trans. Roger Ariew. Indianapolis: Hackett Pub. Co., 2005.

Tolstoy, Leo. 1936. *On Insanity*. Trans. Ludvig Perno. London: C. W. Daniel.

Wahl, Jean. 1944. *Existence humaine et transcendance*. Neuchâtel: Éditions de la Baconnière.

Eric Hoppenot
Poetic Language and Prophetic Language in Levinas's Works

"Kafka said to Janouch that 'the task of the poet is a prophetic task [. . .]'" (Blanchot 1982, 73),[1] determining in the same conversation that the Jewish people live with the voices of Scripture, that these are by no means relegated to the past, and that, on the contrary, they are in the present.

The manuscript of Emmanuel Levinas's "The Servant and Her Master," held in the Maurice Blanchot archive, contains several additions to the published article Levinas dedicated to Maurice Blanchot's narrative *Awaiting Oblivion* (1963). A relatively lengthy addition was to constitute a footnote in the version first published in the celebrated volume of *Critique* from June, 1966,[2] a special issue comprising the first volume of collected articles dedicated to Blanchot, and was subsequently included in Levinas's volume *On Maurice Blanchot* (1975). The footnote reads:

> No ethical element comes into play in Blanchot's work so as to constitute this modality. It is not owing to its impoverished nature, nor to persecution or contempt, that it acquires the privilege of disappearing from the horizon, of transcending it, and then responding from the depths of its absence only to the call of the best. And yet every now and then, transcendence in Blanchot consists of the very uncertainty of presence, "as if she were only present so as to prevent herself from speaking. Then came the moments when, the thread of their relationship having been broken, she recovered her calm reality. It was at those moments that he saw better in how extraordinary a state of weakness she was, one from which she drew that authority which sometimes made her speak" (pp. 25–6). We said earlier that the word poetry referred to the disruption of immanence to which language is condemned in becoming its own prisoner. There is no question of considering this disruption as a purely aesthetic event. But the word poetry does not after all name a species whose genus is referred to by the word art. Inseparable from speech (*le verbe*), it overflows with prophetic meanings. (Levinas 1989, 158–159)[3]

---

[1] The French translation of Gustav Janouch's *Gespräche mit Kafka* uses the word "writer" and not "poet" (see Janouch 1998, 231).
[2] *Critique* 229 (1966), special issue devoted to Maurice Blanchot.
[3] This footnote refers to the sentence: "Such is the scintillating modality of transcendence, of what truly *comes to pass*." (Levinas 1989, 156)

Translation: Translated, from the French, by Ashraf Noor

I thought that I would find other instances in Levinas's work reaffirming this marginal comment that poetry "overflows with prophetic meanings," a statement that one intuits immediately as sounding like a Levinasian expression, so indubitably familiar are we with the recurrence of the verb "to overflow" in Levinas's vocabulary. There is, however, in fact nothing that resonates with this marginal expression. Moreover, the only evocation of the prophetic in Levinas's *Sur Maurice Blanchot* is found in this sole note. Is it possible, though, to articulate something between the poetic and the prophetic in the Levinasian space? Or, further, does the poetic only overflow with "prophetic meanings" in the unique work of Blanchot, as the *hapax* that we have just pointed out seems to underline?

1 Song

In the *Carnets de captivité*, Levinas associates poetry first of all with musicality. "Poetry is therefore like a rhythm. [. . .] Poetry is things set to music" (Levinas 2009, 100). Even more decisively, four pages further, we find this statement: "Rhyme and its technique are neither the obstacle nor the guide of thought. They are the very condition of art." This is a point of view that assumes a relatively conventional, indeed outdated, representation of poetry. No contemporary poet would seriously share this statement. What seems to me entirely worthy of interest in this movement giving birth to thought that begins to become writing is to observe the manner in which the poetic semination, in one of the philosophical potentialities as yet unthought by Levinas, becomes the binding encounter. In a word, and to paraphrase one of Heidegger's titles, poetry is on the way to philosophy, not because it claims in any way to elevate itself to philosophy but because it bears within itself a surge of thought, at least of language. Thus, after having explicated the possibility for poetry to detach itself by its musicality from all objective meaning, Levinas writes "the philosophical concept is also able to de-materialize itself in such a way [as poetry] and become like art itself profound knowledge" (Levinas 2009, 115). Shortly after, Levinas asks himself whether, finally, metaphysics and existence itself are not art.

The first proximity between poetry and prophecy is, before anything else, even before the word, the Said, the offering of song. Both discourses participate in song, something preceding the event of meaning, the voice itself, its intonation, its melody, its rhythm. This is the case from Levinas's first texts, from *Existence and Existents*, where he seeks to describe what he calls *exoticism*, a concept that is nothing if not reminiscent of Baudelaire, whom he cites frequently and with whom *Totality and Infinity* concludes. Exoticism is that which is liable to tear us from the world, and this is how Levinas refers to the arts, particularly to music and to the musicality of poetry. The attraction, the power of art, that which Blanchot calls "the fascination," consists of extricating oneself from perception in order to give way to sensation. It is this confusing of sensation in the image of the object and not in the object itself, which Levinas defines as aesthetics.

In "Reality and Its Shadow," however, *exoticism* takes a completely different turn, and the exotic musicality of poetry, which hitherto harboured fecundity, moves into magic, a relatively rare word in Levinas's vocabulary, or into sorcery: "Rhythm represents a unique situation where we cannot speak of consent, assumption, initiative, or freedom, because the subject is caught up and carried away by it [. . .] for in rhythm there is no longer anything of oneself, but rather a passage from oneself to anonymity [thus to Blanchot's universe! –EH]. This is the sorcery or the incantation of poetry and music." (Levinas 1989, 132–133) The rhythm of song or poetry relegates the subject to a posture that is ecstatic posture, if I may force the word a little, but in a way that condemns it to passivity or fastens it to the present of contemplation. In this essential article, there is no word severe enough for Levinas to characterize the errance into which art, and not only the image, leads us, even if this latter is endowed with a power to fascinate that is stronger than poetry. If poetry, in contrast to the prophetic word, entrances, this is because it maintains a relation of itself to itself and freezes time in a present that does not pass. This is the very definition of fascination: absorbed in poetic literature, the reader, in strict terms, "does not see time passing." It is pleasure, certainly, but pleasure that entrances. Art is the time that freezes things in an eternal present. Prophetic time is completely different. The prophetic word inaugurates a disturbance such that the very concept of the future becomes practically aporetic: an impossible future or impossibility as future. To announce an impossible future is to offer a word that escapes the chain of effects and of causes, the logical course of time, as a consequence of which the prophetic offering announces itself in a language that can be not received by the people to whom it is addressed. This is attested, for example, in the reticence manifested by the Hebrews who at first refuse to leave Egypt. The impossible future founded in the prophetic word implies a word that abstracts entirely from what is, without a hold on the past. Thus for Blanchot: "But prophetic speech announces an impossible future, or makes the future it announces, because it announces it, something impossible, a future one would not know how to live and that must upset all the sure givens of existence. When speech becomes prophetic, it is not the future that is given, it is the present that is taken away, and with it any possibility of a firm, stable, lasting presence." (Blanchot 2003, 79)

If the present is as if "withdrawn," this is because prophetic language sets all categories of representation ablaze. The advent of the prophetic address explodes the very possibility of the present, substituting for the awaited present a word, which in some way uproots and tears away the pleasure of the instant, of the fascination of the poetic song. Prophecy comes to destroy the present, imposing a configuration in which the present already contains the future. Awaiting the Messiah, Levinas writes, "marks the very duration of time" (Levinas 1990, 26).

In *Totality and Infinity*, the critical tones announced in "Reality and Its Shadow" are nearby: "Every work of art is painting and statuary, immobilized in the instant or in its periodic return. Poetry substitutes a rhythm for the feminine life. Beauty becomes a form covering over indifferent matter, and not harboring mystery." (Levinas 1979, 263) In sorcery, one will recognize the song of the Sirens that Ulysses, this antinomian figure to Abraham, has to confront.

But in analyzing Blanchot's writing, Levinas defends the argument according to which the poetic transformation to which the writer makes language submit would have the faculty of overcoming the rustling of the world. Would the song that overwhelms the literary space offer a hypostatic modality to the subject or is it reduced to an illusion, as the motif of bewitchment would suggest? Levinas will emphasize at various junctures, outside the restricted context of his commentaries on Blanchot, the necessity of thinking the poetic event as the possibility offered to language of extracting itself from immanence.

At least two bodies of works, those of Solomon and those of David,[4] realize a discursive coalescence between the poetic and the prophetic. In *Du sacré au saint*, Levinas characterizes the psalms as poetry, and in the part of *Difficult Freedom* devoted to "Messianic Commentaries" one reads: "'King David' is distinguished here from the Messiah. He is the author of the Psalms, where poetry merges with prayer and prayer spills over into poetry. The word has meaning from the moment adoration is produced in this world, where a finite being stands before something which goes beyond him, but where this presence before the Most High becomes the psalm's exaltation" (Levinas 1990, 84). (One can rightfully make a distinction here and hear that the *Psalms* are not prophetic narrations.) It seems to me that it is precisely at this point of encounter that poetry can overflow with "prophetic meanings," this point at which the

---

4 See Levinas, *In the Time of the Nations* (1994, pages 23 and 68, respectively).

discovery of the divine enjoins the necessity of an alternative discursive modality where the poetic song would not, like that of the Sirens, intend to entrance the reader but where the speaking poet would be affected, perhaps disrupted by a language that is not wholly his own. Does this mean to say that poetry would not associate with the prophetic except under the condition that it proclaim praise of the infinite? Would this imply that the coalescence I evoked cannot take place except at the heart of religious, mystical poetry? If we are to believe Levinas's acerbic commentaries on Claudel's work, the religious character of poetry by no means implies this advent of the prophetic as hospitality. And even if he concedes to Claudel his admiration for the work *Les Patriarches*, attentive eyes will see in this once again the reiteration of poetry defined as "sorcery."

One finds, however, from time to time approaches to poetry that are less negative, and this is why, to my mind, it is very difficult to determine the logic of Levinas's discourse on art. Even if the note in *Otherwise than Being,* which I read as an extended echo of "Reality and Its Shadow," rings clearly as a rejection of art:

> The immemorial past is intolerable for thought. Thus there is an exigency to stop: *ananké stenaï*. The movement beyond being becomes ontology and theology. And thus there is also an idolatry of the beautiful. In its indiscrete exposition and in its stoppage in a statue, in its plasticity, a work of art substitutes itself for God. [. . .] By an irresistible subreption, the incomparable, the diachronic, the non-contemporaneous, through the effect of a deceitful and marvelous schematism, is "imitated" by art, which is iconography. The movement beyond being is fixed in beauty. Theology and art "retain" the immemorial past.   (Levinas 1998b, 199)

But let us also be attentive to what can be generous in the description of the poetic act, for example in *Humanism of the Other*: "Language as expression is above all the creative language of poetry. So art is not the lovely madness of man who takes it into his head to make beauty" (Levinas 2003, 17). And describing the poetry of Agnon, which he considers as "pure poetry," he announces: "Poetry *signifies* poetically the resurrection that sustains it: not in the fable it sings but in its very singing" (Levinas 1996, 12). The essence of poetry, contrary to the prophetic message, uncovers, in a way, its essence through the decision to sing even before the word manifests itself as meaning. In poetry, according to Levinas, the word goes first not towards its meaning but rather towards the materiality of the sound. It seems to me that, in this regard, one could also examine the question of the cry such as it is found in certain poets and the cry to which Levinas accords a role in evoking the "ethical revolt" that "begins in prophecy" (Levinas 1998a, 77). This is, of course, the "voice that cries out in the wilderness," without speaking of the written cry that he evokes when proceeding from what Blanchot wrote about the graffiti posted on the walls of Paris in May 1968, where it was also a matter of an expression so often poetic. The cry as a song that derails, as an excess of the voice, would also need to be interrogated in this articulation of poetic/prophetic word.

2 Prophetic Speech, between *Ruah* and *Davar*

The prophet, in a different sense than the poet, is an inspired being. To be inspired consists in thinking that the world has been created, and its creation continued, by the word. Levinas evokes the "disproportionate voice of a God addressing human beings in the prophetic or poetic tongue" (Levinas 1994, 112). God has placed in the prophet the *ruah* that imparts its energy to him. Claude Tresmontant defines *ruah* as "the supernatural dimension proper to Biblical revelation" (Tresmontant 1977, 108). According to the Biblical tradition, however, everyone is capable of being a prophet. For Levinas, the prophetic is even one of the modes of being human. Every person is potentially a prophet, as is announced in a verse in Numbers 11:29: "Would that all Yahwe's people be prophets!" It is due to the *ruah* that the human escapes abandonment, that he discovers he is not alone. It is equally through inspiration that the relation to God is established as dialogue, God's *ruah* speaking with that of humans. André Neher wrote that the *ruah* of God is "pathetic," a characterization that can be affected by all the anthropo-pathic dangers, but that describes very precisely the action of the spoken word. God addresses humans with his *pathos*, manifesting in this way his attention to what is human. It is through *pathos* that he can grasp the prophet and demand that he not stray from his mission. The pathos of poetry, however, evidently shelters something very different.

Nevertheless, the prophet is not only he who responds to the injunction, to the divine *ruah*, but he is also the one who bears the spoken word, the *davar*. *Ruah* and *davar* cannot be disassociated. If the *davar* is an expression of violence, it is also the manifestation of the pleasure of the spoken word, as is testified by the well-known passage in Ezekiel 3:1–3 where Ezekiel delights in eating the book that tastes of honey. In taking up Levinas's comment on Blanchot once again, while inverting it, one could say that the prophetic word overflows with poetic meanings. Without a doubt, poetry is necessary for the prophetic word. The divine language is a word that nourishes, but could one dare to suggest that the poetic word nourishes the effusion for the divine in the same way that prayer does?

In Levinas's eyes, however, prophecy does not hide the truth of existence; it reveals, but only exercises its power under the singular condition that it makes itself, according to the Law and as Benny Lévy said in a seminar on the philosophy of Levinas, the injunction of existence. It is fundamentally of little importance if the prophet has a particular relation to time, at least in its predictive or oracular dimension (cf. particularly Levinas1998b, 96). Where it seems to me that the prophetic never ceases to resonate in his work is in this verse of Amos that he cites abundantly like a refrain inherent to his writing: "The Lord God has spoken; who can but prophesy?" (Amos 3:8). Levinas will say with respect to Amos that his prophetic inspiration manifests itself through his utterance.

At least once in his works, in addition to our initial example of the note on Blanchot, Levinas will commit himself to recognizing not only a proximity but a quasi-identity between the prophetic and the poetic. In a passage from *In the Time of the Nations*, we read: "Completion and authority, the disproportionate voice of a God addressing human beings in the prophetic or poetic tongue. This is an ascent within words, be they the most recent ones, to I know not what antiquity that is already to be translated, already to be deciphered" (Levinas 1996, 112).

The divine word is a shock, it harasses the subject in his entrenchment – let us recall Jonah –and does not cease to summon him. If Blanchot maintains essentially the dynamic of *davar* and its hyperbolic character, it is because the divine word is intrinsically action. It judges, it condemns, it saves, it heals, it commands. In the *davar*, the prophet is not relieved of his language in order to be nothing other than the receptacle and the utterer of the divine word, but he enters into a veritable dialogical configuration with God.

In the manner of God, who creates the world through language, the *nabi*, because he is the divine spokesman par excellence, creates the conditions of a dialogical space and temporality where everything works in the verticality of exchange. The prophet is not only he who listens and transmits; he is not a simple receptacle, for the *nabi* possesses the extraordinary power of appealing to God. In other words, he is both the locus of the appeal and that of the initial response. The prophetic utterance bears the word to the highest point of its engagement, to the extent that it inaugurates a face to face between the people and the word from Outside. With regard to this word that is absolutely other it is necessary to be bound by the responsibility of a decision involving his future and the future of coming generations. How does the resonance of this dialogue manifest itself? According to Levinas: "Prophetism could be the name of this reversal in which the perception of order coincides with the fact that he who obeys it also signifies it. Prophetism would thus be the very psyche of the soul, the Other *within* the Same, where the *within* signifies the *waking up* of the Same by the Other" (Levinas 2000, 200). And once more, still describing the verse of Amos, Levinas will add: "Prophetism as pure witnessing, pure, because prior to all disclosure; this is a subjection to an order prior to the understanding of the order." (Levinas 1998a, 76) This is a statement that cannot but remind us of the "we shall do and we shall hear" of the scene in Sinai.

This is why the prophet is always confronted with the trial of the reception of his own speech, of his power of persuasion. The action of the people is the response to the prophetic *davar*. Poetry is clearly deprived of this pragmatic and injunctive dimension, even if, as Levinas will read and will say with respect to Celan's poetry, poetry is an outstretched hand, or to say this differently, an offering addressed to the other; yet it is also, for Celan, writing in a bottle launched into the sea, its destination fragile and uncertain.

In the same way, prophetic writing is the only one for which a date is set, for it bears its own end within itself (prophetic time is limited). It sets itself forth simultaneously for the present and for the messianic age. Poetic time, the time of art, the time that always remains that of Narcissus, is completely different.

3 Concluding Remarks

To conclude these too rapid remarks, let us examine briefly what distinguishes Levinas's prophetic thought from that of Blanchot. If Blanchot emphasizes the aspect of time in his interpretation of prophecy, Levinas, loyal in this to the rabbinical tradition, prefers the sage to the prophet but above all invites us to think the human condition as prophecy, this being a condition of ethics.

If one agrees with Levinas's thought, it appears that prophecy is not only something that is possible for man but also, and further, that the prophetic is a moment of the human condition that signifies responsibility for the Other. The prophet would not be merely a voice that professes but one that bears the responsibility for his word and in the responsibility for his Saying manifests that for the Other. The prophet's language responds to, and is accountable for, "the epiphany of the face of the Other." One can be sensitive to the distinction Levinas makes between the prophet and the witness, who is not subjected to the order for he anticipates it and responds "Here I am!" before any request. Finally, one understands why in Levinas's thought and in Jewish thought in general the prophet is not glorified – and this holds all the more for the poet! Jewish thought will always prefer the sage to the prophet. Does that mean, as Levinas considers, that Rabbi Akiba will always take precedence over Moses?

If, however, a link could once be established between the prophetic according to Levinas and that described by Blanchot, one would find a trace of this, and by no means a faint one, in *The Writing of the Disaster*, where it is Levinas's very philosophy that Blanchot characterizes as prophecy.[5] According to this, Levinas's Jewish philosophy is prophetic inasmuch as it has yet to be thought. Why? It is because "it bears responsibility for the future" and because it has to "care for hope."[6] In other words, the Jewish word is in some way still to come, it is at play in the attentive study of the oral tradition, which pursues without cease the word inherited from the prophets.[7] It is in addressing his questions to the text that the Jew responds to the call.

Bibliography

Banon, David. *Entrelacs: La lettre et le sens dans l'exégèse juive*. Paris: Editions du Cerf, 2008.
Blanchot, Maurice. *The Space of Literature*. Trans. Ann Smock. Lincoln: University of Nebraska Press, 1982.
Blanchot, Maurice. *The Writing of the Disaster*. Trans. Ann Smock. Lincoln: University of Nebraska Press, 1986.
Blanchot, Maurice. "Prophetic speech", in *The Book to Come*. Trans. Charlotte Mandell. California: Stanford University Press, 2003. 79–85.
Blanchot, Maurice. *Ecrits politiques, 1953–1993*. Paris: Gallimard, 2008.
Draï, Raphaël. *La communication prophétique. Volume I. Le Dieu caché et sa revelation*. Paris: Fayard, 1990.
Janouch, Gustav. *Conversations avec Kafka*. Trans. Bernard Lortholary. Paris: Maurice Nadeau, 1998.
Levinas, Emmanuel. *Totality and Infinity: An Essay on Exteriority*. Trans. Alfonso Lingis. The Hague: Martinus Nijhoff, 1979.
Levinas, Emmanuel. "Reality and Its Shadow." Trans. Alphonso Lingis. *The Levinas Reader*. Ed. Seán Hand. Oxford: Blackwell, 1989. 129–143.

---

5 See Blanchot (1986, note 148). This footnote is sufficiently important to be taken up once more in the form of a quote in the article "N'oubliez pas" (1983), in *Ecrits politiques 1953–1993* (Blanchot 2008, 40).
6 According to Raphaël Draï (1990, 135), there could not be prophecy without hope, even if this is not dominant.
7 One can read profitably, in David Banon's *Entrelacs: La lettre et le sens dans l'exégèse juive*, the chapters "Du prophète au rabbi ou de la voix à la lettre: une lecture d'adultes" (Banon 2008, 19–46), as well as the chapter devoted to André Neher, "André Néher et la Bible. Approche nouvelle et langage neuf" (Banon 2008, 143–157).

Levinas, Emmanuel. "The Servant and Her Master." Trans. Michael Holland. *The Levinas Reader*. Ed. Seán Hand. Oxford: Blackwell, 1989. 150–159.

Levinas, Emmanuel. *Difficult Freedom*. Trans. Seán Hand. Baltimore: Johns Hopkins University Press, 1990.

Levinas, Emmanuel. *In the Time of the Nations*. Trans. Michael B. Smith. London: The Athlone Press, 1994.

Levinas, Emmanuel. *Proper Names*. Trans. Michael B. Smith. London: The Athlone Press, 1996.

Levinas, Emmanuel. *Of God Who Comes to Mind*. Trans. Bettina Bergo. Stanford: Stanford University Press, 1998a.

Levinas, Emmanuel. *Otherwise Than Being or Beyond Essence*. Trans. Alphonso Lingis. Pittsburgh: Duquesne University Press, 1998b.

Levinas, Emmanuel. *God, Death, and Time*. Trans. Bettina Bergo. Stanford: Stanford University Press, 2000.

Levinas, Emmanuel. *Humanism of the Other*. Trans. Nidra Poller. Chicago: University of Illinois Press, 2003.

Levinas, Emmanuel. *Œuvres complètes*. Volume I. *Carnets de captivité et autres inédits*. Eds. Rodolphe Calin and Catherine Chalier. Paris: Grasset/IMEC, 2009.

Tresmontant, Claude. *Le prophétisme hébreu*. Paris:François Xavier de Guibert, 1977.

Vivian Liska
The Poem, the Place, the Jew: Emmanuel Levinas on Paul Celan

A reflection on Emmanuel Levinas's approach to Paul Celan requires an expansion of the field of vision as concerns the two protagonists. One such potential revision would be a constellation of the following names: Levinas, Blanchot, Hölderlin, Celan. These four figures conjoined paratactically form a chiasm with regard to the relationship between the poem, the place, and the Jew. Levinas and Celan meet at the outer poles of this figure of thought, at extremities whose relation is illuminated by the other two names, Blanchot and Hölderlin, which both unite and separate them. This chiasm is complicated by a division that distinguishes between the two thinkers and the two poets. At the centre of the chiasm is a name that is not expressed explicitly but which nevertheless constitutes the axis of this poetico-philosophical constellation: Martin Heidegger. This chiasm will, in what follows, be deployed in terms of a central motif: the question of place, more particularly the conceptual pairs of exile and *Heimat*, errancy and rootedness, homelessness and dwelling, all considered in respect to the poem, to poetry.

In his essay on Celan titled "Paul Celan. De l'être à l'autre" (Paul Celan: From Being to the Other), first published in *La Revue des Belles Letters* in 1972, shortly after the poet's suicide, Levinas implicitly retrieves the central idea of the famous passage in his earlier essay "La Trace de l'Autre" (The Trace of the Other), where he distinguishes between Greek philosophy and Jewish thought via the opposition between Ulysses's and Abraham's respective relations to place. In the earlier text, Levinas writes: "To the myth of Ulysses returning to Ithaca, we wish to oppose the story of Abraham who leaves his fatherland forever for a yet unknown land" (Levinas 1986, 348).[1] Ulysses's journey is directed towards the eventual return to his fatherland, his *Heimat*; for Levinas, this is both a sign of turning in upon oneself and contrasts with Abraham's departure, which, rather than being directed towards return to the land of his birth, is oriented solely towards a foreign destination, a terrain that is, so far, nothing but

---

[1] In the original: "Au mythe d'Ulysse retournant à Ithaque, nous voudrions opposer l'histoire d'Abraham quittant à jamais sa patrie pour une terre encore inconnue" (Levinas 1982, 192). The essay was first published in *Tijdschrift Voor Filosofie* 25.3 (1963): 605–623.

Translation: Translated, from the French, by Ashraf Noor

Open Access. © 2021 Vivian Liska, published by De Gruyter. This work is licensed under the Creative Commons Attribution 4.0 International License.
https://doi.org/10.1515/9783110668926-012

a promise. Between Ulysses and Abraham, as envisaged by Levinas, the fundamental difference between Greek and Jew is at stake, not just between the philosophical logos but also between Homer and the Hebrew Bible. The Greek route remains that of Ulysses, whose protracted, adventure-laden journey through the world is in fact nothing other than a return to himself, to his native island – "complying with the Same, misapprehending the Other" – in contrast to "the biblical movement of the Same towards the Other" (Levinas 1987, 43 (my translation)).[2] In contrast to the closure and totality re-established through the return as final destination in the Greek experience, the Jewish destiny corresponds to an incessant movement towards the other and to what Levinas terms, perhaps somewhat hyperbolically, in "Heidegger, Gagarin et nous" (Heidegger, Gagarin, and Us), an indifference to land and soil: "Judaism has always been free with regard to place" (Levinas 1990, 231).[3] In this, Levinas seems to support the idea of the Jew as the eternal wanderer and to affirm exile as both a mode of existence and a modality of thought opening towards a non-retrievable alterity.

The spirit of Levinas's statement would seem to accord with the writings of several thinkers in the second half of the twentieth century who, in a positive manner, associate Jewishness with exile, exodus, and errancy. In the post-World War II period, the old antisemitic motif of the rootless, parasitic Jew underwent a transformation and came to be invoked for its critical potential for undermining nationalisms of all colours. Understandably, in the years after National Socialism, the idea of the Jew as a homeless, eternal wanderer reactivated the notion of an intellectual rootedness imbedded within the law, the word, and the letter as an alternative to national or geographic rootedness. Many thinkers who, after 1945, allude to the centuries-old narrative of Jewish exile seek, on one hand, to reverse the inimical view of the homeless Jewish people and, on the other, to propagate a universally valid alternative, and even counterforce, to ideologies of "blood and soil" and, ultimately, to all nationalist identities. The simultaneity of these concerns raises fundamental questions: How can one present Jewish exile as positive, indeed as an exemplary condition of extraterritoriality, in light of the history of the Jewish plight, which includes a long and bloody history of suffering partly due to the lack of a "proper place?" And how does one prevent the consciousness of this negative aspect of exile from again becoming a desire for rootedness in the soil, which Levinas associates both with Greek paganism and with Nazi ideology, and which he calls,

---

[2] In the original: "L'itinéraire de la philosophie reste celui d'Ulysse dont l'aventure dans le monde n'est qu'un retour à son île natale – une complaisance dans le Même, une méconnaissance de l'Autre" (Levinas 1987, 43).

[3] In the original: "Le judaïsme a toujours été libre à l'égard des lieux" (Levinas 1983, 350).

in "Heidegger, Gagarin et nous," "the very splitting of humanity into natives and strangers?" (Levinas 1990, 232)?⁴ Moreover, how can one formulate a universal concept while referring to a particular, concrete, historical instance, without falling either into "Judeo-centrism" – the wandering Jew as exemplary and to be emulated by the whole of humankind – or into an annihilation of the concrete singularity of the Jew by means of metaphor, which would be the negation of Jewish history, of exile forced upon the Jews for centuries? And finally, above all in the context of poetry, how can one render justice to the Jewish attachment to the word and to the book – to having no other home than the letter – without idealizing this attribution to the point of forgetting the precarious state of this substitute for a domicile that would promise protection and security?

In my reading of Levinas's text on Celan and of several verses by Celan, I wish to show that it is through the use of poetic language that both the philosopher and the poet devise suggestions that indicate the direction of such a possibility: to think, or rather to write, exile as the ethical refusal to anchor oneself in the soil, without, at the same time, negating the vulnerability of such a state; to conceive the exemplary association of Jewishness and exile while maintaining both its particular and its general dimension, its concrete history and its meaning as a universal predicament; and finally, to convey the vitality of the idea of Jewish dwelling in the word and the letter, but in such a way that the vulnerability of this substitution as well as a hope born from the contesting force of the poetic act remain perceptible.

1 Levinas Reading Heidegger

Given his distrust of poetry,⁵ expressed among other places in his early text "La réalité et son ombre" (Reality and Its Shadow),⁶ why does Levinas rethink the question of place in the context of poetry, particularly that of Paul Celan? A preliminary response to this question presents itself in one of the key expressions Heidegger borrows from the German Romantic poet Friedrich Hölderlin: "Dichterisch wohnet der Mensch auf Erden" (Poetically Man Dwells on Earth).⁷ For Heidegger, the poet is the one who provides man with a dwelling in the

---

4 In the original: "la scission même de l'humanité en autochtones et en étrangers" (Levinas 1983, 350).
5 See, for example, Leslie Hill, "Distrust of Poetry: Levinas, Blanchot, Celan" (2005).
6 See Levinas, "La réalité et son ombre" (1994).
7 See Heidegger, "Poetically Man Dwells . . ." (1975).

"house of being" (Heidegger 2002, 232).[8] Levinas's "Paul Celan. De l'être à l'autre" can be read as a radical contestation of Heidegger's claims, most pertinently those maintained by the later Heidegger of *Holzwege* in 1950. The task of the poet is to provide man with a place, to root the human being in the earth, thus finding again, in and through this dwelling, the ancient splendor of the pagan gods. This task is the response to the question presented in the title of a central text in this collection of Heidegger's articles. The title of the article, "Und wozu Dichter in dürftiger Zeit?" (Why Poets in Times of Distress?), derives from another celebrated verse of Hölderlin. This question, with which Heidegger begins his reflection on the task of the poet in modernity, cites Hölderlin's elegy "Brot und Wein" (Bread and Wine). Heidegger evaluates in Hölderlin's poetry the notion that, after the death of Herakles, Dionysus, and Christ, the world has lost the meaning of its history and of "man's stay within it." Heidegger continues, "in the absence of God notice is given of something even worse. [. . .] The time has already become so desolate that it is no longer able to see the absence of God as a lack" (Heidegger 2002, 200).[9] The world has lost its ground, and, with the abyss that has thus opened, it has lost the possibility of all rootedness, the possibility of inhabiting the earth. It is not possible to reverse this condition unless man places his dwelling in his own being, and it is the task of the poet to lead him there. The conditions of this reversal are linked to a time, a place, a language, and a relation to nature, which all together provide mortals with a dwelling on this earth. If "[i]n the age of the world's night [*Weltnacht*], the abyss of the world must be experienced and must be endured" (Heidegger 2002, 201), it is the task of the poet to experience and endure this abyss.[10] For Heidegger, this *Weltnacht* extends from Socrates to the present. It is the mission of the poet to recall the gods and their absence; it is his task to advance fearlessly toward the abyss, to confront it directly. The poet's calling consists in listening and submitting to the *language that speaks*

---

8 In the original: "Haus des Seins" (Heidegger 1999, 310).

9 In the original: "Der Fehl Gottes bedeutet, daß kein Gott mehr sichtbar und eindeutig die Menschen und die Dinge auf sich versammelt und aus solcher Versammlung die Weltgeschichte und den menschlichen Aufenthalt in ihr fügt. Im Fehl Gottes kündigt sich aber noch Ärgeres an. Nicht nur die Götter und der Gott sind entflohen, sondern der Glanz der Gottheit ist in der Weltgeschichte erloschen. Die Zeit der Weltnacht ist die dürftige Zeit, weil sie immer dürftiger wird. Sie ist bereits so dürftig geworden, daß sie nicht mehr vermag, den Fehl Gottes als Fehl zu merken" (Heidegger 1999, 269).

10 In the original: "Im Weltalter der Weltnacht muß der Abgrund der Welt erfahren und ausgestanden werden. Dazu ist aber nötig, daß solche sind, die in den Abgrund reichen" (Heidegger 1999, 270).

Being in the impersonal neuter, to sing the "god of the vine," who "preserves in it and in its fruit the essential mutuality of earth and sky as the site of the nuptials of men and gods" (Heidegger 2002, 202)[11] and thus to provide human being with its dwelling on this earth.

In "Paul Celan. De l'être à l'autre," Levinas takes up these Heideggerian terms and refutes them one by one: against the *Weltnacht* and its continuity from the pre-Socratic Greeks to our times, Levinas names the "time of distress" the "passion of Israel under Nazism" (Levinas 1978, 16).[12] Against Heidegger's suggestion of continuity, Levinas views Auschwitz as "the interruption of history," that which, precisely, underlies the ruptured harmony in Celan's verses. Against the Heideggerian abyss, Levinas speaks of the "leap across the abyss open in Being" (Levinas 1978, 18).[13] Against the language that speaks in the neuter, Levinas, evoking Celan, describes a "mumbling infancy of discourse," an "awkward entry into the [Heideggerian]'speaking of language,' the celebrated '*die Sprache spricht*'" (Levinas 1978, 16).[14] Against the impersonality of this language, Levinas cites Celan, who describes the genesis of the poem through the "inclination" (*Neigungswinkel*) of the poet's existence. Against the splendour of nature – the pagan idolatry of "the shining forth of pre-Socratic 'physis'" (Levinas 1978, 16)[15] sung by the poet, according to Heidegger – Levinas invokes the dialogue of the two Jews in *Gespräch im Gebirg*, one of Celan's rare prose texts, in which the poet formulates the Jewish negation of paganism in the most simple and direct terms: "for the Jew and nature, they are two" (my translation).[16]

Heidegger's primary metaphor of the *Weltnacht* itself designates a place: the reversal of the night occurs where the mortals inhabit the "site" of Being, where they "come into their own essence," where Being dwells. It is this site that Levinas calls upon us to leave behind as he sets forth on the path of the poem which, in Celan's words cited by Levinas (Levinas 1978, 17), "goes toward the other."[17] On this path, the poem shows the direction to be taken.

---

11 In the original: "[. . .] der Gott der Rebe verwahrt in dieser und in deren Frucht zugleich das wesenhafte Zueinander von Erde und Himmel als der Stätte des Brautfestes für Menschen und Götter" (Heidegger 1999, 271).
12 In the original: "la passion d'Israël sous Hitler" (Levinas 1976, 54).
13 In the original: "saut par-dessus l'abîme ouvert dans l'être" (Levinas 1976, 52).
14 In the original: "Communication élémentaire et sans révélation, balbutiante enfance du discours, bien maladroite insertion dans la fameuse langue qui parle, dans le fameux *die Sprache spricht* [. . .]" (Levinas 1976, 50).
15 In the original: "l'éclat de la *physis* des présocratiques" (Levinas 1976, 50).
16 In the original: "Denn der Jud und die Natur, das ist zweierlei" (Celan 1983, 169–170).
17 In the original: "Le poème va vers l'autre" (Levinas 1976, 51).

A brief excursus will illuminate the extent to which, in Levinas's text on Celan, the critical attitude shown towards Heidegger's paean to the pre-Socratic mythology of *physis* is prefigured in Celan's "Why Poets?," a poem that the Jewish-Romanian poet wrote in his youth. According to Heidegger:

> These, for the poet, are the tracks of the fugitive gods. This track, in Hölderlin's experience, is what Dionysus, the wine-god, brings down for the God-less during the darkness of their world's night. For the god of the vine preserves [. . .] the essential mutuality of earth and sky as the site of the nuptials of men and gods. [. . .] Poets are the mortals who gravely sing the wine-god and sense the track of the fugitive gods; they stay on the gods' track, and so they blaze a path for their mortal relations, a path toward the turning point.
>
> (Heidegger 2002, 202)[18]

In 1942, Celan wrote the poem "Nähe der Gräber" (Nearness of Graves) after learning of his mother's death. This poem of five stanzas points to the indifference of nature in the face of violence and the suffering of victims. Having called upon the water of the river near the internment camp where his mother was killed, and upon the wheat field, the trees, the quaking aspen ([*Zitter-*]*Espe*), the weeping willow ([*Trauer-*]*Weide*), he invokes, in almost naïve fashion, the god Dionysus:

> Und steigt nicht der Gott mit dem knospenden Stab
> den Hügel hinan und den Hügel hinab?   (Celan 2003, 17)

> And does not the god with the bourgeoning stick
> Go uphill and downhill, from summit to valley?[19]

Indifferent to the plight of the victims, Dionysus continues on his path up and down the mountain according to the rhythm of the seasons. And the poem continues:

> Und duldest du, Mutter, wie einst, ach, daheim,
> den leisen, den deutschen, den schmerzlichen Reim?   (Celan 2003, 17)

> And, mother, can you bear as once ago, ah, *daheim*
> The gentle, the German, the painful *Reim*.

---

18 In the original: "Das sind für den Dichter die Spuren der entflohenen Götter. Diese Spur bringt nach Hölderlins Erfahrung Dionysos, der Weingott, den Gott-losen unter das Finstere ihrer Weltnacht hinab. Denn der Gott der Rebe verwahrt in dieser und in deren Frucht zugleich das wesenhafte Zueinander von Erde und Himmel als der Stätte des Brautfestes für Menschen und Götter. Nur im Bereich dieser Stätte können noch, wenn irgendwo, Spuren der entflohen Götter für die gott-losen Menschen zurückbleiben" (Heidegger 1999, 267).
19 The translations from this poem are my own.

The harmonious poetry of the German lyrical tradition has become unbearable, particularly the poetry which Heidegger, in his text written some years later (though perhaps already conceived when Celan composed the poem), envisages as offering a dwelling and a *Heimat* to man in the *Weltnacht*, the night of the world. Celan and Heidegger clearly envisage different nights and different worlds. Celan's poem, written in the darkest night of the Shoah, prefigures Levinas's injunction to tear out the pagan roots – both physically in the earth and metaphorically in myth – of the Greek *physis* and the German residues of its chant.

The question "Why poets in times of distress?" undoubtedly applies to Celan, the poet of the Shoah, but also the poet who is considered to have both sustained and closed the tradition of German lyric poetry that began with Hölderlin. Celan's belonging to this tradition is no doubt due to the philosophical character of his poetry, and to the fact that he, as few others, embraced Hölderlin's major themes: the lament of absence, memory, the task of the poet, the dwelling of man on earth. These are precisely the poetic topoi that Celan reconfigures in the face of the catastrophe. Celan's complex relation to Hölderlin, and particularly to Hölderlin as the late Heidegger conceives him, underlies Levinas's text. This would indeed be the point of departure for Levinas's text on Celan: it is, above all, with and against the understanding of poetry as rooted – and rooting – in the soil, as Heidegger's text describes it, that Levinas addresses Celan. He does so in his own text in the form of an Abrahamic departure without return, which he opposes to the "site of Being." Levinas's entire text is conceived as an invitation to depart from this site and, with it, from Heidegger's world. The departure from this world, which Levinas also calls the Hellenic space of the "truth of being," is effectuated not only by means of a reflection *on* poetry but by a poetic path.

As the subtitle "De l'être à l'autre" – a strange and attractive alliteration in the French – indicates, Levinas's text bears within itself the traits of poetic language: it is an invitation to a transformative passage, in which the Heideggerian vocabulary is invoked, transfigured, and undermined. The epigraph at the beginning of Levinas's text consists of verses by Celan that refer to Heidegger and which dismantle his world:

> alles ist weniger, als
> es ist,
> alles ist mehr.   (Levinas 1976, 49)

> everything is less than
> it is,
> everything is more.[20]

In these verses, Celan proceeds to a negation of Being in its impersonal and neutral form of the *es ist*, which is derived from *sein*. The verb "to be" in the form "is" is also contained in the preceding and following verses, preceded by "everything." These Celanian verses negate Heidegger's thought of Being as a totalizing ontology without anything outside it, and which encompasses both heaven and earth, gods and humans. In Levinas's epitaph, the verse "it is" separates what is less and what is more than being, and at the same time joins them. The poem thereby dismantles the closed totality of being just as much by what "is less," that which is lacking, as by what "is more," that which exceeds the totality, that which is before and that which goes beyond and outside of being.

Levinas's "Paul Celan. De l'être à l'autre" projects the departure from the world of Being into three parts, respectively entitled *Vers l'autre* (Towards the Other), *La transcendence* (Transcendence), and *Dans la clarté de l'utopie . . .* (In the Clarity of Utopia . . .). In "Towards the Other," the text embarks on its path; with "Transcendence," it goes *beyond*, breaching the limits of what is enclosed; and, having left the closed space, arrives without arriving "In the Clarity of Utopia . . ." The ellipsis in this last subtitle indicates the opening to which the text moves: towards the non-place of u-topia.

As announced in Celan's verses, Levinas's text begins with an enactment of the "less" than Being; the first pages move from a suggestion of totality to the description of something deficient, lacking: "Here then is the poem – perfected language." This traditional idea of the poem as complete, absolute, and closed in itself is, in Levinas's description of Celan's poetics, reduced to a series of attributions in a minor key (see Levinas 1978, 16).[21] Referring to Celan's understanding of his own poetry, Levinas describes the poem as a mere "interjection" (interjection), a "handshake" (poignée de main), a "wink" (clin d'œil), a "sign of nothing" (signe de rien); he speaks of "dispossession," of a "gift without revelation" (donation [. . .] sans

---

20 My translation. Interestingly, Melville's translation ("Being and the Other: On Paul Celan," Levinas 1978), cited throughout this article, omits both this epigraph and the essay's dedication to Paul Ricœur. These elements are retained in the version included in Michael B. Smith's translation of *Proper Names* (Levinas 1996, 40).
21 In the original: "Voilà le poème, langage achevé, ramené au niveau d'une interjection" (Levinas 1976, 49).

revelation), of stammering language, a "babbling childhood of speech" (balbutiante enfance de discours), a "clumsy gesture" (maladroite insertion), the "beggar's door" to the "*dwelling of Being*" (entrée de mendiant dans la *demeure de l'être* (italic in original)). To totality, grandeur, pathos, Levinas opposes the "less than being," human language in its imperfection.

After the "transcendence" of the second part, describing the "more than Being," we arrive at the infinite opening, at utopia. "De l'être à l'autre" thus suggests traversing a place that is closed and dark, traversing Being towards a *clearing* (*Lichtung*), an eminently Heideggerian term designating the revelation of Being. This very term, however, is, in Levinas's text, submitted to the transformation towards which the text moves. Here, Levinas implicitly addresses Heidegger, who writes, in "Why Poets?":

> The poet thinks into the place that is determined from that clearing of being which has been stamped as the realm in which Western metaphysics is fulfilled. Hölderlin's thinking poetry has also stamped this realm of the poetic thinking. His poetry dwells in this place more intimately than any other poetry of his time. The place into which Hölderlin came is one where being is manifest, a manifestness which itself belongs in the destiny of being; out of this destiny, the manifestness is intended for the poet.   (Heidegger 2002, 203)[22]

In borrowing Celan's words from his meta-poetical text "Der Meridian" (The Meridian), this clearing is no longer a place, as in Heidegger, but rather the clarity of a utopia, in the light of which the human appears, the other human.[23] "Utopia" designates literally u-topos, non-place. And it is thus that Levinas describes the path that his argument pursues: "The movement thus described – going from place towards non-place, from *here* to u-topia" (Levinas 1978, 18).[24] It is in this last part of his text that Levinas addresses most explicitly the question of place and of non-place. These pages lead us to questions we asked at the beginning: does Levinas, in his distancing from Heidegger, refuse the

---

22 In the original: "Der Dichter denkt in die Ortschaft, die sich aus derjenigen Lichtung des Seins bestimmt, die als der Bereich der sich vollendenden Metaphysik in ihr Gepräge gelangt ist. Hölderlins denkende Dichtung hat diesen Bereich des dichtenden Denkens mitgeprägt. Sein Dichten wohnt in dieser Ortschaft so vertraut wie kein anderes Dichtertum zu seiner Zeit. Die Ortschaft, in die Hölderlin gekommen, ist eine Offenbarkeit des Seins, die selbst in das Geschick des Seins gehört und aus diesem her dem Dichter zugedacht wird" (Heidegger 1999, 273).
23 "Nothing is stranger or more alien than the other man, and it is in the light of utopia that one touches man outside of all rootedness and domestication" (Levinas 1978, 19). In the original: "Rien n'est plus étrange ni plus étranger que l'autre homme et c'est dans la clarté de l'utopie que se montre l'homme" (Levinas 1976, 54).
24 In the original: "Le mouvement ainsi décrit va du lieu vers le non-lieu d'ici vers l'utopie" (Levinas 1976, 52).

implanting in a place, the dwelling of Greek being provided by the poet, to the extent of celebrating unconditionally the modality of exilic existence considered as the Jewish modality par excellence?

Before considering these few pages in the last part of *De l'être à l'autre*, it is instructive to turn to another text by Levinas, entitled "Le regard du poète" (The Poet's Gaze), in which he addresses this question more explicitly. The text is the first piece in the collection *Sur Blanchot* (On Blanchot). In this piece, from 1956, written fifteen years before "De l'être à l'autre," Levinas recognizes the importance of Heidegger's thought for Blanchot's work, stating: "One feels the proximity of the German philosopher in myriad ways, right up to [. . .] the texts by Rilke and Hölderlin that he comments upon."[25] It is thus a question, as Levinas states explicitly, of the later Heidegger, precisely of the one who will be the object of his polemic in the text on Celan. And just as fifteen years later Levinas finds in Celan, particularly in Celan's Büchner Prize address, "Der Meridian," an invitation to leave the Heideggerian world, in the vision of art espoused by Blanchot he reads an opposition to "the Hellenic truth of Being." Levinas writes of Blanchot: "Does [he] not attribute to art the function of uprooting the Heideggerian universe?" (Levinas 1996, 139).[26] He undoubtedly discerns correctly when he distances his friend from Heidegger's pagan temptation, above all where he affirms Blanchot's insistence on nomadism as the human essence. However, the association of the "authenticity of exile" (one of the subtitles of his text) found in Blanchot, with the condition of human being "as a being, as this man here, exposed to hunger, to thirst, to the cold" is in fact that of Levinas rather than of Blanchot, who, Levinas admits, did not place ethics at the centre of his considerations. And what would Levinas have said of a text by Blanchot bearing the title "Traduire" (Translate), first published in 1961, in which Blanchot, in dialogue with Walter Benjamin and his celebrated text on the task of the translator, sings praise of Hölderlin, specifically for having magisterially unified in a "pure language" nothing less than the Greek and the German in his translations of Sophocles, his last works before sinking into madness?[27]

One would also have to turn here to Blanchot's pages on Paul Celan entitled *Le dernier à parler* (The Last to Speak), published in the same issue of the

---

[25] My translation. In the original: "le voisinage du philosophe allemand de mille façons et jusque dans . . . les textes de Rilke et de Hölderlin qu'il commente" (Levinas 1975, 24).
[26] In the original: "Blanchot ne prête-t-il pas à l'art la fonction de déraciner l'univers heideggerien?" (Levinas 1975, 25).
[27] See Vivian Liska, "A Same Other, Another Same: Walter Benjamin and Maurice Blanchot on Translation" (2014, 242).

Revue des Belles Lettres as Levinas's text on Celan, to see where Blanchot's reading situates the Jewish poet with respect to Hölderlin – particularly the later Hölderlin, to whom he refers at various junctures – and implicitly with regard to Heidegger. It will perhaps suffice, however, to suggest that in contrast to Levinas, who brings about a "departure from the Heideggarian world," Blanchot indicates with his title (citing a verse by Celan) that this poet in fact closes the tradition of Hölderlin, but *without leaving it*: for Blanchot, Celan is, rather, "the last to speak," to speak Hölderlin's language, that of Heidegger's Hölderlin. Blanchot indeed leads Celan to the edge of the Heideggerian abyss but without Levinas's injunction to "leap beyond"[28] and above all without setting himself on the way towards the other. The path on which Celan embarks in Blanchot is indeed one directed towards an exterior (*un dehors*), "never already given,"[29] "movement or following a route, a relation without attachments or roots [. . .] indicating the Open, what is empty, free,"[30] it is rather "white at the ground of what is without a ground."[31] Blanchot designates an abyss that is indeed different from that of Heidegger's – the latter being an apocalyptic one, indicating the absence of the gods, but also the possible place of a turn – while in Blanchot's the void remains essentially empty, a different abyss but an abyss just the same. It is an excess, a murmur, the rustling of the outside. But another human face is not to be seen.

The parts of "Paul Celan. From Being to the Other" where Levinas addresses most closely the question of place are found at the beginning of the third and final part, bearing the title "In the clarity of utopia . . ." It is here that Levinas invokes and at the same time goes beyond the non-place, Blanchot's neutral outside, without, however, arriving at another destination. Yet the direction of this destination is nonetheless inscribed there, and in Levinas's language where this is at its most poetic. At the beginning of this third part, Levinas writes, "This exceptional 'outside' is not an other landscape. [. . .] the poem takes a further step" (Levinas 1978, 19).[32] And one might add that in Levinas it perhaps takes a step further than Celan himself. Levinas writes: "the

---

28 In the original: "transcendance – saut par-dessus l'abîme ouvert dans l'être" (Levinas 1976, 52); "transcendence [. . .] a leap across the abyss open in Being" (Levinas 1978, 18).
29 My translation. In the original: "jamais déjà donné" (Blanchot 2002, 83).
30 My translation. In the original: "essai d'un mouvement ou d'un cheminement, rapport sans attaches et sans racines" (Blanchot 2002, 83).
31 My translation. In the original: "blanc qui est au fond de ce qui est sans fond" (Blanchot 2002, 85).
32 In the original: "Ce dehors insolite n'est pas un autre paysage. Au-delà du simplement étrange de l'art et de l'ouverture sur l'être de l'étant – le poème fait un pas de plus [. . .]" (Levinas 1976, 53).

strange is the stranger" (Levinas 1978, 19).[33] It is indeed Levinas himself, and not Celan, who adds that "nothing is stranger or more foreign that the other *human being*" (Levinas 1978, 19).[34] In effect, Celan remains more vague and more abstract in the original German when he writes that the poem goes towards "a foreigner, an other, a totally other" (my translation) without specifying that this is in fact a question of the human other – or, in language that is almost already Biblical, of the neighbour. In any case, it is at this moment that Levinas expostulates: "Outside of all rootedness and all domestication; authenticity as being without a fatherland!"[35] The next paragraph ends with the sentence: "But the dwelling justified by the movement towards the other is essentially Jewish."[36] In this formulation, at the latest, one could gain the certainty that Levinas takes the position of the wandering Jew as an ultimate philosophical theme, as the guarantee of a modality of the ethical being. Yet it is also at this moment that Levinas adopts a language of detours, of zigzags, of propositions and counter-propositions that destabilise his own proposition: "Outside of all rootedness and all domestication; authenticity as being without a fatherland!" It is in "this adventure" – this path towards the other designated by Celan's "Der Meridian" – that "the I dedicates itself to the poem so as to meet the other in the non-place, it is the return that is surprising – a return based not on the response of the summoned relation, but on the circularity of the meridian [. . .]" (Levinas 1978, 19).[37] This is indeed a surprising proposition, for the circularity of the movement leading towards the other described by "Der Meridian" is, Levinas continues, "As if in going toward the other, I were reunited with myself and implanted myself in a soil that would, henceforth, be native; as if the distancing of the I drew me closer to myself, discharged of the full weight of my identity – a movement of which poetry would be the

---

[33] Melville's translation (Levinas 1978) cited here omits the final three words of the sentence, which should read: "the strange is the stranger or the neighbor." In the original: "[. . .] l'étrange, c'est l'étranger ou le prochain" (Levinas 1976, 54).
[34] In the original: "Rien n'est plus étrange ni plus étranger que l'autre homme [. . .]" (Levinas 1976, 54).
[35] Melville's English rendering of this sentence (Levinas 1978) is inaccurate. The version above has been offered by the translator of this article. In the original: "Hors de tout enracinement et de toute domiciliation; apatridie comme authenticité!" (Levinas 1976, 54).
[36] My translation. This sentence is missing in Melville's translation of the text (Levinas 1978). In the original: "Mais l'habitation justifiée par le mouvement vers l'autre est d'essence juive" (Levinas 1976, 54).
[37] In the original: "Hors de tout enracinement et de toute domiciliation; apatridie comme authenticité! [. . .] Mais le surprise de cette aventure où le moi se dédie à l'autre dans le non-lieu, c'est le retour" (Levinas 1976, 54).

possibility itself, and a native land which owes nothing to rootedness, nothing to 'prior occupation': a native land that has no need to be a birthplace. Native land or promised land?" (Levinas 1978, 20).[38] And it is Levinas who asks himself the final question, using a biblical image: "Does it spew forth its inhabitants when they forget the course of one who goes off in search of the other" (Levinas 1978, 20).[39] Would the surprise of the return be that it is necessary to go towards the other in order to end at home with oneself in the Heideggerian "when mortals come into their own essence" (Heidegger 2002, 202)?[40] This is by no means the case if one reads these lines as an act of poetic language: in such a reading, the return does not go back to the same but transforms the same on its path. In these lines, the exclamation that authenticity is to be bereft of a fatherland no longer appears in light of a philosophical or moral affirmation of exile; instead, it leads to the conception of Biblical dwelling that does not allow for forgetting that the relation to the land is neither possession nor rootedness. The land always remains a *promise*, it does not offer a dwelling but rather a *refuge* in order to "pass the night" (Levinas 1978, 20),[41] in order (as Levinas earlier stated, in his text on Blanchot) for shelter from the cold, from hunger, from destitution. A temporary shelter, where, in the words of a severe piece of poetry, there persists both the "[i]nsomnia in the bed of Being" (Levinas 1978, 20)[42] and the "impossibility of curling up to shut one's eyes" (Levinas 1978, 20).[43] As far as concerns the Jewish essence, which could be interpreted as chauvinist particularism: it is defined, in the paragraph that follows, according to Jewish history under Nazism, and as the extreme possibility and impossibility of humanity as such, leading to a vision of human being in its most vulnerable nudity. It is later in this passage that the state of "being without a fatherland"

---

38 In the original: "Non pas à partir de la réponse de l'interpellé, mais de par la circularité de ce mouvement sans retour, de cette trajéctoire parfaite, de ce méridie que, dans la finalité sans fin, décrit le poème. Comme si en allant vers l'autre, je me réjoignais et m'implantais dans une une terre, désormais natale, déchargée de tout le poids de mon identité. Terre natale qui ne doit rien à l'enracinement, rien à la première occupation; terre natale qui ne doit rien à la naissance. Terre natale ou terre promise" (Levinas 1976, 54).
39 In the original: "Vomit-elle ses habitants quand ils oublient le parcours circulaire qui leur a rendu familière cette terre, et leur errance qui n'était pas pour le dépaysement, qui était dépaganisation?" (Levinas 1976, 54).
40 In the original: "Mit den Sterblichen wendet es sich aber, wenn sie in ihr eigenes Wesen finden" (Heidegger 1999, 271).
41 In the original: "pour passer la nuit" (Levinas 1976, 54).
42 In the original: "Insomnie dans le lit de l'être" (Levinas 1976, 54).
43 In the original: "impossibilité de se peletonner pour s'oublier" (Levinas 1976, 54).

loses its aspect of a superior moral position to be imitated and becomes the signum of this idea of the fragile human being, exposed to evil and to destitution, which for Levinas is absent from the Heideggerian world. Levinas's passage ends with a return to Paul Celan and his poetry: against the silence of nature confronted with frail and denuded human being, Levinas writes, "a true word" (*une vraie parole*) is necessary, against the language of the poetry that Heidegger derives from Hölderlin's hymns. It is the word of poetry that expresses and maintains the remembrance of "this particular human being." This is the framework in which the role of the poetic word in Levinas can be linked to his evocation of the relation between the Saying and the Said in *Autrement qu'être ou au-delà de l'essence* (Otherwise than Being, or Beyond Essence). The language that I earlier called poetic language calls sclerotic concepts into question, submits the Said of "place" or "exile" to the movement of the Saying in which the wounds of Jewish experience are exposed. Such a vulnerability, expressed in the poetic word, exposed and as such shared with the other, cannot possess a place, cannot consolidate itself as the supremacy of possession, be it of the land, be it of the content of a concept, of an "essence."

In a remarkable text that appeared in a major collection edited by Danielle Cohen-Levinas, *Le souci de l'art chez Emmanuel Levinas* (The Care of Art in Emmanuel Levinas), Stéphane Habib and Raphaël Zagury-Orly analyse a fragment of this passage and, after a lucid and nuanced deconstructive course of argument, arrive at the convincing conclusion that Levinas's thought cannot be reduced either to a return to the same or to an affirmation of wandering as a position, as a positive modality. They rightly call on the reader to listen to the complication to which Levinas invites him/her, that is, the necessity to think at the same time dwelling and the movement towards the Other. They write that Levinas "is not a philosopher of dwelling, of being at home. But Levinas is also not a philosopher of the wandering of exile."[44] Their conclusion, however, particularly in light of the present context, elicits doubt. Commenting on Levinas's deviating the Jewish essence towards a complex validity – possible and impossible – for all humanity, they write: "Everything takes place as if, in a message towards a universality of insane necessity, Levinas were responding to Saint Paul's famous 'neither Jew nor Greek' by saying 'both Jew and Greek,' one in

---

[44] My translation. In the original: "n'est pas un philosophe de l'habitation, du chez soi. Mais Lévinas n'est pas non plus un philosophe de la poésie de l'errance de l'exil" (Habib and Zagury-Orly 2011, 178).

the other, alteration."⁴⁵ Perhaps in their deconstructive gesture, which attempts at all costs to avoid hierarchy and the primacy of tradition, of one form of thought in relation to another, and above all to avoid any such synthesis into a third, Habib and Zagury-Orly miss what is brought about essentially by the alteration of the thought of place that Levinas allows us to think. It seems to me that Levinas has indeed passed from being to the other; he has not effectuated a symmetrical deconstruction of two equal, opposed positions but has rather instigated a radical modification of the notion of place. Exile, displacement, and the loss of fatherland are indeed authenticity for him, yet this does not ignore the need for refuge claimed for oneself and granted to the other. The circular trajectory towards the other – the path of Celan's meridian, according to Levinas – thus does not end in a return to the same, but this same, like this place, has itself become transformed: it has become refuge and shelter for the naked human being.

It is, therefore, not a question of simply opposing the Greek and the Jew, nor of embedding one into the other so as to have one who is "both Jew and Greek"; rather, it is an invitation, as a travelling companion of Levinas, to follow his Abrahamic path by introducing the Greek into the infinite movement of a departure without return. This movement would, in the course of its journey towards the other, and without supporting a call to re-implant itself, transform the native place of the other just as much as the absence of this place is itself marked as an absence. It is through the angle of this transformation that the poetical word enacts what it conveys and constitutes a place of engagement with the other. This place remains, and must remain, both a promise and, as Levinas puts it, in his text on Blanchot, in reference to the Exodus from Egypt and the feast of Tabernacles, a "hut in the desert" – in order to transform, to translate a Jewish experience into a Greek signifier in the name of *return*. This, while following the path of the same not as a destination but rather as the transformation of being with the Other in view. It is not a case of "both Jew and Greek": it is a Jewish path inviting all those who feel called by this vision to take their place in his hut without, however, stopping their passage towards the Other and towards the promise of a time and of a place, of a truth of Being that signifies justice.

Celan's poetry reveals, in a form condensed to the extreme, that which one finds in Levinas almost in filigree in the passages conceived poetically, or

---

45 My translation. In the original: "Tout se passe comme si, en un envoi vers une universalité d'une exigence folle, Levinas était en train de répondre au fameux 'ni juif ni grec' de saint Paul par un et Juif et Grec, l'un dans l'autre: altération" (Habib and Zagury-Orly 2011, 195).

which at least opens up a reading attentive to the mode of signifying, subverting propositions that could pose problems when conceived purely conceptually (such as the idealisation of being without a fatherland or the proposal of a Jewish essence).

2 Paul Celan's "With Us"

In a poem entitled "Mit uns" (With Us), written on 9 April 1966 and which concludes the cycle "Eingedunkelt" (Darkening Light) (first published in 1968), Celan envisions Jewish exile in similar terms to those of the other authors who wished to reverse the negative associations of the rootless, homeless Jew. As did other thinkers who regarded the Jew as the embodiment of displacement, Celan associates both rootedness and belonging to a place with Heidegger and, beyond that, with the "blood and soil" ideology of National Socialism. Celan, too, links the alternative to this rootedness in the earth with the text and letter. However, he simultaneously blocks the paths to appropriation and self-affirming embellishment of the condition of involuntary displacement, and, above all, enacts an irrefutable resistance to the forgetting of suffering, in particular, the suffering from exile.

MIT UNS, den	
Umhergeworfenen, dennoch	With us, those
Fahrenden:	thrown about, nevertheless
	traveling:
Der eine	
unversehrte,	The sole
nicht usurpierbare,	unscathed,
aufständische	non-appropriable,
Gram. (Celan 2003, 268)	defiant
	grief.[46]

In a short, two-part sentence lacking any verbs, Celan speaks as "we" (or "us") and says what or how it is "with us." The intertextual reference to Heidegger's "Being-with" (*Mitsein*) becomes more explicit in the second line, where he defines the collectivity to which he refers: the we/us are the "thrown about, nevertheless." "We" are, and also are not, the Heideggerian thrown, those thrown into the world as being. "We" are, more precisely, "thrown about" – thrown from one place to the next, displaced, hunted, and expelled. "We" are, above all, those

---

46 My translation.

who *nevertheless*, despite the trauma of persecution and expulsion, eschew searching for a homeland and resist the yearning for a dwelling that would ward off the existential condition of thrownness. "We" are those who "nevertheless" defy that consolation, who turn the passivity of having been thrown by fate and history into a self-determined action: "We" become the "travellers" (*die Fahrenden*), who as such could be Rilke's unplaced, melancholy yet of their own free choice, nomadic wanderers. Celan's "travellers," however, derive their significance from the resistance evoked in the "nevertheless"; they are the expelled and hunted who nevertheless withstand the temptation of remaining in place, who resolutely travel *as resistance* against emplacement. This resistance rests on the only unrelenting, undiminished certainty that remains: "The sole / unscathed, / non-appropriable, / defiant / grief."

The insurmountable, defiant grief uniting anger and mourning binds these travellers and accompanies them. It does not stand for them metaphorically nor does it define an identity; rather, it is *with* them. It is neither to be used nor to be appropriated (as a metaphoric undoing of particularity would have it); it stands upright amidst all movement. As in the poem "Niemals, stehender Gram" (At No Time, Lasting Grief) (Celan 2003, 526), written two years later, it defies the "mimeticists," who, "no matter how lettered," never wrote a word "that rebels" (my translation). The sorrow evoked in "With us" is as defiant as the letter of this poem in which grief (*Gram*) and *Grammaton*, the Greek word for letter, come together in the concrete and singular reality of the poem that is open to all fellow travellers who are touched by it. The sorrow that "With us" evokes is as recalcitrant and rebellious as the letter of these poems, of the poem in which *Gram* and *Grammaton* coalesce in the singular reality of the poem, a reality open to all the fellow travellers who are "with us." Like Levinas in his thought, Celan translates here Jewish experience as well as its rebellious letter, its poetry, into Greek.

Bibliography

Blanchot, Maurice. "Le dernier à parler." *Une voix venue d'ailleurs*. Paris: Gallimard, 2002. 69–108.
Celan, Paul. "Gespräch im Gebirg." *Gesammelte Werke in fünf Bänden*, Vol. III. Eds. Beda Allemann and Stefan Reichert with Rolf Bücher. Frankfurt am Main: Suhrkamp, 1983. 169–173.
Celan, Paul. "The Meridian." *Selected Poems and Prose of Paul Celan*. Trans. John Felstiner. New York: Norton, 2001. 401–414.
Celan, Paul. *Die Gedichte. Kommentierte Gesamtausgabe in einem Band*. Ed. Barbara Wiedemann. Frankfurt am Main: Suhrkamp, 2003.

Habib, Stéphane, and Zagury-Orly, Raphaël. "Abstraire, Arracher, Penser. Levinas et la question du lieu." *Le souci de l'art chez Emmanuel Levinas*. Ed. Danielle Cohen-Levinas. Houilles: Editions Manucius, 2011. 183–195.

Heidegger, Martin. "Poetically Man Dwells . . . " *Poetry, Language, Thought*. Trans. Albert Hofstadter. New York: Harper & Row, 1975. 211–229.

Heidegger, Martin. "Wozu Dichter?" *Holzwege*. Frankfurt am Main: Klostermann, 1999. 265–316.

Heidegger, Martin. "Why Poets?" *Off the Beaten Track*. Trans. and Eds. Julian Young and Kenneth Haynes. Cambridge: Cambridge University Press, 2002. 200–241.

Hill, Leslie "Distrust of Poetry: Levinas, Blanchot, Celan." *Modern Language Notes* 120.5 (2005): 986–1008.

Levinas, Emmanuel. "Paul Celan. De l'être à l'autre." *La Revue des Belles Lettres* 2-3 (1972): 193–199.

Levinas, Emmanuel. "Le regard du poète." *Sur Maurice Blanchot*. Montpellier: Fata Morgana, 1975. 7–26.

Levinas, Emmanuel. "Paul Celan. De l'être à l'autre." *Noms propres*. Paris: Le Livre de Poche, 1976. 49–56.

Levinas, Emmanuel. "Being and the Other: On Paul Celan." Trans. Stephen Melville. *Chicago Revue* 29.3 (1978): 16–22.

Levinas, Emmanuel. "La trace de l'autre." *En découvrant l'existence avec Husserl et Heidegger*. Paris: Vrin, 1982. 187–202.

Levinas, Emmanuel. "Heidegger, Gagarin et nous." *Difficile Liberté: Essais sur le Judaïsme*. Paris: Le Livre de Poche, 1983. 299–303.

Levinas, Emmanuel. "The Trace of the Other." Trans. Alfonso Lingis. *Deconstruction in Context: Literature and Philosophy*. Ed. Mark C. Taylor. Chicago: University of Chicago Press, 1986. 345–359.

Levinas, Emmanuel. "Le sens et l'œuvre." *Humanisme de l'autre homme*. Paris: Le Livre de Poche, 1987. 42–47.

Levinas, Emmanuel. "Heidegger, Gagarin, and Us." *Difficult Freedom: Essays on Judaism*. Trans. Sean Hand. Baltimore: Johns Hopkins University Press, 1990. 231–234.

Levinas, Emmanuel. "La réalité et son ombre." *Les Imprévus de l'histoire*. Montpellier: Fata Morgana, 1994. 123–148.

Levinas, Emmanuel. *Proper Names*. Trans. Michael B. Smith. Stanford: Stanford University Press, 1996.

Liska, Vivian. "A Same Other, Another Same: Walter Benjamin and Maurice Blanchot on Translation." *The German Quarterly* 87.2 (2014): 229–245.

Part IV: **Novel Writers**

Danielle Cohen-Levinas
The Literary Instant and the Condition of Being Hostage: Levinas, Proust, and the Corporeal Meaning of Time

Literature is present everywhere in the philosophical work of Emmanuel Levinas, but this omnipresence does not allow itself to be circumscribed by unique narrative idioms or isolated references. One of the characteristic traits of the modernity of the twentieth century is to elicit a proximity between philosophy and literature with regard to writing and thought and, in this regard, Proust single-handedly represents what Roland Barthes in 1974 called "a complete system of reading the world. [. . .] In our everyday life, there is not an incident, an encounter, a trait, a situation that does not have a reference in Proust" (Barthes 2002, 569).[1]

Emmanuel Levinas did not abandon this tradition, which, as far as France is concerned, is very old; indeed, one should immediately add that few philosophers have been as attentive to literature and poetry as he was. Furthermore, Levinas's great originality, I would even say the radicality of his gesture, is to hold the hypothesis, or at least to let it be glimpsed in his essay "Reality and Its Shadow,"[2] published in *Les Temps Modernes* in 1948, that literature cannot be understood as "art," that the narrative word is not restricted to speaking or immersing itself in the passion of verbalism or psychological satisfaction, but that it is speech manifesting itself in the movement of telling, in the act of writing. In this sense it is already in itself an appeal to the other – that which Levinas understands as the most essential modality of "being wary of oneself," which is, as we know, characteristic of philosophy and criticism. Alongside philosophical preoccupations and priorities, in certain respects modern literature would manifest, more than or just as much as philosophy, what Levinas calls "a more and more acute awareness of this fundamental insufficiency of artistic idolatry" (Levinas 1994, 148). The development to which Levinas attests in an acutely incisive way is not that of literature but that of art, inasmuch as it is not language. Consequently, it does not attain the dignity of the question of truth and of the good, which philosophy after Plato attempts to articulate. The aesthetic

---

[1] Barthes's comment is from an interview by Claude Jannoud, *Le Figaro*, 27 July 1974.
[2] The text is reprinted in Levinas's *Les imprévus de l'histoire* (1994, 123–148).

Translation: Translated, from the French, by Ashraf Noor.

temptation was condemned rigorously by Levinas already in *De l'existence à l'existant* (1947), begun in captivity, in the context of the immediate aftermath of the War, for the reason that it constitutes the very event of the obscuring of being and that it leads to its darkening. This is not comparable to the literary temptation expressed by Levinas in *Les carnets de captivité*, which, I believe, one must take very seriously and probe with great attention. A reader of Proust, certainly, but also of many other writers during this period, whom he interrogates tragically with the formulation inscribed in these notebooks, "What will history say?" (Levinas 2009, 79), Levinas detects in literature the possibility of reintroducing, into the heart of the concept's rigor, an intelligibility of the world in which the notion of "experience" takes a central role. With narrative, which has become the form of the relation to the other, Levinas broaches the status of the subject, of the subjectivity that has to face the trial of alteration, that is, of fissure and devastation. The narratives and the writers who attract his attention are undeniably all pierced by what one could call the extradition of the subject, which is the true motif of the narratives, around which a dramaturgy, what Levinas calls an intrigue, would be woven. Or rather, as he writes in the sixth *Carnet de captivité*: "The fear of being 'duped' – is not such a practical rule, which seems to me to be absolute, purely and simply 'literature' [?] – This sphere of literature enlarges itself infinitely. Does virtue exist?" (Levinas 2009, 161).

Levinas, then, experienced captivity, the condition of the hostage, as he himself calls it – recalling at various junctures that he has known the word "hostage" "since the persecution by the Nazis" (de Saint-Cheron 2006, 31) – "[i]n the total passivity of abandonment, in detachment from all relations" (Levinas 2009, 213), and, at the same time, as a moment where "the true experiences" (Levinas 2009, 203) are revealed. Levinas's narrative has an unheard of force: "Suffering, hopelessness, mourning – certainly. Yet, above all that, a new rhythm of life. We stepped onto another planet, breathing an atmosphere of unknown composition and handling matter that no longer weighs anything" (Levinas 2009, 203).

The singular force of the word "hostage," which at once resonates with that of "captivity," is without a doubt due to the way in which Levinas displaces it in the conceptual register by revealing in it the eminence of a Saying narrating itself while being charged with an irrefutable ethical force. This is an effort striving towards what Levinas, in *Autrement qu'être*, calls a "thematising, thought, history and writing" (Levinas 1974, 20) that necessarily comes to be wounded not only by the trace of signifying, of "designating," and of proximity, but by lived experience and its temporalisation in the process of writing and in the exercise of thought. Levinas, then, experienced captivity.

He was, as one says, a prisoner of war, billeted from 1942 in various *Frontstalag*, in Rennes, in Laval, and in Vesoul; and, from 1942 to the end of his captivity, in 1945, he was prisoner in *Stalag XI B* in *Fallingbostel* in Germany. Here, he was separated from the other French prisoners and forced to work in a special commando reserved for Jews, which left for the forest every day at four in the morning. It was in these inhuman conditions that each day, when he returned from the forest, where he worked as a logger and was shouted at and insulted by the German soldiers, he entrusted notes, aphorisms, and thoughts to a series of small notebooks, which we now leaf through in the attempt to reconstitute, after the event, the genesis of his work. We do so on the basis of the accumulated fragments, in which philosophical reflections intermingle with references to the biblical and Talmudic tradition, excerpts from novelistic texts, which Levinas copied out rigorously, and the drafts of three novels, of which two remained unfinished: *Eros* and *La dame de chez Wepler*. For the condition of being hostage was paradoxical in that it allowed the prisoners, who suffered the most severe mistreatment during the day, to go to the library in the late afternoon. Reading, writing, and copying out excerpts represented for Levinas spaces of survival in the face of "the terrible reality that wove itself back together" (Levinas 2009, 72). Later, in an interview, Levinas will return to this experience, which he likens in the *Carnets de captivité* to a "monastic or moral life," evoking reading that he would never had done had he not been in captivity.

> In making you a hostage, you are punished for someone else. For me, this term has no other meaning, except that it receives in this context a meaning that can be glorious. This misery of the hostage has a certain glory, to the extent that the person who is hostage knows that he runs the risk of being killed for someone else. In this condition of being hostage, however, which I call "the uncondition of the hostage," is there not a supreme dignity beyond the dramatic fate? (de Saint-Cheron 2006, 31)

1 Condition and Uncondition

Is it possible to expose and thematise the figure of the hostage when one is oneself a hostage? Is it possible to pass from the lived experience of the condition of being hostage to the philosophical experience of the *uncondition* of being hostage without letting this question, which was posed in the traumatism of historical time, return within the order of that which Levinas seeks to exceed? What can be made of the transition from the Said of captivity to the Saying of the hostage? Can one translate the other without betraying him? It would be through an *unsaying oneself* that is never attained, always begun anew, that Levinas would come to interpret the meaning of the Said pertaining to the hostage of lived experience, by submitting it to the irreducibility of the Said in the *uncondition* of the hostage. This is the locus where philosophical thought would be developed that would open into what Levinas, in the *Carnets de captivité*, calls the "[c]orporeal meaning of time" (Levinas 2009, 186). Levinas operates this corporeal meaning of time on the basis of the incessant reading of Proust he carries out when he is prisoner of war. In Proust, human being does not derive merely from the dialectic of historical totality and eschatological rupture. It is always in a constitutive tension with the pure meaning of the other, thus excluding objective disclosure and extracting it from a political and historical order. As Levinas notes in the *Carnets de captivité*, "All the history of Albertine as a prisoner is the history of the relation to the other" (Levinas 2009, 72). In the same way, the amorous and erotic approach to the other in Proust is not due to the directness of the face and of the word. It comes to pass in the equivocal and meaningful silence that, in Levinas, will become in *Totalité et infini* the intentionality of the caress as the sensual moment that "transcends the sensual" and that by transcending it allows one to attain the duality proper to the incommensurable mystery of the other. This mystery is for Levinas, from the beginning of the *Carnets de captivité*, "the very basis of love" (Levinas 2009, 114). The motif of sexuality, which is very present in the *Carnets*, is from now on broached as constituting egoity. In 1942, between a reflection on Joseph de Maistre and Alfred de Vigny and an allusion to the festival of *Simhat Torah* (October 4, 1942), Levinas copies this brief passage of *Albertine disparue*:

> I never stopped loving myself, for my daily relations with myself had not been ruptured as had those with Albertine. But what if those with my body, with myself, had also been? Certainly, it would be the same. Our love of life is nothing other than an old liaison that we cannot get rid of. Its force lies in its permanence. But the death that rends it will cure us of the desire for immortality. (Levinas 2009, 77)

One could make a very precise summary of the themes that provide the foundation for Proustian subjectivity and we could place them, in a systematic manner, in relation to Levinassian idioms: love, eroticism, sexuality, sociality, signifyingness and signification, ethical structure of the subjectivity of the one-for-the-other, death as refractory to experience, the moment in which the heterogeneous imposes itself as Other such that it is Wholly Other, the impossibility of recuperating the wholly Other into the same, the feminine assimilated to the figure of the Other "before the Other is another person" (Levinas 2009, 76). These themes can be thought of as narrative-philosophical attestations of which one finds an archaeological and genetic trace in the *Carnets* and which, in *Autrement qu'être*, Levinas articulates around one single question: what becomes of subjectivity when it is exposed to the alterity of the other?

This duality of a subject simultaneously exposed to the alterity of the other and of a subject reposing substantially in itself – that which Levinas calls the *other-in-the same* exposed to an "in-spite-of-oneself" – characterises what we call here the "literary instant." The reading of Proust represents one of the foundational moments of this questioning. Proustian subjects are all determined by a subjective identity that never coincides with itself. Thus, one could inscribe the speculative movement of Levinas's thought into the narrative moments of Proust's writing and deduce from there, on the basis of the three cases of Love, Alterity, and Subjectivity, in the phenomenological sense of the term, what it means to "show what a person is when facing the other" (Levinas 2009, 145). Proust is therefore one of the pivots around which Levinas's rupture with substantialism turns for the benefit of the real emergence of the intersubjectivity of love. This rupture is not possible unless one effects a movement of substitution, a movement by which one passes from the act as the first manifestation of substance to "the voluptuosity that is neither *act* nor thought" (Levinas 2009, 144). Levinas's effort consists in articulating the question of voluptuosity with that of sociality and of radical alterity. He writes:

> When I say that Proust is a poet of the social and that all his work consists of showing what a person is when facing another, I do not want to simply evoke the old theme of the fatal solitude of every being (cf. Estaunié's *Solitudes*) – the situation is different: to a being, all of the other is hidden – but a separation does not result from this. It is precisely the fact of hiding oneself that is the ferment of social life. It is my solitude that interests the other and all his comportment is movement around my solitude. This is Marcel and Albertine. The so voluminous work of Proust culminates in these two themes of Albertine as a prisoner and as possessed, which is not distinct from Albertine who has disappeared and died. The torment that constitutes his relation to her lies in the fact that there are many things about her – simple things, attitudes, gestures, poses – that he will never know. And what he knows about her is dominated by what he will never know, because all the objective evidence is less powerful than the doubts that will remain within him forever – and that comprise his relation with Albertine. (Levinas 2009, 145)

2 Genesis and Genetics of a New Thought

If the appearance of the first volume of Emmanuel Levinas's unpublished writings allows one to trace and reconstitute in a quasi-genetic manner the premises of a thought that investigates the status of writing, it is to a large part thanks to the discovery, in the *Carnets de captivité*, of the explicit abundance of literary references, and above all the discovery of what few interpreters and specialists of Levinas's work knew about: Levinas's ambition, his clearly expressed vocation, to conceive his work as a constellation that articulates philosophy with literature and criticism.

In the first notebook, begun on September 8, 1937, Levinas notes:

My work to be done:
Philosophical :   1) Being and nothingness
                  2) Time
                  3) Rosenzweig
                  4) Rosenberg
Literary: 1) Sad opulence
                  2) Irreality and love
Criticism: Proust (Levinas 2009, 74)

I would like, then, to comment on Proust, emphasising the idea that Levinas indeed expressed the wish to carry out a work of criticism – just like his friend Maurice Blanchot, who, in the 1920s, when they were students in Strasbourg, had introduced him not only to the work of Proust but also to that of Léon Bloy, whose great importance for Levinas one measures with admiring astonishment on reading the *Carnets* and the laudable pages that he devotes to the author of the *Lettres à sa fiancée* (1889–1890). These are two writers from whom Levinas, throughout the five years of his captivity, carefully excerpts fragments of narratives that are like the mimetic possibility of responding in his own language, in wresting it from the impersonal and inhuman *il y a* of the condition of being hostage, in such a way as to let surge forth the materiality of language having become thing, the *experience* thing, which, in the seventh and last notebook, Levinas calls the "corporeal meaning of time" (Levinas 2009, 186).

Many writers file past in the course of the notebooks, too many to be cited in the general economy of my remarks, but Léon Bloy, whom I shall not dwell on, and Marcel Proust each require a gesture of writing that is a powerful movement of transcendence within immanence. There is a way in which Levinas considers this movement of transcendence, this liberating of the Heideggerian immanence of being, as being carried out in the literature of Bloy and Proust. Levinas does not hesitate to express a sentence with respect to Bloy that we should meditate upon at length, for it brings about the defection from the Husserlian intentionality that Levinas decries: "He knows things that are not in phenomenology" (Levinas 2009, 162). This is an admirable perception of narrative time in search of a true beyond-being, which draws its inspiration from a meditation on the negativity of death, dismissing momentarily the spiritualism of German Idealism, which sees in it, in the nothingness of death, the condition of the life of the Spirit. It is thus at an extreme point of excess and of exceeding that Levinas, in captivity, reads and excerpts Bloy and Proust, and, even if he denies this, one cannot exclude the possibility that he lived this literary instant as an experience of "consummation," such as the one he speaks of in *De l'existence à l'existant*.[3] This would be the possibility of descrying absolute exteriority from the very interior of his reflection, the exteriority that he will attain in the final chapter of *Autrement qu'être*. So, too, in Proust, the emotion and the meaning borne by writing are constantly released by a movement of reflexivity with respect to his own emotion, "and even more often," Levinas says in speaking of Proust, "by reflection on the emotion of the other. Still better: this reflection is this very emotion" (Levinas 2009, 71).

Once more, the trope of excess contained in the idea of a reflection as the paradigm of an emotion induces in Levinas a reading of Proust, an aspect of which we already know in the essay he devotes to him in *Noms propres* (1976), "L'Autre dans Proust." Indeed, Levinas always weaves his discourse on Proust and on what develops from him by connecting him to an ambivalent interpretation dividing itself into two contrary movements[4] at the heart of transcendence, thus calling forth an irreconcilable diachrony in the temporality of the narrative. I shall borrow from Jean Wahl the designations he forged on the basis of the word "transcendence" in attempting to describe a double transcendence he detected in Kierkegaard's relation of subjectivity to the absolute. The first movement, "transcendence," would correspond, as its name indicates, to the return, to falling back to what lies before being, in the *il y a* that is obsessional and from which there is no way out, just as being rooted in the primordial earth or being rooted in the flesh, which would always presuppose the unpredictability of the interpellation of a word come to rupture and interrupt this rootedness. These are the moments in which, according to Levinas, Proust engages in the concrete, even exotic descriptions where the ethical structure of the loving face-to-face disappears or is diluted. This is the moment in which, in Proust's work, "magic begins, like a fantastic Sabbath, once ethics has finished" (Levinas 1976, 119). In the *Carnets de captivité*, these are the moments in which Levinas underlines the paradoxical and unattainable character, the enigma of the irrepressible attraction Albertine effects in all her nihilating power, which would be the annulling of

---

3 See Levinas, *De l'existence à l'existant* (1986, 93 and following).
4 The two expressions proper to these two contrary movements, "transdescendence" and "trans-ascendence," derive from Jean Wahl, *Immanence et transcendance*, "La transcendance intériorisée," *Traité de Métaphysique*. Paris: Payot, 1957.

the face. This annihilation would open onto a nothingness that would itself lead to nothing but the incommensurability of a subordination to an other that no longer recognises the traversing of alterity or, to speak like Hegel, a subordination that no longer recognises a thought of death that has to face the trial of nothingness by "looking it in the face" (Hegel 1988, 26) – a Hegelian reflection from which Levinas has broken. However far she abandons or extends herself, whatever the objective and loved alterity to which she refers, Albertine always remains identical with herself. She is, one could say, identity par excellence. Levinas comments:

> What is Albertine (and her lies), if not the very evanescence of the other, her reality made from her nothingness, her presence made from her absence, the struggle with the ungraspable? And beside this – the calm of Albertine sleeping, of the vegetal Albertine. The "character," the "solid" = thing. (Levinas 2009, 72)

Three fragments further on, Levinas continues his reflection, alternating between commentaries and extracts copied from *Albertine disparue*:

> It is no longer a question of deciding between a certain pleasure – which has become almost nothing through habit or perhaps because of the mediocrity of its object – and other pleasures, which are on the contrary tantalizing, ravishing, but between those pleasures and something that is much stronger than them, the pity felt for suffering. Proust, *Albertine disparue*, I, p. 22. (Levinas 2009, 73)

The second movement, that of "trans-ascendence," designates the metaphysical movement towards the Other, the movement of being affected by the other which happens through the body, through its temporal meaning and by the impossibility of quenching the metaphysical desire for the other – from whence the idea that sensibility is defined by vulnerability. This distinction between transdescendence and trans-ascendence is not truly thematised by Levinas. Yet it permeates Levinas's relation to literature; the relation is not identifiable as a philosophical proposition (*énoncé*) but as its perlocution (*énonciation*). It is the narrative Saying that acts deep below the philosophical Said. It is not a matter of a discourse of truth but of a word on the absolute ambiguity contingent upon the opposition between alterity and knowledge. Certainly, it is in death that the Other is most fertile, gnaws at us the most, that his alterity is the most unattainable, the least reducible to the mastery of knowledge. Levinas writes:

> The illness itself *is* this thought of death (and aging and boredom) 2) Proust conceives this thought *through* illness or aging, which are a positive (and appropriate) access to a concept and without which we could only have a negative concept.
> (Levinas 2009, 72ff.)

Albertine's nothingness is therefore not a nothing. It is that which, as Levinas underlines in his essay on Proust, "discovers her total alterity." Death is not only her own death, "it is the death of the other, contrary to the contemporary philosophy attached to the solitary death of the self" (Levinas 1976, 122)

This essential step taken by Levinas, this step not beyond (Blanchot), would have been in part, not exclusively, due to literature and in particular to the work of Proust. This is remarkable in never dividing between transdescendence and trans-ascendence. In it the two movements, in a single piece, join in their shared refusal to yield to Heideggerian being. It is the fact of leaving the ambivalence to a total ethical tension that makes the work of Proust at the same time "more and less than being" (Levinas 1976, 55). To me, this is the essential and decisive role of Levinas's reading of Proust in captivity. It is the locus where a paradoxical, although completely Husserlian, reflection on the question of experience is constituted, which Levinas will later take up in this extraordinary sentence that I place immediately in relation to the question of the temporal meaning of time: "The great 'experiences' of our lives were never, properly speaking, lived" (Levinas 2010, 294).

3 The Corporeal Meaning of Time

One finds here the Husserlian analysis of inner time-consciousness again, but this is articulated in the modality of the corporeal meaning of time, in lived experience, in the incessant passage of the Said to the Saying and to the Unsaying, inner time-consciousness no longer coming to support totally the concept of a transcendental egoic consciousness and intentionality. The important experiences of one's life, which are never properly speaking lived, are situated at the point of intersection where the inner consciousness of time is caught in the ellipse of temporal meaning, pushing it towards the extreme limits, to the point of rupture with the intentional objects that no longer belong to consciousness as constitutive moments but are rather recognised in their full transcendence and ideality. Experience is thus of a perceptive nature, pre-predicative, completely transformed by the flowing temporality of lived experience and of intentional acts. The phenomenon of the retention of lived experience flowing and flowing away in the protention of what is about to be and at the same time has not yet come always remains suspended in the coming or occurrence of an event, in an "awakening" that has nothing to do with a phenomenon of recollection or with a synthesis of recognition.

The decisive gesture carried out by Levinas consists in no longer thinking in two temporal registers – the one active, i.e., retention, the other passive, i.e., protention – but in apprehending the subject as "passivity in its very origin" (Levinas 1974), which will not become active again save in a secondary and lateral manner. The important experiences of our life that we have not experienced – and all Levinas's work is an admirable exemplification of this, or a true narrative phenomenality – are such because the passivity of the subject is no longer thought as the Same that has already been constituted, that will subsequently encounter the other. The passivity of the subject is thought originally as the Other-in-the-Same, the Other, which, according to Hegel, has opened the Same to the Other. In the case of Proust, according to Levinas's reading in captivity, the interest consists not in a perception that would reduce the sources of consciousness in impressions to a psychological analysis of characters and of action. The interest lies, as Levinas determines, "in the theme: the social" (Levinas 2009, 72).

The manner in which Levinas introduces the motif of sociality is completely remarkable, for this does not enter into contradiction with the idea of a subject-hostage who undoes the relation of retention to protention, who undoes the precise moment in which the intentionalities, as intention and event, coincide. The other motif must be re-introduced here, that of passivity, of a passivity more passive than all passivity, according to the expression that Levinas never ceases to rearticulate.[5]

The subject-hostage exposes itself to the other without an intended expectation, without a destination already present in inner time-consciousness. His passivity is without assumption, like "a skin exposes itself to that which hurts it" (Levinas 1974, 63). Faced with assignation by the other, passivity does not retrench itself in a time behind time. Passivity is to be understood as a return to time itself, thus a social time, which cannot be counted before its limits. This does not mean, however, that it issues forth from nowhere or out of no time. Passivity is not negativity, either. It is just as infinite as responsibility or proximity and is thus just as difficult to grasp. That is why passivity is responsible for a time-lag that it cannot fill. Nothing synchronic is possible, no symmetry, because it is at the same time the *retaining* and the *protaining* of what will never coincide. The passivity of the subject-hostage is passive despite itself. It lives off its "total patience" (Levinas 1974, 86) and in doing so it reaches the other without ever showing itself. Passivity has thus renounced being contemporary to what it wishes to reach and touch. From this comes

---

[5] See Levinas, *Autrement qu'être* (1974, 18 and *passim*).

the idea, very present in Levinas in the *Carnets de captivité*, that erotic desire, which he calls "human sexuality," is of the order of an irritation (Levinas 2009, 182). *Eros* is the basis of this irritation just as it is the basis of sociality for Levinas. It is the issue of a central question, of a dimension of Levinas's thought that the *Carnets de captivité* reveal to us in a decisive manner. On one hand, Levinas defines his philosophy, since the period of his captivity, as a philosophy of the face to face, of *panim el panim*, which in Hebrew is said not in the singular but in the plural – faces to faces. On the other hand, this face to face, which is proper to the erotic relation, exceeds the general motif of existence. In Levinas, the motif of existence means affliction, subjugation, languor of being, and not passivity. This presence of myself for a subjugated self constitutes a hope for Levinas. If *eros* is at the origin of the social, it is because the social is already in being. It is the very basis of the duality of I-for-myself and of the mystery of the other that opens to an intimacy not synonymous with fusion. It is on the basis of the motif of carnal concupiscence that Levinas describes the process of this duality. This duality, not understood, not heard as the phenomenon of fusion, thus opens onto an intimacy that is "the sum of the individuals" (Levinas 2009, 66), in other words, the social. The double relation here temporalises the relation of the I-for-myself to the other by freeing it from itself. The duality is already in itself a figure of time, of a dramatic time, because it is always confronted by the mystery of the other, which it will never reach or join. Yet precisely this temporal detachment between the duality of I-for-myself proper to sexuality as constitutive of egoity and the mystery of the other is the condition that allows one to go beyond the antagonism between egoism and altruism. Here there is "[r]upture with the ancient conception of love" (Levinas 2009, 114), thus the possibility of a true exteriority. This opening belongs to two orders, simultaneously the sexual and the social. Erotic desire temporalises the relation to the other that prevents being from foundering and taking its pleasure in its annihilation. Levinas names this hope for a freed present the "caress": "It is not loquacious, it does not say that things will be better – but it redeems in the present itself. Now, with the caress – we have (the) tender and the carnal. Corporeal meaning of time" (Levinas 2009, 186).

Pure suffering, therefore, is not a category. It is not the consequence of a pure sensation. It is in suffering and in submitting, in this absolute passivity, more passive than passivity, that the shivering of election lies, in the sense in which *eros* bears you towards the other, in the sense "of the love of a person who softly touches (caresses) you" (Levinas 2009, 180). This being carried towards – which is the very opposite of an arbitrary vision of the world, the very opposite of the numbness of the being to being, the very opposite of one being that is two – opens to a horizon of sociality and filiality, because the passage from one being that is two to "two beings in the instant" (Levinas 2009, 178) takes place in a relation of asymmetry. Levinas makes it more precise: "One can let go here." And he adds: "But one does not let go" (Levinas 2009, 178).

Here it is, the drama of the temporalisation of the subject's time. The latter seeks to interrupt this synthesis of voluntary, active, and triumphant cognition by opposing a passive synthesis to it that would be the synthesis of the very temporality of passivity. The only possibility – the only hope! – of interrupting the muffled and tenacious perseveration of being in its being and of overcoming the ontological obstinacy of the being-in-itself and for-itself. What then becomes of the relation of transcendence? Would it not be the hope for the for-the-other in the being that posits itself?

If lived experience can only be thought proceeding from the relation of the for-the-other, on the basis of the question that is posed as much by the mortality of the Other as by the metaphysical and erotic desire for the Other, then the relation of transcendence is always referred to a social continuity, which Levinas presents as a relation of delay, of the irreconcilable gap between who comes, who goes, and who is already here. To have a rendezvous with the other is always to be late for him, whatever happens. In taking one's point of departure in Blanchot's formula – "together and still not" – one could say that for Levinas it would be a question of being together and yet *never*.

The pages of Proust on which Levinas comments show well that the passive and inordinate relation of love tied to Albertine is always already concealed in the society to which the subject belongs. This is why ultimate and radical passivity, Levinas's so extravagant gesture, is necessary in order to think of "madness" (Levinas 1974) – that which assaults the human and conditions his relation to time imperatively, that which he cannot approach without desisting from it at the same time.

For Levinas, then, calling on the interiority proper to Proustian narration is not a way of escaping lived experience; rather, it is a means of penetrating deeper into the exigencies of the ethical vocation of the narrative beyond the facticity of the history always seeking to utter itself or not to utter itself in thematising itself. Ultimate meaning escapes it, however, for the relation of the subject-hostage to the other is dissymmetrical, just as is the irreversibility of time. The indelible traces of this in the structure of the meaning narrated do not belong to any formal logic but derive from an infinite moment of *un-saying* and of *re-saying* that is one of the characteristics of the *disinterestedness* of love.

Bibliography

Barthes, Roland. *Œuvres Complètes*, vol. 3. Paris: Seuil, 2002.
Hegel, *Phänomenologie des Geistes*. Eds. Hans-Friedrich Wessels and Heinrich Clairmont. Hamburg: Meiner, 1988.
Levinas, Emmanuel. *Autrement qu'être ou au-delà de l'essence*. The Hague: Nijhoff, 1974.
Levinas, Emmanuel. *Noms propres*. Paris: Vrin, 1976.
Levinas, Emmanuel. *De l'existence à l'existant*. Paris: Vrin, 1986.
Levinas, Emmanuel. *Les imprévus de l'histoire*. Montpellier: Fata Morgana, 1994.
Levinas, Emmanuel. *Oeuvres*, 1: *Carnets de captivité et autre inédits*. Eds. Rodolphe Calin and Catherine Chalier. Paris: Grasset/IMEC, 2009.
Levinas, Emmanuel. *En découvrant l'existence avec Husserl et Heidegger*. Paris: Vrin, 2010.
de Saint-Cheron, Michel. *Entretiens avec Emmanuel Levinas (1992–1994)*. Paris: Le livre de poche, 2006.

Jan Bierhanzl
Ideology, Literature, and Philosophy: Levinas as a Reader of Léon Bloy

> To admit the effect that literature has on men is perhaps the ultimate wisdom of the West in which the people of the Bible may recognize themselves.
> Levinas, *Difficult Freedom* (53).

1 Introduction

Reading *Carnet* 6 of the *Carnets de captivité et autres inédits* – published in 2009 and containing long quotes from, and comments on, Léon Bloy's *Lettres à sa fiancée*, in which literature, philosophy, and religion are conjoined – provokes a sort of embarrassment in the reader today. This is linked to the tension between, on one hand, Levinas's admiration for this writer and the trace of a profound inspiration for all of his work provided by his reading of Bloy, and, on the other hand, the profoundly disturbing context in which this reading took place. In his article "Salvation through Literature: Levinas's *Carnets de captivité*," Seán Hand sketches the tension between these two paths of reading. On one hand, he insists on these two authors' simultaneously thematic, stylistic, and methodological proximity as well as the reasons why Bloy's "pensée absolue" could exercise such a fascination on Levinas: "The extreme and almost ecstatic pronouncements about suffering, the female, glory, and the absolutization of thought [. . .] as operating in profound dialogue with Levinas's own thematical developments and even exegetical strategies" (Hand 2013, 58). On the other hand, he also evokes the more than disturbing context in which Levinas read Bloy. It was in 1944, when Levinas was in captivity:

> [. . .] The contextual isolation of Bloy at this precise moment and place can [. . .] be called uncanny. For less than 50 miles away, at exactly the same time, another diarist is engaged in a similarly intense meditation on Bloy's writing. This writer is none other than Ernst Jünger. This professional soldier, author of the first world war account

---

Note: The present text is published as a part of the grant project "Image and Music in 20th Century Thought", financed by GA ČR, No. P401 19-20498S.
Translation: Translated, from the French, by Ashraf Noor.

Open Access. © 2021 Jan Bierhanzl, published by De Gruyter. This work is licensed under the Creative Commons Attribution 4.0 International License.
https://doi.org/10.1515/9783110668926-014

Storm of Steel (*In Stahlgewittern*), self-conscious diarist, and friend and correspondent of Heidegger and Carl Schmitt, is more particularly a captain and senior member of the German military occupation in Paris." (Hand 2013, 61)

Recently, Sarah Hammerschlag has pointed out that this disturbing context could be explained in part by the accessibility of literature in the camps. The *Comité international de la Croix Rouge* distributed book packets in the POW camps, some of which even had libraries. All books, however, were scrutinized by the censor. While all authors in exile, communists, and Jews were prohibited, Catholics like Léon Bloy were accessible.[1] Now, what disturbs the reader of *Carnet 6* and, parallel to this, of the *Lettres à sa fiancée*, lies not only in the historical context of Bloy's remarks taken up and approved by Levinas, but equally in the ideological content of certain judgments that Levinas seems never to have called into question philosophically (even in his mature works). We are thinking here particularly of Levinas's concept of the Feminine (or feminine), which is profoundly inspired by Bloy's idea of Woman. As we shall see, certain passages of the *Lettres à sa fiancée* copied by Levinas bear witness to a particularly violent sexist ideology. For example, when Bloy describes his project of a coming book on Woman[2] in one of his letters to Jeanne Molbech, his fiancée, he associates the feminine with women's physiological sex, while this is not the case for the masculine. "The central concept of this book is the physiological sex of the woman around which her whole psychology is wrapped and reeled implacably. In brief, the woman depends on her sex just as the man depends on his brain" (Bloy 1922, 79). Before scrutinizing this central problem concerning the ideological content of Levinas's concept of the feminine, from his being inspired by Bloy, in greater detail and considering the possibility of going beyond this in literature and in philosophy (with the aid of certain concepts deriving from Barthes and Blanchot), we will attempt to retrace the relations between philosophy, literature, and religion that allowed Levinas as a reader of Bloy to achieve a new style of thought, that is, a new philosophical intelligibility, in accordance with the progressive development of his mature work.

---

1 See Sarah Hammerschlag, *Broken Tablets: Levinas, Derrida, and the Literary Afterlife of Religion* (2016, 200, note 36).
2 What is meant here will be his major work, the novel *La femme pauvre*, published in 1897, that is to say eight years after writing the letter to his fiancée in which he mentions his project of a book on Woman, an "important work" of "extreme audacity." See *Lettres à sa fiancée* (1922, 78), and *La femme pauvre* (2013).

2 Bloy and the Style of Levinas's Thought

In the preface to the *Carnets de captivité*, the editors, Catherine Chalier and Rodolphe Calin, state that the style of Levinas's thought, that is, the new philosophical intelligibility he created in accordance with the construction of his work, is the product of a "conjunction" between the literary concern for "descriptions of concrete situations" and the "religious" concern for transcendence. This "conjunction will constitute the very style of Levinas's thought" (Levinas 2009, 25). Now, his reading of Léon Bloy plays a major part in putting this "conjunction" into place. Levinas, reading Bloy, paid a great deal of attention to what Bloy calls the "connectivity" between the prosaic and the spiritual: "the miraculous connectivity that exists between the Holy Spirit and the most lamentable, the most despised, the most soiled human creature, the Prostitute" (Bloy 1922, 82).[3] This is also the way he links indissolubly his vocations as writer and exegete: "I would have thus given to my manner as an artist and according to my vision as an exegete the two cruelly symbolic faces of the truth of the divine drama" (Bloy 1922, 80). Another way to formulate this conjunction of what is on this side, as literature, and beyond, as religion, is their common tendency to escape the light. Chalier and Calin speak of the "sense in Bloy of the transcendence of the mystery that is contained in empirical situations, of transcendence understood as that which escapes the light" (Levinas 2009, 25). Levinas notes to this effect, with regard to Bloy, in a formulation prefiguring his path in *Otherwise than Being or Beyond Essence* that links the phenomenological method of concretization and the stylistic figure of emphasis, which he elevates to the rank of a philosophical method: "And this order of mystery to which concrete situations are returned – is only there – is only justified by this admiration that goes as far as tears" (Levinas 2009, 151).

Levinas shares with Bloy the exegete the performative strategy of interrupting the system of "professors' categories" with this wholly literary concern for concrete situations coupled with attentiveness to "religious" transcendence, noting admiringly with regard to the *Lettres à sa fiancée*: "the professors' categories are replaced by the very transcendence of the order of mystery" (Levinas 2009, 151). In this interruption of the system of categories, the *Lettres à sa fiancée* contain the trace of Bloy's major project of a definitive destruction of bourgeois speech in *Exégèse des lieux communs*. This two-volume work collects bourgeois speech comprised of stock expressions while interrupting it, destroying it performatively through repetition and ideologically "religious" exegesis, and accompanying this with a joy in the destruction,

---
[3] Levinas copies this passage, in *Carnet* 6 (2009, 157).

with a felicity of expression, which are eminently literary. Here is the utterance of the stock expression in a part of the *Lettres à sa fiancée* where Bloy describes his project of a book on Woman to his fiancée: "All the women whom I have come to know in my country, all, without exception, have an idea that must be universal [. . .]. This idea is that they have a secret to which no man is capable of acceding. – 'Sir, you will never be able to know a woman; there is something about her that will always escape you'" (1922, 76). This idea, corresponding to the combination of exegesis and exorcism that Bloy carries out in *Exégèse des lieux communs,* constitutes at the same time a philistine platitude and a profoundly vertiginous truth about the "unknown Woman." Bloy continues: "I have heard that a thousand times, and those who said it were often, I assure you, inexpressibly stupid. Poor creatures, who would, it is certain, indeed be embarrassed if they had to explain their famous secret to themselves, that is, unless their thoughts contained turpitude and nonsense, as is probable. It is clearly ridiculous, yet they are right, without knowing it" (1922, 76).

Before coming to the feminist critique of the ideological concept of the feminine in Bloy and Levinas, let us note that Bloy's exegesis is a way of conjoining literature and "religion" close to Levinas's method, carried out in particular in *Totalité et infini,* which he calls "concretization." This issued forth from the phenomenological method in a broad sense and consists of deducing from formal relations the concrete life in which these relations and the terms of these relations are brought to our attention. He thus explains this method of concretization, which he also calls "*deduction* – necessary and yet non-analytical," in the preface to *Totality and Infinity* "The break-up of the formal structure of thought (the noema of a noesis) – into events which this structure simulates, but which sustain it and restore its concrete significance, constitutes a *deduction* – necessary and yet not analytical. In our exposition it is marked by terms such as 'that is' or 'precisely' or 'this accomplishes that' or 'this is produced by that'" (Levinas 1979, 28).[4] Here, then, is the concretization of

---

[4] Didier Franck is the author of the most precise and rigorous analysis of this method of non-analytic deduction. Cf. Didier Franck, *L'un-pour-l'autre. Levinas et la signification* (2008, 52): "The use of the expression 'under the aspects of. . . .' indicates consequently the very particular relation that obtains, in the manner in which Levinas proceeds, between the example and the meaning, for the former can be mistaken for the latter, for the former is the staging and the operating theatre of the latter in virtue of a radicalization of the principle of all phenomenology according to which '*access to the object is part of the object's being*'. If one intends by literature an order of the Said where the meaning cannot be disassociated from the dramatic situations that articulate it and where the echo of the Saying can always be found in one way or another, Levinas's descriptions, which link examples in as many meanings, have a literary character while excluding any lack of proper conceptual rigour. Once again, without knowledge of this method and this style everything here remains and will remain incomprehensible."

the expression "to know a woman" penned by Bloy, when he continues to present his project of a book on Woman: "The central concept of this book is the physiological sex of the woman around which her whole psychology is wrapped and reeled implacably" (Bloy 1922, 79).

In order to do justice to the originality of Levinas's philosophical project, it is necessary to mention here that this method of concretization is not solely of phenomenological or literary inspiration but that he derives it equally from Talmudic texts. Indeed, in such a text, the concrete example does not play the role of an illustration or of a particularization of the concept of which it is an example; rather, it contributes to extending and bursting the concept into an irreducible multiplicity of meanings. In other words, the example creates a new meaning, which is not contained in the concept: "[. . .] in Talmudic texts multiple meanings coexist; it is a way of thinking in which the example is not the mere particularization of a concept but in which the example holds together a multiplicity of meanings [. . .]" (Levinas 1990, 60). Now, in the precise context of the concretization of the expression "to know a woman," we can in the same way suppose a Biblical inspiration, a source common to Bloy's Catholicism and to Levinas's Judaism. For in Biblical language, "to know" does not mean purely intellectual knowledge; to know someone can mean prosaically "to have a sexual relation with someone," as witnessed by the current expression "to know someone in the Biblical sense." In *Theology of the Body*, John Paul II explains:

> To know in Biblical language does not only mean purely intellectual knowledge but also a concrete example like, for example, the experience of suffering, of sin, of war and of peace. [. . .] 'Knowledge' penetrates into the domain of relations between persons when it concerns the solidarity of the family [DT 33,9] and especially conjugal relations. It is precisely in referring to the conjugal act that the term underlines the paternity of illustrious persons and the origin of their descendants [Gn 4,1; Gn 4,17–25; Is 1,19] as significant facts of genealogy, to which the tradition of priests (hereditary in Israel) attributed great importance. The term 'knowledge' could equally refer to all the other sexual relations, even the illicit ones [Nb 31,17; Gn 19,5; Jg 19,22].   (Jean-Paul II, 1980)

Gn 4, 1–2 speaks only of the knowledge of woman on the part of man as if to emphasize the latter's activity ("Man knew Eve, his woman. She was with child and gave birth to Cain"). But one can also speak of the reciprocal character of this "knowledge" in which man and woman participate by means of their body, of their sex. Since the verb could be used for both sexes, as in "The two daughters of Lot had not known men," it is not necessarily the case in the Bible that one has to consider woman as an object (of knowledge) of which man takes possession.

To return to *Lettres à sa fiancée* and to the "concretization" of the expression "to know a woman" according to which "woman depends on her sex" (Bloy 1922, 79), we can already notice in the text Levinas read very carefully in

1944 a philosophical-literary trait that he will develop in the work of his maturity. This concerns the radicalization of the method of concretization through emphasis. The concretization of the idea of knowing a woman through the sexual relation with a concrete woman is immediately followed, under Bloy's pen, by a methodological remark justifying the use of emphasis in order to reach the "absolute truth," "absolute thought" in "absolute expressions" (Levinas 2009, 159): "The idea is not new, but it is possible to renew it and even to give it a terrifying expression by pushing it to the most extreme consequences, and it is this I propose to myself in the hope of encountering absolute truth." (Bloy 1922, 79) In the same way, the emphatic passage from "suffering with" to "suffering in others" – an authentic Christian figure of the person in whose heart "there are all human hearts" (Levinas 2009, 158; Bloy 1922, 89) and which recalls in many respects the concretization and the emphasis of *one-for-the-other* in the vulnerability of *the other in the same* of maternity in *Otherwise than Being* – constitutes another profound resonance between Bloy's text and the expression of Levinas's late thought. After having shown that the originality of the style of Levinas's thought resides in the connection between literature defined formally as "a regime of the Said where the meaning cannot be dissociated from the dramatic situations in which it is articulated" (Franck 2008, 52) and the "religious" attention to transcendence, both of which traits can be found in reading Léon Bloy, it is now necessary to make the content of the two terms of this connection more explicit. In what way do Levinas's concepts of "religion" and of "literature" bear a trace of his reading of Bloy?

Let us begin with the conception of religion. In *Carnet* 6, Levinas notes with regard to Bloy's conception of Catholicism: "Everyone dwells in the categories of Catholicism. The same work has to be done for J." (Levinas 2009, 151) Or in an analogous passage: "Existence as a whole is integrated into the divine drama." (Levinas 2009, 153) In a parallel, Levinas has thus drawn from Bloy the idea according to which Judaism is not a category of religious belonging but an ontological category that makes of this religion "the locus of a new interpretation of man and of his subjectivity" (Levinas 2009, 22). Other notes in the same *Carnet* develop this idea of a new interpretation of man within Judaism and allow us to note retrospectively the importance of this philosophical concept of Judaism for the expression of Levinas's thought in all his work up to that of his maturity: "to take the point where one begins in Dasein or in J[udaism]. Judaism as a category" (Levinas 2009, 22); to interpret man and his subjectivity beginning in "I am" or the " 'I' understood from the outset from the past of creation and of election" (Levinas 2009, 22). Hammerschlag, in connecting three aspects – the Catholic sources in the *Carnets*, *Être Juïf* of 1947, and the definition of religion in *Otherwise than Being*, notes: "We can thus trace a line connecting three moments: Levinas's interpretation of Catholic sources during the war, his formulation of *Being Jewish* in 1947, and his definition of religion in *Otherwise than Being*. This is not to say that the Catholic sources are necessary to the later thought, or to argue their priority over the Jewish sources, but only to reveal the connection between the comments from the notebooks and a mature expression of Levinas's thought" (Hammerschlag 2016, 49) As far as the conception of subjectivity being elected from the outset is concerned, formulated in the *Carnets* as the sentiment imposed on the Jew particularly by Hitlerism as being "ineluctably riveted to his Judaism" (Levinas 2009, 21), an idea concretized and radicalized in the "sacrificial turn" of *Otherwise than Being*, it is not short of echoes. Here, again, we find a context that is more than disturbing, apprehending the suffering of the Jews as an extension of Christ's redemptive works. Hammerschlag, too, underlines the attention paid by Levinas, the reader of Bloy, to the connection between suffering and election: "Levinas's interest in Bloy is, on one level, not surprising. Bloy's 1892 *Salvation by the Jews* had revived the notion that the suffering of the Jews was redemptive, a carrying on of the work of Christ. While such a view functioned to justify Dreyfus's suffering in such a way that it was itself a redemptive event, it was, nonetheless, for some a powerful counter account to Drumont's." (Hammerschlag 2016, 300, note 36)

As far as the second part of our analysis is concerned, the literary dimension of Levinas's thought, we shall try to show that the regime of the Said does not only constitutes a modality of Levinas's phenomenological method, but that it equally bears a content that is at the same time ideological and ontological. On the ideological level, the concept of literature is intimately linked to the concept of the feminine, inspired to a large extent by Bloy's idea of Woman. On the ontological level, literature is a regime of the Said, allowing one to lay bare "the most brutal materiality" of the *il y a*.

3 Woman and the Feminine

Here is an emblematic passage concerning this point, which is decisive for our argument.

> Neither does this mystery of the feminine – the feminine: essentially other – refer to any romantic notions of the mysterious, unknown, or misunderstood woman. Let it be understood that if, in order to uphold the thesis of the exceptional position of the feminine in the economy of being, I willingly refer to the great themes of Goethe or Dante, to Beatrice and the *ewig Weibliches*, to the cult of the *Woman* in chivalry and in modern society (which is certainly not explained solely by the necessity of lending a strong arm to the

weaker sex) – if, more precisely, I think of the admirably bold pages of Léon Bloy in his *Letters to his Fiancée*, I do not want to ignore the legitimate claims of the feminism that presupposes all the acquired attainments of civilization. I simply want to say that this mystery must not be understood in the ethereal sense of a certain literature; that in the most brutal materiality, in the most shameless or the most prosaic appearance of the feminine,[5] neither her mystery nor her modesty are abolished. Profanation is not a negation of mystery, but one of the possible relationships with it. (Levinas 1987, 86)

We will analyze this link, at the same time ideological and ontological, between the feminine and the *il y a* by drawing on certain feminist critiques.

Bloy and Levinas indeed share a brutally reductive dualism regarding the subject of Woman or the feminine. In the *Carnets de captivité*, Levinas copied a long passage on Woman from Bloy's *Lettres à sa Fiancée*, preceded by the note "the basis of his ideas" (Levinas 2009, 156). Here is the beginning of this passage: "For woman, a creature temporarily, provisionally inferior, there are only two ways of being: the most august maternity or the title and the quality of an instrument of pleasure, pure or impure love. In other words Holiness or Prostitution; Mary Magdalen before or Mary Magdalen after" (Bloy 1922, 80). Setting aside the passage in *Time and the Other* in which Levinas lays claim explicitly to Bloy's conception of Woman, which he associates with "the most brutal materiality, [. . .] the most shameless or the most prosaic appearance of the feminine" and which he opposes to "mystery of the feminine" in "the ethereal sense of a certain literature," the description of the "feminine face" in section IV of *Totality and Infinity* (cf. 1979, 260–264), which bears the title "Beyond the Face," is also the imprint of a sexist dialectic that approaches "rape culture." Michel Lisse has indicated precisely this logic of the feminine in Levinas, "where the chastity and the decency of the face is maintained at the limit of the obscene that is still repulsed but is already very close and full of promise" (Levinas 1987, 260): "The feminine is at the same time mystery and the animal, the Virgin and the child, inviolable and violable at the same time, the saint and the whore, even if these two latter words are not those of

---

5 These formulations on the part of Levinas concerning the prosaic character of the apparition of the feminine translate in a highly precise manner the "terrifying impression" that Bloy gives to the idea of Woman in making it depend on her sex. On the other hand, Levinas owes to Bloy the vertiginous idea according to which the profanation of the mystery is not its negation but constitutes a possible relation with this mystery. Transgressing Catholic orthodoxy, Bloy attributes the cult of *latréia*, which relates solely to God, to Woman and pushes the sacrilege to the extreme by linking the cult with prostitution: "For example, the cult, the true latreian cult of woman, as virtuous as one supposes her to be, for the exterior sign of her sex, which she unconsciously values as being equal to Paradise. Imagine it, this cult, in immediate conflict with the absolute necessity of venal prostitution. Push this idea to the extreme, this conception of sacrilege, and the proudest of men will tremble before the monster that his spirit will have evoked" (Bloy 1922, 79).

Levinas [. . .]. Hence Levinas's logic of thinking the feminine [. . .], virginity and the loss of virginity, the membrane and its perforation, respect and the desire for profanation, the untouchable at the same time the purest and most impure." (Lisse 2015, 299)

Stella Sandford has shown that the feminine in Levinas is associated (being an heir to Bloy) with sexual difference and with eros (as well as with "childhood without responsibility" and the "pure life ´a little stupid`" of animality (Levinas 1979, 263 and following)) in a way that the masculine, for its part, is not:

> [. . .] it would be ludicrous to ascribe to Levinas, the man, the view that he does not believe women to have human status. Nevertheless, the implication of these texts is indeed that the feminine is opposed to the human in a way 'the masculine' is not. To the extent that Levinas attaches an increasing importance to the distinction between the truly 'human' in its apparent neutrality from the being of the human in his or her sexuate incarnation or the human being under the mark of sexual difference, the unequal status of the feminine and the masculine becomes more and more apparent. Only the feminine being appears in her sexuate incarnation or under the mark of sexual difference. As a consequence the human and the masculine are conjoined in such a way that the former loses its claim to neutrality. (Sandford 2000, 53)

Sandford also insists on the fact that Levinas's retrospective proposal, in the "Preface" to *Time and the Other*, dating from 1979, to enlarge his concept of femininity as "a difference contrasting strongly with other differences" to masculinity or virility, that is to say to "the difference between the sexes in general" (Levinas 1987, 36), cannot operate on such a basis of inequality: "[. . .] it is particularly obvious in this discussion that no reversal of genders could turn it into an abstract point about sexual difference [. . .] (one could not, that is, seriously say: 'The masculine essentially violable and inviolable, the 'Eternal masculine' is the virgin or an incessant recommencement of virginity')." (Sandford 2000, 53) In the same way, Levinas's recognition of the legitimate claims of feminism precisely in the passage of *Time and the Other* in which he also refers to the concept of Woman in Bloy does not seem convincing, not only because of its brevity. As Lisse notes, "[. . .] it is indeed woman as 'the weak sex' to whom the man has to lend a 'strong hand' who serves Levinas as a reference in order to think the feminine. Feminism finds itself at the same time celebrated, acknowledged, and dismissed in the space and the time of a proposition." (2015, 298)

Despite the evolution of Levinas's thought on this question from *Totality and Infinity* to *Otherwise than Being* and the introduction of a feminine element – maternity – into the very heart of ethical subjectivity, Catherine Chalier and Stella Sandford show, each in her own way, that the fundamental dichotomy proposing to non-metaphorical women only two alternatives – the irresponsibility of the lover and the protective mother – is far from eluded in the work of the philosopher's maturity. Chalier evokes the non-metaphorical women "who do not want to recognize themselves either in the inverted face of the lover or in maternal succour" (1982, 35) and their right to speak, to choose for themselves a name that they would like to bear. And they indicate the risk of justifying in philosophical language an injustice and a violence that are indeed historical in Levinas's discourse on maternity as election, before any choice, to suffer for the other.

> It is not surprising to note how they have so often understood themselves in effacement before the other. For them it was, in fact, an election before any choice. To say this election, an election by the Good to which they can but respond, is to interrupt their silence on the question. History also says, very simply but this time very violently, that they really did not have a choice. To consecrate them as women was to consecrate them as holders of a body they did not have to say because it was an offering. (Chalier 1982, 44–45)

Chalier remains a follower of Levinas to the extent that she proposes to women a correction of this ultimate meaning of the feminine in the context of a Levinasian ethics, which is an ethics of the face without metaphor. The Saying that does not say a word, in the later Levinas, is also the relinquishment by women of "all the metaphors" (Chalier 1982, 45) alluding to them. "Neither the Virgin Mary nor even Beatrice, a woman has to also hear her name in the ethical utopia, where language speaks as justice and resistance towards the Same. For this, it is incumbent on them to put an end to their effacement of themselves behind metaphors that they have not chosen." (Chalier 1982, 44–45)

Sandford, for her part, formulates a radical critique of Levinas's whole philosophical project as a philosophical, more precisely a phenomenological, justification of a metaphysics of eros, and she contends that maternity in *Otherwise than Being* does not represent a true alternative to the meaning of the feminine in *Totality and Infinity*.[6] "Once this community, and the wisdom of love that informs it, appear in *Otherwise than Being*, the trope of maternity drops out, much as the

---

[6] We will leave aside here the connection between the feminine and hospitality that is also present in *Totality and Infinity*, just as the Derridean interpretation of this motif, given that Levinas does not owe this stereotype associating the feminine and the economic sphere of the house directly to Bloy. It is interesting to note that Derrida attempts a "feminist" interpretation of this motif. Lisse summarises this interpretation in the following terms: "Derrida shows that Levinas's claim generates two possible readings: either an androcentric hyperbole, marked by a vision of the feminine orientated towards the masculine point of view, or a feminist hyperbole that would maintain the feminine as the condition of possibility of welcoming in general, of absolute hospitality, thus as the 'pre-ethical origin of ethics' [(Derrida 1999, 83)]." (Lisse 2015, 301) Since Derrida has the tendency to understand this masculine point of view as that of someone who "writes like a man" in the biological sense of the term, one has to specify that it is rather a question of an ideological position that can therefore equally be shared by an individual of the feminine sex. With respect to this, see Sandford (2000, 62).

feminine ceases to play a role in *Totality and Infinity* after the elaboration of fecundity as fraternity" (Sandford 2000, 91). Although Levinas substitutes the term of "relation" to that of "paternity," this relation does not represent a true alternative feminine relation. As Sandford explains, "Levinas's text has not been able to effect or install an alternative feminine parenthood because ultimately maternity must and does give way to paternity, that is to the law of the father. Maternity, indeed, as associated with the particularity of the feminine, is outside of any parenthood when this is understood as paternity is, as the institution of a universal order of the human, of sociality, community and philosophy." (2000, 92)

4 The Ideological Content of the Concept of the Feminine and its Possible Overcoming in Literature

This reconciliation between philosophy as "wisdom of love in the service of love" and paternity, of which the ideological content of the concept of the feminine constitutes the hidden face, does not constitute, according to our argument, the only philosophical approach in Levinas's work. There is also, above all in his late works such as *Otherwise than Being* or *Of God Who Comes to the Mind*, a dimension that is subversive of philosophy, irreducible to all ideology, including the ideological content of the sexual difference, which one can characterize as literary, following Didier Franck's analyses or – much earlier than the latter's brilliant analyses in *L'un-pour-l'autre* – following Roland Barthes's interpretation of Bloy as well as that of Levinas by Maurice Blanchot.

According to Roland Barthes, despite the ideological content of Bloy's texts, these participate in literature in the proper sense of the term, with "its resistances to order, its power to oppose being recuperated, and the permanent scandal that it has constituted with respect to collectivities and their institutions [. . .]" (Barthes 1995, 46). In the same way, despite the ideological content of the concept of the feminine in Levinas, the descriptions of the feminine, in their "literary" dimension as Barthes conceives it, are at the origin of a return from the *il y a* that threatens the institution of ethics as first philosophy impassably. Or, to say this inversely and more precisely, literature as an ambiguous form of language (in the later Levinas, the literary force of his thought is marked by an ambiguity between *il y a* and *illéité*, between Saying and Said, between reason and scepticism), as an irreducible multiplicity, eludes any recuperation by a duality between the masculine and the feminine – which in fact sets one back to the dual unity of masculine privilege. It is in this way that ambiguity, which is elevated to the level of a method in Levinas's later works and is practiced with such joy,[7] reintroduces a rupture of the system into philosophical discourse, a rupture that foils all duality, including the duality of sexual difference. It is Blanchot, in *L'Écriture du désastre*, who allows such an interpretation of ambiguity as philosophical method doing justice to the resistance to order, which is the meaning of literature.

> The question that is always to be questioned: 'Does the multiple amount, finally, to just two?' One answer: whoever says two, only *repeats* One (or dual unity), unless the second term – inasmuch as it is the Other – is infinitely multiple. Or unless the repetition of One maintains only to dissipate unity (perhaps fictively). Thus there are not two discourses: there is discourse – and then there would be dis-course, were it not that we 'know' practically nothing. We 'know' that it escapes systems, order, possibility, including the possibility of language, and that writing, perhaps – writing, where totality has let itself be exceeded – puts it in play. (Blanchot 1986, 134)

Simon Critchley follows Blanchot in his interpretation of literature in Levinas. He poses the following rhetorical question: "Is literature ever decisively overcome in the establishment of ethics as first philosophy?" (Critchley 2005, 83). The answer is, of course, negative. Literature, inasmuch as it is an ambiguous form of language making meaning and non-meaning, *il y a* and *illéité*, Saying and Said, reason and scepticism, alternate, is never exceeded in a linear manner by ethics as first philosophy. If, despite the ideological (that is, metaphysical) presuppositions never called into question philosophically (in particular the ideological concept of the feminine that associates this latter with eros and sexual difference and is thus contrasted to the human in another way than the concept of the masculine), Bloy and Levinas continue to fascinate us or to make us share their passion, the reason is the radically literary dimension of their thought, in the sense that Barthes or Blanchot gives to literature – literature that "strikes the ideological choices [. . .] of a sort of inconsistent irrationalism" (Barthes 1995, 47). This is because in the "space" of this ambiguity practiced with true happiness and without any limit of objects (including, particularly in *Of God Who Comes to the Mind*, the ambiguity of God and the *il y a*, that is, in "the sombre paradox of God's malevolence," the ambiguity of good and evil), we can question again the totality of Levinas's ideological choices.

---

7 In "Difficile éthique," the preface to my book *La rupture du sens*, Gérard Bensussan proposes enlarging "the power of equivocation," to which Levinas's analyses of the erotic in *Totality and Infinity* "give a hyperbolic extension," up to the whole of the meta-conceptualities of Levinas's ethics. According to Bensussan, this extended equivocation is practiced "with true joy." See Bensussan, "Difficile éthique" (2017, 9).

If we continue today to share Bloy's passion, it is not for his ideological choices but for the "happiness of expression" that he practiced with such vivacity.

> [. . .] this style so carried away and primed that says nothing other, finally, than the passion of words [. . .]. The systematic invective carried out without any limit of objects (the surrealist slap given to Anatole France's corpse is quite timid compared with Bloy's profanations) constitutes in a certain way a radical experience of language: the happiness of invective is nothing other than a variety of this happiness of expression that Maurice Blanchot has justifiably turned into the expression of happiness. [. . .] It is without a doubt this invincible voluptuousness of language, to which an extraordinary 'richness' of expressions bears witness, that afflicts Bloy's ideological choices with a kind of inconsistent irreality: that he was furiously Catholic, offending in a jumbled way the conformist and modernist Church, the Protestants, the Freemasons, the English, and the democrats [and, we can add, women], that this fanatic of the incongruous fell for Louis XVIII or Mélanie (the shepherdess of La Salette) is nothing more than variable matter that does not abuse any of Bloy's readers. The illusion is composed of the ideas, the choices, the beliefs, the declarations, the causes; the reality is composed of the words, the eroticism of language, that this poor writer, bereft of a salary, practiced furiously and of which he makes us still today share the passion. (Barthes 1995, 47)

That which, in the same way, continues to fascinate us in Levinas is his writing, which captivates us and holds us in the ambiguity of the experience of literature in Blanchot's sense (an experience that is metaphysically and ideologically "neutral" without being for that matter impersonal (cf. Critchley 2005, 83)). "[. . .] might not the fascination (a word favoured by Blanchot) that Levinas's writing continues to exert, the way that it captivates us without our ever feeling that we have captured it, be found in the way it keeps open the question of ambiguity, the ambiguity that defines the experience of language and literature itself for Blanchot, the ambiguity of the Saying and the Said, the skepticism and reason, of the il y a and illeity, that is also to say – perhaps – of evil and goodness?" (Critchley 2005, 80). The question remains open whether, in our experience of the ambiguity of literature, that is, in the experience of the neutral in Blanchot's sense, where we have lost all ideology and all metaphysics of the feminine, we have not also lost transcendence itself (which is, however, so characteristic of Levinas's style of thought). Blanchot would say that the experience of the neutral, which is infinitely multiple, also eludes being recuperated by the conceptual pair of immanence and transcendence.[8]

---

[8] See Critchley (2005, 87, note 35): "Blanchot's reservations on the subject of whether the neuter can be described as transcendent should be noted here. In *The Infinite Conversation*, he writes: 'One of the essential traits of the neutral, in fact, is that it does not allow itself to be grasped either in terms of immanence or in terms of transcendence, drawing us into an entirely different sort of relation'(p. 463)."

Bibliography

Barthes, Roland. *Oeuvres complètes*, Volume III: 1974–1980. Paris: Editions du Seuil, 1995.
Bensussan, Gérard. "Difficile éthique," Preface to *La rupture du sens: Corps, langage et non sens dans la pensée de la signifiance éthique d'Emmanuel Levinas*, by Jan Bierhanzl. Paris: Mimésis, 2014. 7–10.
Blanchot, Maurice. *The Writing of the Disaster*. Trans. Ann Smock. Lincoln: University of Nebraska Press, 1986.
Bloy, Léon. *Lettres à sa fiancée*. Paris: Librairie Stock, 1922.
Bloy, Léon. *La femme pauvre*. Clermont-Ferrand: Ed. De Borée, 2013.
Chalier, Catherine. *Figures du féminin. Lecture d'Emmanuel Lévinas*. Paris: La nuit surveillée, 1982.
Critchley, Simon. "*Il y a* – Holding Levinas's Hand to Blanchot's Fire." *Emmanuel Levinas: Critical Assessments of Leading Philosophers*, Volume I: *Levinas, Phenomenology and His Critics*. Eds. Claire Elise Katz and Lara Trout. London: Routledge, 2005. 75–87.
Derrida, Jacques. *Adieu to Emmanuel Levinas*. Trans. Pascal-Anne Brault and Michael Naas. Stanford: Stanford University Press, 1999.
Franck, Didier. *L'un-pour-l'autre. Levinas et la signification*. Paris: PUF, 2008.
Hammerschlag, Sarah. *Broken Tablets: Levinas, Derrida, and the Literary Afterlife of Religion*. New York: Columbia University Press, 2016.
Hand, Seán. "Salvation through literature: Levinas's *Carnets de captivité*." *Levinas Studies* 8, no. 1 (2013): 45–68.
John Paul II. https://w2.vatican.va/content/john-paul-ii/fr/audiences/1980/documents/hf_jp-ii_aud_19800305.html.
Levinas, Emmanuel. *Totality and Infinity: An Essay on Exteriority*. Trans. Alphonso Lingis. The Hague / Boston: Nijhoff, 1979.
Levinas, Emmanuel. *Time and the Other*. Trans. Richard A. Cohen. Pittsburgh: Duquesne University Press, 1987.
Levinas, Emmanuel. *Nine Talmudic Readings*. Trans. Annette Aronowicz. Bloomington: Indiana University Press, 1990.
Levinas, Emmanuel. *Œuvres complètes*, Volume I: *Carnets de captivité et autres inédits*. Eds. Rodolphe Calin and Catherine Chalier. Paris: Grasset/IMEC, 2009.
Lisse, Michel. "L'hymen de Levinas." *Debating Levinas' Legacy*. Eds. Andris Breitling, Chris Bremmers, and Arthur Cools. Leiden/Boston: Brill, 2015. 296–306.
Sandford, Stella. *The Metaphysics of Love: Gender and Transcendence in Levinas*. London / New Brunswick: The Athlone Press, 2000.

Luc Anckaert
Goodness without Witnesses: Vasily Grossman and Emmanuel Levinas

Life and Fate, the impressive novel on the battle of Stalingrad by the Jewish-Russian author Vasily Grossman, was first published in 1980, by *L'Âge d'homme* in Lausanne (Garrard & Garrard 2012). Grossman had earlier submitted it in 1960, in a rather naive way, for publication in the post-Stalin period. Under the Khrushchev regime, there was little tolerance for criticizing Stalinism or comparing it to Nazism. However, instead of Grossman being arrested, as had happened to Boris Pasternak, it was the novel's manuscript, along with all copies and carbon papers of it, that were confiscated. The text – an *emulation* of Tolstoy's *War and Peace* (Emerson 2012) – subsequently lived an underground life. Levinas, after finishing his main works, read the Russian edition when he was 75 years old. In 1987, in the Poirié interview (Levinas 2001a, 80), he stated: "The great book which impressed me a lot, is the book by Vasily Grossman, *Life and Fate*, translated from the Russian, which I read in Russian."

Although written in the same decade as *Totality and Infinity* (Levinas 1969), *Life and Fate* is not a source for Levinas. Nevertheless, it is interesting to confront the novel with some of Levinas's insights. In his post-1980 writings, Levinas refers several times to Grossman. Most of these texts are interviews. Sometimes, it concerns a short allusion, but there is an important exception: the Talmudic reading *Beyond Memory* (Levinas 1994a). For a discussion of the relation between Grossman and Levinas, I refer to two important books by Michael Morgan, *Discovering Levinas* (2007) and *The Cambridge Introduction to Emmanuel Levinas* (2011).

I concentrate on three topics. Two of them are represented by protagonists in Grossman's novel: the holy fool Ikonnikov and the childless mother Sofya Osipovna. The third is a reflection on the difference between both authors.

The ambiguous relation between individual goodness and structural justice is, in a divergent way, present in the works of both authors. I will investigate how Levinas integrates and critiques the socio-political intuitions of Grossman: the refusal of collaboration; the critique of ideologies and totalitarianism; the necessary injustice of just institutions; the violence of great ideas; the small goodness without witnesses; the goodness as radix of social life. I illustrate this in quoting Grossman and in indicating how Levinas 'uses' or reinterprets the literary texts of Grossman in his philosophical reflections. The thesis is that Levinas not only reads Grossman as an illustration or confirmation of his ideas, but that he develops an intellectual gesture by which Grossman's intuitions are changed in their radicalness and thereby integrated into the already elaborated ethical thinking after 1980. For example, the small goodness – in Grosmann, a critique of ideology – is reinterpreted as a source and a correction of the necessary institutions.

At a more fundamental level, Grossman and Levinas speak of the mystery of the human soul. This topic allows for delving into the deeper philosophical foundations of both authors. I am convinced there exists an unconscious congeniality between them – fostered by their experiences of violence and of goodness. This congeniality existed before Levinas read Grossman, as becomes evident in comparing some of Grossmans main intuitions with a Talmudic reading.

But there is also an unbridgeable gap: the individual protest against the violence of society – in a world that is no place and in the era of the wolfhound – finds in Grossman its immanent sources in the indestructible power of human life; in Levinas, human life is opened by the alterity of certain old and sacred words.

1 Goodness and Justice

When Levinas refers to Grossman, it is almost always to the person of Ikonnikov, who is the incarnation of the small goodness. In chapter 67 of the novel's first part, we read a discussion, in the concentration camp, between some Mensheviks and the old Bolshevist Michael Mostovskoy. Mostovskoy is confronted with the thesis that "it's precisely Stalin's monstrous inhumanity that makes him Lenin's successor. As you love to repeat – Stalin is the Lenin of today" (LF, 285). The legitimacy of the violent terror as way of realization of the Marxist-Leninist ideal is at stake. During this ideological discussion Ikonnikov-Morzj comes to the fore, "a holy fool, that seeker after God" (LF, 304), a character type of which there are many in the work of Tolstoy. Ikonnikov's life represents the small goodness in a radical way. He gives Mostovskoy "some dirty sheets of paper covered in writing" (LF, 287) and asks him to read them. For the confrontation with Levinas, two intertwined topics are important: the radical refusal of the violence of the great ideologies and the plea for a humble goodness.

The Modest Refusal to Complicity

Ikonnikov expects his own death. He knows that the wells he was forced to dig are intended for gas chambers. By doing so, he is preparing the terror. He resolutely refuses to cooperate with this death machinery, although this refusal means his own death. In the subsequent encounter with the priest Gardi, reminiscent of and an inversion of the passage "The Grand Inquisitor" in Dostoevsky's *The Brothers Karamazov,* he goes in against the statement that everyone participates and that God will forgive.

> Ikonnikov reached up and grasped the bare foot of the priest sitting on the second tier of boards. "Que dois-je faire, mio padre? Nous travaillons dans una Vernichtungslager." Ikonnikov looked round at the three men with his coal-black eyes. "Tout le monde travaille là-bas. Et moi je travaille là-bas. Nous sommes des esclaves," he said slowly. "Dieu nous pardonnera." "C'est son métier," added Mostovskoy. "Mais ce n'est pas votre métier," said Gardi reproachfully.
>
> "Yes, that's what you said, Mikhail Sidorovich," said Ikonnikov, speaking so quickly he almost tripped up over his own words, "but I'm not asking for absolution. It's wrong to make out that only the people in power are guilty, that you yourself are only an innocent slave. I'm helping to build an extermination camp; I'm responsible before the people who are to be gassed. But I'm free. I can say 'No!' What power can stop me if I have the strength not to be afraid of extinction? I will say 'No!' Je dirai non, mio padre, je dirai non!"
>
> Gardi placed his hands on Ikonnikov's grey head. "Donnez-moi votre main," he said. "Now the shepherd's going to admonish the lost sheep for his pride," said Chernetsov. Mostovskoy nodded. But, rather than admonishing Ikonnikov, Gardi lifted his dirty hand to his lips and kissed it. (LF, 288–289)

Ikonnikov refuses his responsibility to slide under the guise of a deadly command structure and comes on for his own freedom. This freedom is the source of the small goodness. It becomes manifest in the protest against the inevitable injustice. A few chapters later, the bed of Ikonnikov, who turns out to have been executed, is empty: "The holy fool? The man you used to call the blancmange? He was executed. He refused to work on the construction of an extermination camp. Keyze was ordered to shoot him" (LF, 515).

The Violence of the Great Ideas

The famous text fragments on the dirty sheets of paper held by Ikonnikov-Morzj are the subject of a discussion between the Communist prisoner Mostovskoy and the SS officer in command, Liss. In a well-written way, Grossman confronts the small goodness with the two great totalitarian visions of "the good," namely, Communism and Nazism. Do not the fascist Empire and the Socialist state exhibit a deep similarity? And are not both parties convinced of their own idiosyncratic truth? Each one acts always from a particular vision of the great good. "Even Herod did not shed blood in the name of evil; he shed blood in the name of his particular good" (LF, 389). The jarring insight that the idea of the good "sinks into the mire of life" (LF, 390) shows Grossman's unbelief "in the sermons of religious teachers and prophets, in the teachings of sociologists and popular leaders, in the ethical systems of philosophers" (LF, 391).

The problem of the good that leads to totalitarianism can be interpreted starting from Hannah Arendt. Although Arendt analyzes Nazism and Stalinism in her magisterial work *The Origins of Totalitarianism* (1951), we will start with *The Human Condition* (1969). Arendt differentiates three important aspects of human existence, each of which are connected with the human condition. Man is a product of nature; he is situated in a spatio-temporal environment in which he can build a world; and he lives together with others. Active life is a threefold answer to this condition. By labor, man keeps the human metabolism alive; by work he produces culture; and by acting he realizes a political society.

Work has a specific structure. In ancient Athens the craftsman and the artist were respected as those who create sustainable and unique products. It is a form of technique in which one realizes a pre-existent idea in the materiality. To this end, one needs certain means and resources. The means are extrinsically effective for the purpose. It is said that the neo-Platonic Michelangelo understood art production in the same way. The artist sees the ideal, projects it in the marble, and then strips away the unnecessary pieces. The realization of an artifact has to do with the imitation of an idea. The artist is inspired by a *tupos*. The concrete object is an imitation of a pre-existing example, a model, an idea. One can call this an onto-typological structure: a certain ideal or *tupos* is pressed upon the concrete things.

Acting has a different structure. As an interaction between people, acting does not intend to reach an extrinsic goal. The goal of action falls together with itself. For the Greeks, political action is the main example. Politics happens between free citizens and exists in the discussion between various interests. In politics, one not only realizes goals with all possible means, but also, especially in a democracy, one tries to achieve, by conversation, the common good. As such, political action is the opposite of the onto-typology of the technician.

However, Plato saw politics as the realization of pre-existing ideas. According to him, the fundamental structure of the work fits in another field of action of man, namely, politics. It was Plato, in *The Republic*, who first explained politics as a form of *poièsis* (that is, an act like a craftsman). He binds politics to a pre-existing idea, a paradigm, whose imitation or *mimèsis* ensures development of the good republic. The philosophers are inevitably the best rulers, because they are best-suited to a true understanding of the idea. Plato opposes the democracy because it is subject to discussion, to the undecidable plurality of opinions and the *doxai*.

When the ideas of the philosophers in the line of Plato predetermine how politics should appear, a radical distortion of the politics arises. Politics becomes the technical realization of a particular ideal. This happened in Communist Russia, where the idea and the aim of a non-alienated society determined all means (Popper 2003). Grossman writes:

> I have seen the unshakeable strength of the idea of social good that was born in my own country. I saw this struggle during the period of general collectivization and again in 1937. I saw people being annihilated in the name of an idea of good as fine and humane as the ideal of Christianity. I saw whole villages dying of hunger; I saw peasant children dying in the snows of Siberia; I saw trains bound for Siberia with hundreds and thousands of men and women from Moscow, Leningrad and every city in Russia – men and women who had been declared enemies of a great and bright idea of social good. This idea was something fine and noble – yet it killed some without mercy, crippled the lives of others, and separated wives from husbands and children from fathers.
> (LF, 390–391)

When acting is understood theoretically, the paradoxical result is that the ideal becomes murderous. Film lovers can think of the impressive scene from *Doctor Zhivago* in which a thunderous train, decorated with red flags, steams straight to the target. The dominance of the alleged ideal destroys everything on the road.

The Small Goodness

Opposite the weft of evil that lets explode history from the inside and destroys the human mysteries, there is the hidden force of the small goodness. The small goodness is placed in front of both systems, represented in Liss and Mostovskoy. Grossman makes a clear distinction between the good (*dobro*) and the goodness (*dobrota*). He believes only in the goodness that is focused on concrete men. The small goodness is the treatment of the other, regardless of any system and concept of the good. It is most strongly expressed by Ikonnikov: the dingy leaves he gives to Mostovskoy, accursed by his own regime, forms a tract on the small goodness. Ikonnikov offers them as "an inheritance without testament." Opposite the destructive power of the historical ideologies, based on the ideal of the great good, Ikonnikov describes the small "goodness without witnesses":

> Yes, as well as this terrible Good with a capital "G," there is everyday human kindness. The kindness of an old woman carrying a piece of bread to a prisoner, the kindness of a soldier allowing a wounded enemy to drink from his water-flask, the kindness of youth towards age, the kindness of a peasant hiding an old Jew in his loft. The kindness of a prison guard who risks his own liberty to pass on letters written by a prisoner not to his ideological comrades, but to his wife and mother.
>
> The private kindness of one individual towards another; a petty, thoughtless kindness; an unwitnessed kindness. Something we could call senseless kindness. A kindness outside any system of social or religious good.
>
> But if we think about it, we realize that this private, senseless, incidental kindness is in fact eternal. It is extended to everything living, even to a mouse, even to a bent branch that a man straightens as he walks by.
>
> Even at the most terrible times, through all the mad acts carried out in the name of Universal Good and the glory of States, times when people were tossed about like branches in the wind, filling ditches and gullies like stones in an avalanche – even then this senseless, pathetic kindness remained scattered throughout life like atoms of radium. (LF, 391–392)

Levinas also stresses this goodness as opposed to the idea of the good:

> The good rises, merely by the fact itself that, in the encounter, the other counts above all else. The Relationship where the I encounters the You is the original place and circumstance of the ethical coming [avènement]. The ethical fact owes nothing to values; it is values that owe everything to the ethical fact. The concreteness of the Good is the worth [le valoir] of the other man. (Levinas 1998, 225)

Levinas's Reading of Grossman

The confrontation with Levinas can be elaborated on different levels. I will not discuss Levinas's interpretation of the relation between Nazism and Stalinism, although it is quite akin with Grossman. More relevant is Levinas's assessment of the small goodness and its relation to structural justice. It is clear that Grossman does not believe in any form of organized goodness. All institutions are based on sometimes good and brilliant ideas of justice, but in reality they are dehumanizing and monstrous. Levinas is impressed by the concept of the small goodness and he sees within it a challenge for his own thinking. Levinas, however, has a different view on structural justice.

In Levinas's view, man is an interiority who, in meeting the other, is called to an endless responsibility. Although the call for responsibility is radical, it is limited by the presence of the many others. The ethical responsibility is not only the exclusive encounter between two people. There is also the third, the quantitative other, he who is not present in my life-circle; yet he is also the qualitative other, who escapes from any possibility to call me to responsibility. The thirds are these people who are not involved in the I–Thou relation. They can be absent in time and space. It is the aspect of the illeity. Although the thirds are unable to call for responsibility, they are also an object of responsibility. This kind of responsibility is not immediate, but must be mediated by institutions.

Within ethical dynamics, the thirds have an important place, in that their presence introduces the social dimension into ethics. Seen from the intimate I–Thou relation, the thirds mean a disruption in the personal ethical commitment. But the thirds show that the ethical commitment towards the singular other bears in itself the possibility of injustice. When one responds to the call of the other and thus becomes the unique person taking up the responsibility for the unique other, one does injustice to the many others. This is the tragedy of the small goodness. The ethical choice for the unique other necessarily implicates exclusion of the third.

Therefore, the responsibility must be organized in a structural way (Burggraeve 2015). The social and political field of action is, in a certain sense, the result of the appearance of many thirds, which cry for some degree of equality. Levinas's social ethics displays, in outline, the following structure. Man is self-directed (*conatus essendi*) and in meeting the other he is called to an endless responsibility. This infinite responsibility, however, is restricted by the appearance of the thirds, who also have their own rights. A potential conflict between the rights of the second other and the third others leads to the institution of a more or less just system. In *The Other, Utopia and Justice*, a text that mentions Grossman, Levinas states:

> But the order of justice of individuals responsible for one another does not arise in order to restore that reciprocity between the I and its other; it arises from the fact of the third who, next to the one who is an other to me, is "another other" to me. The I, precisely as responsible for the other and the third, cannot remain indifferent to their interactions, and in the charity for the one cannot withdraw its love for the other. [. . .] Behind the unique singularities, one must perceive the individuals of a genus, one must compare them [. . .]. This is the hour of inevitable justice [. . .]. The hour of justice, of the comparison between incomparables [. . .]. (Levinas 2001f, 205–206)

Thus, Levinas integrates the economic and political system into his thinking. The incomparable uniqueness of the many thirds can be valuated only by organizing a system of equality. In this way, responsibility receives a social structure.

The presence of the many others asks to organize responsibility. The individual responsibility is turned into a social solidarity. The paradox and tragedy of the organized solidarity consists in the fact that everyone is considered as equal. Any system overlooks the concrete face of the other. The system that seeks to ensure justice for the many becomes dehumanizing. This is the critique of Grossman, who wrote that even Herod initially acted from the idea of the good. But Grossman stresses that the little act of goodness (*la petite bonté*) from one person to his neighbor is lost and deformed as soon as it seeks organization, universality, and systemization.

For Levinas, this is not a reason to condemn the system. The totalizing aspects are absorbed as much as possible by a secondary instance of goodness. Since any system overlooks the concrete face of the other, the system needs to be continually corrected. Levinas is well aware of the totalizing compulsion inherent in the system. Responsibility for others becomes concrete in a world of power, money, and corruption. Therefore, the system that is necessary to organize the goodness must be put under permanent critique. In doing so, it can be corrected. This correction can happen in the small goodness. It is the refuge of the good in being.

> This leads to a justice always to be perfected against its own harshness. Legislation always unfinished, always resumed, a legislation open to the better. It attests to an ethical excellence and its origin in goodness. (Levinas 2001, 206–207)

Grossman and Levinas offer similar descriptions of the ethical commitment. For Grossman the small goodness is a critique against the fate of totalitarian systems. For Levinas, this goodness is the radix of the legislation that in its necessary calculation always disrupts the goodness. Levinas interprets the small goodness to be a correction of the impersonality of a system that both tries to realize justice but also disregards the invisible tears of people who, despite all their efforts, fall outside of this whole.

2 The Small Goodness and the Mystery of the Soul

The first part of this discussion was thematic. After reading *Life and Fate*, Levinas was struck by the concept of the small goodness and understood it as a challenge for his own ethical thinking. For Grossman, freedom remains possible in an inhuman world of violence. This freedom realizes itself as small goodness. For Levinas, ethical responsibility is the refutation of war (Levinas 1969, 21). At first sight, one might think to oppose freedom in Grossman to responsibility in Levinas. Rather than explore this potential yet superfluous antithesis, I wish to look for an unconscious congeniality between the two authors, both of whom link the small goodness to the mystery of the soul.

In his description of the small goodness, Grossman labels it the immortal secret of human existence that manifests itself in the deepest darkness.

> The powerlessness of kindness, of senseless kindness, is the secret of its immortality. It can never be conquered. The more stupid, the more senseless, the more helpless it may seem, the vaster it is. Evil is impotent before it. The prophets, religious teachers, reformers, social and political leaders are impotent before it. This dumb, blind love is man's meaning. (LF, 394)

> But the more I saw of the darkness of Fascism, the more clearly I realized that human qualities persist even on the edge of the grave, even at the door of the gas chamber.
> (LF, 394)

Sofya Osipovna, a childless doctor, is on the threshold of the gas chamber, on the edge of the abyss. The goodness happens between people and is not chronicled in the annals of history. It originates in the secret of the soul and is located in the cryptic caving of "the anus mundi" (Kielar 2009):

> For a moment this sense of her past blotted out everything present, blotted out the abyss. It was the very strangest of feelings, something you could never share with any other person – not even your wife, your mother, your brother, your son, your friend or your father. It was the secret of your soul. However passionately it might long to, your soul could never betray this secret. You carry away this sense of your life without having ever shared it with anyone: the miracle of a particular individual whose conscious and unconscious contain everything good and bad, everything funny, sweet, shameful, pitiful, timid, tender, uncertain, that has happened from childhood to old age – fused into the mysterious sense of an individual life. (LF, 527)

Sofya Osipovna recognizes the eternal secret in another woman, Deborah:

> The machinist's wife was walking along beside her; in her arms the pathetic little baby, its head too large for its body, was looking around with a calm, thoughtful expression. It was this woman, Deborah, who one night in the goods-wagon had stolen a handful of sugar for her baby. The injured party had been too feeble to do anything, but old Lapidus had stood up for her [. . .]. No one had wanted to sit near him – he was always urinating on the floor. And now Deborah was walking along beside her, holding her baby in her arms. And the baby, who had cried day and night, was quite silent. The woman's sad dark eyes stopped one from noticing the hideousness of her dirty face and pale crumpled lips. "A Madonna!" thought Sofya Levinton. (LF, 528–529)

The topic of the secret of the soul expresses the common unconscious intuition that structures the economy of the texts of both authors. Levinas reflects on the mystery of the human soul in his Talmudic commentary *And God Created Woman* (Levinas 1990; Anckaert 2009). The Hebrew word *vayyitzer* (creates) contains an orthographic failure: the word is written with a double *yod*. Why? Levinas stumbles on this detail: it must have a meaning. His final proposal is that the double *yod* refers to a double face. This interpretation is taken not from Genesis, where it would mean the faces turned to each other and the erotic attraction of man and woman, but from Psalm 139:5, which explains the anomaly: "You hedge me before and behind; You lay Your hand upon me." Man has a double face. With one face, the back of the subject's head remains hidden as a shelter for dark thoughts. With two faces, everything is visible and there remain no mental reservations. God's gaze sees man in all directions, into life and death. There is no refuge or hidden place left. God's hand seizes and leads man everywhere. There is no escape to the left or to the right, up or down. From the contexts of the Psalm verse it seems to be impossible to escape from God or not to be present to his eye without sleep. This look, however, is no misfortune but rather an obsessive election. It is a complete visibility of man to the eye of the invisible. Later in the text this is called "the mystery of the human psyche" (Levinas 1990, 170). Man's secret is no hidden and impenetrable unconsciousness, but the complete visibility of the face to God's eye.

The (in)visibility can be understood according to two modalities (Derrida 1995). Something which is invisible can be made visible by a change of position or a revelation (e.g., the back of a cupboard or the contents of a box). The lifting of this invisibility by *Abschattungen* (Husserl) leads to the constitution of an ideal object. There is a further invisibility which cannot be lifted because the invisible is beyond visibility (e.g., a smell). In the Psalm text every darkness or secrecy becomes visible to God's eye and there is no escape left. There is a visibility of the first order. And yet this visibility is there only to the eye of the transcendence. To one's fellow man there is still invisibility. As with Gyges, the mystical relationship, where everything becomes visible, is invisible to the outside world. But the transparency to God's eye does not mean that man can see God. Although the subject is visible, God remains invisible.

The parabola of the double face has yet a deeper meaning. The infinity, which sees through the finite, refers to the neighbor whose face calls for a new responsibility. Under God's eye without sleep one is the bearer of another subject. The mysterious being seen by God is a responsibility for the other. The gift of the Torah consists in an ethical commitment. When the skin completely turns into a face, the being experiences a shelling. This synonym for decomposition refers to a hidden inner core which is exposed. The naked existence to God's eye – by which the whole skin becomes visible and there can be no secrecy left – is the place where responsibility for the neighbor is registered. The double face means the impossibility of pretending that one does not see the other's need.

This mystery is a responsibility. The infinity refers to the other whose face calls for a responsibility. Under God's eye, one is the bearer of another subject. Being born by infinity means the task to bear the other. The woman bears the child:

> Sofya Levinton felt the boy's body subside in her hands. Once again she had fallen behind him. In mine-shafts where the air becomes poisoned, it is always the little creatures, the birds and mice, that die first. This boy, with his slight, bird-like body, had left before her. "I've become a mother," she thought. That was her last thought. (LF, 538)

3 Goodness without Hope or Hope without Promise

In the previous section, I alluded to a possible congeniality between Grossman and Levinas. There is an underground source of their thoughts: their mutual understanding of the mystery of the human soul. This mystery is the confrontation with the suffering and death of the other as source of the goodness without witnesses. But the difference is great: atheism and despair versus religion and hope. This becomes clear in Grossman's interpretation of the Madonna and Levinas's interpretation of the *rahamim*.

In 1955 Grossman wrote the splendid short text *The Sistine Madonna* (Grossman 2010). The painting in question, by Rafael, had been stolen by the Red Army from the Dresden Art Gallery and removed to Moscow. Before its return to Dresden, the painting was exhibited in May 1955 at the Pushkin Museum. Grossman was struck by the immortality of the painting: "I realized that I had, until this moment, been careless in my use of this awesome word 'immortality'" (Grossman 2010, 181). The secret of the painting is that the body and the face of the young woman show her soul: "Everyone who looks at her can see her humanity. She is the image of the maternal soul" (Grossman 2010, 183). The Madonna is completely human, without any divine participation (Garrard 2012, 328). The child also has his own lucidity. The spectator can perceive the child's fate through his sad and serious expression, directed simultaneously ahead and within himself. Mother and child feel their own Golgotha; they can be seen in the hell of Treblinka:

> This was how mothers and children looked, this was how they were in their souls when they saw, against the dark green of the pine trees, the white walls of the Treblinka gas chambers. (Grossman 2010, 187)

> How many times had I stared through darkness at the people getting out of the freight wagons, but their faces had never been clear to me. Sometimes their faces had seemed distorted by extreme horror, and everything had dissolved in a terrible scream. Sometimes despair and exhaustion, physical and spiritual, had obscured their faces with a look of blank, sullen indifference. Sometimes the carefree smile of insanity had veiled their faces as they left the transport and walked towards the gas chambers. And now at last I had seen these faces truly and clearly. Rafael had painted them four centuries earlier. This is how someone goes to meet their fate.
> (Grossman 2010, 187–188)

> It was she, treading lightly on her little bare feet, who had walked over the swaying earth of Treblinka. (Grosmann 2010, 187)

> The power of life, the power of what is human in man, is very great, and even the mightiest and most perfect violence cannot enslave this power; it can only kill it.
> (Grossman 2010, 191)

Grossman reads the soul of the mother in a completely atheistic way. He interprets human life and freedom as the only seat of humanity. Only this humanity has eternal value and can resist inhumanity. The text concludes:

> Seeing the Sistine Madonna go on her way, we preserve our faith that life and freedom are one, that there is nothing higher than what is human in man. This will live forever and triumph. (Grossman 2010, 192)

Whereas Grossman believes in a goodness without hope, Levinas is driven by a hope without promise. Here we discover the decisive difference between the two authors: in Levinas's intuition that the secret of humanity is born by the alterity of transcendence. In Grossman, man dwells in a desperate world wherein he can keep his humanity by realizing small goodness. But the mother Osipova bears a death child. There is no hope for the future.

Levinas integrates his great reference to Grossman in the context of the Shoah. In his Talmudic reading *Beyond memory* he states "that war of Gog and Magog may have already begun in this century of *Shoah*" (Levinas 1994a, 88). Levinas explicitly links the small goodness with two Hebrew words. The first word of difference is the *ahavat Israel* (the love for Israel), the hope escaping from the abyss of despair (Levinas 1994a, 89). The *ahavat* Israel "may be the original tenderness for the other, the compassion and mercy" (Levinas 1994a, 89). This *ahavat* is contributed to Abraham, the father of many nations (Anckaert 2008). It is a promise without hope: "What a paradox Holy History is – in which the announcements to Abraham implies the certainty of the cruelty of the Pharaohs" (Levinas 1994a, 88).

The second word of difference is the *rahamim*, translated here as mercy. In its Hebrew form it is used in *The Bible and the Greeks*, another text in which Levinas refers to Grossman. It is "the goodness of one person toward another, the little kindness I have called mercy, the *rahamim* of the Bible" (Levinas 1994b, 135). It is "an invincible goodness" that "bears witness, in the mode of being our Europe, to a new awareness of a strange (or very old) mode of spirituality or a piety without promises, which would not render human responsibility – always my responsibility – a senseless notion. A spirituality whose future is unknown" (Levinas 1994b, 135). *Rahamim* is the mercy of a human being who bears another human being, like a woman bearing a living child in her womb (*Rehem*, in Hebrew). It is the utmost passivity that precedes goodness. This passivity is the hope without promises that prevents human responsibility from being a senseless notion. The goodness is the sign of a still unknown God. The unknown God is not Heidegger's (Heidegger 2000), but He is the God of a very old text – the Torah, which is older than the world. Humanity is made possible by a word that is created before the creation of the world.

4 Conclusion

The small goodness is the crux in comparing Levinas and Grossman. This tender form of humanity has a different place in the topicality of the two authors' respective socio-political texts. On a deeper level, one can discover an unconscious congeniality. The small goodness is the revelation of the mystery of the human soul. This soul is the feminine secret of Sofya Osipovna and of the created man. The ultimate difference that constitutes Levinas and Grossman's mutual congeniality is the unknown God of the sacred text. Levinas's thinking starts from the verses; the pages of Grossman contain none (Levinas 1994b, 135).

> Are these truths present in a forgotten corner of some letters or syllables from Scripture, waiting to become God's word in the Jewish and the non-Jewish suffering of the twentieth century, in a time without promises and with a God who doesn't offer a shelter?

Bibliography

Texts of Levinas Referring to Grossman

Levinas, Emmanuel. "Paix et proximité." *Les cahiers de la nuit surveillée* 3. Lagrasse: Verdier, 1984. 339–346.
Levinas, Emmanuel. "Entretien (propos receuillis par L. Adert et J.-C. Aeschlimann)." *Répôndre d'autrui*. Ed. J.-C. Aeschlimann. Boudry-Neuschâtel: La Baconnière, 1989. 9–16.
Levinas, Emmanuel. *De l'oblitération. Entretien avec Françoise Armengaud à propos de l'oeuvre de Sosno*. Paris: La Différence, 1990.
Levinas, Emmanuel. "Beyond Memory." *In the Time of the Nations*. Trans. M. B. Smith. London: The Athlone Press, 1994a. 76–91.
Levinas, Emmanuel. "The Bible and the Greeks." *In the Name of the Nations*. Trans. M. B. Smith. London: The Athlone Press, 1994b. 133–135.
Levinas, Emmanuel. *God, Death, and Time*. Trans. B. Bergo. Stanford: Stanford University Press, (2000).
Levinas, Emmanuel. "Interview with François Poirié." *Is it Righteous to Be?: Interviews with Emmanuel Levinas*. Ed. J. Robbins. Stanford: Stanford University Press, 2001a. 23–83.
Levinas, Emmanuel. "Interview with Myriam Anissimov." *Is it Righteous to Be?: Interviews with Emmanuel Levinas*. Ed. J. Robbins. Stanford: Stanford University Press, 2001b. 84–92.
Levinas, Emmanuel. "The Vocation of the Other." *Is it Righteous to Be?: Interviews with Emmanuel Levinas*. Ed. J. Robbins. Stanford: Stanford University Press, 2001c. 105–113.
Levinas, Emmanuel. "Being-Toward-Death and 'Thou Shalt Not Kill.'" *Is it Righteous to Be?: Interviews with Emmanuel Levinas*. Ed. J. Robbins. Stanford: Stanford University Press, 2001d. 130–139.
Levinas, Emmanuel. "In the Name of the Other." *Is it Righteous to Be?: Interviews with Emmanuel Levinas*. Ed. J. Robbins. Stanford: Stanford University Press, 2001e. 188–199.
Levinas, Emmanuel. "The Other, Utopia and Justice." *Is it Righteous to Be?: Interviews with Emmanuel Levinas*. Ed. J. Robbins. Stanford: Stanford University Press, 2001f. 200–210.
Levinas, Emmanuel. "The Proximity of the Other." *Is it Righteous to Be?: Interviews with Emmanuel Levinas*. Ed. J. Robbins. Stanford: Stanford University Press, 2001g. 211–218.

Other texts

Anckaert, Luc. "The Secret of Abraham and its Repetition. A Narrative Reflection on the Relation between Faith and Ethics." *Responsibility, God and Society. Theological Ethics in Dialogue. Festschrift Roger Burggraeve*. Eds. J. De Tavernier, J. Selling, J. Verstraeten, and P. Schotsmans. Leuven: Peeters, 2008. 25–48.
Anckaert, Luc. "L'être entre les lettres. Creation and Passivity in 'And God Created Woman.'" *Radical Passivity: Rethinking Ethical Agency in Levinas*. Ed. B. Hofmeyr. Dordrecht: Springer Academic Publishers, 2009. 143–154.
Anckaert, Luc. "The Thunderbolt of Evil and Goodness without Witnesses: In Conversation with Vasili Grossman, *Life and Fate*." *Religija ir Kultura* 18–19 (2016): 22–37.
Arendt, Hannah. *The Human Condition*. Chicago: University of Chicago Press, 1969.

Arendt, Hannah. *The Origins of Totalitarianism*. San Diego: Harcourt, 1994.
Burggraeve, Roger. "Ethics as Crisis: Levinas' Contribution to a Humane Society." *Emmanuel Levinas: A Radical Thinker in the Time of Crisis*. Ed. R. Serpytyte. Vilnius: Vilnius University Press – Vilniaus Universiteto Leydikla, 2015. 9–26.
Derrida, Jacques. *The Gift of Death*. Trans. D. Wills. Chicago: The University of Chicago Press, 1995.
Emerson, Caryl. "War and Peace. Life and Fate." *Common Knowledge* 18.2 (2012): 348–354.
Garrard, John, and Carol Garrard. *The Life and Fate of Vasily Grossman*. South Yorkshire: Pen & Sword, 2012.
Grossman, Vasily. *Life and Fate*. Trans. Robert Chandler. London: Vintage Books, 2006. (LF)
Grossman, Vasily. "The Sistine Madonna." *The Road: Short Fiction and Articles*. Trans. Robert Chandler and Elizabeth Chandler with Olga Mukovnikova. London: MacLehose Press, 2010. 181–192.
Heidegger, Martin. "Spiegel-Gespräch mit Martin Heidegger [23. September 1966]." *Gesamtausgabe*, Band 16: *Reden und andere Zeugnisse eines Lebensweg*. Frankfurt am Main: Vittorio Klostermann, 2000. 652–683.
Kielar, Wieslaw. *Anus Mundi. Fünf Jahre Auschwitz*. Trans. Wera Kapkajew. Frankfurt am Main: Fischer, 2009.
Levinas, Emmanuel. *Totality and Infinity. An Essay on Exteriority*. Trans. Alphonso Lingis. The Hague: Martinus Nijhoff, 1969.
Levinas, Emmanuel. *De Dieu qui vient à l'idée*. Paris: Vrin, 1998.
Levinas, Emmanuel. "And God Created Woman." *Nine Talmudic Readings*. Trans. Annette Aronowicz. Bloomington: Indiana University Press, 1990. 161–177.
Morgan, Michael L. *Discovering Levinas*. Cambridge: Cambridge University Press, 2007.
Morgan, Michael L. *The Cambridge Introduction to Emmanuel Levinas*. Cambridge: Cambridge University Press, 2011.
Popper, Karl. *The Open Society and Its Enemies*. London: Routledge, 2003.

Tammy Amiel Houser
Reading Fiction with Levinas: Ian McEwan's novel *Atonement*

What does it mean to read fiction through the lens of Levinas's ethics? How does literary criticism benefit from Levinas's philosophy? In this article I explore the relevance of Levinas's thought to contemporary ethical criticism as exemplified by a reading of Ian McEwan's novel *Atonement* (2001). Ethical criticism is not a new field of inquiry. Rather, "for roughly 2500 years, ethical references constituted the starting point (and often the ending point) for most literary commentary" (Marshall 2010, 273). However, with the rise of literary theory during the twentieth century, traditional forms of ethical criticism were challenged and repudiated.[1] Since the late 1980s, a general turn to philosophical ideas in literary studies has led to the reemergence of ethical criticism, a shift in which Levinas's ideas have played a major role. Levinas's notions of subjectivity, otherness, responsibility, and signification have deeply affected the discourse of literary criticism and inspired critical reexamination of the ethical possibilities of literary texts.

On one hand, Levinas's thought constitutes a departure from the ethics of empathetic reading which was central to nineteenth-century traditions of ethical criticism,[2] and was later advanced by the neo-humanist strand in literary studies.[3] According to this tradition, empathetic reading is an aesthetic experience with ethical affect: by entering into the feelings and thoughts of various characters, the readers open their eyes to new perspectives and expand their understanding of both other people and themselves.[4] By contrast, for Levinas, rather than being ethically significant, empathetic imagination presents the common tyranny of the "same": it involves a presumptive knowledge of the other, based on a denial of his/her special uniqueness that enables comprehension and identification.[5]

---

1 See Gregory Marshall (2010, 273–277); Dorothy Hale (2007, 187–188);
2 On Victorian ethical criticism see Rohan Maitzen (2005, 151–185) and Rae Greiner (2012).
3 For more on this approach see Martha Nussbaum (2001, 59–77). See also Namwali Serpell (2014, 293–302).
4 See, for example, Gregory Currie (1995, 257), Noël Carroll (2002, 3–26), and Mary-Catherine Harrison (2008). See also the collection edited by Meghan Marie Hammond and Sue J. Kim, *Rethinking Empathy through Literature* (2014).
5 For a critical view of empathy in Levinas's thought, see Tammy Amiel Houser and Adia Mendelson-Maoz (2014, 199–218).

∂ Open Access. © 2021 Tammy Amiel Houser, published by De Gruyter. This work is licensed under the Creative Commons Attribution 4.0 International License.
https://doi.org/10.1515/9783110668926-016

On the other hand, Levinas does not see the other as the marginalized construction of a dominant system, caught up within an oppressive order from which it should be liberated. As Shameem Black notes, this view of otherness underlies critical theories in literary studies that focus on "hegemonic domination and representational violence" (Black 2010, 3). What Levinas's thought offers to these approaches is an acknowledgment of alterity that is not dependent or reduced to the dynamics of logo-centrism, phallocentrism, or Western imperialism: "the other absolutely other" (Levinas 2002 [1969], 41). In Levinas's philosophy *Autrui* "does not negate the same" and does not function as a constituent of self-consciousness (Levinas 2002 [1969], 203). Rather, human otherness signifies a special uniqueness that disturbs "the being at home with oneself," while demanding answerability and producing responsibility for the other (Levinas 2002 [1969], 39). Thus, instead of focusing on the submission and exploitation of the other and on relations of oppression, Levinas calls attention to "the access to the alterity of the Other" and the unconditional responsibility this access to the other creates (Levinas 2002 [1969], 121).

This approach to alterity and responsibility has inspired intriguing investigations in the literary field, for it raises important questions: can literature enable an encounter with the singularity of the other? In what ways and forms? Or, as Jill Robbins formulates it in her illuminating book on Levinas and literature: "Does the work of art give access to the ethical, as Levinas understands it?" (Robbins 1999, 75). Notably, although Robbins makes it clear that Levinas's response should be understood as "a resounding *no*" (Robbins 1999, 75; italics in original) since literary representation cannot deal with the non-representational essence of alterity, she and other literary scholars believe that it deserves further scrutiny.[6] Indeed, this investigation has become the major concern of poststructuralist ethical criticism, as scholars try to overcome the limits that Levinas placed on the relations between literature and ethics, without abandoning his view of the ethical.

It is worth noting that in his treatment of language, Levinas himself suggested that literature could be further explored as giving access to the ethical. Derrida's early deconstructive reading of *Totality and Infinity* drew attention to the relationships between language and ethics in Levinas's thought and opened the door for literary scholars to engage in the debate. In his essay "Violence

---

[6] Robert Eaglestone began to explore this question in his *Ethical Criticism* (1997), which was published before Robbins's book. For later studies see the collection *In Proximity: Emmanuel Levinas and the Eighteenth Century*, edited by Melvyn New with Robert Bernasconi and Richard A. Cohen (2001), and *Levinas and Nineteenth-Century Literature: Ethics and Otherness from Romanticism to Realism*, edited by Donald R. Wehrs and David P. Haney (2009).

and Metaphysics," Derrida appraises Levinas's important challenge to Western metaphysics, claiming that *Totality and Infinity* aims at acknowledging the "unthinkable truth" of the face-to-face relation, "the truth to which the traditional logos is forever inhospitable" (Derrida 1978, 90). However, Derrida concurrently criticizes Levinas's style of writing: by its ontological terminology and linguistic tendency to clearly represent the unthinkable ethical relation, it joins the metaphysical violence that it opposes. Levinas's later *Otherwise than Being or beyond Essence* is often understood as an implied response to Derrida's analysis of the relations between language and the violence of ontological thought.[7] In this book, Levinas attempts to escape the phenomenal terminology of his early writings by translating the face-to-face relation into linguistic terms that are actually performed in the text. He insists that the ethical command be enacted in discourse, in the linguistic relation between the self and the other.

This understanding of the ethical is based on Levinas's distinction between the content of speech, meanings and themes, what Levinas terms the Said ["*dit*"], and the performative dimension of the linguistic address to another, termed the Saying ["*dire*"]. The *Saying*, which is interwoven with the *Said*, amounts to a special register of language; it is a modality of responsiveness and contact created through speech without any conscious intention on the part of the speaking subject (see Levinas 1991a [1974], 48–49). Hence, a discursive event brings the face-to-face relation into being, creating "the contact of saying" with the other (Levinas 1991a [1974], 85), to whom the speaking subject answers with the ethical declaration "here I am." According to Levinas, this biblical declaration expressed by Abraham to acknowledge his total obedience to God's command,[8] is embodied in the linguistic relation that admits the infinite obligation of the speaking subject to her addressee.[9]

This Levinasian conception of language is crucial for literary criticism, which deals with linguistic constructions. If the Said and the Saying are interwoven in discourse, then literary works cannot be seen as devoid of the ethical, as Levinas often suggests (Robbins 1999, 77–78). Rather, as Robert Eaglestone claims, "the Saying can be understood as occurring in literary discourse as

---

[7] This interpretation of *Otherwise than Being* was suggested by Robert Bernasconi and Simon Critchley in their collection *Re-reading Levinas* (1991, xiii). See also Critchley (1999, 12). See also Eaglestone's discussion of the literary style of *Otherwise than Being* (Eaglestone 1997, 136–146). Levinas's explicit response to Derrida is presented in his essay "Wholly Otherwise" (1991b [1973], 3–8).
[8] See for example Genesis 22:1–14.
[9] On the biblical l expression "me voici" (Here I am) and its ethical importance see Levinas (1991a [1974], 64–67, 142, 228–232).

much as in philosophical discourse" (Eaglestone 1997, 163). Literature, therefore, can be explored as a linguistic construction that extends beyond the totalizing structures of representation and is able to signify the ethical obligation to the other. For Joseph G. Kronick this remains the main challenge for literary ethics: "Can literature perform the equivalent of extracting the *otherwise than being* from the Said in which it comes to light? Can it undo the thematization in which what cannot be thematized is represented?" (Kronick 2016, 266). Kronick argues that "for literary criticism, this means that any reading that remains thematic operates on the level of the Said and cannot account for the original relationship to the Other or the ethical" (Kronick 2016, 270). However, it should be recalled that the Saying always operates through the Said and is intermingled with the thematic level of discourse. Therefore, accounting for "the original relationship to the Other" requires working through the thematic level of the literary work, exploring the disruption of the Said, or as Simon Critchley writes, "the ways in which the Said can be unsaid" (Critchley 1999, 8).

In the last few decades, Levinas's conception of the ethical relation as embodied in the linguistic Saying has led to a resurgence of poststructuralist ethical criticism. Drawing on Levinas, literary scholars have explored the ways in which "the face accomplishes its breakthrough or divestiture of form" in various literary contexts (Robbins 1999, 24–25). Derek Attridge, for example, looks into "how otherness is engaged, staged, distanced, embraced, how it is manifested in the rupturing of narrative discourse" in J. M. Coetzee's fiction (Attridge 2004, 670); and Rachel Hollander analyzes "the profound ambivalence about the ability of the realist form to do full justice to an ethics of otherness" as developed in George Eliot's *Daniel Deronda* (Hollander 2009, 284). Even critics who are not committed to Levinas's thought are often deeply affected by "the Levinasian tradition of conceptualizing ethical obligation" (Black 2010, 44). Black in particular draws on Levinas in her search for a literary "breakthrough that allows for the encounter with significant otherness once considered impossible" (Black 2010, 44).

Reading fiction through Levinas thus requires a willingness to undergo the disturbing experience of being in touch with the impossible and the incomprehensible. It is difficult because, as David Palambu-Liu writes, "storytelling attempts to 'bridge' the distance between self and other" (Palambu-Liu 2012, 29). Reading a story is indeed a process of bridging: an attempt at decoding and connecting, understanding, and circumscribing different signs into coherent structures of meaning. It is also a process of relating with unknown characters and narrators in ways that make the stranger become familiar and comprehensible. Radical otherness, however, thwarts this process of bridging and understanding, by affecting what Palambu–Liu describes as "the crisis of representation" (Palambu Liu 2012, 30) and what Judith Butler characterizes as "that very disjunction that makes representation impossible" (Butler 2004, 144). Thus, the encounter with the singularity of the other rests on an ongoing negotiation in the reading process between sameness and difference, between the desire to comprehend and the willingness to endorse the incomprehensible. It demands an awareness of the reader's desire for empathetic identification – that connection which rests on similarity – and a contrary willingness to face what "destroys and overflows" such a connection (Levinas 2002 [1969], 51). In what follows, I examine this approach through a Levinasian reading of Ian McEwan's *Atonement*, a novel that puts forward a metafictional reflection on the relations between literature and the ethical.

1 Giving Access to the Ethical: Ian McEwan's *Atonement*

Written at the beginning of the new millennium, and looking back at the history of Europe in the twentieth century, *Atonement* is a good test for ethical criticism because it engages with questions of responsibility and ethical repair. Is there a way to atone for crimes against a fellow creature? Is it possible to restore justice after it has been violated? And can fiction contribute to these attempts at ethical rehabilitation? The protagonist of the novel, Briony Tallis, is guilty of giving false testimony that sends her elder sister's boyfriend, Robbie Turner, to prison for molesting her cousin Lola. Although the novel centers on a personal relationship, its scope is more than a private affair, since it links the local story to a larger social and cultural context and to the pervasive sense of anxiety around World War II. I argue that beyond the thematic preoccupation with ethical questions, in its structure and narration the novel also explores the possibility of giving access to the "pre-original saying" of the human condition (Levinas 1991 [1974], 6).

The thematic center of the novel is a transgression. It unfolds in the first section of the novel, told by an omniscient third-person narrator who looks closely at the main characters – Briony, her sister Cecilia, and Robbie – while shifting between their separate perspectives. The transgression occurs on a hot summer day in 1935 when a family gathering at the Tallises' aristocratic estate turns into a nightmare. The elitist serenity with its "impression of timeless, unchanging calm" (McEwan 2002, 19) – based on the Tallises' disregard for both personal and social tensions and injustices[10] – collapses abruptly when the

---

10 On class experience in *Atonement* see Ian Fraser (2013).

twin cousins disappear, Lola is attacked, and thirteen-year-old Briony accuses Robbie – the son of the cleaning woman, and Cecilia's new lover – of committing the sexual attack.

The second section of the novel takes Robbie's perspective and tells of his experience as a soldier in the awful retreat to Dunkirk in 1940. Robbie's story reveals how his life has been ruined by Briony's accusation, which led to his incarceration. He sees the war as just another facet of his own decline: "A dead civilization. First his own life ruined, then everybody else's" (McEwan 2002, 217). Tyrannical forces of destruction seem to win the day in both the private sphere and the public life of Western civilization.

In the third section as well, personal events are closely connected to the larger social and cultural context of conflict and anxiety. The focalizer is Briony, who works as a nurse during the war, tending to wounded soldiers in an effort to make amends for her own crime. Briony dreams of meeting Robbie and caring for him: "she would dress his wounds" and thus hopefully be forgiven (McEwan 2002, 98). Implicitly, the cruelty of Briony's crime is connected to the cruelty of war, and Briony's early misjudgment seems to form part of the general bleak picture of twentieth-century European history, in which initially poor judgments of Fascism and Nazism had horrible effects.[11] Some of these effects are seen in the hospital in bodily images of a terrible pain. However, when Briony dares to contact her sister, she learns that the effects of her own crime have been somehow mitigated: Robbie and Cecilia have recovered and are reunited, and they will live together happily ever after (McEwan 2002, 338).

Yet, at the end of the novel the readers learn that Briony, now seventy-seven years old and a successful novelist, is the fictional implied author of the whole novel, and that "it is only in this last version that my lovers end well" (McEwan 2002, 370). The readers have been deceived. The promised ending of "happily ever after" is a fictional lie. Briony outlines another version of the story, one in which Robbie dies at Dunkirk and Cecilia is killed by a bomb in London three months later (McEwan 2002, 370). Martin Jacobi refuses to accept this elimination of the happy ending as the definitive interpretation of the novel and claims that the narrative leaves open the possibility that Robbie and Cecilia "did survive and flourish" (Jacobi 2011, 68). Yet, the crucial revelation of Briony's fictional authorship and the "convenient distortion[s]" she admits to having included in her narrative (McEwan 2002, 356)

---

[11] See Brian Finney, who notes "a connection between the microcosm of the lives that Briony has disrupted and the macrocosm of a world at war" (Finney 2004, 73). See also Dominic Head (2007, 171).

make the readers suspicious of such a happy ending. As Jonathan Kertzer writes, poetic justice rests on "a willing suspension of disbelief," in that the readers accept the supposition of a justice "unavailable in ordinary life" (Kertzer 2010, 11). *Atonement* destroys this suspension of disbelief and makes the just outcome – Robbie and Cecilia's reunion – part of Briony's immoral deceitful storytelling: she seems to force poetic justice so as to create hope and satisfaction in a cruel and hopeless world.

The unexpected twist at the end of the third section pulls the rug from under the realistic reading of the novel and destabilizes the coherent picture constructed by the readers. It is true that metafictional elements permeate the novel as of its first pages (Finney, 2004). Nonetheless, the concluding section turns the novel into "a self-conscious, self-reflexive novel employing a character narrator who is herself a novelist" (Phelan 2007, 109), which produces an unsettling shock for most readers. I believe that this shock plays an important role in the novel's engagement with the ethical, as it upends the knowing ego of the readers, dismantles the narrative construction, and calls attention to essential dimensions of humanity that exceed representation and narration while still demanding responsibility and responsiveness.

The questioning of the knowing ego develops early in the novel, in the complicity that McEwan creates between closed and totalizing structures of representation – such as those that the young Briony adheres to – and egoistic, imperialistic subjectivity that is blind to the suffering of others. As the first section reveals, Briony's false accusation against Robbie is driven by her passion for such closed narratives with their aesthetic, neat form that provides clear meaning and coherence to the world. An emerging author, the young Briony writes romantic short stories and dramas that reveal "her wish for a harmonious, organized world" (McEwan 2002, 5). As the narrator explains, her desire is "to have the world just so" (McEwan 2002, 4), and therefore she invents schematic and hermetically sealed stories that satisfy "her controlling demon" (McEwan 2002, 5). Thus, when Briony bumps into Lola on that dark night and sees "a figure [. . .] backing away from her [Lola] and beginning to fade into the darker background of the trees" (McEwan 2002, 164), she immediately creates a sealed story, in which Robbie, whom she has already crowned as an "incarnation of evil" (McEwan 2002, 115), is the perpetrator: "Everything connected. It was her own discovery. It was her story, the one that was writing itself around her. 'It was Robbie, wasn't it?'" (McEwan 2002, 166) In Briony's well-connected story, Robbie, the son of the Tallises' servant, who earlier that day had sent Cecilia an obscene love letter that Briony interprets as "brutal" (McEwan 2002, 113), becomes Lola's rapist. Stripped of his unique individuality, Robbie turns into the missing link in Briony's imaginative chain: he is the obvious villain.

Briony has no doubt, because "the affair was too consistent, too symmetrical to be anything other than what she said it was" (McEwan 2002, 168). Briony's story also overlooks Lola's perspective, since Briony "cut[s] her [Lola] off" (McEwan 2002, 166), filling in the gaps before Lola dares to speak and explain what actually happened. Although she was only a witness, and a partial witness, Briony turns herself into a reporter who gives a full account of the event. Earlier we are told that in Briony's childish stories "[a] love of order [. . .] shaped the principles of justice" (McEwan 2002, 7). Yet, when Briony authors reality according to these principles, her well-organized and connected story leads to a terrible miscarriage of justice. As Brian Finney writes, "forcing life to conform to the aesthetic orderliness of art can have actual tragic consequences" (Finney 2004, 80).

When analyzed through the prism of Levinas's philosophy, these tragic consequences seem to point to crucial connections between some uses (or abuses) of language – as in the case of Briony's reasonably structured and closed narratives – and the relation to the other person as a mere other-than-self. McEwan highlights these connections early in the novel, when the young Briony reflects on the mysterious existence of other minds: "was everyone else really as alive as she was? For example, did her sister really matter to herself, was she as valuable to herself as Briony was?" (McEwan 2002, 36). Critics of the novel often argue that Briony's tragic construction of the story of Lola's rape derives from her childish inability to imagine just that: the fact that other people are "as alive as she was." As Finney writes, her problem is "a failure of imaginative projection (into the other)" (Finney 2004, 80). David K. O'Hara also interprets Briony's fault in terms of her inability to step into the shoes of the other, reading it in light of McEwan's own declaration that "imagining what it is like to be someone other than yourself is at the core of our humanity" (O'Hara 2011, 84).

In this view, the ethical vision of the novel is found exactly here – in Briony's gradual process of learning to imagine the inner perspective of others, which she eventually succeeds in completing: "the novel that we read and that took her [Briony's] adult lifetime to write is her attempt to project herself into the feelings of the two characters whose lives her failure of imagination destroyed" (Finney 2004, 80). O'Hara develops this idea by reading *Atonement* through the writings of Levinas, Merleau-Ponty, and Zigmunt Bauman. As he writes: "it is Briony's actual *writing* of the novel that may be her vital act of atonement," since by her fictional writing, the mature Briony is able to convey "what it is like to be other than yourself" (O'Hara 2011, 84; italics in original). Thus, O'Hara suggests seeing Briony as a culmination of Levinas's "being-for," in her "[attempt] to imagine the reality of an Other's experience" (O'Hara 2011, 93).

Unlike these interpretations of *Atonement*'s ethical stance, my contention is that the novel actually rejects both the ethics of empathy and the idea that Briony's fault lies in her inability to project herself into the feelings of others and simulate their inner perspective. I also reject the argument that Briony's later ability to do so constitutes her moral growth. On the contrary, McEwan turns the readers' attention to the ethical problematics of such an imaginative projection: the elderly Briony sees her novelistic self as having an "absolute power" (McEwan 2002, 371) in a way that corresponds to Levinas's description of "imperialist subjectivity" (Levinas 1991 [1974], 146) rather than his ethical "being-for." The above interpretations assume that imaginative projection into others not only facilitates an understanding of other minds but also promotes ethical relationships and behavior.[12] However, McEwan questions this idea when he endows Briony with the ability to imagine the independent existence of others before she commits her terrible crime against Robbie and Cecilia, and not after it. This is a crucial point: imaginative projection is an aesthetic development in Briony's initiation story, but it should not be confused with an ethical relation to the other.

Briony's aesthetic change occurs when she witnesses the scene by the fountain and considers how she might turn it into a story. At first she is startled: Cecilia and Robbie meet near the fountain, quarrel over a vase (which then shatters), after which Cecilia removes her clothes and jumps into the water (McEwan 2002, 38–39). This unexpected and incomprehensible unfolding seems "illogical" to Briony, but she then has a sudden realization that helps her gain control over the surprising episode: she can describe it in a narrative by "[entering] these different minds" and representing the scene "from three points of view" (McEwan 2002, 40). McEwan is careful to describe Briony's change in aesthetic terms, leaving the readers to reflect upon the ethical implications: "[she] had written her way through a whole history of literature, beginning with stories derived from the European tradition of folk tales, through drama with simple moral intent, to arrive at an impartial psychological realism which she had discovered for herself, one special morning during a heat wave in 1935" (McEwan 2002, 41).

Briony's understanding of the aesthetic value of "[entering] these different minds" (McEwan 2002, 40) is an important phase in her development as a writer. It is also a process that corresponds to the aesthetic development of Western literature and the emergence of ethical realism:[13] a tradition that offers

---

12 On this twofold dimension of empathy see Amy Coplan and Peter Goldie (2011, ix–xvii).
13 On the literary teleology here, see Serpell (2014, 96).

readers a sense of ethical elevation by letting them share the inner perspective of different human beings. However, McEwan implicitly questions the ethical connotations of empathetic realism. Does Briony's new aesthetics make her a better person? Does it make her recognize her own limits regarding other human beings? The unfolding of the plot points to a negative answer. A moment later Briony betrays Robbie, reading his love letter to Cecilia and turning him into "a maniac," despite having known him all her life as a good, kind person. Later that day she will reduce Robbie to a violent criminal in her story of rape, thereby ruining both his and Cecilia's lives. Aesthetic development, McEwan seems to argue, should not be equated with ethical growth.

Instead of viewing the ethical core of the novel as an affirmation of empathetic imagination, I suggest reading it in terms of Levinas's notion of "bearing witness" to the enigma of the other that "strips the ego of its pride and the dominating imperialism characteristic of it" while producing infinite responsibility (Levinas 1991a [1974], 110). Hence, Briony's fault does not lie in her (in)ability to enter the inner world of others, but in her way of turning the encounter with the mystery of the other into an intellectual inquiry that produces a plot with a clear explanation. Indeed, when Briony witnesses the scene at the pond she finds herself confused, and faces what Levinas describes as the "traumatism of astonishment" (Levinas 2002 [1969], 73), i.e., the experience of shock that arises from the encounter with "something absolutely foreign" (Levinas 2002 [1969], 73). Briony is agitated by seeing a scene that she does not understand – a mysterious happening between her sister and Robbie. She cannot interpret it, but "it was extraordinary that she was unable to resist it" (McEwan 2002, 38). Yet, Briony is also unable to resist the temptation to solve the mystery and defy the shock of the incomprehensible by turning it into a story: "Blackmail? Threats?" she wonders (McEwan 2002, 38). As of her first questions Briony begins to form a plot, and she continues by calming herself: "she could see the simple sentences [. . .] she could write the scene three times over" (McEwan 2002, 40). When confronted with what Levinas terms "the horror of the radical unknown" (Levinas 2002 [1969], 41), Briony resorts to constructing stories, thus turning the other into an intelligible character rather than recognizing her own limitations and obligations in this incomprehensibility.

By the end of the novel it is clear that Briony has gone a long way from her childish folktales of villains and princesses to writing the absorbing novel we have just read with its varying focalizations and realistic impressions. Nevertheless, the surprising revelation of her authorship further undermines the ties between empathetic imagination of other selves and ethical concern for the other. It is true that "her narrative so sympathetically enters into the consciousness of the other characters" (Phelan 2007, 122). However, her signature at the end of the third section highlights the fabrication behind any sympathetic simulation of another person's perspective. In fact, Briony's construction of the stories of Robbie and Cecilia – which is acutely beautiful and convincing – relies upon her own perspective, her understanding of the events and her interpretation of their experience. Indeed, it is "her [Briony's] absolute power" that constructs every aspect of the story, every character and perspective, amounting to the position of "God" (McEwan 2002, 371) – a dominating force that determines everything in the represented world.[14]

McEwan's suggestion of the God-like position of the author hints at his own position as the author of *Atonement* and at the broader issue of the ethics of fiction writing. This is why Dominic Head notes that "the actions of the novelist might *always* be morally dubious" (Head 2007, 166; italics in original). However, I believe that *Atonement* points to another possibility rather than concluding with moral skepticism. In the invitation to re-read the novel, which arises from the surprising revelation of Briony's authorship, McEwan points to a different vision of the ethical – behind Briony's authority and beyond the language of representation and empathetic understanding. In this second reading we can see the novel's exploration of both the evil spirits populating European history and those that operate in the individual soul – as part of its insistence on the obligation to care for the singularity of the other person. In the double reading of *Atonement*, the novel appears not only to acknowledge the human desire to provide a definitive explanation for the world, but also to insist on the impossibility of doing so and the obligation that arises from this impossibility.

In the second section of *Atonement*, Robbie considers the impossibility of giving witness to his war experiences: "[. . .] – the place was rubble and it was impossible to tell. Who would care? Who could ever describe this confusion [. . .] No one would ever know what it was like to be here. Without the details there could be no larger picture" (McEwan 2002, 227). The response to Robbie's skepticism emerges in Briony's attempts to achieve representation in her many drafts of the novel. Briony tries hard to believe that she can tell; that she can present the larger picture, enter Robbie's perspective, and convey his experience of war. However, the delayed revelation of her authorship of the novel indicates that this representation is in fact a lie, a deceitful depiction. The structure of *Atonement* is witness to the fact that literature cannot paint the larger picture and do justice to the truth of history or the individual experience

---

[14] Moreover, as Phelan argues, McEwan "actually call[s] attention to the fact that [Briony's] long delay in finishing her novel has also been a way to avoid taking the one concrete step toward atonement available to her: the public admission of her crime [. . .] and the effort to clear Robbie's name" (Phelan 2007, 126).

of "what it was like to be [there]." Moreover, the novel forces the readers to face their own complicity with Briony's deception: just like Briony we were eager to believe that we can "know what it was like to be [there]." Yet just like Briony, we cannot. We can only fake this knowledge and pretend to share the experience of war. As Serpell argues, "we [the readers] are accused – framed – by the text" (Serpell 2014, 88).

Reading *Atonement* through Levinas is thus a process of self-critique that demands awareness not only of the readers' desire for a happy ending, just like Briony's, but also their desire to enjoy the consolation of stories that "bridge the distance between self and other" (Palambu-Liu 2012, 29). These are stories that organize human reality into a meaningful and comprehensible framework, what Levinas describes as a "system – complete, perfect, denying or absorbing the differences that appear to betray or limit it" (Levinas 1996, 5). Yet *Atonement*'s unexpected conclusion dismantles this complete and perfect system, thus allowing the readers to see their attachment to it and recognize their complicity with Briony's efforts to turn the unknown and the unimaginable into comprehensible components of this perfect system.

In addition, however, apart from the question of knowledge, the preceding quote also raises the question of caring: "Who would care?" In the first reading of the novel, caring seems completely dependent on knowing: if it is impossible to tell and to know, then no one will care. By contrast, in the second reading, this relationship between knowing and caring are seen as part of Briony's attitude and her authorial domination: she, as an author, is resolved to determine what is known and what is cared for. However, in the story of Robbie's trial another view about caring is hinted at: namely, the obligation to care that emanates precisely from the impossibility to tell and to know, the responsibility to that human suffering that cannot be described and shared.

This obligation emerges early in Robbie's section when he comes across "the unexpected detail" of a human leg in a tree (McEwan 2002, 191). The encounter replicates Briony's experience of the shock of the unexpected when she witnesses the scene near the pond, but here the development is different:

> The leg was twenty feet up, wedged in the first forking of the trunk, bare, severed cleanly above the knee. From where they stood there was no sign of blood or torn flesh. It was a perfect leg, pale, smooth, small enough to be a child's. The way it was angled in the fork, it seemed to be on display, for their benefit or enlightenment: this is a leg.
>
> (McEwan 2002, 192)

Unlike Briony's puzzlement when witnessing the incomprehensible spectacle, here the image is very clear and simple: "this is a leg." Nevertheless, it is a horrifying image for both Robbie and the readers. Rereading the novel, the readers already know that Briony is describing everything. Thus, it is significant that unlike her early rush to invent a story after seeing the shocking episode near the pond, here the story pauses. Witnessing does not turn into storytelling. There is no narrative, no plot, no explanation. There is only a sign: "this is a leg." Although the leg is "on display," there is a great deal that cannot be seen and cannot be said: the novel does not tell the story of how the leg came to be there. The story of the human being, perhaps a boy who lost his leg, is also missing.

The leg is a dreadful image. J. Hillis Miller discusses its horrifying effect in terms of the "traumatic doubling" that attentive readers experience when associating this leg with an earlier image of Briony's mother's leg in the first section of the novel (Miller 2013, 97). But even more so, it is the untold violence and unrepresented suffering that cause the shock here. Indeed, the leg determines the limits of representation of Briony's narration and of McEwan's writing. The text seems to declare the impossibility of giving an account of the deep suffering experienced by the human being who lost a leg. The "perfect leg," with "no sign of blood or torn flesh," signifies horrific pain, which, contrary to Briony's aim of telling all, cannot be told. Thus, the leg is a synecdoche for the face, which itself is "abstract" and "invisible" even as it signifies the precariousness of the other. Levinas describes several parts of the body in these terms when he refers to a scene in Vasily Grossman's novel *Life and Fate* in which the human back, neck, and shoulders become painfully expressive and ethically demanding.[15]

In *Atonement*, Robbie is deeply disturbed by the leg: "All he wanted [. . .] was to forget about the leg" (McEwan 2002, 193), but it does not stop haunting him: "He was trying to push it away, but it would not let him go" (McEwan 2002, 194). The leg pervades Robbie's thoughts and hallucinations and at times it seems as though it is speaking to him, pointing to what is missing: "a vanished boy. Vanished" (McEwan 2002, 202). All that can be told is a lacuna, a void.

Yet near the end of this section, something else develops, when the wounded Robbie, probably in his dying moments, acknowledges the command emanating from the leg and its missing story: "He must go back and get the boy from the

---

15 See Levinas's reference, in "Peace and Proximity," to an episode in Grossman's novel when the backs and raised shoulders of people in a line at Lubyanka prison embody the vulnerable enigma of the face (Levinas 1996a, 167). In later interviews Levinas refers again to this episode and points to the nape of the neck as an expression of the face (Levinas 2001, 192, 208).

tree" (McEwan 2002, 262). Here, the unknown and the ineffable provoke the obligation to care. Robbie's feverish delusions continue with a vision of his reverse journey:

> So he would go back the way he had come, walk back through the reverses of all they had achieved, across the drained and dreary marshes, past the fierce sergeant on the bridge, through the bombed- up village, [. . .] and next day, in yellow morning light, on the swing of a compass needle, hurry through that glorious country of little valleys and streams and swarming bees, and take the rising footpath to the sad cottage by the railway. And the tree. Gather up from the mud the pieces of burned, striped cloth, the shreds of his pyjamas, then bring him down, the poor pale boy. (McEwan 2002, 262)

Robbie dreams of undoing the plot of war, reversing the narrative step by step so that he can return to that vanished boy. It is the undoing of all that has been done that can change everything, reverse the extreme violence that severed this leg from a living human being, annul the crimes of the terrible war, and overturn Briony's accusation of Robbie. This is Robbie's fantasy, or perhaps Briony's, or McEwan's dream of rewinding the traumatic record of the twentieth century and re-writing the history of Europe. The readers know that this cannot be done. Literature cannot change the past, cannot atone for crimes, and cannot offer a full accounting of human lives and the distinct experience of others.

However, in re-reading the novel another possibility takes shape in this dream of undoing. Robbie's dream is driven by the bond of responsibility, and it is this bond that *Atonement* tries to convey. The dream of undoing the plot is also the dream of undoing the Said of the narrative, so that the Saying can be approximated: the infinite responsibility for the suffering of another human being whose pain can never be fully narrated or shared. Judith Butler comments that "the human is indirectly affirmed in that very disjunction that makes representation impossible [. . .]. There is something unrepresentable that we nevertheless seek to represent, and that paradox must be retained in the representation we give" (Butler 2004, 144). McEwan's *Atonement* addresses exactly this paradox, giving Briony the authority to represent but then admitting that representation is necessarily limited, misleading, and flawed. Yet even if representation and narration necessarily miss or distort the otherness of the other, *Atonement* nonetheless tries to articulate the essential indebtedness of its narrative to "what is precarious in another life" (Butler 2004, 134).

Robbie's fantasy of rewinding the plot, like Briony's wish of amending her crime, can be read as the novel's fantasy of undoing the said of its representation to signify the plot of proximity, the ethical "for-the-other." This primal responsibility of the self to the other is the basic relation that is ignored and rejected in both Briony's plot of accusation and the historical plot of the terrible war. As the novel sends the readers to re-read its plot, after the surprising ending, it also invites the readers to realize that the crime of overlooking the singularity of the other is at the root of human atrocities.

Reading *Atonement* through the ethical perspective of Levinas's thought thus calls for an effort to reach beyond Briony's captivating narration, beyond the understanding of others promised by realism, and beyond McEwan's skeptical suggestion that storytelling is always deceptive and misleading and thus, as Head claims, "morally dubious" (Head 2007, 166). Instead, the novel draws attention to the potential of fiction to bear witness to the infinite indebtedness to the singularity of the other. It demands being attentive to narrative lapses, absences, omissions, duplications, and inconsistencies – discursive features that disrupt the narrative construction and the fluidity of reading – where the relation to "the other than self" can be approached as the unsaid of what is said. *Atonement* explores this potential of fiction. Beyond the well-connected plot, the novel calls upon its readers to re-read this basic relation to the other person as part of the act of narration itself that is committed to and embedded in the vulnerability of human life.

Works Cited

Amiel Houser, Tammy, and Adia Mendelson-Maoz. "Against Empathy: Levinas and Ethical Criticism in the Twenty-First Century." *Journal of Literary Theory* 8.1 (2014): 199–218.
Attridge, Derek. "Ethical Modernism: Servants as Others in J. M. Coetzee's Early Work." *Poetics Today* 25.4 (2004): 653–671.
Bernasconi, Robert, and Critchley Simon (Eds.) *Re-reading Levinas*. Bloomington: Indiana University Press, 1991.
Black, Shameem. *Fiction across Borders: Imagining the Lives of Others in Late-Twentieth-Century Novels*. New York: Columbia University Press, 2010.
Butler, Judith. *Precarious Life: The Powers of Mourning and Violence*. New York: Verso, 2004.
Carroll, Noël. "The wheel of Virtue: Art, Literature and Moral knowledge." *The Journal of Aesthetics and Art Criticism* 60.1 (2002): 3–26.
Critchley, Simon, *The Ethics of Deconstruction: Derrida and Levinas*. Edinburgh: Edinburgh University Press, 1999.
Coplan, Amy and Peter Goldie. "Introduction." *Empathy: Philosophical and Psychological Perspectives*. Eds. Amy Coplan and Peter Goldie. Oxford: Oxford University Press. 2011, IX–XLVII.
Currie, Gregory. "The Moral Psychology of Fiction." *Australian Journal of Philosophy*. 73.2 (1995): 250–259.
Derrida, Jacques. "Violence and Metaphysics: An Essay on the Thought of Emmanuel Levinas." Trans. Alan Bass. *Writing and Difference*. Chicago: The University of Chicago Press, 1978, 79–153.

Eaglestone, Robert. *Ethical Criticism: Reading after Levinas*. Edinburgh: Edinburgh University Press, 1997.
Finney, Brian. "Briony's Stand against Oblivion: The Making of Fiction in Ian McEwan's *Atonement*." *Journal of Modern Literature* 27.3 (2004): 68–82.
Fraser, Ian. "Class Experience in McEwan's *Atonement*." *Critique* 54.4 (2013): 465–477.
Genesis. *The New Oxford Annotated Bible*. Ed. Michael D. Coogan. New York: Oxford University Press, 2007.
Greiner, Rae. *Sympathetic Realism in Nineteenth-Century British Fiction*. Baltimore: Johns Hopkins University Press, 2012.
Hale, Dorothy J. "Fiction as Restriction: Self-Binding in New Ethical Theories of the Novel." *Narrative* 15.2 (2007): 187–206.
Hammond, Meghan Marie, and Sue J. Kim (Eds.). *Rethinking Empathy through Literature*. New York: Routledge, 2014.
Harrison, Mary-Catherine. "The Paradox of Fiction and the Ethics of Empathy: Reconceiving Dickens's Realism." *Narrative* 16.3 (2008): 256–278.
Head, Dominic. *Ian McEwan*. Manchester and New York: Manchester University Press, 2007.
Hollander, Rachel. "*Daniel Deronda* and the Ethics of Alterity." *Levinas and Nineteenth-Century Literature: Ethics and Otherness from Romanticism through Realism*. Eds. Donald R. Wehrs and David P. Haney. Newark: University of Delaware Press, 2009. 264–287.
Jacobi, Martin. "Who Killed Robbie and Cecilia? Reading and Misreading Ian McEwan's *Atonement*." *Critique* 52.1 (2011): 55–73.
Kertzer, Jonathan. *Poetic Justice and Legal Fictions*. Cambridge: Cambridge University Press, 2010.
Kronick, Joseph K. "Levinas and the Plot against Literature." *Philosophy and Literature* 40.1 (2016): 265–272.
Levinas, Emmanuel. *Otherwise than Being or beyond Essence*. Trans. Alphonso Lingis. Dordrecht: Kluwer Academic, 1991a [1974].
Levinas, Emmanuel. "Wholly Otherwise" [1973]. Trans. Simon Critchley. *Re-reading Levinas*. Eds. Robert Bernasconi and Simon Critchley. Bloomington: Indiana University Press, 1991b. 3–8.
Levinas, Emmanuel. "Peace and proximity." *Basic Philosophical Writings*. Eds. Adriaan T. Peperzak, Simon Critchley, and Robert Bernasconi. Bloomington: Indiana University Press, 1996a. 161–170.
Levinas, Emmanuel. *Proper Names*. Trans. Michael B. Smith. Stanford: Stanford University Press, 1996b [1975].
Levinas, Emmanuel. *Is it Righteous to be? Interviews with Emmanuel Levinas*. Ed. Jill Robbins. Stanford: Stanford University Press, 2001.
Levinas, Emmanuel. *Totality and Infinity: An Essay on Exteriority*. Trans. Alphonso Lingis. Pittsburgh: Duquesne University Press, 2002 [1969].
Maitzen, Rohan. 'The Soul of Art': Understanding Victorian Ethical Criticism. ESC: *English Studies in Canada*, 31.2–3 (2005): 151–185.
Marshal, Gregory. "Redefining Ethical Criticism: The Old vs. the New." *Journal of Literary Theory* 4.2 (2010): 273–302.
McEwan, Ian. *Atonement*. London: Vintage, 2002 [2001].

Miller, J. Hillis. "Some Versions of Romance Trauma as Generated by Realist Detail in Ian McEwan's *Atonement*." *Trauma and Romance in Contemporary British Literature*. Eds. Susana Onega and Jean-Michel Ganteau. New York: Routledge, 2013. 90–106.

New, Melvyn, Robert Bernasconi, and Richard A. Cohen (Eds.). *In Proximity: Emmanuel Levinas and the Eighteenth Century*. Lubbock: Texas Tech University Press, 2001.

Nussbaum, Martha C. "Exactly and Responsibly: A Defense of Ethical Criticism." *Mapping the Ethical Turn: A Reader in Ethics, Culture, and Literary Theory*. Eds. Todd F. Davis and Kenneth Womack. Charlottesville: University of Virginia Press, 2001. 59–77.

O'Hara, David K. "Briony's Being-For: Metafictional Narrative Ethics in Ian McEwan's *Atonement*." *Critique* 52.1 (2011): 72–100.

Palambu-Liu, David. *The Deliverance of Others: Reading Literature in a Global Age*. Durham: Duke University Press, 2012.

Phelan, James. "Delayed Disclosure and the Problem of Other Minds: Ian McEwan's *Atonement*." *Experiencing Fiction: Judgments, Progressions, and the Rhetorical Theory of Narrative*. Columbus: The Ohio State University Press, 2007, 109–132.

Robbins, Jill. *Altered Reading: Levinas and Literature*. Chicago: Chicago University Press, 1999.

Serpell, C. Namwali. *Seven Modes of Uncertainty*. Cambridge: Harvard University Press, 2014.

Wehrs, Donald R., and David P. Haney (Eds.). *Levinas and Nineteenth-Century Literature: Ethics and Otherness from Romanticism to Realism*. Newark: University of Delaware Press, 2009.

Part V: **Literary Theory**

Shira Wolosky
Emmanuel Levinas: Metaphor without Metaphysics

Levinas's treatment of metaphor and figural language in his posthumously published notebooks and conference lectures clarifies its status and implications in his formal published writings. These *Notes* are exploratory. They show him thinking through language about thinking through language. One of his first premises is, indeed, that thought happens in language, a linguistic turn that goes back to Nietzsche. Derrida later develops as a sign theory the intrinsic role of signifiers in formulating meaning, not as "reference" to a signified idea prior to them, as mere vehicles to thought, but rather to other signifiers in an ongoing chain of signification.[1] As Levinas writes: language does not just "communicat[e] a prefabricated thought" (Levinas 2012, 319). "The word does not evoke an object by a sign . . . there is no signification that so to speak exists outside of all language" (Levinas 2009, 334) and of which language would merely be a "servile translation" (Levinas 2009, 375).

The structure of metaphor is both a basis for and has traditionally reflected the sign-theory of signified expressed through or represented by a signifier, as tenor to vehicle, or abstract to concrete, or figural to literal.[2] As Derrida analyzed in "White Mythology," traditional metaphor reproduces ontological structures to which it is also foundational.[3] As in traditional metaphor, so in traditional metaphysics, a signifier is taken to be a "vehicle" to a signified as "tenor," assuming them to share a pre-given common feature to justify the transfer. Levinas in his war notebooks likewise exposes and recasts metaphor in its ontological implications. Metaphor there is not a particular rhetorical

---

[1] "Communication presupposes subjects (whose identity and presence are constituted before the signifying operation) and objects (signified concepts, a thought that the passage of communication will have neither to constitute nor by all rights transform)" (Derrida 1972, 23).
[2] I. A. Richards introduced the terms vehicle and tenor, picked up by Ricoeur for example in *The Rule of Metaphor* (1987), where the terms of metaphor are assigned as concrete and abstract (Rule 298), vehicle and tenor (Rule 294), and particular and general (Rule 300). Metaphor of course is a large topic in philosophical as well as literary analysis.
[3] Derrida, in "White Mythology," claims that the terms traditionally assigned to metaphor to reproduce classic ontological distinction between sensible and intelligible, visible and invisible, with metaphoric transferring from the first to the second (Derrida 1982, 225–226). Ricoeur, in *The Rule of Metaphor*, disputes Derrida's account, claiming that metaphor can be employed metaphysically but need not be (Ricoeur 1987, 336–348).

figure, but a figure for all figures and ultimately for language itself. In language generally, there is no signified prior to signifiers, determining their meanings. There is no prior idea or object whose meaning is merely conveyed by language. Instead of language as signifiers corresponding or referring to prior signifieds, signification in Levinas unfolds through a procession of signifiers, each of which refers to each other in ongoing inter-relationships. Metaphor in the broad sense of figuration becomes not a mere subtrope as comparison, but the model of language altogether: "Far from an exceptional phenomenon of language, as a figure or style among others, metaphor coincides with the phenomenon of language itself or of signification" (Levinas 2009, 337). All language is, from the outset, figural. Each signifier is a figure for each other, with no signified outside or beyond the unfolding of signification.

The traditional terms for metaphor thereby dissolve. There is no "literal" against "figural" meaning, whose usages in fact are confusing and inconsistent. For, in the history of exegesis where the terms originate, "literal" points to a historical signifier for a prior and truer spiritual meaning, as both Nietzsche and Derrida expose.[4] In ordinary usage, however, "literal" indicates what is actual, often physical, with "figural" some further sense granted to it. Levinas's recasting of the terms clarifies and situates the meaning of a signifier in the sign-chains of their inter-relationality, which can take place on a variety of planes of order and hence a variety of senses. Signs mean in ways that Wittgenstein calls language games. There is no pre-given "signified" outside of signifying chains or networks of meaning. As signifiers signifying signifiers, each term of language is then a "figure" or signifier for another. The sense of any word emerges within the inter-relationality of signifiers in the unfolding signification in which each appears. Each of these signifying networks offers one or more levels or configurations of meaning.

Levinas here accords with Nietzschean language theory, as well as many twentieth-century thinkers writing after Nietzsche. When Nietzsche famously says in "Truth and Lying in an Extra-Moral Sense": "What then is truth? a mobile army of metaphors, metonyms, and anthropomorphisms, in short, a sum of human relations," his claim is that language, rather than signifying metaphysical truth, is relational to human meaning, "a sum of human relations"

---

4 Nietzsche, in *The Dawn*, lambasts biblical typology's absorption and unification of all "literal" images of the Old Testament into the "figural" meaning of the New: "Wherever any piece of wood, a switch, a ladder, a twig, a tree, a willow, or a staff is mentioned, this was supposed to indicate a prophecy of the wood of the cross" (Nietzsche 1968, # 84). Derrida, in *Of Grammatology*, exposes the "literal" as itself a "figure" (Derrida 1974, 15). See also Wolosky, "Religion and Literature" (2018).

(Nietzsche 1989, 250). His lecture notes on "Ancient Rhetoric" declares all "words" to be "tropes . . . with respect to their meanings" "Tropes" are the "proper nature," the "proper meaning" of words (Nietzsche 1989, 23–25). In *Philosophy in the Tragic Age of the Greeks* he similarly writes: "Words are but symbols for the relations of things to one another and to us" (Nietzsche 1962, 83). Nietzsche is here critiquing traditional claims that language is an "adequate expression" of a pregiven truth, as he puts it in "Truth and Lying" (Nietzsche 1989, 248).[5] But he is also offering a positive claim of language, redefining the very meaning of meaning. Rather than deriving in "truth" in any metaphysical sense, Nietzsche is pointing towards the generation of linguistic meaning in human terms, as hermeneutic, interpretive action.

Levinas, like Nietzsche, Merleau-Ponty, and other post-Nietzschean philosophers, challenges not only traditional theories of metaphor and language, but also the ontological structures upon which they are based and which they reflect. Traditional theory structures metaphor as reflecting an ontological hierarchy of concrete/abstract, literal/figural, signifier/signified. This reproduces the Platonist ontology of an intelligible, unchanging eternal ideal realm of true Being which temporal material realm of Becoming reflects as a lesser and less true reality. Levinas rejects this two-world system. This Nietzschean overcoming of metaphysics resituates language in Levinas away from the two-world system of intelligible/material, unchanging eternal/temporal historical worlds. In Levinas there are no two worlds, no higher ontology beyond time governing a lower, thinner ontology as shadowy copy whose reality, substance, meaning, and truth derive in the higher world. Meaning, for Levinas, is situated within the phenomenal world of time, matter, history, as the interrelationship among its particulars. There is "*rapprochement* of meaning and another meaning," but not "correspondence," which "no longer has anything in common with the system in which meaning laterally posits itself" (Levinas 2012, 321). Meaning is horizontal, "lateral" and not vertical, which is to say not invoking or referring to essences or universals shared or common among particulars.

What Levinas here outlines is a switch from a *referential* to a *relational* theory of language, as Nietzsche did, as Wittgenstein does, and as Derrida later formulates in terms of signifying chains, a term Levinas also introduces. "Language is not a group of names designating essences of things acts and relations" but instead it "already exceeds "this is" (*en tant que*) (as, like, as if)

---

5 Maudemarie Clark offers a detailed discussion of Nietzsche and correspondence theory in *Nietzsche on Truth and Philosophy*, disputing that Nietzsche rejects correspondence theory as the majority of commentators claim, but also redefining correspondence theory in more pragmatist directions as correspondence to "common sense" (Clark 1990, 34–38, 61).

another thing" (Levinas 2009, 337). As Levinas continues, language theory here is deeply hermeneutical. The sign-chains that situate meaning act as interpretive frameworks in which each signifies, what Levinas describes as a Heideggerean "world:" "The fact that every signification signifies in a context, or as Heidegger says in a world" (Levinas 2009, 337). Signifiers hermeneutically mean within interpretive frameworks that indeed define what the given [donnée] even is as well as what it means. "Like language, experience too no longer appears to be made up of isolated elements . . . and each signify by itself. They signify on the basis of the 'world' and of the position of the one that looks at them" (Levinas 1987, 78), Levinas clarifies in "Meaning and Sense," a published essay to emerge from these notes.

Yet Levinas's hermeneutics or frameworks of interpretation are not contained within the models of phenomenology, when these entail that understanding is how consciousness grasps experience as a unity of intentionality and intuition. Neither metaphor nor language nor understanding itself is for Levinas a moment of integrative intuition of which language, as a linear unfolding part by part in time, would inevitably be an inferior mode (Levinas 2009, 360). Signification is not "an ideal essence or a relation offered to intellectual intuition" (Levinas 2009, 370). Likewise metaphor, as both model and instance, is "not a modification of a signification which exists outside of language," and signification is "not born out of thought or simple correlatives of intuition. It refers already to significations" (Levinas 2009, 332). The mind no longer encloses or is enclosed in an "intentional structure of thought" (Levinas 2009, 337) against, as Levinas often repeats, Plato's reminiscence in which "the soul only receives what is already there, returning to itself" (Levinas 2009, 339). Levinas would break through this enclosure of self as an "interiority that is intuitive" (Levinas 2009, 379).

Levinas's distinctive contribution is to direct language theory beyond ontological, epistemological, or phenomenological analysis to ethics. In doing so, he challenges not only ontological structure, but its foundational presupposition of unity. As a figure of comparison, metaphor works in resemblance, which traditionally is seen to assume a shared essence common and prior to both of the compared terms. As Levinas writes: traditional metaphor projects "resemblance to resemblance as if entities existed prior to their comparison within an analogical structure pre-establishing likenesses: a resemblance of resemblance, . . . as if establishing coincidence between beings, objects and situations that reveal an analogy" (Levinas 2009, 326). Such analogical structure underwrites Platonist ontology itself: whether as in Republic X the world is a copy representing Ideas, or in Plotinus where world is emanated as shared Being through attenuating gradations of likeness. At the apex is unity: Plato's

Ideas, as unchanging, must be non-multiple as well as immaterial: the multiplicity that the changingness of matter in time results in is precisely what defies its being what it is, true to itself as identical to itself. Plotinus's elevation of unity to the ultimate principle is plainly announced in calling it the One, beyond being since even being, unchanging as it essentially is, is in Plato's Ideas still multiple. Metaphor would be a glimpse through these multiple refractions to the unity thought to underlie them.

Levinas, however, moves meaning from such unitary Being to the time, change, materiality, and multiplicity which Platonism demoted as Becoming. He does so not firstly as an accusation of falsehood, what Nietzsche accuses as "the equation of what is dissimilar," thus erasing the "unique, absolutely individualized original experience" of particulars to "fit countless, more or less similar cases" which, however, "are never identical, and hence absolutely dissimilar" (Nietzsche 1989, 249). This erasure of unique particulars is to Levinas not only falsifying, but ethically violating. Unity is erasive. It must deny or destroy whatever cannot be incorporated into it. Thus, it generates as well as justifies violence. The appeal to unitary truths, Levinas writes in notes made as a prisoner of war of the Nazis, becomes a form of "colonization," of imposing one cultural mode onto another as if it were universal in ways that "serve exploitation and violence" (Levinas 2009, 381). Analogy consumes difference. The signifier is absorbed into the signified, its purpose of transmission fulfilled. Discourse itself can become the self reflecting on itself, the relation with the interlocutor one of "domination as the self retrieves its own memory" (Levinas 2009, 343). As Levinas writes elsewhere in his lecture notes: "The conception in which language merely transmits thought . . . is a philosophy of mastery, every human relation becomes inevitably a relation of power" (Levinas 2009, 80). Unity appropriates and effaces difference, an appropriation performed in a kind of conceptualization that subsumes difference in a drive to assimilation. Consolidation, *Aufhebung*, subsuming terms into each other while effacing their distinction, is a conceptual drive Levinas repeatedly and consistently sees to unfold throughout the traditions of Western ontology and truth. And he deeply suspects its ethical implications, as one of power and appropriation.

Unity of mind and being threatens violence against whatever lies outside it – multiplicity, temporality, difference, the particular. Yet, abandoning all norms other than hermeneutics of cultural practices – Richard Rorty's position – may open another danger, that of sheer relativism.[6] Levinas concurs with Nietzsche in

---

[6] Richard Rorty, in urging not the "desire to know the truth" but "the desire to recontextualize," concedes "this is the desire to be as polymorphous in our adjustments as possible, to

rejecting a Platonic definition of signification that is "separate from the world of becoming" (Levinas 2009, 381). But he also warns against the denial of all norms except those of cultural practices, norms that would make possible adjudicating among different cultural contexts and their hermeneutics of signification. In a concluding note to "La Métaphore," Levinas summarizes: "Metaphor in the sense of comparison as the structure of all cultural signification" results in the "purely relative." He then, however, asks: "Doesn't there exist signification in an other sense, one which is apprehensive of words and their cultural activities" (Levinas 2009, 346).

In seeking this "other" signification, Levinas proposes instead of unity an ontology and an ethic of multiplicity in which each signifier is other from any other. Signifiers would have a double relationality of both distinctiveness yet connection, connection in terms of the specific sign-chains in which they appear and are linked to each other. It would be a nominalism that would not rely on an ultimate ground that is, however, beyond reach, as in the medieval kind[7] but rather a post-metaphysical nominalism that locates relationships within the changing world of particulars.[8] Resemblances can of course still be drawn, but they would be relational, not essential, through what Rorty calls "recontextualization." Yet unlike Rorty, Levinas introduces a transcendence that ruptures any context, that exceeds it, rupturing also any analogical reification within it.

Multiplicity here becomes a norm, rather than a failure of unity or sign of disorder, chaos, and meaninglessness, as is traditionally the case. The closed system of self-reflection and analogical ontology Levinas ruptures by a transcendence that will not be encompassed within it, interrupting totality and generating multiplicity but not as a fall: as a creative good. Transcendence acts, first, as an incursion within the signifying system. Each signifier transcends each other. In the unfolding of signification, then, there is an assertion of the distinctive integrity of each signifier, different from every other in which it is in relation. Difference thus becomes intrinsic to meaning, not as a dispersion that must be overcome but as a way signifiers relate to each other. Signifier terms are then no longer units "in a system of metaphoric relation which privileges the transfer of identical senses across a multiplicity they have in common" as background to be consolidated out of (Levinas 2009, 335).

---

recontexualize for the hell of it" (Rorty 1991, 110). He also states: "The pragmatist admits he has no ahistorical standpoint from which to endorse the habits of modern democracy he wishes to praise" except through our practice to "privilege our own group" (Rorty 1991, 29).
7 See Hans Blumenberg, *The Legitimacy of the Modern Age* (1983, 151 and following).
8 See for example Nelson Goodman and W. V. Quine, "Toward a Constructive Nominalism" (1947).

"A literal meaning is inseparable from the figurative meaning," he writes more imagistically, "and neither vanishes nor is absorbed in the meaning that nourishes it, but the two meanings glimmer in the same dawn, both turned to the light" (Levinas 1987, 67). Indeed, this passage both describes and demonstrates self-reflexively Levinasian metaphor. A sign-chain of words involving light intercrosses with a sign-chain of words involving language, forming a new sign-chain of inter-relational terms which nevertheless retain their difference. New relationships emerge, not subordinating or incorporating the distinctive language webs out of which these new relationships are built. Thus signifiers are launched in new differential relationships, but not as subsumption, nor as dialectical or metaphoric synthesis.

Within the unfolding of signifiers, relationality is not the same as identity. Two identical terms would not be in relation; they would be identically the same. Relationality entails connection, but between distinct terms. There is a double relation of connection and distinction, proximity and distance, with difference taking precedence as the very condition of meaning. "Differences between signs concern thought before the identity of these signs" (Levinas 2009, 359). Levinas here accords with Saussure's differential relationality of signs, but rejects the notion of a "signified" to describe it, as Derrida does as well. As a differential relationality among signifiers, all language is figural. This relationality can be a comparison, as in a specific metaphor: such that two chains of signifiers crossover, bringing each chain into relation with the other through an intersecting term. Comparison would, however, also always retain difference. The transfer is never complete, with one term subsumed into the other.

"No given would bear identity forthwith," but would always appear within hermeneutic interpretation, just the way language means: as a "word that receives the gift of being understood from a context to which it refers" (Levinas 1987, 77). Levinas thus concurs with contemporary anti-Platonism, in language as in ontology and epistemology, refuting unitary Ideas as governing meaning. He, however, goes beyond other contemporary theorists, with the possible exception of Derrida, who in fact draws on Levinas, to address and outline an ethics of language precisely in theorizing it as inter-relational multiplicity.

This ethical turn is particularly marked and dramatized in a uniquely Levinasian shift in the models of signification. For in Levinas, discourse and its hermeneutics is not only a structure of relational signifiers as these reflect interpretive frameworks, but a relationship among the interpreters themselves. Beyond signifiers as structural units, Levinas insists on signifiers in a different sense: the persons who signify, who actively signal to each other and are thus inseparable from how, what, why, and for whom meanings occur. "Language is the only system of signs that does not turn back/refer only to the signified that it expresses but breaks the system to manifest the meaning that delivers the signs" (Levinas 2009, 369). Words are not "congealed into a literal meaning. In fact there would be no literal meaning." Words instead refer "laterally . . . to other words" as used in different contexts, for example in their etymology (Levinas 1987, 77). This is to move metaphor from a vertical structure to a horizontal one: "laterally" along and between sign chains or language networks. Levinas then further extends figural meanings beyond structure toward the "positions of the listeners and speakers." Signification occurs only among speakers/responders. "Language [even as] signifying thought is to someone, supposes the other . . . Language is not just instruction, but a call to the other" (Levinas 2009, 81). Speaker/responders, too, are signifiers as actors; signification via signifiers is their act. And as signifier-sayers, actors launching signs, they always exceed structure, stand outside its incorporation and systematization.

To insist on speaker/responders reaffirms the historicity and contingency of signification – "the contingency of their history" (Levinas 1987, 77). Yet, it also opens signification to the ethical dimension, which is Levinas's ultimate concern, a dimension that entails an absolute of ethical demand above all contingency. The differences which enter into a differential diachronic system, what Levinas quite technically calls "diacritics," in which "a sign points laterally to another sign" (Levinas 2009, 359; see also Levinas 2009, 378), also break out of the system. The interlocutors as signifiers in their address and response to each other – with each addresser a responder, each responder an addresser in the ongoing unfolding of discourse – also emerge relationally to each other. Yet they also exceed relation. Linked by the very language they address and respond to but are also absolutely and irrevocably separate from each other, they are other to each other beyond any signifiers they interchange, are ultimately unknown and unknowable to each other in any complete grasp or intuition of consciousness.

The relation among signifiers is not one of interiority through shared thought but "a relation with what is exterior" (Levinas 2009, 343), an "original relation with an exterior being," not as a "regrettable failure of intuition" but precisely as the "rightness of relation" (Levinas 2009, 371). It is this exteriority of multiple signifiers which do not erase, absorb, or incorporate each other but stand in relationships that both connect and distinguish that constitutes Levinasian ethics. Ethics is not recognition of self in self, empathy, identification, or universalization. Rather, it is the recognition and respect of the other as beyond grasp, claim, or full knowledge. But this is exactly to elevate multiplicity over unity: the multiplicity of signifiers "countless" beyond any possibility "to seize by inventory"; and the multiplicity of signifiers as speakers/ responders linked by language but across an absolute distance in which each is unique, each from the "position of the one that looks at them" (Levinas 1987, 77–78), a diversity of positions that cannot and should not be consolidated into one. Ethically, such diversity is experienced as it affirms uniqueness: each distinct signifier/person is unique, transforming or, rather, exposing the self-enclosed self as interlocutor speaker/responder: "the uniqueness of the I is the fact that no one can answer for me" (Levinas 1987, 97). "Multivocity, polyvalence, is the internal character of meaning." This extends beyond any "system" including metaphor as "this like that," which would assert fixed analogies. Rather, there would be genuine transformation and newness, newness possible only through openness to the truly different and other, "a germination which is meaning and not some kind of preference for the signified," where instead one object "responds to other objects by which it can be something other than what it is." In this, as in Levinas's ethics, radically and against all the philosophical centuries governed by analogical unity, "the multiplicity opened [would] in itself be intelligibility" (Levinas 2012, 321).

What then is metaphor? Rodolphe Calin has argued that metaphor in the Notes ultimately verges into what Levinas later calls trace – actually, Levinas himself introduces "trace" in his "Notes on Metaphor" (Levinas 2012, 328), asking this very question: "Does the excess of metaphor not come from the trace?" (Calin 2012, 136). Levinasian metaphor, like trace, is always in motion, never fixed essence, never final. Metaphor is an "excess of every going towards on High (*Hauteur*)" in "refusal of the end point" (Levinas 2012, 329). Metaphor in this sense does "come from the trace" which marks the passage of the other that remains ever beyond signifiers left in its wake, to which speakers and responders, signifiers in an active sense, speak and respond. The relation between speakers and responders then also exceeds itself. Each stands to the other outside their relationality. Levinas speaks of movement as against static correspondence, a "movement towards the infinite" (Levinas 2012, 325) that breaks through all closure and correlation: "There is a movement in language toward the infinite and there is no language without this movement. And this movement comes from the other insofar as language is response to another and excess of that which is said" (Levinas 2012, 328).

Metaphor, then, has a double status in Levinas. On one hand it is a term for the specific figures of comparison, not, however, as referring to a common essence but as linking together different sign-chains through terms that crossover between them: that is, establishing new links which continue to shift among further links as well as further differences and distinctions. On the other, metaphor is a term for all figuration, much as it is in Nietzsche's "Truth and Lying," where all language is seen to be metaphorical, that is, as figural whose meaning derives in networks of signifiers.

Levinas does not attempt to deny the possibility of analogy. But he rejects its foundational status, insisting that this "call of likeness to likeness" cannot exhaust metaphor's "role" (Levinas 2009, 326). Signification entails difference, but it also requires connection, which can include resemblance. Thus it is not accurate to say that Levinasian metaphor must "transcend all resemblance," as if to be "no longer situated in words, to divest of all reference," leaving only the "invocation of other that precedes all exchange of verbal signs" (Calin 2012, 132–134). The Height which exceeds metaphor does not refute it, leaving words behind into a higher silence as a "silent word" [*parole silencieuse*] (Calin 2012, 137); a word without what is Said [*la parole sans Dit*] (Faessler 2012, 152), a "speaking silence" [*silencieusement parlante*] (Guibal 2012, 171). There is a danger here to re-ontologize the beyond as if it were another higher state, displacing and demoting immanent experience and language. This would be to return to a two-world dualism not only ontologically but linguistically, where, as in traditions of negative theology, nothingness becomes a term for the higher world beyond immanence and beyond language, traditionally represented by silence.[9]

But Levinas protests the "mistrust of language" that is intrinsic to the Platonic tradition, its "exaltation of silence" and "distrust of language," where silence functions as a foundational trope for Being as a higher ontology (Levinas 2012, 132, 134). Levinas does insist that the ultimate other is beyond language as it is beyond being, but this is not to devalue language. It is to define its proper domain and role. Levinas elevates language as the arena of human interaction and ethics. "The world is significant in language" (Levinas 2009, 334), Levinas writes. Significance includes both signifiers in the sense of what is "Said," as Levinas later calls designation, that is, cognitive communication. It also intends signifiers as participants who address and respond, what Levinas later calls "Saying," which in Levinas is prior to, although it does not negate what is Said. "The signification of the interlocutor as interlocutor is not a signification like one that translates words . . . that constitute the world"; it is first address and response to the other: "the other belongs to the order of the world through the role it plays there . . . in the discourse in which I respond to the mundane signification" (Levinas 2009, 342). Language returns to "thought" but also consists in the

---

9 See Shira Wolosky, "Two Types of Negative Theology" (2017).

"aim of the one to whom language addresses itself" (Levinas 2012, 326). The challenge is "at the same time to signify and not be enveloped in intellection" (Levinas 2009, 342), to affirm the "simultaneity of this designation and this transcendence itself" (Levinas 2012, 323).

Language thereby becomes both conduct and model to signification including signifier elements and signifier-sayer actors. Each opens another dimension, "a miraculous surplus" (Levinas 2009, 325). Surplus then reaches beyond signification, a "surplus that appears in the less" (Levinas 2009, 341). In transmitting "the call of the other," the sign not only "signifies significations, but resonates in language through which the Other presents as Other" (Levinas 2009, 368). To present as Other is an oxymoron: the other is what cannot be presented or present. It breaks into what is present, preventing determinate closure into system, including between speaker/responders. The other transcends whatever is experienced, as a break that disrupts and disorients any totalization and fixation, any unification of meaning. In terms of language Levinas comes to call this the "Unsaid," *dedire* as an absolute interruption of both Said and Saying, in which "the Infinite shuts itself up in a word and becomes a being but already undoes its dwelling and unsays itself without vanishing into nothingness" (Levinas 1998b, 145).

Levinas, in a break with Platonist tradition, rejects not only a two-world ontology, but a two-world language dualism. There is absolute distinction, that between the human world and transcendence. Although transcendence incurs into this world, breaking the grip of phenomenological consciousness as possessing others, this world cannot be transcended into another one. That is what transcendence means: the impossibility of transcending this world, and the error of trying to. "The beyond is not a simple background [as in Heidegger] . . . is not "another world" behind the world [as Nietzsche accuses Plato]; the beyond is precisely beyond the world: beyond every disclosure" (Levinas 1987, 102). Levinas speaks of metaphor as "movement to the beyond" (*vers l'au dela*): that is, movement *to* but not *into*. The beyond remains beyond, so that metaphor's movement is not "lost in the thought which absorbs in resemblance as in a static essence" (Levinas 2012, 325), "without stopping in a fixed correspondence which, instead of piercing into a higher signification would entrap in the closed world fixated in objects" (Levinas 2009, 340–341). Yet this world remains the arena for language. Metaphor at once exceeds a determinate given, yet is a way to affirm meaning within the "sensible and concrete significations" that "exceeds experience, remaining part of what it transfigures" (Levinas 2009, 326).

Metaphor, then, is redefined in Levinas in terms of a general theory of language as differential interrelationship of signifiers of which comparison is one sort, always, however, stretched across differentiation that is never fully overcome. Yet Levinas also emphasizes rupture that breaks even relational differentials, that exceeds all structure and system, all comprehension and grasp. This is his ethical check: putting beings altogether outside and beyond each other, as an ultimate respect of untouchable mystery, what he calls enigma. Enigma, again, is not then hypostasized into an alternative state beyond language as silence. Yet silence does penetrate language as marking its boundaries and resisting efforts to uphold each particular, each signifier. Although there is rupture, this mystery also institutes order, norms – the norm of preserving and respecting distinct particulars as valuable and never to be incorporated. It is enigma that sustains exteriority as against identification, but to generate the movements of meaning, not negate them. Levinas, interestingly, speaks of both disorientation and orientation: of the disorientation in rupturing closed and fixed systems; but as opening towards another "orientation," a "movement towards on high" which he also calls "God" (Levinas 2012, 322). Transcendence disorients, breaking into closed system; but it also reorients, through respect of difference in multiplicity that must be embraced and affirmed against the violence of unity. The claim to a direct or privileged contact with the world of Ideas is possible which, claiming "the emancipation of minds" can be used as "a pretext for exploitation and violence" (Levinas 1987, 101). This is not to chastise the ego as autonomous consciousness, but to affirm that the self, when "it loses its sovereign self-coincidence," is "not reducible to a negative moment" but marks the discovery of an "orientation [to be] infinitely responsible" to the Other (Levinas 1987, 97).

This ongoing, open back-and-forth between connection and distinction, never resolved into a dialectic subsumption but rather driving forward in an infinite generation without resolution through and beyond metaphor, is not a failure of coherence but a production of value in life. Indeed, this is how signification unfolds: as relationalities among the particulars in the world, including a concrete "diacritics" of the body "which signifies," an "expression of the body signifying laterally from sign to sign" (Levinas 2009, 362, 378). Above all, meaning unfolds as relationship across difference between signifiers who address and respond to each other. It points to a "beyond which it announces but does not represent, [to] language as a passage to an altogether other alterity" (Levinas 2009, 337). Rather than appeal to a unifying universal, signification launches inter-relations between particulars, "the generation of a particular from a particular" (Levinas 2012, 321) which Levinas also calls "trope" (Levinas 2012, 321). In this sense the "meta" of metaphor is a speaking beyond itself. Ultimately it an address to an Other which is the core of

Levinasean ethics of language. We look beyond the signification of the words toward the Other who addresses but is never encompassed by us. All language is then meta-phorical, pointing from signifier to signifier and ultimately to its sign-givers and receivers.

1 Enigma

Metaphor thus is redefined to affirm multiple inter-relationships without closure and pointing beyond analogy. Yet another term comes to be introduced to safeguard such incompletion and insist on unintegrated difference: enigma. Enigma denotes the rupture that opens all inter-relation to new, further, infinite, unfinished, and multiple significations.

Levinas's essay "Phenomenon and Enigma" associates enigma, like metaphor, with trace. Like trace, enigma is not "like signs which recapture the signified" (Levinas 1987, 65). Enigma's "signifyingness" is one that is "absent from the very terms in which it was signaled" (Levinas 1987, 71). Enigma underscores the non-analogical in signification, the rupture that at once secures signification and also breaks through it into the ungraspable.

Enigma contests the rule of traditional metaphor, and the hermeneutics and phenomenology it both implies and constructs. Levinas's formulations can be interestingly compared to Paul Ricoeur's, whose *The Rule of Metaphor* is a central text of metaphor theory. In it, analogical structures retain their commanding role, indeed rule, such that "the same operates in spite of the different" (Ricoeur 1987, Rule 196). Levinas, however, insists on difference as it withstands and disturbs the same. Interestingly, Ricoeur refers to "enigma" as precisely the "tension, contradiction, and controversion" of usages "to which the metaphorical meaning offers the solution" (Ricoeur 1987, Rule 194–195). What Ricoeur calls "enigma" is a site of inconsistencies "the reconciliation of which metaphor 'makes sense'" (Ricoeur 1987, Rule 195). Resisting such reconciliation is precisely Levinas's project. Enigma does not "resemble terms of an already familiar order" (Levinas 1987, 62), an order which Levinas (like Ricoeur) identifies with phenomenology. Phenomena as apprehended in consciousness he describes as an appearing which "assembles" time and manifestation as contemporaneous, present within the "understanding of being" that has defined philosophy (Levinas 1987, 61, 63). But enigma ruptures such contemporaneity and correlation in ways that cannot be recovered or reconciled. As in its etymological sense of "riddle," enigma counters phenomenology as an "impossibility of manifesting" (Levinas 1987, 66, 62), a "transcendence which ventures beyond being" and "beyond thought" (Levinas 1987, 62).

"Enigma and Phenomena" reiterates Levinas's critique or language theory in the Platonist tradition. There is no "signified" as a pre-given meaning that happens outside of discourse, which language would represent as secondary signifier. As Levinas puts it, "language does not come to double up phenomena" (Levinas 1987, 69). Phenomena do not "indicate an order of 'things in themselves' of which [there] would be signs." There is no structure of "signifieds" prior to and independent of signifiers. There are no "signs which recapture the signified" (Levinas 1987, 65), no "conjuncture" or "simultaneity between the indicated and indicated terms" (Levinas 1987, 65).

Articulation is signification that emerges among signifiers interrelationally, without some prior signified they would express, indicate, or represent, what he calls a "chain of significations which constitute the world" (Levinas 1987, 62), a "rational enchainment of its significations" (Levinas 1987, 70). These signifiers do not represent an ontologically independent signified, but instead unfold meanings through lateral interrelation. The function of signifiers is not to offer representation and ultimately phenomenological comprehension and hermeneutic integration. Chains of signifiers, even as metaphors, never complete representation, never offer a "simultaneity of one single order," nor even a "meeting of two series of significations that each, with equal rights, lay claim to the same phenomenon" (Levinas 1987, 67–68). Even in the substance of a communication, Levinas's "Said," the chain does not signify a signified prior to it and is never fully constituted, but is always ongoing, open, open to rupture and to whatever exceeds its enclosure. "The enchainment of an account is exposed to interruption" (Levinas 1987, 69), writes Levinas. This is the interruption of enigma. It marks a discourse which does not fulfill "the structure of an intentional correlation" (Levinas 1987, 73), running counter to a "signifyingness . . . that awaits a concept capable of finding and grasping it" in a "sphere that is present" (Levinas 1987, 71).

Such interruption breaks through differentials within a diachronic system. It announces an absolute otherness which is never recuperated, which breaches all closures, "cutting the threads of the context" (Levinas 1987, 65). This first occurs in that every sign system is also enacted as address/response, with speakers/responders multiplying positions that open the senses of signs beyond any closed intention. This ultimate ungraspability breaks into not only sign-system but relation between interlocutors who remain other to each other, enigma to each other. Levinas refers to this as "withdrawal," foreseeing the *Dedire*, the Unsaying of *Otherwise than Being*, which he there associates with enigma as "unsaying in the ambiguity or the enigma of the transcendent, in which the breathless spirit retains a fading echo" (Levinas 1998b, 44). The infinite, exceeding all determination, is a "withdrawal like a farewell which is signified" not "to inundate it with light, but in being extinguished in the incognito" (Levinas 1987, 71–72). Enigma as trace does not "signify [] as a sign." It is the very emptiness of an irrecuperable absence, . . . the gaping open of emptiness that is not only the sign of an absence . . . but the very emptiness of a passage" (Levinas 1987, 65–66).

Enigma thus exceeds and disrupts the signified/signifier correlations of both classical sign-theory and theories of metaphorical resemblance. Enigma is ungraspable, both in terms of representation of what is "said" and the other which "Saying" addresses/responds to. As absent signified or signified absence enigma marks "the intervention of a meaning which disturbs phenomena but is quite ready to withdraw" as "footsteps that depart [as] transcendence itself, the proximity of the Other as Other" (Levinas 1987, 70).

Ricoeur directly contests Levinas's radical alterity. In *Oneself as Another* (1992), Ricoeur insists on an interchangeability or transfer between self and other. The "irreducible disturbance" Levinas insists on as unbridgeable by analogical relations that metaphor sustains (Levinas 1987, 63), Ricoeur sees as unraveling sense altogether. Of Levinas, Ricoeur writes: "to the extent that the other represents absolute exteriority with respect to an ego ('moi') defined by the condition of separation . . . The other absolves himself of any relation. This irrelation defines exteriority as such" (Ricoeur 1992, 188). Exteriority as denying analogical substances as in metaphor and intentional consciousness seems to Ricoeur to threaten "irrelation," the loss of relationship altogether. Ricoeur thus complains that Levinas, in his radical transcendence expressed as absence, void, and negation, allows "no middle ground, no 'between' secured to lessen the utter dissymmetry between the Same and the Other" (Ricoeur 1992, 338).

> To mediate the opening of the Same to the Other and the interiorization of the voice of the other in the same, language must have its resources of communication, i.e., reciprocity. Doesn't dialogue require superposing relation on "absolute distance" so-called between the separate me and teaching other?　　　　　　　　　　　　(Ricoeur 1992, 339)[10]

As Ricoeur writes in *The Rule of Metaphor,* loss of represented signified anchored in analogical ontology threatens loss of significance and discourse itself, a fall into relativism and willfulness: "When the reference to objects set

---

[10] Here Ricoeur and Levinas echo and reenact an old theological dispute, that between Aquinas and Maimonides, where Maimonides insists on an absolute non-analogy between the divine and creation and Aquinas insists on the mediation of analogical *via eminentiae* where, as Faessler notes, scholastic ontology affirms "the path of analogy where formal beings resemble supra-eminent divine Being" (Faessler 2012, 157).

over against a judging subject is suspended, is not the very structure of utterance shaken?" (Ricoeur 1987, Rule 306).

But Levinas, while refusing Ricoeur's "interiorization of the voice of the other in the same" still does not defeat relationship, such that enigmatic trace would be only a "sign of a remoteness" (Levinas 1987, 65). Instead, he redefines relationship as across absolute distinction – distance *and* relation, what he calls "unrelating relation" (Levinas 1969, 295). He thus rejects the submergence of transcendence into a "totality which gives it meaning." Yet he does not concede that "to refuse this primordial order of contemporaneousness" means "ceasing to signify" (Levinas 1987, 63). What emerges is a different mode of signification from that of representation, which Levinas sees ultimately as a mode of narcissism. Levinas insists: "the Other cannot also not appear without renouncing his radical alterity, without entering into an order" (Levinas 1987, 64). Neither through metaphor nor symbol, the other is not shown in any phenomenological sense: "The infinite is an inassimilable alterity, a difference and absolute past respect to everything that is shown, signaled, symbolized, announced, remembered, and thereby 'contemporized' with him who understands" (Levinas 1987, 71).

But how then is positive relation, signification itself possible? Levinas's radical shift from ontology to ethics moves from representation to response as address/response to otherness. The relation to the other is not one of cognition or correlation or participation but rather of ethical regard: the approach to the Other as "beyond cognition and disclosure in enigma is ethics" (Levinas 1987, 73). "Enigma is ethics," as response that "break[s] the undephasable simultaneity" of representation (Levinas 1987, 63). Enigma as unsaying initiates an "extravagant response," which "think[s] more than one thinks, to think of what withdraws from thought" (Levinas 1987, 72). Yet this is also a "summons to moral responsibility" precisely in failing to claim to encompass, grasp, or finalize analogy (Levinas 1987, 72). As "summons," enigma affirms relation; but as unsaying it "withdraws," thus sustaining difference, the transcendence which safeguards the other, so that "morality is the enigma's way" (Levinas 1987, 72).

Levinas's view of metaphor would thus be one in which, as in his ethics, the alterity of the other is never absorbed into the artwork as a self-sufficient representation. It would be to enact a "relationship with the infinite" that does not have the structure of "correlation," that breaks the "simultaneity of representation," pursuing instead an "approach" that "signifies itself without revealing itself," "that retracts, withdraws, fails to be grasped" (Levinas 1987, 72–73). Enigma projects poetry not as representation nor as formal closure, but instead as exposing and resisting any total account or comprehension. Enigma, like unsaying, ruptures the language event, and so safeguards its generativity. Insisting on areas that signifiers and those who signify them, the Said and Saying, cannot reach, that transcend human linguistic grasp and must not be claimed, it opens aesthetics towards ethics.

2 The Enigmatics of Marianne Moore

Levinas's enigma opens a different avenue into the analysis and experience of poetic texts than traditional metaphorics does. It is especially suitable to certain kinds of modernist and post-modernist writing, which also grapple with post-metaphysical challenges to what had been for centuries the governing rule of analogical being. As an example I will take Marianne Moore.

Moore's poetry is regularly described as ethical. Her ethical commitments can be felt through many of her characteristic poetic techniques: its practices of quiet attention to features otherwise often overlooked, such as her almost inaudible yet exquisite half- rhymes which respect even insignificant syllables and parts of speech, and her careful counting of inaudible metrical syllabic patterns, enact as form a respectful and grateful attention and appreciation of language and world. Her figure of the poet similarly proposes a self in abeyance, undramatized, whose craft configures myriad, often diminutive, details, as opposed to sublime visions. Often she echoes others' voices in direct and indirect citations, drawing on traditions that she also recasts. What emerges is an aesthetic of trace, of concealment/revelation, as an affirmation of mystery: a sense of further dimension, never fully commanded or completed, where the spiritual beckons to further meanings, as does the poetic. There is never totalized expression, but rather a procedure that recalls Levinasian notions of interruption and breach, through linguistic positing and retraction as enigma. I take Moore's "By Disposition of Angels" as an example:

> Messengers much like ourselves? Explain it.
> Steadfastness the darkness makes explicit?
> Something heard most clearly when not near it?
>   Above particularities,
> these unparticularities praise cannot violate.
>   One has seen in such steadiness never deflected,
>   how by darkness a star is perfected.

> Star that does not ask me if I see it?
> Fir that would not wish me to uproot it?
> Speech that does not ask me if I hear it?
>   Mysteries expound mysteries.
> Steadier than steady, star dazzling me, live and elate,
>   no need to say, how like some we have known; too like her,
>   too like him, and a-quiver forever.
>
>   (Moore 1994, 142)

This poem's careful craft is characteristically concealed, in oblique but pleasurably traceable formal disciplines. The rhyme scheme is irregular and partial: rhyming "it," "explicit," "near it," and "violate." "Particularities," in the fourth line of the first stanza, matches "Mysteries" (itself interesting), in the fourth line of the second stanza, as do the fifth lines of each stanza ("violate"/"elate"). Each stanza concludes with its own couplet ("deflected"/"perfected"; "her"/"forever"). Syllable counts match in Moore's own odd quantitative way: in each stanza, lines 1, 2, 3, and 7 have ten syllables, line 4 has eight syllables, and lines 5 and 6 have fourteen syllables.

As to text, Moore begins with the Hebrew meaning of angel as messenger, not only as sent from God to address humans, but as a messenger in an ordinary sense. In this sense, angels are like us. Yet the first line sets out to investigate the word "like." "Explain it" is an invitation, or imperative, to hermeneutics – which if undertaken through fusions of horizons, and mediating unities between distinctives – Moore's "particularities" – is something Levinas suspects. Moore's "like" is equally cautious and self-effacing, marking less a relation of similarity and continuity then of difference and distance. What seems to need explaining is just how "Messengers" are "much like ourselves," given the ineffaceable difference between the two. "Steadfastness," which demarks loyalty but not identity, is made in an oxymoron "explicit" by "darkness." "Explicit" here plays against its rhyming "Explain it," both as question and as suggesting emergence rather than explication, and in any case via "darkness"; as continued mystery and not complete illumination. Hearing is similarly most clear "when not near it," across distance.

This "not near" in fact inaugurates what will be in the text a pattern of negatives, always enacting distances and hence performing integrities of difference. Thus, if the messengers are "Above particularities," they gain specification only by retraction as "unparticularities," not by leaping into universals. Removed from language – "praise cannot violate" them – words move into distance as remote, unlike; yet always retaining their value, never negated into silence. "Darkness," here repeated, becomes a scene of emergence, while perfection itself is made ongoing and temporal in tense, as process: "how by darkness a star is perfected." To be remote and not completely penetrable is part of the star's radiance.

The second stanza pursues this remoteness. It affirms three expressions of "not" ("would not" and twice "does not"). One pertains to the world, as a limit on our power over it: "Fir that would not wish me to uproot it?" denies us the right to uproot what is given in the world. Here our inevitable personifying is interrupted by negation: the tree "would not wish" retracts, in its self-exposure and denial, the personification it offers. Immediately before and after that line, the stanza twice bids to "not ask me," first of the star, then of speech itself. This is not, however, to deny address, but to establish it: the speaker sees and hears without first asking. The initiative comes from outside. It can be thought of as an interlocutionary although not symmetrical "Saying," in Levinas's terms, from other to self. What follows is a series of phrases that do not claim likeness. The poem in fact offers little by way of analogy. "Steadier than steady" intensifies but does not compare. What there is "no need to say" is exactly "how like some we have known." Instead of knowledge in or as likeness, there is mystery, also intensified in grammatical iteration. If "Mysteries expound mysteries" this leads not to clarification, but rather opens toward further depths that are never fully fathomed. Light itself yields a darkness that, however, also elates, uplifts. "[S]tar dazzling me" recalls a persistent mystical trope of revelation, but which here is not unitive, but keeps the self in an accusative and distinct state. "[T]oo like her, / too like him" extends to both genders but also paradoxically confutes them: how can it be like both in their difference? Finally, "a-quiver forever" again verges on oxymoron, joining temporal quivering with eternity – or is it infinity in a Levinasian untotalized sense?

The title of this text – "By Disposition of Angels" – uncannily recalls Levinas's problematic of deposing, which he calls an ethical "positing of the self as a deposing of the ego" (Levinas 1998b, 58) although in the name of a "uniqueness" of each responsive, responsible self. Levinas asks: "is not the very opening of the dialogue already a way for the I to . . . deliver itself, a way for the I to place itself at the disposition of the You?" (Levinas 1998a, 150). In the poem, "disposition" points towards a paradoxical placing that also displaces grants and disposes. Moore's title points to but keeps apart. The angels as messengers remain between poles, displaced but at the disposal of those before whom they appear and disappear, like and unlike, never fully grasped within the integrations of analogy.

Bibliography

Blumenberg, Hans. *The Legitimacy of the Modern Age*. Cambridge: MIT Press, 1983.
Calin, Rodolphe. "La Metaphore absolue. Un faux depart vers l'autrement qu'etre." *Levinas: au-delà du visible. Études sur les inédits de Levinas des* Carnets de captivité *à* Totalité et Infini. Eds. Emmanuel Housset and Rodolphe Calin. *Cahiers de philosophie de l'Université de Caen* 49 (August 2012): 125–141.
Clark, Maudemarie. *Nietzsche on Truth and Philosophy*. New York: Cambridge University Press, 1990.
Cohen, Richard. "Levinas on Art and Aestheticism: Getting 'Reality and Its Shadow' Right." *Levinas Studies* 11 (2016): 149–194.
Cools, Arthur. "Trace and Resemblance in the Face of the Other: On the Problem of Metaphor in Levinas's Philosophy." *Metaphors in Modern and Contemporary Philosophy*. Eds. Arthur Cools, Walter Van Herck, and Koenraad Verrycke. Antwerp: University Press, 2013. 243–258.
Derrida, Jacques, *Positions*. Trans. Alan Bass. Chicago: University of Chicago Press, 1972.
Derrida, Jacques. *Of Grammatology*. Trans. Gayatri Spivak. Baltimore: The Johns Hopkins University Press, 1974.
Derrida, Jacques. "White Mythology: Metaphor in the Text of Philosophy." *Margins of Philosophy*. Trans. Alan Bass. Chicago: University of Chicago Press, 1982. 207–272.
Faessler, Marc. "Metaphor et Hauteur." *Lévinas: au-delà du visible. Études sur les inédits de Levinas des* Carnets de captivité *à* Totalité et Infini. Eds. Emmanuel Housset and Rodolphe Calin. *Cahiers de philosophie de l'Université de Caen* 49 (August 2012): 143–160.
Goodman, Nelson, and W. V. Quine. "Toward a Constructive Nominalism." *The Journal of Symbolic Logic* 12.4 (December 1947): 105–122.
Guibal, Francis. "En chemin vers le sens du langage." *Lévinas: au-delà du visible. Études sur les inédits de Levinas des* Carnets de captivité *à* Totalité et Infini. Eds. Emmanuel Housset and Rodolphe Calin. *Cahiers de philosophie de l'Université de Caen* 49 (August 2012): 161–178.
Levinas, Emmanuel. *Totality and Infinity*. Trans. Alphonso Lingis. Pittsburgh: Duquesne University Press, 1969.
Levinas, Emmanuel. *Collected Philosophical Papers*. Trans. Alphonso Lingis. Dordrecht: Martinus Nijhoff Publishers, 1987.
Levinas, Emmanuel. *Of God Who Comes to Mind*. Trans. Bettina Bergo. Stanford: Stanford University Press, 1998a.
Levinas, Emmanuel. *Otherwise than Being*. Trans. Alphonso Lingis. Pittsburgh: Duquesne University Press, 1998b.
Levinas, Emmanuel. *Parole et Silence, Oeuvres 2*. Eds. Rodolphe Calin and Catherine Chalier. Paris: Grasset, 2009.
Levinas, Emmanuel. *Notes on Metaphor*. Trans. Andrew Haas. *International Journal of Philosophical Studies* 20: 3 (2012): 331–347.
Moore, Marianne. *Complete Poems*. New York: Penguin Books, 1994.
Nietzsche, Friedrich. *Philosophy in the Tragic Age of the Greeks*. Trans. Marianne Cowan. Washington, D.C.: Regnery Publishing, 1962.

Nietzsche, Friedrich "The Dawn," *The Portable Nietzsche*. Trans. Walter Kaufmann. New York: The Viking Press, 1968. 73–75.

Nietzsche, Friedrich. *Friedrich Nietzsche on Rhetoric and Language*. Eds. Sander L. Gilman, Carole Blair, and David J. Parent. New York: Oxford University Press, 1989.

Ricoeur, Paul. *The Rule of Metaphor: Multi-Disciplinary Studies of the Creation of Meaning in Language*. Trans. Robert Czerny with Kathleen McLaughlin and John Costello. New York: Routledge, 1987.

Ricoeur, Paul. *Oneself as Another*. Trans. Kathleen Blamey. Chicago: University of Chicago Press, 1992.

Rorty, Richard. *Objectivity, Relativism, and Truth: Philosophical Papers, Vol. 1*. New York: Cambridge University Press, 1991.

Wolosky, Shira. "Two Types of Negative Theology." *Negative Theology as Jewish Modernity*. Ed. Michael Fagenblat. Bloomington: Indiana University Press, 2017. 161–179.

Wolosky, Shira. "Religion and Literature." *Palgrave Macmillan Handbook on Philosophy and Religion*. Ed. Barry Stocker, New York: Palgrave Macmillan, 2018. 645–664.

Ashraf Noor
Apparition: Aesthetics of Disproportion in Levinas and Adorno

In memory of Werner Hamacher

1 The Question of Apparition

Levinas and Adorno explore the question of apparition as the mode of being of the work of art, Levinas approaching the question as an intrinsic problem, Adorno considering it in addition with explicit reference to Benjamin. In reflections on Max Picard, Levinas writes that encountering what is "an *apparition*, but *strangely real*" is "perhaps the very definition of a poetic experience."[1] Adorno determines in his *Ästhetische Theorie*: "Not the least of the difficulties of art today is that it is ashamed of apparition without being able to divest itself of it. Having become transparent to itself in its constitutive appearing, considering this appearance in its transparency as untrue, art gnaws at its own possibility, no longer being, in Hegel's language, substantial."[2] The disruptive force that can emerge in apparition is elicited by Levinas and Adorno from these forms of tension. In the manner in which they work through the central theme "apparition", the lineaments and the limits of the critical affiliation in their thought with respect to art can be discerned. Levinas's use of the term is intimately linked to the phenomenological exploration of the problem of the phenomenon. Adorno is both cognisant of this context and responsive to Benjamin's discussion of the phenomenon and appearance in his *Ursprung des deutschen Trauerspiels*, "Goethes Wahlverwandtschaften", and other writings.

Both Levinas and Adorno emphasise the need for the philosophical accompaniment to the work of art. In one of the "Paralipomena" to his *Ästhetische*

---

[1] "[. . .] une *apparition*, mais *étrangement réelle*. C'est là peut-être la définition même d'une expérience poétique." (Levinas 1976, 111). The article "Max Picard et le visage" is based on a lecture Levinas gave in 1966.
[2] "Unter den Schwierigkeiten von Kunst heute ist nicht die letzte, daß sie der apparition sich schämt, ohne sie doch abwerfen zu können; sich selbst durchsichtig geworden bis in den konstitutiven Schein, der ihr in seiner Durchsichtigkeit unwahr dünkt, nagt sie an ihrer Möglichkeit, nicht länger, nach Hegels Sprache, substantiell." (Adorno 1990, 127).

Theorie, Adorno writes "Every work of art needs, in order to be experienced fully, thought and thus philosophy, which is thought that does not allow itself to be reined in."[3] Levinas refers to this thought in his article "La réalité et son ombre" of 1948, as "critique". He carries out a rapprochement between the critical enterprise and philosophy in his article "Intentionalité et métaphysique" of 1959, where he connects the evocation of non-objectifying intentionality in Blanchot's critical writings with its use in contemporary philosophy of art. He writes of this aspect of Blanchot: "literature is not the approach towards ideal Beauty, not one of the ornaments of our life, not the witness to an epoch, not the translation of its economic conflicts, but the ultimate relation with being in an anticipation, almost impossible, of what is no longer being".[4] It is this opening of literature to that which is "no longer being" that Levinas interprets in his own thought, particularly in his later work, as the site of the oscillation to which he refers as "clignotement". In this blinking between being and that which goes beyond it, "the ontological proposition remains open to a certain reduction, disposed to unsay itself and to mean in a completely different way."[5] This "completely different" meaning is opened for Levinas in the relation to the other that enacts the radical unsettling of ontology.

Critique for Levinas elicits the trace of that which coagulates into the Said, into the work frozen in time, but which is beyond the being of the coagulated. In following the trace by means of non-objectifying thought, as he underlines in his endorsement of Blanchot's critical writing, the resulting discourse nevertheless remains open to a community of actual or potential interlocutors. For Adorno, critique is "necessary for works of art";[6] it deciphers the spirit constituting the process in which the tensions of the work's elements become manifest, and it goes beyond the aesthetic configuration to the spirit, *Geist*, which is its truth-content. The moment of apparition is the rupture of the objective form that cannot contain the spirit. Both for Levinas and for Adorno the work of art as apparition is a tension that points beyond itself. Levinas uses critique to

---

3 "Jedes Kunstwerk bedarf, um ganz erfahren werden zu können, des Gedankens und damit der Philosophie, die nichts anderes ist, als der Gedanke, der sich nicht abbremsen läßt." *Ibid.*, p. 392.
4 "[. . .] la littérature n'est ni l'approche du Beau idéal, ni l'un des ornements de notre vie, ni le témoignage de l'époque, ni la traduction de ses conflits économiques, mais la relation ultime avec l'être dans une anticipation, quasiment impossible, de ce qui n'est plus l'être [. . .]." (Levinas 2010, 199).
5 "[. . .] la proposition ontologique reste ouverte à une certaine réduction, disposée à se dédire et à se vouloir tout autrement dite." (Levinas 1986),. The article "Façon de parler" was first published in 1980.
6 "Darum ist Kritik den Werken notwendig." (Adorno 1990, 137).

show that the phenomenon of the work of art is an enigma. Adorno determines that manifestation is in itself a negation: "If the spirit of works of art shines forth in their sensuous appearance, it shines forth only as their negation, in union with the phenomenon and at the same time its Other. The spirit of works of art adheres to its form, but it is only spirit if it points beyond it."[7] Both the enigma and the negation are movements that put the being coagulated in the work of art into question.

2 Levinas: Disproportion, Ethics, and the Work of Art

For both Levinas and Adorno, apparition is an event that contains a paradoxical movement of presentation and dissolution, a tension within appearance itself. In apparition, the phenomenon is turned against itself in the non-coincidence to which Levinas refers as "anachronism". This is the "pure passage" of the other as "trace". The manner in which the trace disturbs the phenomenon as its interruption, the disruption of the phenomenon by that which cannot appear, is explored by Levinas under the title of the "enigma". His examination of the irruption of "expression" in the phenomenon, interrupting its "indiscreet and victorious appearance",[8] is part of his exposition of the "face", the proximity in which the other is approached. This is the context in which, for example, he considers poetry in his discussion of Agnon's writing. Levinas sets up a parallel to the relation between the phenomenon and relation in general. He determines the following: "It belongs to the essence of art to signify between the lines – in the intervals of time – between time – like a trace that would be anterior to the step or like an echo that would precede the repercussion of a voice."[9] Levinas proposes a complement to this "anachronism" of a signifying whose meaning is always before, this

---

7 "Leuchtet der Geist der Kunstwerke in ihrer sinnlichen Erscheinung auf, so leuchtet er nur als ihre Negation, in der Einheit mit dem Phänomen zugleich dessen Anderes. Der Geist der Kunstwerke haftet an ihrer Gestalt, ist aber Geist nur, insofern er darüber hinausweist." *Ibid.*
8 "l'apparoir indiscret et victorieux". (Levinas 1990, 291). The article "Enigme et phénomène" was first published in 1965.
9 "Il appartient à l'essence de l'art de signifier entre les lignes – dans les intervalles du temps – entre temps – comme une trace qui serait antérieure à la marche ou comme un écho qui précéderait le retentissement d'une voix." (Levinas 1976, 12). The article "Poésie et resurrection" was first published in 1973.

side of the thematic object of a sign, of an indication. The complement is exegesis. Already in his article "Réalité et son ombre" Levinas had determined critique as the activity that returns the representation of reality frozen in an image – the idolatrous doubling that binds sensation in a rhythm constituting an ontological dimension of its own – to discourse open to the community with others. The perspective of the relation to the other in the philosophy of art is the final, named but as yet unexplored dimension of the exegesis envisioned in this early text. Here he writes that "being could not be said in its reality, that is in its time"[10] without this widened perspective. The analysis in Levinas's text *Le temps et l'autre*, consisting of lectures of 1946/7, underlies this position of the saying of being, reality, and time depending on the other, and it is here that he takes the further step indicated in "Réalité et son ombre". In these lectures, as elsewhere in his work, for example in *De l'existence à l'existant*, he returns repeatedly to Shakespeare, writing that "it sometimes seems to me that all philosophy is nothing but a meditation of Shakespeare"[11] and citing *Macbeth* and *Hamlet* to show respectively the *hypostase* of liberty in the present moment and the impossibility of assuming death into a present. Levinas states that *Hamlet* is a "lengthy testimony"[12] to the latter theme. He invokes these literary works as part of his development of this theme to the thought on sexuality and paternity with which his lectures approach alterity and sociality. The perspective of the relation to the other as testified by literature is central to his meditation on Agnon of 1973, where he takes up his earlier critique of the image and his earlier concern about the responsibility he sees abrogated in aesthetic transport – now, however, in the context of responding to an alterity "wholly other than being"[13] by means of non-objectifying thought.

At the end of his article "La poésie et l'impossible" of 1969, one of his several discussions of Paul Claudel's writing, Levinas poses a series of questions that mark the coordinates of his own thought on literature. He asks whether politics constitutes the ultimate horizon of being and the guide of action. Stating that there is a "poetic vision" that transcends politics, he asks whether poetry is condemned to being "belles lettres" and to "perpetuating fantasms". Finally, he asks whether "contrary to this" it is not "the very definition of

---

10 "perspective [. . .] sans laquelle l'être ne saurait être dit dans sa réalité, c'est à dire dans son temps". (Levinas 1994, 148).
11 "[. . .] il me semble parfois que toute la philosophie n'est qu'une méditation de Shakespeare." (Levinas 1983, 60).
12 "un long témoignage", *Ibid.*, 61.
13 "tout autre que l'être". Emmanuel Levinas, "Poésie et résurrection", 14.

poetry" to be what "makes language possible".[14] As the very possibility of language, as a Saying that demands exegesis, poetry signals the "[i]mpossibility of remaining silent"[15] that is the responsibility of those who have survived the historical event that cast the Jews "into the most profound depths of the abyss into which all humanity was thrown between 1939 and 1945".[16] Levinas's thought on art addresses an enigma. On the one hand, as in the articles that compose the volume *Difficile Liberté*, where Judaism is explored in multiple ways as "the substitution of the letter for the soil",[17] he emphasises the commitment this entails to "creating a type of man who lives in a demystified world, freed from enchantment".[18] This position militates against art, both as the pagan rootedness in the earth that Levinas invariably links to Heidegger and in the versions of petrification, of role-fulfilment, of figure that, for example, he identifies in Claudel's Christian images of sacred history and that he contrasts with the liberty of the human as person.[19] The terms in which he invokes lucidity as against the intoxication of chthonic or religious rapture pertain in this perspective equally to art. This is the sense in which Levinas writes in *Totalité et infini*[20] of the manner in which the "poetic activity", though – as he previously also underlined in his article "La réalité et son ombre" – "conscious", becomes transformed, suffused by rhythm, the artist being transported by the work or becoming the work itself in the Dionysian fashion evoked by Nietzsche. Here, in *Totalité et infini*, Levinas addresses the "rhythm that enraptures and abducts the interlocutors" and to this he opposes "prose" as the "discourse" that "is rupture and commencement". In contrast to the "enchantment by the rhythm" that "envelops" and "cradles" the activity in question, Levinas emphasises the prosaic disruptive interruption of such enrapturing distortion that imposes a

---

14 "Mais la politique constitue-t-elle la trame ultime de l'être et le guide unique de l'action? La vision poétique qui la transcende est-elle à jamais vouée à demeurer 'belles lettres' et à perpétuer les fantasmes? N'est-elle pas au contraire – et c'est probablement la définition même de la poésie – ce qui rend le langage possible?" (Levinas 1976, 204). 204.
15 "Impossible de se taire. Obligation de parler." *Ibid.*
16 "au plus profond de l'abîme où, entre 1939 et 1945, fut jetée l'humanité." *Ibid.*, 200.
17 "la substitution de la lettre au sol". (Levinas 1976, 211). The article "Simone Weil contre la Bible" was first published in 1952.
18 "créer un type d'homme qui vit dans un univers démystifié, désensorcelé". (Levinas 1976, 90). The text "L'arche et la momie" was presented at a round table discussion broadcast on radio in 1958.
19 See "Personnes ou figures (À propos d'"Emmaüs' de Paul Claudel)", *Ibid.*, p. 185. The article was first published in 1950.
20 "rythme qui ravit et enlève les interlocuteurs"; "charme du rythme"; "envelopper"; "bercer". (Levinas 1980, 221).

role on the poetic "initiative". The freedom at issue, defended against the manner in which "influences surge forth unbeknownst to us",[21] is formulated in this passage in *Totalité et infini* in a manner that clearly echoes Levinas's critique of Claudel, where he wrote more than twenty years earlier: "We distrust the poetry that already rhythmically imbues and puts a spell on our gestures, all that which, in lucid life, is at play in spite of us."[22]

Already in one of Levinas's early articles, however, in "De l'évasion", published in 1935, he presents another possibility, which opposes the aspect of appearance that seduces the producers and the recipients of, the participants in, the work of art. Here, he examines the theme of escape from oneself, the need to "*break the most radical, the most indispensible chain there is, the fact that the ego is itself*".[23] This theme, which, he states, is prevalent in contemporary literature, opens onto fundamental philosophical questions, above all that of being as being. Levinas designates with the term of "excendance" the need experienced by the human being to escape imprisonment in being, to be extricated from being fused to oneself. He examines in this context the feelings of shame and nausea, both of which force the self into being itself while wanting to escape itself. Levinas writes here of the nudity to which the self is reduced, a nudity that is "*the very experience of pure being*".[24] In situating the human being in this experience, Levinas writes of shame that it is "one and the same as nausea".[25] Here, he determines the importance of Céline's work *Voyage au bout de la nuit*. Sartre, with whose novel *La nausée* Levinas's essay shares central themes, was to preface his text precisely with a quote from Céline's *Voyage*. Levinas writes "What is of great interest in *Voyage au bout de la nuit* by Céline is to have divested the universe, in a sad and desperate cynicism, thanks to a marvellous art of language."[26] Here, the enigma of art is brought to the fore. Céline's language is "marvellous" but in such a way that it breaks through the

---

21 "où des influences surgissent, à notre insu". *Ibid.*, 222.
22 "Nous nous méfions de la poésie qui déjà scande et ensorcelle nos gestes, de tout ce qui, dans notre vie lucide, se joue malgré nous." "Personnes ou figures", 188.
23 "le besoin de sortir de soi-même, c'est à dire *de briser l'enchaînement le plus radical, le plus irrémissible, le fait que le moi est soi-même*." (Levinas 1982, 98).
24 "*l'expérience même de l'être pur*", *Ibid.*, 116.
25 "Le phénomène de la honte de soi devant soi [. . .] ne fait qu'un avec la nausée." *Ibid.*, 117.
26 "C'est le grand intérêt du *Voyage au bout de la nuit* de Céline que d'avoir, grâce à un art merveilleux du langage, dévêtu l'univers, dans un cynisme triste et désespéré." *Ibid.*, 112. In his article "Langage quotidien et rhétorique sans éloquence" of 1981, Levinas discusses Céline in the context of "anti-literature" and of "anti-humanism", stating that his work was "perhaps a signal" (peut-être [. . .] le signal") of the former and that this "anti-literature" was a reason for the latter. (Levinas 1987, 190).

vestments with which the nudity of being is concealed. It is noteworthy that Levinas underlines this function of Céline's writing in the *Voyage*, in which "sad and desperate cynicism" serves to reveal the harsh and sordid reality of war, colonialism, urban poverty, and human relations in general, where the figures representing the good are unlikely beacons of hope both acknowledged as such and invariably betrayed by the narrating figure. The good is given unconditionally, however incapable the recipient is of responding adequately to it. The novel is enigmatic because the narrating figure both breaks through the images governing social reality and the self while himself succumbing to his own distorting abrogation of responsibility. In one of the most powerful episodes, the narrator, a doctor in an impoverished quarter of Paris, leaves a young woman, who is bleeding to death as the result of a backstreet abortion, to the mercy of her parents, who in their egotistical moral hypocrisy refuse to call for an ambulance because they are only interested in saving face with respect to their neighbours. The historical circumstances of the *Voyage* differ – notoriously – from those of Céline's later writing. While the style of *Nord*, for example, is still that of "sad and desperate cynicism" and there is still a ductus of unveiling, the narrator is a self-proclaimed "collabo" on the run and the milieu described is that of other collaborators and proponents of National Socialism facing the end of the regime they had celebrated and supported. The self-understanding of the narrator as collaborator is thematised in a dialogue that prefaces one of the chapters, where an unidentified voice asks him, whether he indeed calls himself a narrator, and when he affirms that he does, he is asked whether he does not feel shame in doing so. It is left open whether this shame should be felt by the instance that claims to frame a narrative as such, i.e. that claims a narrative is at all possible when facing contemporary reality, or rather one concerning the specific events involving the narrator and his fellow collaborators. The evaluation of the extent to which the narrator's tone of aggrieved self-pity should be regarded as part of the stripping away of concealing vestments or rather as further concealment using the style and language of such an unveiling is central here. In the terms of "De l'évasion" only the former would be acceptable. These terms are confirmed in the sustained reflection on the role of literature and of art in general with regard to its representation of reality found in Levinas's article "La réalité et son ombre".[27]

---

[27] The importance of this text for Levinas's thought has been underlined by commentators such as Hent de Vries, in a chapter on Levinas and art added to the new, English language edition of his book *Theologie im pianissimo: Zur Aktualität der Denkfiguren Adornos und Levinas'* (1989), *Minimal Theologies. Critiques of Secular Reason in Adorno and Levinas* (de Vries 2005), Fabio Ciaramelli, in his article "L'appel infini à l'interprétation. Remarques sur

The question of the relation of philosophy to literature in Levinas's work often emerges from passages such as the following sequence of thoughts in the text "Signature", with which *Difficile Liberté* ends. Levinas delineates here the way in which the experience of the other is "expérience par excellence". His preface to *Totalité et infini* of 1961 had already indicated with this expression that the conception of the experience involved in his thought on alterity is problematic since there could be no experience, at least no "objective experience", of the infinite, of that which is always exteriority. This means, he stated, that one should speak of "the relation to the infinite in other terms than those of objective experience."[28] The expression "expérience par excellence" is employed by Levinas to designate this other experience, the experience of the other. In his article "La trace de l'Autre" of 1963, Levinas explores the theme of "the heteronomous experience"[29] as a "movement without return", one "*of the Same towards the Other that never returns to the Same.*"[30] Since the status of experience *qua* experience is always in question,[31] the terms in which Levinas refers to it are accompanied by a displacing of the objectifying tendency that, according to his claim, characterises occidental philosophy. This displacing is active in Levinas's critique of the general application of Husserlian intentionality in its noetic-noematic structure, of the, in his view, cognitive structure of Heideggerian fundamental ontology, and indeed of Buber's conception of the

---

Levinas et l'art" (Ciaramelli 1994), and Jacques Colleony in his article "Levinas et l'art: La réalité et son ombre" (Colleony 1991).

28 "[. . .] il faudra dire la relation avec l'infini en d'autres termes qu'en termes d'expérience objective. Mais si expérience signifie précisément relation avec l'absolument autre – c'est-à-dire avec ce qui toujours déborde la pensée – la relation avec l'infini accomplit l'expérience par excellence." (Levinas 1980, XIII).

29 "l'expérience hétéronome". (Levinas 2010, 266). The article was first published in 1963.

30 "*un mouvement du Même vers l'Autre qui ne retourne jamais au Même.*" Ibid., 266–267.

31 It is in question to such an extent that Levinas writes in "Éthique et l'esprit", an article published in 1952, "the vision of the face is not an *experience*, but an exit from oneself" ("la vision du visage n'est pas une *expérience*, mais une sortie de soi"). (Levinas 1976, 26). In this text, Levinas formulates the thought on the impossibility of murder that later constitutes one of the most challenging passages in *Totalité et infini*. Murder is impossible, he states. Yet, he continues, "In reality murder is possible. But it is possible when one has not looked the other in the face. The impossibility of killing is not real, it is moral." ("[. . .] en réalité, le meutre est possible. Mais il est possible quand on n'a pas regardé autrui en face. L'impossibilité de tuer n'est pas réelle, elle est morale." *Ibid.*, 26. This is why he writes that "the vision of the face is not an *experience*" for what he will later emphatically characterise as going beyond ontology is at stake. The question of disproportion and its implications for ontology is already present at this point of Levinas's thought.

experience of alterity. The steps Levinas takes in "Signature" proceed via determinations of disproportion. Just as the idea of infinity Descartes introduced in the third *Méditation* "overflows", *déborde*, the thought presented in the Cartesian theory of the mind, "the Other is out of proportion to the power and the freedom of the Ego".[32] The characterisation of disproportion Levinas undertakes connects this determination to ethics: "The disproportion between the Other and the Ego is precisely ethical consciousness."[33] The next two steps that he takes distinguish "ethical consciousness" first from an "experience of values" and second from a "modality of psychological consciousness". He contrasts ethical consciousness with the first as "an access to external being" and with the second "the condition and, first of all, even inversion" of such a psychological consciousness. To experience the Other means "that the freedom that lives by consciousness inhibits itself in front of the Other".[34] Both are forms of exteriority. The Other is, Levinas underlines, "external being par excellence".[35] This external being calls the force, the spontaneity of the Ego into question. The Other as the face is the calling into question of the joyous force of this spontaneity. Levinas's final move here is to cite two passages from literature, the first from Tolstoy's *War and Peace* and the second from Pushkin's *Boris Godounov*, which embody this experience of the face, the experience par excellence.

Levinas's elucidation of this experience, which is "fundamental", he states, because it is supposed by objective experience, takes place both in discursive concepts, of which *Totalité et infini* is the systematic presentation, and with reference to literature. The question is whether the literature that Levinas cites here and elsewhere, for example in his adducing of Sonia Marmeladova's "insatiable compassion" for Raskolnikov in Dostoyevsky's *Crime and Punishment*,[36] is a mere illustration of what he otherwise expounds using discursive, conceptual means or whether the "disproportion" invoked above can be experienced on literature's own terms.

---

32 "[. . .] Autrui est hors proportion avec le pouvoir et la liberté du Moi." (Levinas 1976, 437).
33 "La disproportion entre Autrui et le Moi – est précisement la conscience morale." *Ibid.*
34 "[. . .] la liberté qui vit par la conscience s'inhibe devant Autrui." *Ibid.*
35 " l'être extérieur par excellence". *Ibid.*
36 "Désir d'Autrui". Levinas, "La trace de l'Autre", 270.

3 Adorno: Aesthetic Immanence and the Configuration of Transcendence

In Adorno's inaugural lecture at the University of Frankfurt, "Die Aktualität der Philosophie" of 1931, the terms in which he develops the guiding idea of "interpretation", *Deutung*, pertain to the movement from the theoretical to the practical attitude towards the world. Adorno invokes the idea of dialectics here, which, he underlines, is the necessary condition for philosophical *Deutung*. He states in lapidary fashion: "The interpretation of the reality that obtains and its suspension are in a mutual relation. Reality is not, however, suspended in the concept; but from the construction of the figure of reality follows promptly the demand for real change to it."[37] The acquaintance with reality does not "remain within the closed space of knowledge"[38] but is "imparted", *erteilt*, by "Praxis". This is the trajectory from Adorno's initial determination that there is an "essential connection"[39] between "interpretative philosophy" and materialism. Adorno's conception of philosophy as he outlines it in his exposition of the idea of *Deutung* is opposed to the claim of idealism that "reality is founded in the ratio" and that tracing back to the primary axioms of autonomous rational laws would enable the rational architectonic of being to be established. In contrast to this, philosophy has to respond to the "irruption of the irreducible".[40] Being breaks through the autonomous rational imposition of laws. It interrupts the movement back to first principles and forces thought to confront the concrete historical moment. Adorno conceives a dialectical philosophy here that responds to the "force of reality" in the form of the essay. His delineation of this philosophy develops the position he maintained in his critique of Kierkegaard's aesthetics in his work *Kierkegaard. Konstruktion des Ästhetischen* of 1933, the published version of his *Habilitationsschrift* of 1931. In contrast to Kierkegaard's claim that abstracting from what is historically specific and attaining what is temporally invariant constitutes the immortality of the most distinguished works of art, Adorno emphasises precisely the historically particular. He writes: "Works of art do not obey the force of the generality of ideas. Their centre is the

---

37 "Die Deutung der vorgefundenen Wirklichkeit und ihre Aufhebung sind aufeinander bezogen. Nicht zwar wird im Begriff die Wirklichkeit aufgehoben; aber aus der Konstruktion der Figur des Wirklichen folge allemal prompt die Forderung nach ihrer realen Veränderung." (Adorno 1969, 338).
38 "im geschlossenen Raum von Erkenntnis". *Ibid.*
39 "wesentliche[r] Zusammenhang"; "deutende[. . .] Philosophie". *Ibid.*
40 "Einbruch des Irreduziblen". *Ibid.*, 343.

temporal and the particular, to which they orientate themselves as its figure; whatever they mean beyond this, they mean solely in the figure."[41]

This position is developed in its linguistic, logical, and ontological ramifications in Adorno's *Ästhetische Theorie*. He connects Benjamin's thoughts on the "intensive direction of expression into the core of innermost muteness"[42] with the final section of Wittgenstein's *Tractatus* and delineates the dialectical structure that determines the relation of the particular and the general in the work of art. This latter is closest to the universal, he underlines, the closer it comes to language. The mimetic dimension of the work of art is that aspect in which it is similar to language. However, the work gains its "general loquacity"[43] in its specificity, the further away it is from the general. The work of art both says and does not say the general. This paradox lies in the fact that "being opaque and specific, the mimetic instance through which it says it at the same time opposes the saying".[44]

In Adorno's address "Die Aktualität der Philosophie", he delineates a kind of thinking that responds to the collapse of what philosophy had hitherto assumed, i.e. "that it is possible to grasp the totality of reality through the power of thought".[45] This assumption, he states, is revealed as illusory, at worst deceptive ideology, by a reality whose "order and form"[46] defeat any "claim of reason"[47] to encompass it. In terms whose proximity to Benjamin, to whom Adorno planned to dedicate the published version of the address, is not fortuitous, Adorno points to the "traces and ruins", which are the only aspects of this reality in which "it permits the hope that it will at some time become right and just".[48] Adorno begins his address by pointing to a kind of thought that seeks out and follows these "traces and ruins" and ends his exposition of this idea of philosophy by characterising its power to "explode the measures of the mere

---

41 "Kunstwerke gehorchen nicht der Macht der Allgemeinheit von Ideen. Ihr Zentrum ist das Zeitliche und Besondere, auf welches hin sie als dessen Figur sich ausrichten; was sie mehr bedeuten, bedeuten sie einzig in der Figur." (Adorno 1979, 34).
42 "die intensive Richtung der Worte in den Kern des innersten Verstummens hinein". (Benjamin 1966, 126–127), quoted in Adorno 1990, 305.
43 "beredt allgemein". *Ibid.*
44 "[. . .] daß jenes Mimetische, durch welches sie es sagt, als Opakes und Besonderes dem Sagen zugleich opponiert." *Ibid.*
45 "[. . .] daß es möglich sei, in Kraft des Denkens die Totalität des Wirklichen zu ergreifen." (Adorno 1969, 325).
46 "Ordnung und Gestalt". *Ibid.*
47 "Anspruch der Vernunft". *Ibid.*
48 " [. . .] sie nur in Spuren und Trümmern die Hoffnung gewährt, einmal zur richtigen und gerechten Wirklichkeit zu werden." *Ibid.*

existent". In both cases, at the beginning and at the end, the thought he espouses is set against philosophy's previous claim to totality, be it that of German Idealism or of Heidegger's phenomenological fundamental ontology, Adorno's initial account of the presumption of Idealism with regard to reality being developed into a parallel critique of the presumption of fundamental ontology with respect to Being. This is responsible for the terms in which he formulates his final characterisation of the thought he has in view in contrast to such presumption: "For spirit is indeed not capable of producing or grasping the totality of reality; but it is capable of penetrating in miniature, to explode in miniature the dimensions of the merely existent."[49] The thought Adorno conceives here is concerned with the concrete. That which he denominates as "interpretation", *Deutung*, is contrasted with research, *Forschung*, which is what the individual empirical sciences undertake. The former bears, he determines, an affinity to materialism, the "kind of thought" that "most rigorously rejects the idea that reality is intentional or significant".[50] The thought Adorno calls *Deutung* is faced with the fact that the symbolic constructs of philosophy have lost their power to give meaning to the world. He regards this thought as having an affinity to materialism inasmuch as it distances itself from the "'meaning' of its objects"[51] and no longer itself refers to "implicit [. . .] meaning",[52] an example of which, he states, would be that of religion. The emphasis on the concrete is related intimately to this. Since the "symbolic function",[53] in which the particular represented the general in Idealism, has collapsed, any reference to totality is no longer to be found in symbolic representation of the "total question",[54] but "in a concrete diagnosis of an individual case".[55]

Adorno characterises the work of art in an early version of the Introduction to his posthumously published work *Ästhetische Theorie* as the "crystallisation" of a "process" and contrasts this with its attributes as an existent, *Seiendes*. This determination forms a central aspect of his delineation of the role of the work of art in negating the regnant state of the world. It is in this negation, he maintains, that the work of art constitutes itself as spirit, *Geist*. This

---

49 "Denn wohl vermag der Geist es nicht, die Totalität des Wirklichen zu erzeugen oder zu begreifen; aber er vermag es, im kleinen einzudringen, im kleinen die Maße des bloß Seienden zu sprengen. *Ibid.*, 344.
50 "[. . .] Art von Denken [. . .], die die Vorstellung des Intentionalen, des Bedeutenden von der Wirklichkeit am strengsten abwehrt". *Ibid.*, 336.
51 "'Sinn' seiner Gegenstände". *Ibid.*
52 "impliziten [. . .] Sinn". *Ibid.*
53 "symbolische Funktion". *Ibid.*
54 "totale Frage". *Ibid.*
55 "in einem konkreten Befund". *Ibid.*

constitution is dialectical construction, Adorno writes, "inasmuch as" spirit informs it. The character of the work of art as process manifests itself here: "Works of art, as much as they appear to be existents, are crystallisations of the process between that spirit and its other."[56] In the later Introduction to the last version of the *Ästhetische Theorie*, he emphasises the task of "interpretation", *Deutung*, with respect to art as an activity that follows the latter's movement in its relation to its other: "Art can only be interpreted in the law of its movement, not through invariants. It determines itself in relation to what it is not."[57] Adorno emphasises the contrast between this characteristic and the central contention of Hegel's aesthetics, i.e. the positing of the exteriorisation of the spirit as at the same time the recognition of its identity with this exteriorised other. For Hegel, the movement of self-alienation and self-recognition as identity takes place within the totality of spirit. In contrast to this, Adorno reveals the rupture that the dissolution of this "Generalthesis" – as he puts it, using the term from Husserl's seminal inauguration of transcendental phenomenology, the *Ideen* of 1913 – implies for the work of art. If spirit can no longer be seen as reincorporating its self-alienation as exteriority into a totality, it constitutes only a part of the work of art and is inextricably related to the other as the "historically and socially preformed" materials and procedures that the work of art bears within itself as the heterogeneous moments that resist unity. The tension between this resistance and the striving for unity is what is manifested as dissonance. Adorno underlines the unstoppable, *unaufhaltbare*, movement in the history of art that has come to make dissonance its centre. His following determination is crucial. In this dissonance he sees a participation in suffering. In the unity of the process at work in art, he discerns the attempt of suffering to be expressed in language. The terms he employs here are graphic: "to feel its way to language".[58] Dissonance and suffering are linked in expression.

In Adorno's determination that "expression can hardly be imagined as anything other than that of suffering", which in the immanence of the work of art "resists immanence under the law of form",[59] making expression into "the

---

56 "Die Kunstwerke sind, mögen sie noch so sehr ein Seiendes scheinen, Kristallisationen des Prozesses zwischen jenem Geist und seinem Anderen." (Adorno 1990, 512).
57 "Deutbar ist Kunst nur an ihrem Bewegungsgesetz, nicht durch Invarianten. Sie bestimmt sich im Verhältnis zu dem, was sie nicht ist." *Ibid.*, 12.
58 "zur Sprache tastet". *Ibid.*, 512.
59 "Läßt Ausdruck kaum anders sich vorstellen denn als der von Leiden [. . .], so hat Kunst am Ausdruck immanent das Moment, durch welches sie, als eines ihrer Konstituentien, gegen ihre Immanenz unterm Formgesetz sich wehrt." *Ibid.*, 168–169.

lamenting face of works",[60] porous in their dissonances to alterity, there is a proximity to Levinas's thought. In the section "Visage et éthique" in *Totalité et infini*, Levinas explicates the idea of expression as the revelation of infinity in the face of the other. In sub-section 2, Levinas follows the question of the disproportion between infinity and the capacity of the subject to the point at which he exposes infinity as "the original *expression*".[61] For Levinas, the question of apparition is intimately linked to the question of being. This is, in turn, inextricably connected to the theoretical attitude, which he views as predominant in occidental philosophy. The point at which Levinas's own trajectory begins concerns the question of whether all meaning is restricted to this relation. He puts this succinctly in his lecture-series "Dieu et l'onto-théologie" of 1975/76, where he writes: "One can ask oneself, however, whether the manifestation where all signification has the form of an ontological event exhausts the meaning of the signification, whether everything is exhausted by this form."[62] In this late adumbration of Levinas's thought, where he seeks to "inscribe a dis-quiet",[63] to think language as a questioning of the priority of ontology, as the question of whether all meaning derives from being, apparition is firmly situated at the point at which being "makes itself into presence in a consciousness"[64] and thereby affirms itself.

Levinas characterises the primary focus of occidental philosophy repeatedly as "the apparition of a given content"[65] represented in the signification of the Said and communicated to others as such. The sense of signification, he determines, is "a way of representing being in the absence of being".[66] Apparition of a given fulfils signification. The task Levinas sets himself is to seek a signification that does not achieve its end in ontology. This he finds in the responsibility for the other, which he explicates in his later thought in a series of ever more emphatic locutions for the "nudity" this involves for the subject exposed to the other. This hyperbolic intensification results in passages such as the following, the language of which borders on provocation: "In this responsibility,

---

60 "Ausdruck ist das klagende Gesicht der Werke." *Ibid.*, 170.
61 "Cet infini, plus fort que le meutre, nous résiste déjà dans son visage, est son visage, est l'*expression* originelle, est le premier mot: 'tu ne commettras pas de meutre'." (Levinas 1980, 173).
62 "Mais on peut se demander si la manifestation où toute signification a la forme d'un événement ontologique épuise la signifiance de la signification, si tout est épuisé par cette forme." (Levinas 1993, 187).
63 "inscrire une in-quiétude". *Ibid.*, 148.
64 "se faire présence dans une conscience". *Ibid.*, 147.
65 "l'apparition du donné". *Ibid.*, 180.
66 "un mode de représentation de l'être en l'absence de l'être". *Ibid.*

the ego does not pose itself but loses its place, deports itself or finds itself deported. The substitution for the other is like the trace of exile and of deportation."[67] The Saying in which this takes place is the signification prior to that which appertains to the synchronisation in which the synthetic gathering of the temporal manifold is effected in transcendental apperception, in Kant's terms, or as the subjective pole of identification in the intentional relation to an object, in Husserl's terms. For Levinas, the Saying that is prior to the Said is, in contrast to what he understands as Kant and Husserl, diachronic. He determines that this Saying is to bear witness to Infinity, which cannot appear. In witnessing, he writes: "Infinity reveals itself without appearing, without *showing* itself as Infinity."[68] The disproportion between the way this witnessing relates to infinity, which Levinas names glory, *gloire*, is pre-temporal and pre-semantic. In the non-coincidence of the terms of the relation with the other, temporality that cannot be reduced to simultaneity and meaning that cannot be reduced to the concept are at play.

Expression and its role in opening up a passage to the other in a language prior to the language frozen in concepts is a central theme in Adorno's thought on the work of art. In the *Ästhetische Theorie* he analyses the aporetic situation of contemporary art, which, on the one hand, he regards as in danger of giving up its autonomy and succumbing to the "mechanism of existing society",[69] while, on the other hand, if remaining enclosed within itself, it risks being neglected and considered peripheral and thus "harmless". Here, he introduces a criterion of the excellence of the work of art. The fact that the contemporary work of art withdraws from communication is, he claims, merely the necessary condition for its refusal to comply with ideology. He determines that the "central criterion" of the "power of expression", *Ausdruck*, has to be added to this. The implications of this terminological and thematic use of *Ausdruck* are manifold and they concern the kind of speech that does without words. Adorno writes: "The central criterion is the power of expression, through the tension of which works of art become eloquent with a wordless gesture. In expression, they reveal themselves as social stigmata. Expression

---

[67] "Dans cette responsabilité, le moi ne se pose pas, mais perd sa place, se déporte ou se trouve déporté. La substitution à l'autre est comme la trace de l'exil et de la déportation." *Ibid.*, 184.
[68] "[. . .] l'Infini se révèle sans apparaître, sans se *montrer* comme Infini." *Ibid.*, 229.
[69] "Betrieb der bestehenden Gesellschaft." (Adorno 1990, 352).

is the social ferment of their autonomous form."⁷⁰ He cites Picasso's *Guernica* as the "chief witness", *Kronzeuge*, for this way in which form reveals the wounds of the world. When Adorno invokes the term "Ausdruck" in this passage, there are various contexts in which it could be understood. For one, it contains a reminiscence of the Leibnizian monad as the "expression" of the monadic community, an idea that is further transmitted to German Idealism via Shaftesbury and Herder. At the same time, he connects the term to that of "tension", *Spannung*, which could bear a relation to one of the central elements of the use of language and images in Expressionism. The closest connection to Adorno's thought, however, while retaining both of the latter contexts, is provided by Benjamin's use of the term in the epistemological convolute of the *Passagen-Werk*. Here, Benjamin writes in the fragment N1 a, 6 of his striving to construct the "relation of expression", *Ausdruckszusammenhang*,⁷¹ between the economy and culture, while in the fragment N 10 a, 3 he locates his conception of the "dialectical image" at the point "where the tension between the dialectical opposites is greatest."⁷² Adorno's judgement on *Guernica* emphasises its force in this respect, stating that the painting gains "that expression [. . .] that sharpens it into social protest beyond any contemplative misunderstanding while being strictly incompatible with realism by decree, precisely through inhuman construction".⁷³ What is important in the current context is the conception of the "stigmata" as the wordless expression of social suffering.

This theme finds its concentrated formulation in the final sentence of the *Ästhetische Theorie*: "What kind of historiography would art be if it shook off the memory of accumulated suffering."⁷⁴ Formally a question, the sentence is an expostulation that amplifies what he had earlier identified as "the character of art as

---

70 "Zentrales Kriterium ist die Kraft des Ausdrucks, durch dessen Spannung die Kunstwerke mit wortlosem Gestus beredt werden. Im Ausdruck enthüllen sie sich als gesellschaftliches Wundmal; Ausdruck ist das soziale Ferment ihrer autonomen Gestalt." *Ibid*, 353.
71 (Benjamin, 1982, 573).
72 "[. . .] wo die Spannung zwischen den dialektischen Gegensätzen am größten ist." *Ibid*., 595.
73 "[. . .] bei strikter Unvereinbarkeit mit dem verordneten Realismus, gerade durch inhumane Konstruktion, jenen Ausdruck [. . .], der es zum sozialen Protest schärft jenseits aller kontemplativen Mißverständlichkeit." (Adorno 1990, 353). This judgement may require further differentiation in the light of Carlo Ginzburg's discussion of Picasso's painting, which emphasises precisely its relation to the iconographic tradition. See Ginzburg *Das Schwert und die Glühbirne. Picasso's 'Guernica'* (Frankurt am Main: Suhrkamp, 1999.
74 "Was aber wäre Kunst als Geschichtsschreibung, wenn sie das Gedächtnis des akkumulierten Leidens abschüttelte." (Adorno, 1990, 387).

unconscious historiography".⁷⁵ He had explicated the latter expression as: "anamnesis of the defeated, repressed, perhaps possible."⁷⁶ This historiographical character of the work of art is given an alternative formulation in one of the "Paraligomena" that accompany Adorno's unfinished text of the *Ästhetische Theorie*. The remembrance that takes place in the work of art is intimately connected with its form, indeed to such an extent that the existence of the latter depends on the former: "Even in a legendary better future art would not be permitted to deny remembrance of the accumulated horror, for otherwise its form would be nullified."⁷⁷ "Form", when Adorno employs this term in his *Ästhetische Theorie*, is not set over against "matter" in an abstract opposition, as if it were imposed onto something inchoate. The role that both form and matter play in the work of art is rather dialectical, each of these basic aspects being mediated in the tension Adorno views as constitutive for the work's dynamic.

"Form" is a determining moment of the work's relation to the world. Adorno states this in lapidary fashion: "The unresolved antagonisms of reality return in works of art as the immanent problems of their form."⁷⁸ He conceives this relation as one of question and answer. The work of art is in this sense an answer to the "interrogative form", *Fragegestalt*, of what impinges upon the subject's experience "from the outside", *von außen*.⁷⁹ Experience is thus imbued with the process of question and answer, and in this process the answer given by the work of art itself becomes in turn a question. The task of the commentator, or of the philosophy of art, is to make this relation explicit. In "Voraussetzungen", an article on Hans Helms, which contains one of Adorno's most concentrated discussions of the philosophical implications of modern literature and art in general, he writes that the task of the commentator is to follow the "tensions that are sedimented in the work of art". He refers to what is implied by "the aesthetic concept of understanding"⁸⁰ as "a kind of tracing"⁸¹ of these tensions that uses concepts but does not reduce the work by translating it into concepts.

Here, just as in "Die Aktualität der Philosophie", in his important article "Der Essay als Form", and in his *Ästhetische Theorie* Adorno emphasises that

---

75 "Charakter der Kunst als bewußtloser Geschichtsschreibung". *Ibid.*, 384.
76 "[. . .] Anamnesis des Unterlegenen, Verdrängten, vielleicht Möglichen." *Ibid.*
77 "Selbst in einer legendären besseren Zukunft dürfte Kunst die Erinnerung ans akkumulierte Grauen nicht verleugnen; sonst würde ihre Form nichtig." *Ibid.*, 479.
78 "Die ungelösten Antagonismen der Realität kehren wieder in den Kunstwerken als die immanenten Probleme ihrer Form." *Ibid.*, 16.
79 *Ibid.*
80 "der ästhetische Verstehensbegriff". (Adorno, 1973, 109).
81 "eine Art von Nachfahren", *Ibid.*

the activity of understanding he has in view is irreducible to a fixed hierarchy of concepts. For his theory, the concepts used in commentary and criticism, particularly in the form of writing that is the essay, do not subsume the "matter at issue", *Sache*, under comprehensive higher concepts but enter into the particular movement of the tensions at work in art. As he puts it in "Der Essay als Form", they do not see through the particular to the general concepts it embodies. Rather, they reflect upon and name the experientially grasped matter at issue in its relation in the individual configuration of form and matter. On the other hand, the essay also cannot be equated with a work of art in its own right.[82]

4 Appearance, Language, and the Law

Following Benjamin, Adorno seeks to understand the truth of the work of art as being intimately connected to its "temporal core", *Zeitkern*.[83] It partakes, he

---

[82] This is one of the points on which he considers himself as differing from Lukács' early understanding of criticism in *Die Seele und die Formen*. In Lucács' Florentine letter to Leo Popper of 1910, published under the title "Wesen und Form des Essays" in 1911, he had stated that the essay "faces life with the same gesture as the work of art". ("steht dem Leben mit der gleichen Gebärde gegenüber wie das Kunstwerk"), (Lukács 1971, 31). The question of how justified Adorno's criticism of Lukacs is in this matter cannot be developed here. It should be noted, however, that Lukacs is careful to qualify his comparison and does not equate the critical essay with the work of art *tout court*. Moreover, Lukács writes: "The essay is a trial but the judgment is not indeed what is essential and decisive with respect to value (as in the system), but rather the process of judging." ("Der Essay ist ein Gericht, doch nicht das Urteil ist das Wesentliche und das Wertentscheidende an ihm (wie im System), sondern der Prozeß des Richtens.") *Ibid*. This emphasis on process is close to what we find in Adorno's thought, despite the latter's criticism of Lukacs' position here. Adorno's reflection on Lukacs' early thought accuses him of excessive aestheticism in his treatment of the conceptual component of the essay as form, while in the *Ästhetische Theorie* and elsewhere he emphatically opposes Lukacs' later advocacy of socialist realism and denunciation of formalism.

[83] "If art could rid itself of the illusion of permanence once it has seen through this, if it could incorporate its own transience in sympathy with the ephemeral quality of living things, this would be consonant with a conception of truth that does not consider it as something that perdures abstractly but becomes aware of its temporal core." ("Entschlüge sich Kunst der einmal durchschauten Illusion des Dauerns; nähme sie die eigene Vergänglichkeit aus Sympathie mit dem ephemeren Lebendigen in sich hinein, so wäre das einer Konzeption von Wahrheit gemäß, welche diese nicht als abstrakt beharrend supponiert, sondern ihres Zeitkerns sich bewußt wird.") (Adorno 1990, 50).

specifies in the *Ästhetische Theorie*, in the "secularisation of transcendence". As such, it is involved, he determines, in the dialectics of Enlightenment, and this is why, in contemporary art, the form of anti-Art, *Antikunst*, continues the work of de-sacralisation. Art that responds to the historical moment points beyond itself, it confronts its own problematic status by configuring its evanescence. Levinas, for his part, seeks to place the work of art in the context of the perspective that ruptures history. He writes in *Totalité et infini*: "When man really approaches the Other, he is torn out of history".[84] As will be shown in this section 4 and in section 5 below, Levinas refers this relation explicitly to motifs from the Bible, the Jewish tradition, and sees concrete historical events against this background. When he writes the words, cited in the above, "[s]ubstitution for the other is like the trace of exile and deportation", this is what is at work. In his articles on Agnon and on Celan collected in *Noms Propres* he poses both the question whether poetry is a form of rhetoric that foments illusion and the question whether it is an "unheard of modality of the *autrement qu'être*".[85]

The relation of subjectivity to Jewish religious tradition informs Levinas's approach to art. Rigorous in his rejection of the sacred, Levinas also repudiates what he refers to as the "desacralized world in which the sacred is still degenerating".[86] The equivalence of the ecstasy of the sacred to the suspension of the law is also found here, in "appearance at the *very heart* of truth", in "the equivocal that seems to be an enigma".[87] In order to distinguish what Levinas names

---

[84] "Quand l'homme aborde vraiment Autrui, il est arraché à l'histoire." Levinas 1980, 23).
[85] "une modalité inouïe de l'*autrement qu'être*". (Levinas 1976, 56). The article "Paul Celan. De l'être á l'autre" quoted here was first published in 1972. 56). While Levinas's article "la réalité et son ombre" makes the term "expression" exclusively the preserve of the ethical in distinction from art, there are passages where this distinction seems less rigorous. An example of this would be his evocation, in the interviews comprising *Ethique et infini*, of the "literature" that "brings about a rupture in being" (opère une rupture dans l'être), where "through all literature [. . .] the human face speaks." (à travers toute littérature parle [. . .] le visage humain.). (Levinas 1982, 114). Levinas speaks further of the "eminence of the human face expressed in Greek letters and in our letters that owe everything to them" (l'éminence du visage humain exprimé dans les lettres grecques et dans nos lettres qui leur doivent tout, *Ibid.*, 115) and goes on to say that all national literatures "participate in sacred Scripture" (participation à l'Ecriture sainte dans les littératures nationales, *Ibid.*). See also the important article "Langage et proximité" and Levinas's discussion of the "extension of tenderness" to language and traced letters: "tenderness extends to all things from the human face and skin" (sur toutes choses, à partir du visage et de la peau humains, s'étend la tendresse). (Levinas 2010, 319).
[86] "monde désacralisé, où toujours dégénère le sacré". (Levinas 1977, 121).
[87] "apparence *au cœur même* du vrai"; "les équivoques senties comme des énigmes". *Ibid.*, 93.

the "holy" from the "sacred" in his terms, the ramifications of the dissimulating appearance and of the equivocal have to be traced, identified, and opposed. He writes: "The sacred that is degenerating is worse than the sacred that passes away."[88] Levinas is attentive to the gradations of dissimulation that are present in the transformation of the sacred into sorcery. He goes as far as identifying sorcery with this dissimulation, in the epoch of history in which "*seeming* alters the *appearing*",[89] with "the modern world". Here "nothing is identical with itself; no one is identical with himself [;] nothing is said, because no word has its proper meaning; every word is a magic afflatus; no one listens to what you say; everyone suspects behind your words the not-said, conditioning, ideology."[90] This is the matter Levinas had in view in his article "La réalité et son ombre" and that art of necessity partakes in because it is apparition. The words with which he asks in "Poésie et resurrection", his article on Agnon, "Are eternity and resurrection through poetry exempt of all illusion? Is the ultimate meaning of the human language and poetry?"[91] are written on this background. It is with respect to this question of ultimate meaning that Levinas will discern in Agnon's writing "the indication of an order more ancient than the Saying".[92] It is in this context that he will discern in Celan's work "the interruption of the ludic order of the beautiful and of the play of concepts and of the *play of the world*",[93] that he will stipulate the necessity of "a true word",[94] and will identify Celan's trajectory of the poem towards the other as "essentially Jewish".[95] To partake in this is to make appearance submit to a *retournement,* to the *Wende* that is also a return and a form of remembrance. It is in this movement, delineated in *Autrement qu'être* as "the turning from thematisation to an-archy"[96] in

---

88 "Le sacré qui dégénère est pire que le sacré qui disparaît." *Ibid.*, 109.
89 "l'*apparance* altère l'*apparaître*". *Ibid.*
90 "La sorcellerie, c'est cela: le monde moderne; rien n'est identique à lui-même; personne n'est identique à lui-même[;] rien ne se dit, car aucun mot n'a son sens propre; toute parole est un souffle magique; personne n'écoute ce que vous dites; tout le monde soupçonne derrière vos paroles du non-dit, un conditionnement, une idéologie." *Ibid.*, 107–108.
91 "L'éternité et la resurrection par la poésie sont-elles exemptes de toute illusion? La signification ultime de l'humain est-elle langage et poésie?" (Levinas 1976, 19).
92 "l'indication d'un ordre, plus ancien que le Dire". *Ibid.*, Levinas's article "Poésie et résurrection. Notes sur Agnon" was first published in 1973. 20.
93 "l'interruption de l'ordre ludique du beau et du jeu des concepts et du *jeu du monde*". *Ibid.*, p. 56.
94 "une vraie parole". *Ibid.*, p. 55.
95 "d'essence juive". *Ibid.*, p. 54.
96 "le retournement de la thématisation en an-archie". (Levinas 1986, 155).

the approach to the other that Levinas finds an echo of the return to the "order more ancient than the saying".

Levinas enters into this dimension already in his comparatively early thought, when he writes in 1949 in "La transcendence des mots", a meditation on *Biffures* by Leiris, that "human existence is creature". In this consideration of literature, visual art, and language, which continues his remarks in "La réalité et son ombre", Levinas moves from a determination of what is fixed, frozen, in beauty, be it the visual marks of painting or in the written word, to what is living, contrasting the "frozen words" with the "living word".[97] He elaborates what the expression, the spoken word that does not close itself in the "spectacle" of the finished work of art, opens up. The "interruption" that takes place here disrupts "my existence as subject and master".[98] The subject becomes herein both subject and object. This differs, however, from the manner in which the subject is situated in a work of art. To be related to the other in the address is a disruption of the position of the subject at the heart of a "spectacle", be this also a subject-object. To be situated with respect to the other, Levinas underlines, is to lose this position. This is due to "the first fact of existence", which is "neither the *in itself* nor the *for itself*, but the *for the other*".[99] This, however, takes Levinas to the point where he states that "human existence is creature".[100] In a step further he writes: "By the proffered word, the subject that poses itself exposes itself and, in a way, prays."[101] The expression "in a way" joins all the other occasions in Levinas's work where the status of an assertion is both maintained and rendered enigmatic.

The association of the enigma with the dimension evoked by the word "pray" is a central aspect of Levinas's later thought. It is important to discern, however, how the act of proffering speech here in this early text, opens up in the particular event of transcendence into a dimension that is always already a source of meaning that suffuses the trace. Levinas's article on Agnon indicates retrospectively how this is possible. In a central passage, he writes of the Hebrew word as ambiguous or enigmatic. With reference to the *melitsa*, the rhetorical form in which a word evokes Biblical turns of phrase without explicit reference to its doing so, Levinas comments on Agnon's use of this linguistic possibility as "the rupture of a certain ontology".[102] In this form, "the word

---

97 "'paroles gelées'"; "parole vivante". (Levinas 1987, 202).
98 "mon existence de sujet et de maître". *Ibid.*, 203.
99 "le fait premier de l'existence n'est ni l'*en soi*, ni le *pour soi*, mais le 'pour l'*autre*'". *Ibid.*
100 "l'existence humaine est créature". *Ibid.*
101 "Par la parole proférée, le sujet qui se pose s'expose et, en quelque manière, prie." *Ibid.*
102 "la rupture d'une certaine ontologie". Levinas, "Poésie et résurrection", 13.

signifies both in the context of the locution in which it is enunciated and, as a counterpoint, according with the Scriptures, points to an unrepresentable past. The enigmatic modality of a language beginning in its own trace!"[103] This characterisation of the resurrected trace is elaborated further to encompass the manner in which the liturgical ritual of Judaism suffuses Jewish life and creates "a de-substantialising of being, an excluded third between life and non-life where limits extinguish themselves."[104] Religion becomes, as Levinas writes, "probable", *vraisemblable*, where "the nature of things and of beings has issued forth from the symbol". As such, he continues, "the delimitation of their rigorous essence is less true than their symbolism".[105] He specifies "religion" to mean Judaism. The effect of this interlacing of Jewish life and liturgical rites is radical: "The symbolism of ritual, as the enigma of Jewish saying, extracts the core, the ultimate solidity beneath the plasticity of forms, which is taught by occidental ontology".[106] In the following development of Levinas's thought in this article, he passes via a reflection on how Agnon can be read as "poésie pure" to the idea that the Jewish life that finds voice here is song that has a meaning of an other kind than as a vehicle for contents. Furthermore, it is not a product of the imagination, not a representation in the form of an image. He writes: "the Unrepresentable will not be represented in the poem. It will be its poetry. Poetry *signifies* poetically the resurrection that bears it: not in the story that it sings but by its very singing".[107] This characterisation of poetry, imbued with the meaning Levinas gives to the Saying in *Autrement qu'être*, undergoes a further twist in Levinas's thought that follows a parallel sense of historical and literary crisis in Agnon's writing. It is a parallel that has its immediate context in the reference to Jewish tradition. "In a world in which living community is disappearing, who will be able to transmit the tradition itself – who will be able

---

[103] "le mot, sans imiter aucun modèle, signifie et dans le contexte du propos où il s'énonce et, en contrepoint, selon les Écritures, pointé vers un passé irreprésentable. Modalité énigmatique d'une langue ressuscitée commençant dans sa propre trace!" *Ibid.*
[104] "une désubstantiation de l'être, un tiers exclu où entre vie et non-vie, les limites s'éffacent". *Ibid.*, 14.
[105] "la nature des choses et des êtres est issue du symbole et [. . .] la délimitation de leur rigoureuse essence est moins vraie que leur symbolisme". *Ibid.*
[106] "Le symbolisme du rite, comme l'énigme du dire hébraïque, dénoyaute la solidité ultime sous la plasticité des formes, qu'enseigne l'ontologie occidentale." *Ibid.*
[107] "l'Irreprésentable ne sera pas représenté dans le poème. Il en sera la poésie. La poésie *signifie* poétiquement la résurrection qui la porte: non pas dans la fable qu'elle chante, mais par son chanter même." *Ibid.*, 17.

to read the scriptures?"[108] The fragility of this tradition lays bare the nature of poetry. Levinas interprets Agnon's story "The Seal" in which Ibn Gabirol, the dead poet, composes a poem for the person mourning the community exterminated in his native town. Transported by the poem, the living poet forgets its words. Levinas's comment on this cuts to the quick of literature and the modernity to which it responds. "The mortality of tradition reveals the rhetoric that poetry – this last refuge of transcendence in occidental humanism – dissimulates."[109] The fear that Agnon expresses in the story is ultimately that the literature that could resurrect the moribund Jewish tradition is facing its end, for this literature is confronted with the crisis of occidental humanism. In his comments, the step that Levinas takes with respect to this crisis is crucial, and the context in which he places them serves as a touchstone for the possibility of finding meaning even in the recent historical Jewish experience of being subjected to industrial murder, which indicates a complete absence of meaning. Even here Levinas avers that there is in Agnon's story "perhaps [. . .] the indication of an order more ancient than Saying, through which the non-sense of death can be contested".[110] This order is embodied in the Tora and its injunction of the Law of justice and love for the other. The "perhaps" with which Levinas begins this comment joins the "in a way" in "La transcendence des mots" cited earlier. As Levinas's final remarks on Agnon underline, death still bears within it the "mystery" of its "meaningless meaning", which can never be restricted by comprehending it within the limits of life. This is its "surplus", ever surpassing the limits and, Levinas submits, "exalting life".[111] While literature can engage with the trace, can be remembrance of that which withdraws from reminiscence, Levinas's comments here and in his article on Leiris show that this is constantly in question. For Levinas to reveal that Leiris falls short because he subordinates expression to thought, making it part of the communication of thought, and for him to refer to the "rhetoric" of poetry, which is the last refuge of transcendence in humanism, indicates that he continually subjects literary language to the rigorous criterion of rendering the echo of the Saying in the works created.

---

[108] "Dans un monde où disparait la communauté vivante, qui pourra transmettre la tradition elle-même – qui pourra lire les écritures?" *Ibid.*, 19.
[109] "La mortalité de la tradition révèle la rhétorique que dissimule la poésie – cet ultime réduit de la transcendance dans l'humanisme occidental." *Ibid.*
[110] "peut-être [. . .] l'indication d'un ordre, plus ancient que le Dire, par lequel le non-sens de la mort se conteste". *Ibid.*, 20.
[111] "sens insensé"; "surplus"; "exalte la vie". *Ibid.*, 21 *passim*.

It is a remembrance related to this language of the echo that Adorno has in view when he explores art as Mnemosyne, as that which expresses the paradox in the work of art as being what is evanescent and that which maintains itself. This takes place in various ways. The work of art is both the surpassing of the chthonic tremor, in the forming process of Enlightenment as truth, and the maintenance of the sense of what was overcome. It is the evanescence of the apparition as that which comes to be and passes away, which withdraws itself in the instant, but which is at the same time "expressive appearance".[112] Anamnesis enters into the trace of this expression. It seeks to make it speak. In order to reveal what is required by this anamnesis, Adorno undertakes a rigorous critique of theories that infer aesthetic realism from philosophical materialism. He argues against the conception of Mimesis that requires the work of art to imitate the reality that it finds outside itself. The aim of providing a "photographic" reproduction of an "outside" reality delivers the work of art up to a heteronomy that deprives it of its own way of knowing truth. In contrast to this, Adorno seeks to reveal a dialectic at work in which both the autonomy of the work of art and its particular opening onto reality are maintained. He does this be adumbrating a structure of immanence in which the complexity of the moments comprising it is bound by a tension that pushes it out and beyond itself. The work of art, just as the subject, according to Adorno's argument, is "socially mediated within itself".[113] The concentration of the work of art on itself and on the formal problems that present themselves therein individuates it. This concentrated configuration embodies at the same time a position taken in a specific historical moment to the reality that lies outside it. If Adorno writes "[a]rt has its other [. . .] in its immanence",[114] then it is because transcendence takes place in its "own procedure",[115] orientated towards "objectivation". It is form that carries out transcendence.

Adorno thematises the dialectical movement that takes place here as language. With respect to art, he writes: "It has to bring its latent social content to speak: to go inside itself in order to go out beyond itself."[116] The idea of calling forth the language latent in something is a theme that is encountered in other important related contexts in Adorno's *Ästhetische Theorie*. To take a salient example, he writes in the section of his work devoted to the aesthetic theory of

---

112 "ausdrückende[. . .] Erscheinung". (Adorno, 1990, 126).
113 "in sich gesellschaftlich vermittelt". *Ibid.*, 386.
114 "Kunst hat ihr Anderes [. . .] in ihrer Immanenz" *Ibid.*
115 "eigene[. . .] Verfahrensweise". *Ibid.*
116 "Zum Sprechen bringen muß sie ihren latenten gesellschaftlichen Gehalt: in sich hineingehen, um über sich hinauszugehen." *Ibid.*

natural beauty that the immanent structure of the work of art is what enables one to bring nature, which is mute, to speak. Against Hegel's argument in his lectures on aesthetics that the idea of beauty cannot be applied to natural objects but only to artefacts, Adorno argues that it is possible to experience nature in a way that neither deforms it as myth does nor reifies it as a mere material resource to be exploited. To wish to imitate nature in the work of art renders it vulnerable to both of these aberrations. The experience of nature embodied in the work of art that Adorno conceives in contrast to this is one in which the human sensuous engagement with the material world elicits a response from it by transforming it. He writes: "Art seeks to realise the speaking of the nonhuman by using human means."[117] Adorno develops this idea as a precise formal correlation to the dialectical structure he delineates with regard to the social content of the work of art.

It is from the perspective of the philosophy of history that Adorno examines language, situating it with regard to the human emergence from myth and with the attendant change in the relation to nature. This stratum of his thought on language is represented in the work *Dialektik der Aufklärung*. In an undated text, which, however, probably stems from the beginning of the thirties, Adorno writes in a reflection on Max Scheler's philosophy: "All deceptive ontology must be exposed particularly through the critique of language."[118] This sentence, which could equally be found both in the early and the later Wittgenstein, is the culmination of a series of theses in which Adorno elaborates the connection of language with history, with the concrete historical moment. The seventh thesis, which in the thought of "Konfiguration" points to Adorno's use of this term with regard to the work of art thirty years later in the *Ästhetische Theorie*, exemplifies this tendency. Adorno writes: "Today, the philosopher is confronted with disintegrated language. His material consists of the ruins of words, to which history binds him; his freedom consists merely in the possibility of configuring them according to the coercive force of truth in them. He may as little think a word as predetermined as he may invent one."[119] The configuration that takes its point of departure in the subject is nevertheless orientated towards the "coercive force of truth" that inhabits words. If the

---

117 "Kunst möchte mit menschlichen Mitteln das Sprechen des nicht Menschlichen realisieren." *Ibid.*, 121.
118 "Alle trügende Ontologie ist sprachkritisch zumal zu entlarven." (Adorno, 1969, 371).
119 "Es steht heute der Philosoph der zerfallenen Sprache gegenüber. Sein Material sind die Trümmer der Worte, an die Geschichte ihn bindet; seine Freiheit ist allein die Möglichkeit von deren Konfiguration nach dem Zwange der Wahrheit in ihnen. Er darf so wenig ein Wort als vorgegeben denken wie ein Wort erfinden." *Ibid.*, 368–369.

philosopher may neither regard a word as being "predetermined" nor as something he can invent, this passage marks the place in which Adorno will later insert the thought of dialectic. He will denote this as yet still empty space as the locus of mediation.

5 The Play of Mirrors, the Cage, and Aesthetic Responsibility

"It is not fortuitous that the dissolution of reality that had become song grew, in Cervantes' prose, into the lightness filled with suffering of great epic narrative"[120] – Georg Lukacs' analysis of epic form from the perspective of the philosophy of history is not only seminal for Benjamin and Adorno, but it marks the epochal confrontation of interiority with the other and with the demonic that is at issue in art for Levinas and Kafka. In *Totalité et infini*, Levinas writes of the "rectitude", *droiture*, of the relation to the other that characterises the "face-to-face", *face à face*. Here he writes that this is not "a play of mirrors"[121] but "my responsibility". To consider art as more than a play of mirrors, with respect to which Levinas maintains a constant suspicion, requires a reflection on its relation to responsibility.

Levinas weaves the question of appearance, disproportion, and the work of art together in a meditation on *Don Quixote*, identifying Cervantes' picaresque novel – in a parallel to Descartes' exposition of the *cogito* and the threat of the *Malin Génie* – as a crucial expression of modern man's fear of the spell of bewitchment. The trajectory of Levinas's reflection is made evident when he writes "In truth, only God is the metaphor that suffices to say the disproportion."[122] His focus on *Don Quixote* is part of an analysis of secularisation understood as the combat between the search for truth and the spell of myth. It is an analysis that should be compared in detail with that of Horkheimer and Adorno on the Enlightenment. Levinas's consideration of technology here as the "destroyer of the *gods of the world* and of the *god-things*"[123] indicates that

---

120 "Es ist kein Zufall, daß das Zerfallen der liedgewordenen Wirklichkeit in Cervantes' Prosa zur leiderfüllten Leichtigkeit der großen Epik erwuchs [. . .]." (Lukács, 1975, 50).
121 "Ce n'est pas un jeu de miroirs, mais ma responsabilité, c'est-à-dire une existence déjà obligée." (Levinas, 1980, 158).
122 "À vrai dire, seul Dieu est métaphore suffisante pour dire la *dis-proportion*." (Levinas, 1993, 195).
123 "déstrutrice des *dieux du monde*, des *dieux-choses*", *Ibid.*, 196.

although it serves to counter the spell of myth it is also liable to mystification. Both technology and the attempts at sobriety and rigour in the humanities are vulnerable inasmuch as they can become ideology. Levinas states, however, evoking *Genesis* 1:3, that it is above all technology that falls prey to "the possibly seeming that lies coiled in all appearing".[124]

In an exegesis beginning with Chapter XLVI in the first part of *Don Quixote*, Levinas first shows how the eponymous knight attempts to convince those surrounding him that the everyday figures who have confined him in a cage in order to bring him back to his village are really spirits and that everyone has been put under a spell. Sancho Pansa is depicted as recognising the delusion to which his master has fallen prey. In a radical interpretation of Don Quixote's "imprisonment within the labyrinthine spell",[125] Levinas contends that he undergoes an experience of the *cogito* at the heart of this illusion. In the words that Don Quixote says with regard to his experience of certainty Levinas discerns what he denominates "an other secularisation",[126] to which the awareness of, and openness to, the hunger of others and the vulnerability and exigencies of the lived body responds. Levinas interprets this as a transcendence that is "non-ontological or at least would not have its origin or its measure in ontology".[127] The parallel he sets up here is trenchant: "Ontology reduces the visible gods but it would place us in the position of Don Quixote and of his labyrinthine imprisonment if there were not this other transcendence".[128] In the words of Don Quixote, where the imprisoned knight says that he knows that he is under a spell and that if this were not the case it would be cowardly to be hiding in a cage while others are afflicted and in need of his help, Levinas discerns "in the humility of hunger" an opening. It is a "non-ontological transcendence that begins in the lived bodies of men."[129] He underlines that it is in this movement and "[o]nly in this movement that goes towards the other man"[130] that responsibility is primarily to be found.

---

124 "l'apparance possible qui se love dans tout apparaître de l'être". *Ibid.*
125 "enfermement dans l'enchantement labyrinthique". *Ibid.*, 197.
126 "une autre sécularisation". *Ibid.*, 198.
127 " [. . .] non ontologique ou du moins non trouvant pas son origine ni sa mesure dans l'ontologie." *Ibid.*, 198.
128 "L'ontologie réduit les dieux visibles, mais elle nous placerait dans la position de Don Quixote et de son enfermement labyrinthique s'il n'y avait pas cette autre transcendance." *Ibid.*
129 "une transcendence non ontologique qui commence dans la corporéité des hommes". *Ibid.*
130 "Seulement dans un movement qui va vers l'autre homme et qui est d'emblée responsabilité." *Ibid.*

Within the text of *Don Quixote* and within the figure of the imprisoned knight, at the heart of illusion, a non-spatial exteriority is opened. In hunger a second secularisation of the world takes place, and it is in this, in its extremity, that an appeal is issued to subjectivity. Using the terms of *Autrement qu'être*, it is in subjectivity, the sensibility of the subject to the hunger of the other, that "substitution" takes place. The experience in question is profoundly enigmatic. Levinas writes: "Secularisation through hunger is a question on God and to God – and thus at the same time more and less than an experience. It is a pre-orational question, a question without a response and like an enigmatic or ambiguous echo of the question. One will have to be more specific and say that with this analysis it is not a case of subjectivising transcendence but of being astonished by subjectivity."[131]

With regard to *Don Quixote* as a work of art, Levinas hence elucidates an immanent complexity and tension that, in a parallel to Adorno's analysis of the monadic tensions in modern art, opens a fissure within representation. One could refer to this not only as depicted responsibility, but as itself embodying the responsibility that is possible for the work of art in engaging with appearance by challenging it.

Such a possibility can be found in Kafka's *Nachlaß* text that bears the title, conferred by Max Brod, "Die Wahrheit über Sancho Pansa". In his essay on Kafka of 1934, Benjamin comments on this text in the context of his discussion of Bucephalus and of the studying – in contrast to the practice – of the Law. The "gates of justice"[132] are constituted by the Law as studied and not as practiced. In Benjamin's reading, Kafka could not envisage the promise that tradition attached to the Tora. Hence, Benjamin writes, the figures of the assistants and the students in his work (in *Das Schloß* and *Amerika* respectively) are detached from what would otherwise be their place in Jewish life, where the former would be serving the community in the synagogue and the latter would be learning the Tora. The text by Kafka bearing the title "Die Wahrheit über Sancho Pansa" was written in 1917, at a time when Kafka was considering the publication of a collection of stories under the title *Verantwortung*, Responsibility. Benjamin's introductory comment on this text is singular in the degree of his estimation for this short piece. He writes that in contrast to

---

[131] "La sécularisation par la faim est question sur Dieu et à Dieu – et ainsi à la fois plus et moins qu'une expérience. Elle est question pré-orationnelle, question sans réponse, et comme un écho énigmatique ou ambigu de la question. On précisera cependant qu'avec cette analyse il ne s'agit pas de subjectiviser la transcendance, mais de s'étonner de la subjectivité." *Ibid.*, 199–200.

[132] "Pforte der Gerechtigkeit". (Benjamin 1991, 437).

the "empty happy journey" that the *Gehilfen* and the *Studenten* were now free to begin, Kafka found the law, *Gesetz*, of his own. He was able "at least one sole time" to slow down the "breathtaking speed" of this journey and make it conform to "an epic walking pace".[133] In other words, this is a Haggada that modifies the Halacha. Benjamin writes: "He entrusted it to a text, which became his most accomplished, not least because it is an exegesis".[134] To compare Kafka's exegesis with Levinas's commentary on *Don Quixote* is to encounter a further turn in the question of the responsibility of the work of art with respect to apparition.

"Die Wahrheit über Sancho Pansa" consists of two sentences, both of which begin with the words "Sancho Pansa". In the first sentence, the action carried out by the subject Sancho Pansa, which consists of providing a quantity of novels of chivalry and of brigandage, *Ritter- und Räuberromane*, and thereby distracting his devil from him and rendering it harmless, is broken up by a series of relative clauses. These slow the pace and become a labyrinthine syntactical structure. The action is in effect carried out by the literature. Its function is to divert the harm that the unconstrained, unrooted, *haltlos*, devil could do in objectifying the subject. As in the story "Das Schweigen der Sirenen", which Kafka wrote into the third *Oktavheft* three days after inscribing "Die Wahrheit über Sancho Pansa" there, the text centres on a medial procedure employed by men to escape harm from mythical forces. Both involve foresight, preparation, and strategy involving technical means. In the case of Sancho Pansa, these consist of narrative, the provision of form for what would be otherwise random events, and the creation of worlds of the imagination. As far as the subject of the second story, Odysseus, is concerned, "childlike means", *kindische Mittel*, are employed to effect "salvation", *Rettung*. While the means may be "childlike", they involve strategic planning.

In the second sentence, the devil is referred to as Don Quixote. The change that consists in the denomination is mentioned in a relative clause that constitutes one of turns in the syntax of the first sentence. This change is, however, not innocent. There is one sole reference to "Don Quixote" and this is in the form "dem Don Quixote", which in this locution has the function of familiarisation in the German language. By doing this, the language itself does what the

---

133 "Nun hält sie nichts mehr auf der 'leeren fröhlichen Fahrt'. Kafka hat aber das Gesetz der seinen gefunden: ein einziges Mal zumindest, als es ihm glückte, ihre atemraubende Schnelligkeit einem Paßschritt anzugleichen, wie er ihn wohl sein Lebtag gesucht hat." *Ibid*.
134 "Er hat es einer Niederschrift anvertraut, die nicht nur darum seine vollendetste wurde, weil sie eine Auslegung ist." *Ibid*.

object referred to is: it expresses the fact that "Don Quixote" is a "familiar", a personal demon.

The subject of the second sentence, Sancho Pansa, is immediately qualified as "a free man", and the sentence goes on to describe his relation to the devil, "Don Quixote". He "followed", *folgte*, Don Quixote's riotous deeds "with equanimity", *gleichmütig*, and – crucially – "perhaps out of a feeling of responsibility".[135] Finally, the reader is told that Sancho Pansa derived from this "great and useful entertainment".[136] The objectification of the devil as "Don Quixote" is thus characterised with an epithet that looks very much like the Horatian *prodesse et delectare* with which the task of literary art was characterised in a certain tradition.

Kafka's text is a mise-en-scène of the replacement of the practice of appeasement and expiation with respect to mythic or demonic forces by the techniques of the imagination. No longer in thrall to the spell cast by myth, the subject as "a free man" can follow the disruptive forces from the distance afforded by this replacement. To do this "perhaps out of a feeling of responsibility" is to retain the memory of what the possibilities realised by the imagination have overcome. If Benjamin can write of "Die Wahrheit des Sancho Pansa" that it is Kafka's "most accomplished, not least because it is an exegesis", he is according it the seriousness similar to that of the commentary of a holy text. This is how he himself characterised his own commentaries on Brecht. In Kafka, it constitutes a radical further step in the inversion of appearance that Levinas's commentary on *Don Quixote* contains. In Cervantes' work, Don Quixote imagines that the barber, the priest, and those who accompany them are spirits and that everyone, himself included, is under a spell. Levinas enters into the labyrinth of Don Quixote's immanence to find the moment of fissure that inverts the appearance and opens to the other. In Kafka, one twist further, Sancho Pansa, who is an imagined figure, frees himself from the thrall of Don Quixote, who is also an imagined figure, by using the techniques of the imagination provided by narrative. Imagination, turning further into itself, provides the moment of fissure. In both cases, apparition in the work of art points beyond itself as a kind of disproportion. For Levinas, the affliction of the other calls forth from within the illusion. For Kafka, the liberation from the devil in the play of the imagination shifts, as Benjamin writes, the tectonic plates of world-epochs. Levinas states in "Désacralisation et désensorcellement": "Veritable de-sacralisation would try to separate positively what is true from appearance, perhaps to separate what is

---

[135] "vielleicht aus einem gewissen Verantwortlichkeitsgefühl". *Ibid.*, 438.
[136] "eine große und nützliche Unterhaltung". *Ibid.*

true from the appearance *essentially* mixed with truth."[137] If this is the case, the work of imagination, as in Kafka's text, can embody and realise discernment, *krinein*, the separation that is the task of critique. It is necessary to think Levinas's determinations of responsibility in art further in the light of such evocations of apparition and aesthetic disproportion as realised in "Die Wahrheit des Sancho Pansa". The exegesis of *Don Quixote* by both Levinas and Kafka reveals how responsibility can be embodied in the work of art as *vigilance* in the labyrinth of apparition.

In Adornos's comprehensive Introduction to his central work on Husserl's thought, *Zur Metakritik der Erkenntnistheorie*, published in 1956, he delineates crucial ways in which the "idea of philosophical critique" that he opposes to the concepts of epistemology inherited from tradition opens up the possibility of transformative praxis. Here, as in his later important article "Voraussetzungen" of 1961, he distinguishes between the concepts in which scientific semantics translates language into logic, on the one hand, and the speculative philosophy and semantics that "would make logic speak",[138] on the other hand. It is not fortuitous that in both of these loci in Adorno's work the movement in which objectifying thought is brought to a point beyond itself, undermining its own claim to dominance, is traced in intimate proximity to his exploration of how works of art enact meaning. It is also not fortuitous that Adorno connects in both the analysis of the surpassing of objectifying cognition and of linguistic meaning that goes beyond the fixed semantics of concepts with the ideas of "unconscious historiography", of remembrance, and of suffering that play such a important role in his *Ästhetische Theorie*.

In the Introduction to his *Metakritik*, Adorno writes, echoing Marx and Benjamin, "If the epoch of the interpretation of the world has passed and it is now the task to change it, philosophy takes its departure, and in departure concepts stand still and become images."[139] Philosophy, as Adorno sketches it here, brings these images to life and makes them speak by tracing the movement configured within them. This is the perspective in which Adorno, for his part, approaches Kafka, revealing how Kafka pushes the logic of the distorted world that he encounters to its limits and by doing so undermines these through a kind of

---

137 "La véritable désacralisation tenterait de séparer positivement le vrai de l'apparence, peut-être même de séparer le vrai de l'apparence *essentiellement* mêlée au vrai." (Levinas 1977, 90).
138 "die Idee philosophischer Kritik"; "die Logik zum Sprechen zu bringen". (Adorno, 1971, 47).
139 "Ist das Zeitalter der Interpretation der Welt vorüber und gilt es [,] sie zu verändern, dann nimmt Philosophie Abschied, und im Abschied halten die Begriffe inne und werden zu Bildern." *Ibid.*

mimicry. The dialectic that Adorno sees enacted here is such that Kafka corroborates the claims of the world on the subject to the point that they turn against themselves. For Adorno, Kafka seeks salvation by incorporating the power of the world of mythical forces, opposing the reification that has cast its spell on the subject by himself reifying the subject in his work, bringing myth to deconstruct itself in its mirror-image. In revealing the ways in which Kafka's writing employs this cunning, with which he seeks to reconcile myth, Adorno seeks to trace in his work the kind of responsibility that art enacts. Adorno rejects the translation of Kafka's writing into philosophical propositions that would be expressed in concepts. At the end of his article "Voraussetzungen", he explores the manner in which the hermetic works of art of modernity form within themselves the breach between the work of art and the world. By pushing the conflict between subjective expression and meaning grasped in concepts to the extreme, the work – "loving and hoping" – makes of the breach the agent of the work's form and the figure of the truth-content that transcends it. To discern this movement in the work of art is the task of the critic; to embody this figure is, for Adorno, the responsibility of the work of art.

Bibliography

Adorno, Theodor W.. "Die Aktualität der Philosophie". *Philosophische Frühschriften*. Gesammelte Schriften, Vol. 1. Ed. Rolf Tiedemann. Frankfurt am Main: Suhrkamp, 1973 (1931). 325–344.
Adorno, Theodor W.. "Thesen über die Sprache des Philosophen". *Philosophische Frühschriften*. Gesammelte Schriften, Vol. 1. Ed. Rolf Tiedemann. Frankfurt am Main: Suhrkamp, 1969. 366–371.
Adorno, Theodor W.. *Kierkegaard. Konstruktion des Ästhetischen*. Gesammelte Schriften, Vol. 2. Ed. Rolf Tiedemann. Frankfurt am Main: Suhrkamp, 1979 [1933].
Adorno, Theodor W.. *Zur Metakritik der Erkenntnistheorie*. Gesammelte Schriften. Vol. 5. Eds. Gretel Adorno and Rolf Tiedemann. Frankfurt am Main: Suhrkamp, 1971 [1956].
Adorno, Theodor W.. "Der Essay als Form". *Noten zur Literatur*. Gesammelte Schriften, Vol. 11. Ed. Rolf Tiedemann. Frankfurt am Main: Suhrkamp, 1991 [1958]. 9–33.
Adorno, Theodor W.. "Voraussetzungen. Aus Anlaß einer Lesung von Hans H. Helms". *Versuch, das Endspiel zu verstehen*. Frankfurt am Main: Suhrkamp, 1973 [1961]. 107–126.
Adorno, Theodor W.. *Ästhetische Theorie*. Gesammelte Schriften, Vol. 7. Ed. Rolf Tiedemann. Frankfurt am Main: Suhrkamp, 1990 [1970].
Benjamin, Walter. "Franz Kafka. Zur zehnten Wiederkehr seines Todestags". Gesammelte Schriften. Vol. II,2. Eds. Rolf Tiedemann and Hermann Schweppenhäuser. Frankfurt am Main: Suhrkamp, 1991 [1934, (409–432)]. 409–438.
Benjamin, Walter. *Briefe*. Eds. Gershom Scholem and Theodor W. Adorno. Frankfurt am Main: Suhrkamp, 1966.

Benjamin, Walter. *Das Passagen-Werk*. Gesammelte Schriften, Vol. V,1. Ed. Rolf Tiedemann. Frankfurt am Main: Suhrkamp, 1982.
Céline, Louis-Ferdinand. *Voyage au bout de la nuit*. Paris: Gallimard, 1952 [1932].
Céline, Louis-Ferdinand. *Nord*. Paris: Gallimard, 1960.
Ciaramelli, Fabio. "L'appel infini à l'interprétation. Remarques sur Levinas et l'art". *Revue philosophique de Louvain* XCII (1994): 32–52.
Colleony, Jacques. "Levinas et l'art: La réalité et son ombre". *La part de l'œil* 7(1991): 81–90.
Ginzburg, Carlo. *Das Schwert und die Glühbirne. Picasso's "Guernica"*. Frankfurt am Main: Suhrkamp, 1999.
Kafka, Franz. "Die Wahrheit über Sancho Panza". *Sämtliche Erzählungen*. Ed. Paul Raabe. Frankfurt am Main: Fischer, 1970 [1931]. 304.
Levinas, Emmanuel. *De l'évasion*. Paris: Le livre de poche, 1982 [1935].
Levinas, Emmanuel. *De l'existence à l'existant*. Paris: Vrin, [1947].
Levinas, Emmanuel. *Le temps et l'autre*. Paris: PUF, 1983 [1948].
Levinas, Emmanuel. "La réalité et son ombre". *Les imprévus de l'histoire*. Montpellier: Fata Morgana, 1994 [1948]. 123–148.
Levinas, Emmanuel. "La transcendence des mots". *Hors sujet*. Paris: Le livre de poche, 1987. [1949]. 197–203.
Levinas, Emmanuel. "Enigme et phénomène". *En découvrant l'existence avec Husserl et Heidegger*. Paris: Vrin, 2010 [1949]. 283–302.
Levinas, Emmanuel. "Personnes ou figures (À propos d' 'Emmaüs' de Paul Claudel). *Difficile Liberté. Essais sur le judaïsme*. Paris: Le livre de poche 1976 [1950]. 184–189.
Levinas, Emmanuel. "L'arche et la momie". *Difficile Liberté*. Paris: Le livre de poche, 1976 [1958]. 90–92.
Levinas, Emmanuel. *Totalité et infini*. The Hague: Nijhoff, 1980 [1961].
Levinas, Emmanuel. "La poésie et l'impossible". *Difficile Liberté. Essais sur le judaïsme*. Paris: Le livre de poche, 1976 [1969]). 196–204.
Levinas, Emmanuel. "Simone Weil contre la Bible". *Difficile Liberté. Essais sur le judaïsme*. Paris: Le livre de poche, 1976 [1963]. 205–217.
Levinas, Emmanuel. "Intentionalité et métaphysique". *En découvrant l'existence avec Husserl et Heidegger*. Paris: Vrin 2010 [1969]. 189–200.
Levinas, Emmanuel. "La trace de l'autre". *En découvrant l'existence avec Husserl et Heidegger*. Paris: Vrin 2010 [1969]. 261–282.
Levinas, Emmanuel. *Autrement qu'être ou au-delà de l'essence*. Dordrecht: Martinus Nijhoff, 1986 [1974].
Levinas, Emmanuel. "Max Picard et le visage". *Noms Propres*. Paris: Le livre de poche, 1976 [1975]. 111–116.
Levinas, Emmanuel. "Poésie et resurrection. Notes sur Agnon". *Noms Propres*. Paris: Le livre de poche, 1976 [1975]. 11–21.
Levinas, Emmanuel. "Dieu et l'Onto-théologie". *Dieu, la mort et le temps*. Paris: Le livre de poche, 1993 (1975/76). 137–279.
Levinas, Emmanuel. "Désacralisation et désensorcellement". *Du sacré au saint*. Paris: Les editions du Minuit, 1977. 82–121.
Levinas, Emmanuel. "Façon de parler". *De Dieu qui vient à l'idée*. Paris: Vrin, 1986 [1980]. 266–270.
Levinas, Emmanuel. "Langage quotidien et rhétorique sans eloquence". *Hors sujet*. Paris: Le livre de poche, 1987 [1981]. 183–193.

Levinas, Emmanuel. *Éthique et infinie*. Dialogues avec Philippe Nemo. Paris: Le livre de poche, 1982.
Lukács, Georg. *Die Seele und die Formen*. Neuwied/Berlin: Luchterhand, 1971 [1910].
Lukács, Georg. *Theorie des Romans*. Neuwied/Berlin: Luchterhand, 1975 [1916].
De Vries, Hent. *Minimal Theologies. Critiques of Secular Reason in Adorno and Levinas*. Baltimore: Johns Hopkins University Press, 2005.

www.ingramcontent.com/pod-product-compliance
Lightning Source LLC
Chambersburg PA
CBHW020324170426
43200CB00006B/261